"As a participant in D-Day, a student of the Civil War, and a resident of rural America, I found Jacob and Emeline's letters to be a tremendously moving and literate story of the Civil War that will touch all those who read it. Jacob's stunned emotions while walking through battlefields were similar to all front line men. His dramatic writing of the war, coupled with Emeline's trial of keeping the farm, raising four small children, and dealing with family suffering, provide an emotional view of life back home that sets this book apart from other Civil War books. A must-read for both Civil War fans and general readers."

—Ken Russell, Paratrooper, 82nd Airborne (D-Day)
Featured in *D-Day, June 6, 1944: The Climactic Battle of World War II; The Victors: Eisenhower and His Boys; Americans at War;* and *Citizen Soldiers,* all by Stephen Ambrose, and *Voices of D-Day* by Ronald Drez

---

"For history buffs, Civil War devotees, Americana enthusiasts, or even for those interested in a good old-fashioned love story, this is a dream come true. The letters are superb, extraordinary . . . among the best of their kind that I have ever seen . . ."

—Philip R. Hinderberger, Historian, 17th Missouri Infantry USA
Major, USMCR (Ret.)

"Captain Jacob Ritner's letters provide a fresh look at General W. T. Sherman's campaign through Georgia and the Carolinas, including the occupation of Savannah. His vivid descriptions include the Pulaski Monument, 'the finest thing I ever saw,' church edifices 'said to be the finest in the United States,' and palmettos, 'the greatest curiosity I ever saw' He hated fresh oysters ('Ugh! The nasty things!') but enjoyed a visit to Bonaventure Cemetery, 'one of the most picturesque places I was ever in . . . the final resting place of fallen greatness.' The replies of Jacob's wife Emeline give a rare feminine view of the war and home front, making this both a valuable Civil War reference, and a compelling love story."

—Margaret Wayt DeBolt
Author, *Savannah Spectres and Other Strange Tales*

"RICHLY TOLD. AN IMPRESSIVE WORK of research that all Americans can cherish as part of their national family inheritance. This tale of letters provides an intimate glimpse into our past."
—John Pellicano, Historian, Author
CONQUER OR DIE; The 39th New York Volunteer Infantry: Garibaldi Guard. A Military History.

Love and Valor
The Intimate Civil War Letters
Between Captain Jacob and Emeline Ritner

Captain Jacob B. Ritner

1st Iowa Infantry
25th Iowa Infantry
15th Army Corps—Army of the Tennessee

Wilson's Creek, Chickasaw Bayou, Arkansas Post,
Grant's Canal, Vicksburg, Lookout Mountain,
Chattanooga, Ringgold, Resaca, Dallas, Battle of
Atlanta, Ezra Church, Jonesborough, Sherman's
March to the Sea, Occupation of Savannah,
Burning of Columbia, Bentonville,
Grand Review In Washington

Edited by Charles F. Larimer

Sigourney Press

For a single copy of this book, please contact:
Sigourney Press, Inc.
P.O. Box 414, Western Springs, IL 60558
Web Site: http://www.sigourneypress.com
E-mail: cfraser@sigourneypress.com

Book design, production, and cover art by:
The Floating Gallery, 331 W. 57th St., #465, New York, NY 10019
Phone & Fax: 212-399-1961, E-mail: FloatinGal@aol.com

Ritner, Jacob R.
    Love & Valor : the intimate Civil War letters between Captain Jacob and Emeline Ritner / Jacob B. Ritner (and Emeline Ritner} ; edited by Charles F. Larimer. -- 1st ed.
    p. cm
    Includes bibliographical references and index.
    "1st Iowa Infantry, 25th Iowa Infantry, 15th Army Corps--Army of the Tennessee. Wilson's Creek, Chickasaw Bayou, Arkansas Post ...."
    LCCN: 99-72882
    ISBN 0-9673863-1-4

    1. Ritner, Jacob R.--Correspondence.
2. Ritner, Emeline--Correspondence. 3. History--Civil War, 1861-1865--Personal narratives.
4. Unites States--History--Civil War, 1861-1865--Personal narratives. 5. United States.--Army.--Iowa Infantry Regiment, 1st (1862-1865) 6. United States--History--Civil War, 1861-1868--Women.
I. Ritner, Emeline. II. Larimer, Charles F.
III. Title

E507.5 1st.R58 2000   973.7'477
                    I99-1433

Dedicated to
Emeline Bereman Ritner

Thank God for the token! One lip is still free,
One spirit untrammeled, unbending one knee!
Like the oak of the mountain deep rooted and firm,
Erect when the multitude bends to the storm.

—Lines Written on Reading Governor Ritner's Message of 1836
John Greenleaf Whittier

Contents

Introduction

Jacob B. Ritner was born December 16, 1828 on Birch Farm in Washington County, Pennsylvania. Seven years later, his grandfather, Joseph Ritner, was elected Governor of Pennsylvania. When Governor Joe Ritner lost his re-election bid in 1838, amidst charges of vote fraud perpetrated by his opponents, Federal troops were called to quell the rioting in Philadelphia and Harrisburg. Jacob's father Henry, deciding that farming was a more honorable and stable profession than politics, gathered his growing family and moved to Iowa.

Jacob's wife, Emeline Bereman, was born in Kentucky in 1831, but her father moved the family to Indiana because of his opposition to slavery. In 1845 the Beremans moved again, this time to Mt. Pleasant, Iowa where Jacob and Emeline met at Howe's Academy, a school run by a former high school teacher of William Tecumseh Sherman. Jacob and Emeline married in 1851 and Jacob supported his wife and new family by working as a teacher in southeast Iowa.

Immediately after the Civil War erupted, Jacob responded to Lincoln's call for 75,000 volunteers and enlisted for 100 days in the Union cause. Many people thought the war would be over by the end of this term. The war soon engulfed Jacob's and Emeline's families: two of Jacob's brothers, all six of Emeline's brothers, and Emeline's father joined the Union Army; Emeline's mother worked as a nurse in St. Louis.

During his 100-day term with the 1st Iowa Infantry, Jacob saw action with General Nathaniel Lyon in the Battle of Wilson's Creek in Missouri, where General Lyon suffered fatal wounds. After his initial enlistment expired, Jacob became a recruiting officer, and then re-enlisted in the 25th Iowa Infantry, where he was mustered as First Lieutenant of Company B. During the Vicksburg campaign, his superior officer resigned, and Jacob was promoted to Captain of Company B.

The 25th Iowa Infantry participated in many of the major campaigns of the western theater as part of the 15th Army Corps, Army of the Tennessee. They were with Generals Grant and Sherman for the siege of Vicksburg. After Vicksburg came Chattanooga and the

Battle of Lookout Mountain. Jacob was wounded at Ringgold, Georgia, just south of Chattanooga. The 25th Iowa participated in the siege and capture of Atlanta, and then were part of Sherman's famous "March to the Sea." After capturing Savannah, they marched north through the Carolinas. At the war's conclusion, Jacob marched in the Union Army's Grand Review in Washington, D.C.

The 15th Army Corps, which included Jacob and the 25th Iowa Infantry, was originally led by General William Tecumseh Sherman. It remained under Sherman's authority as he next became commander of the Army of the Tennessee, and then the head of all the western armies.

Throughout the war Jacob and Emeline corresponded with each other, and their letters demonstrate that they both drew much of their emotional strength from each other. Both would encourage the other to write long, detailed correspondence of their daily trials. This not only provides us with life in the field of a soldier during the Civil War, but also portraits of the Iowa women who stayed behind and cared for their families.

The creation of this book was a family project that spanned over sixty years—over 145 years if we date back to Jacob's letter to Emeline just before they were married in 1851. In piecing this story together, I found the actual body of letters in three different places.

My grandmother's sister, Nellie Chase Price, first transcribed and typed Jacob's wartime letters in the late 1930s; these serve as the main body of this book. In 1961, the 100-year anniversary of the start of the Civil War, my grandmother introduced me to the typed copies of Jacob's letters. Who would guess that what so fascinated an eight-year-old would seem even more engaging some thirty-two years later? My initial work was based on Nellie's typed copies, but following cryptic correspondence written in the 1940s, I eventually found Jacob's original wartime letters at the Iowa Historical Society in Iowa City, located just two blocks from my college apartment. Unbeknownst to me at the time, during my last two years at the University of Iowa in the 1970s, I walked past Jacob's original letters every day on my way to classes.

In my search to find the original letters, my father adamantly urged me to contact his long-lost cousin, Martha Lou Price Bugbee. "Where is Martha Lou?" I would ask, and my father would say, "Well, she lives on a turkey farm in North Dakota somewhere, at least she did 25 or 30 years ago, and you really do need to find her." After scratching my head for several months, in a burst of determination I was able to track down Martha Lou, who had recently moved to a senior citizen home with her husband. Underneath her bed, Martha Lou had stored boxes containing some of her most important possessions, which included additional Civil War family correspondence and photos of Jacob, Emeline, and their families. This set of letters included Jacob's letters to Emeline before and after the war, and other family writing throughout the war.

But at this point, and for several years later, I did not have any letters written by Emeline, which I thought no longer existed. The most consistent response I received from reviewers of earlier drafts of this book was the lament that it did not contain any of Emeline's letters. Without the Internet it would have remained that way.

There is an Internet Web Site regarding Iowa and the Civil War, where genealogists can post the name and regiment of their soldiers. Through this I have come in contact with ancestors of several people mentioned in Jacob's letters, including a great-granddaughter of Second Lieutenant Baron Crane, Ann Crane Farrier. Jacob mentions Baron and the Crane family throughout his letters. Eventually Jacob and Baron had a falling out, probably over the trivial matter that Baron received many more letters from home than Jacob did, which made Jacob feel all the more lonely. I suspect that Baron must have teased Jacob about this, and that Jacob took it the wrong way. My sincere apologies to the Crane family for Jacob's comments, for in my studies I have come to believe that Baron was a good soldier and true patriot, just like the rest of the men of the 25th Iowa Infantry.

But my most amazing set of correspondence on the Internet came from Civil War enthusiast Ken Smith from Sandy, Utah. Ken found Jacob's and my name on the Web Site, and then sent me an e-mail telling me that he had obtained copies of Jacob's and Emeline's letters about 15 years earlier. I was stunned. In the early 1980s, Ken's mother had found a woman (who turned out to be the wife of my father's cousin) who had several Civil War letters. Eventually Ken met this woman, who allowed Ken to make copies of the typed version of Jacob's letters, and then to make copies of Emeline's original letters. Without Ken, this book would be absent of all Emeline's letters. Ken transcribed Emeline's first nine letters and also provided a review of my manuscript.

This work would never have been done without the help and direction of my father, Robert Chase Larimer, who guided me through much of his genealogical works that included reference books he had collected regarding Iowa and Henry County during the Civil War. During the last year of his life we shared Jacob's journey together.

A special thanks to Margaret and Frank DeBolt of Savannah, and Roger Durham of Midway, Georgia who showed me around the Savannah area, and provided reviews of that section of the book; and to Ann Crane Farrier, Bruce Allardice, Ken Smith, Jeff Dukes, Becky Peterson, Kevin Wolf, Jerry Zizook, Edmund Zizook, Mike Moreland, Don Young, Don Elder, Neal Nelson, Jeffry Burden, Matthew Schaefer, Peter Binkley, and Philip Hinderberger who helped review my draft manuscripts. Thanks to Savannah sculptor Haywood Nichols, great grandson of Alfred Haywood, the ice merchant of Savannah, for providing stories and pictures of Alfred.

I have included with these letters the official Historical Sketch of the 1st Iowa and 25th Iowa regiments, published in the first decade of the 1900s in the *Roster and Record of Iowa Soldiers in the War of the Rebellion*. I used these to provide necessary and interesting background to understand Jacob's letters. I have also included articles from *The Mt. Pleasant Home Journal* and the *Burlington Hawkeye* newspapers, other historical perspectives and anecdotal information to help explain Jacob and Emeline's tale.

In presenting these letters, I have removed parts of family correspondence that strayed beyond the main story line, and where individuals were mentioned that I could not identify. In reading Jacob's handwriting, I gave him the benefit of the doubt in questions of spelling.

I hope that you will enjoy reading Jacob's and Emeline's letters and the historical reports as much as I have. They open to you the thoughts and heart of an Iowa soldier, farmer, and teacher and a loving and strong pioneer woman.

—Charles F. Larimer, 1999
Great-Great-Grandson of Jacob and Emeline

Family Trees

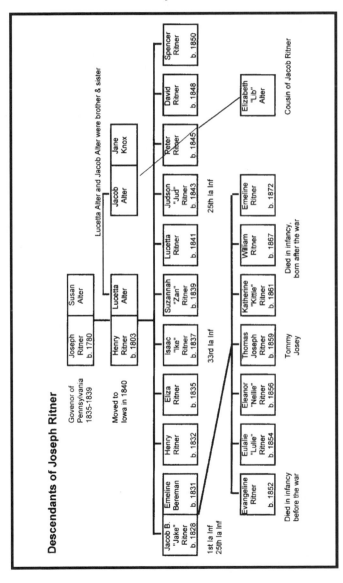

Descendants of Joseph Ritner

Joseph Ritner b. 1780 — Governor of Pennsylvania 1835-1839 — Susan Alter

Henry Ritner b. 1803 — Moved to Iowa in 1840 — Lucetta Alter

Jacob Alter — Jane Knox

Lucetta Alter and Jacob Alter were brother & sister

Children of Henry Ritner and Lucetta Alter:
- Jacob B. "Jake" Ritner b. 1828 — 1st Ia Inf, 25th Ia Inf — Emeline Bereman b. 1831
- Henry Ritner b. 1832
- Eliza Ritner b. 1835
- Isaac "Ike" Ritner b. 1837 — 33rd Ia Inf
- Suzannah "Zan" Ritner b. 1839
- Lucetta Ritner b. 1841
- Judson "Jud" Ritner b. 1843 — 25th Ia Inf
- Peter Ritner b. 1845

Children of Jacob Alter and Jane Knox:
- Peter Ritner b. 1845
- David Ritner b. 1848
- Spencer Ritner b. 1850

Elizabeth "Lib" Alter — Cousin of Jacob Ritner

Children of Jacob B. "Jake" Ritner and Emeline Bereman:
- Evangeline Ritner b. 1852 — Died in infancy before the war
- Eulalie "Lulie" Ritner b. 1854
- Eleanor "Nellie" Ritner b. 1856
- Thomas Joseph Ritner b. 1859
- Katherine "Kittie" Ritner b. 1861
- William Ritner b. 1867
- Emeline Ritner b. 1872 — Died in infancy, born after the war

Tommy
Josey

Descendants of Samuel E. Bereman

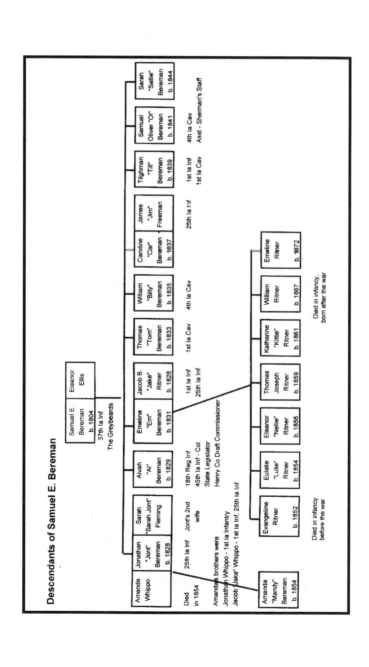

Photos

Emeline Bereman Ritner

Jacob B. Ritner

Eleanor Bereman
Emeline's Mother

Samuel E. Bereman
Emeline's Father

Henry Ritner
Jacob's Father

Henry Ritner
Jacob's Brother

Isaac Ritner
Jacob's Brother

Alvah Bereman
Emeline's Brother

Eber Crane   Baron Crane

George Stone (Iowa State   Alfred Haywood (Ice Merchant
Historical Society—Des Moines)   of Savannah, Georgia)

Elizabeth "Lib" Alter
Jacob's Cousin

Eliza Alter
Jacob's Cousin

Chapter One
Before the War

Danville [Iowa]
March 14, 1851

Dearest Emeline,

According to promise, I take my pen to write you a few lines to let you know where I am and what I am doing. If you are as anxious to hear from me as I am to hear from you, I am sure you will receive them with pleasure. And it has been just one week today since we parted. Would you believe it? Doesn't it seem like an awful long time to you. It does to me. I assure you I had plenty today to write to you, but I could hardly wait till it came. It had seemed to me sometimes, Emeline, that it was too hard to be reparted from you so long. Was it not cruelly? Did we not do an unjustifiable violence to our own feelings when we parted for so long a time. How ardently have I desired to see you once more. If it was only [for] a few minutes. I have sometimes almost come to the conclusion that I <u>would</u> get up there at all hazard and see you once more before we meet to part no more. But, I suppose I had better not. One week is gone. Every day the time to draws more near. Oh how I long for the time to come when I shall clasp you once more in my arms. But, there is one thing gives me unspeakable happiness and satisfaction to me, that is a firm belief that you love me. I doubt not but that even now while I am writing, you are thinking of me. The longer I am separated from you, the more I feel my heart drawn out towards you and the better I love you. I thank God that by his providence he even brought us together. The thought that you love and have consented to be mine causes a thrill of pleasure to pass through my soul that would repay me for months of separation. But, my heart is full . . .

I left town in the stage about two o'clock and got to Messengers about sundown. I there learned that the Baptists were holding a protracted meeting at the "Center" and that our folks would all be there. So, I went to a meeting in place of going home and I have not done anything but go to meetings since . . . The church is thoroughly received and is coming up to the help of the Lord again. The mighty hardened sinners are rowing at the boat of the cross. Satan trembles before the advancing cause of Christ and the Kingdom of Darkness is fast giving way.

As for myself, I feel rather cold and indifferent. I do not enjoy myself in the subject of religion as well it is my privilege to do. I have sometimes almost doubted whether I was not deceived and had never been adopted into the family of the saints. Perhaps it is because I [have] so much else upon my mind that I cannot think of religion.

But, I suppose you are anxious to hear what "our folks" say to the "match"—well, I will tell you all about it. I had not been home long before I "divulged the mighty secret." It came rather unexpectedly, of course. But, neither of them had any objection at all. They said they were glad I had concluded to settle myself, then appeared to be every bit as well pleased as your folks are. Father said if we would come down here and live, he would build a house for us and let me have as much land to work as I wanted for nothing. But, I told him that I did not think you would like to live down here and that your mother wanted us to stay in that neighborhood and that I would rather live there myself than here. They now have no objections to our living up there and will help us all they can . . .

Now Emeline, my dearest Emeline, we must part again.— Remember that my life is bound up in your love. I feel myself under infinite obligation to love, honor and protect you as long as life shall last. I have much to say, but cannot say it now. Only this, doubt not my constancy and be ready to go with me to the altar when I come. I almost think I feel the grasp of your hand, but farewell, my Emeline. May God be with you and protect you.

Your humble unworthy lover,
Jake

Emeline and Jacob married three weeks later, on April 3, 1851. After their marriage, Jacob became a teacher and moved his family to Ft. Madison, Iowa, close to the Missouri border.

A Rattlesnake—From Jacob to Emeline's Father

Fort Madison, Iowa
December 27, 1857
Mr. S. E. Bereman

Dear Sir:
    . . . Well, my school continues to flourish like a pumpkin vine in a garden . . . I have only had between 50 and 60 scholars so far on this quarter (the real number that came last quarter was 98). But, a great many are coming in after the New Years and I have no doubt that this quarter will average better than the last . . .
    These people are afraid of the Slavery Question as if it were a rattlesnake. It is the most pro-slavery hole I ever saw. Some have intimated to me that it would not be a prudent to speak out very freely on that subject.
    The next question—"Resolved that the Constitution of Iowa should be amended." The principle discussion will be on the subject of banks, but I intend to move to strike out the word "white." There are scarcely enough free soilers here to save the city from being made an example like Sodom, but for five righteous it is spared . . .
    Some of you write soon. Give my love to ma and all the rest left (except Aunt).

Yours intensively,
J.B. Ritner

From Henry A. Ritner to Jacob

Lebanon, Warren Co. Ohio
June 25, 1860

Dear Brother,
    . . . and remember that the Democratic party has gone under.
Douglas is nominated, but the convention has split and the south
will not support him. "Honest old Abe" is destined to be <u>President</u>
of the <u>United States</u>. Our nation delivered from bankruptcy, our
people from anarchy and civil war and our <u>territories</u> protected
from the jaws of the monster slavery. Huzza for Lincoln &
Hamlin[1].

Your affectionate brother,
H. A. Ritner

1. Hannibal Hamlin of Maine was Lincoln's running mate in 1860.

Chapter Two
Wilson's Creek, Missouri

In 1908, the State of Iowa printed the Roster and Records of Iowa Soldiers in the War of the Rebellion, published under the authority of the Iowa General Assembly, which presented historical sketches of each Iowa regiment. Included with these letters are the appropriate sections of the sketches of the 1st Iowa Infantry and the 25th Iowa Infantry.

Historical Sketch—1st Iowa Infantry

In the first great drama of the War of the Rebellion, Iowa soldiers played a conspicuous part. The first hostile shot was fired in Charleston Harbor on the morning of April 12, 1861. A few days later, President Lincoln issued his proclamation, calling for 75,000 men for the suppression of the armed rebellion against the government of the United States. In response to this call, the First Regiment of Iowa Volunteers went forth as the vanguard of the mighty host that followed from the State under the subsequent calls of the President. (Roster and Record of Iowa Soldiers in the War of the Rebellion; Published under the authority of the Iowa General Assembly)

Two of those responding to Lincoln's call for 75,000 men were Jacob Ritner and Emeline's brother Tilghman Bereman, who enlisted as privates in the 1st Iowa Infantry. Lincoln was able to bypass Congress and make this call for the state militias by using the authority granted to him by a law enacted in 1795. This law limited the president's use of the state militias to only 100 days, which is why the term of the 1st Iowa Infantry was set at three months.

Keokuk, Iowa
May 9, 1861

Dear Emeline,

    I take the present opportunity to write you a few lines, to let you know how we get along. In the first place we got to Burlington all right. They marched us up to the Lawrence House and told us to take possession of it, which we immediately proceeded to do. We expected to get a boat that night for here, so we sat up most all night, and when we went to bed we were three in a bed and with our clothes on, so we did not get any sleep. Yesterday at Burlington I got a pair of pants and each of us got a new gray shirt, a hat, two pair of socks and a tin water flask with a strap to hang it around the neck. No boat came along till nearly night, when the *William L. Ewing* came down with two companies of soldiers on board. We left Burlington about sundown. We had 300 soldiers aboard besides a good many other passengers. You may know we had a pretty strong time. We got here about midnight. We stopped on the street a while and got a good thick blue blanket apiece, and then came here to our quarters, which is a room about sixty feet long by 18 wide, in the third story of a brick house. There are four other companies in the same building, and the whole regiment is near here. We have some hay scattered over the floor to sleep on and nothing else in the room except what we brought along. We got in about 3 o'clock, and all piled down and slept till morning.

This morning at 6 o'clock they marched us all in a body about 3 squares from here and then single file up a pair of stairs to breakfast. We just stood up with our hats on and pitched in. Every man had a tin pan, knife and fork, with a tin cup full of coffee, but nary cream. We have nothing more to do today till noon. I am trying to write here at the quarters, but it is almost impossible to do so; the men are all walking, talking and jamming round—some playing cards, some reading, some carrying in baggage, some bringing in hay, &c, &c.

So you must excuse me for not writing you much of a letter this time. I have to write with a pencil this time. We will be better fixed before long. Write to me soon and let me know how you get along. I like soldiering very well so far.

> Good-bye for the present,
> J.B. Ritner

[Mt. Pleasant, Iowa]
May the 12th, [1861]
Sunday Night

Dear Jake,

I received your letter yesterday morning and almost cried when I got through reading because it was so short. I hope you will send me a good long one when you get a good place to write. Oh dear hasn't this been a long lonesome week! You have been gone ever since last Tuesday. Oh how I did hate to come home that day. I felt as if I had been to a funeral. Well you are gone—and I must train myself, and get used to it. As long as you are there I shall feel a little comforted, but when you leave I shall be <u>lonely indeed</u>—

We are all well, Billy went to Jefferson[1] yesterday, and we went to Fathers and staid till this evening. Ma, Father, Ol & Manda are all going to Jefferson tomorrow and stay all week to plant sugar cane (I expect I will die with the blues while they are gone). Billy is to milk the cows and bring the milk here.

Look here Jake, Old Jimmy Malles is searing mad about his money, he went over to Fathers and called around there till he got him (Father) mad and he sauced him a little. He thinks you are no gentleman or you would have come and told him that you were going. He is very uneasy, thinks he must take the house, but don't want it, but must have the money. Father thinks perhaps you made arrangements with your Pap to pay it, if so let us know something about it . . .

Well I think Billy will hardly go to the war, as they don't want any more volunteers for less than three years, and he is not in for that long. He says he can do his fighting up in less time than that. I don't know what the rest will do. They were out on the prairie here yesterday parading. Now I want you to promise me good that you will come back when your three months are out, will you? If I know that you will come home at that time I will try and bear it. If not I will just—

I hope you will be a good boy and not learn to play cards, and <u>say bad words</u> like some of the rest but improve your spare moments in reading that little book in your shirt pocket and remember that you are a believer in its doctrines and that it teaches you no such bad habits but Jake I am not afraid <u>I can trust you</u>. . . . Tommy says tell Pa he has "dot a tore pinner, burnt it right on the end"—Good Bye, wish you would come up some Saturday night. (kiss)

Em

You must tell me where to direct letters after you go away from there.

1. The town of Jefferson, located between Trenton and Wayland, (then called Marshall) no longer exists. (Correspondence with Ann C. Farrier)

Keokuk, Iowa
May 16, 1861

Dear Emeline,

I received your letter last Tuesday and have read it three times—it was a dear good letter and done me more good than anything that has happened to me for some time. I only wish it had been about four times as long. This is Thursday morning just after breakfast, and it is one hour and half till roll call. They call the roll at half-past eight, at two, and at nine o'clock every day. The companies were all examined by the United States officers on Monday; on Tuesday we were sworn into the U.S. service. We are now governed by the articles of war, which are very strict. A man may be shot now for doing things which would hardly be noticed before. We have not got our guns yet, and we know nothing about when we will get them or when we will leave here. We expect to get tents soon, and then we will camp out and go it on our own hook.

We had very poor grub at the place I spoke of in my other letter. There was plenty of it, but it was cooked so nasty and dirty that
we cóuld not eat it. So we raised a row and seceded. We have a
first-rate place now; we have seats to sit on, good coffee for breakfast and tea for supper with cream in them, good fresh bread, fresh
beef, ham, beans, dried apples, onions, radishes, sausages,
molasses, &c. We still sleep in the same place. I sleep very well
and enjoy as good health as ever I did. All the boys of our acquain-
tance are well. A great many of the men swear and play cards, and
some of them drink, though they cannot get drunk without getting
punished. You are right in thinking that you can trust your Jake. I
have too much respect for myself and my dear sweet wife and children and I intend always to so live as to be worthy of your love and
confidence. I went to a religious meeting twice last Sunday, and
read two chapters in the Testament every day. The only bad thing I
have done is to smoke three cigars every day!!

Half past 10 o'clock—just got in from drill and will finish my
letter. You want me to promise to come home at the end of three
months. Well, I will, certain. It will be three months from the time
we were sworn in here. I think by that time I will have done my
duty to my country. I feel that I have made a great sacrifice in many
respects for the sake of helping to sustain our government and
institutions, and I am not sorry that I have done so; I am proud of
my position and hope that I may be able to render some efficient
service to the good cause before the time is out. We have no certain
knowledge yet where we will go when we leave here. Some think
we will not go at all, but I think we will.

About Old Malles I will only say that he did know that I was
coming away. I told him that I would get half of it for him right
away if I could, but that he should have it all at the end of the next
six months at any rate, and he made no reply and I supposed that
he was satisfied. I will write to Tom[1] and Pop[2] about it in a few
days, don't you be uneasy about it—just let him rip.

Now, Emeline dear, you must write me a great long letter next
Sunday. I shall be thinking all day that you are writing to me. Tell
Tommy[3] that Pa wants to see him and kiss his sore finger. I want to
see Lulie[3] and Nellie[3] and kiss them too. Tell them they must be
good girls. Tell me all the news, how the trees grow, the garden and
grass, what everybody says. Oh, Emeline, I would like to see you,
but I am a soldier now, and glad of it, and determined to do my
duty. If I can get my first month's pay in time, I will send it to you,

and have you and the baby[3] and Billy[1] come down to see me. Give my respects to Billy and all the rest and tell them to write to me.

Your Jake

1. Thomas Bereman, age 28, and Billy Bereman, age 26, were Emeline's brothers. Thomas would serve in the 1st Iowa Cavalry and Billy in the 4th Iowa Cavalry.

2. Henry Ritner was Jacob's father, age 58. Jacob also had a brother named Henry.

3. Jacob and Emeline's first child, Evangeline, died in infancy. Their four living children were two-year-old Tommy, seven-year-old Eulalie (Lulie), five-year-old Lucetta Eleanor (Nellie), and an as yet unnamed daughter born in February 1861. This unnamed daughter, whose naming is discussed in future letters, survived to adulthood.

Keokuk
May 19/61

Mr. T. E. Bereman

Dear Sir:

This is Sunday morning and I will write to you a few lines to let you know how we get along and writing in the country now which is a very nice place and has been fixed up for the soldiers to send and write their letters in. We are supplied with paper to write and also all kinds of books and newspapers to read and we have prayer meeting here every morning and evening.

We expected to go into camp yesterday, but did not get ready. We will go tomorrow. We received 84 tents a few days ago and found last night each tent holds six soldiers. We have also received 60,000 cartridges and 2,000 guns. The guns came last night and have not been distributed yet. They are just like Brunaugh's Flintlock except that they have been changed to percussion locks[1] and scoured up. Will kill both ways. The men do not like it much. For my part, I would rather have a better gun, but I did not come here to dictate to the government the terms on which I would fight. I am ready to go in with whatever they give me. All I am afraid of is we'll not have a chance to use them. It would be a great bore to have to stay here all summer.

I suppose you heard that we had "seceded" from our first boarding place—Well, we had another secession movement night before last.

The commissary had the two Burlington companies, our company and one from Cedar Rapids (400 men in all) in the second and third stories of a large brick house. Some of the men were suspicious of the building all the time. The night before last, we concluded that it was about to fall down. The front wall cracked in several places and the west wall was bulged out about three or four inches. The Burlington companies left for the other quarters en masse. Some of our men went to the medical college and slept on the floor. Most of them remained, as it was not considered very dangerous after two companies had gone out.

I never enjoyed better health than since I came. I feel that I am deprived of a great many comforts and privileges especially the society of my family and friends. But, if I can be of any use in sustaining our country and our flag, I shall consider myself well paid. My only regret is that a set of scoundrels and thieves has made it necessary to resort to such means to preserve our glorious institutions and all I want is a chance to see them through. We are all "spilling" for a chance to fight.

Emeline says that Old Malles is making a fuss about that money I owe him and is threatening to sue. I suppose I had a fair understanding with him before I came away and that he was to wait another six months for the money. He knew I was coming away and I told him I would pay him 5% in advance if he would renew the note. He said he would not do it unless I would pay him half, as he wanted to lend it to Watt Dorman. I told him that it was a fair understanding when I got the money that if he didn't need it himself at the end of the time, he would renew the note. But, if I could get the money for him I would. If not, he would have to wait. He made no reply. If he wants to do anything, fight it as long as possible.

Write to me soon. Direct to Company F instead of G, as we have been promoted. Let Emeline see this letter. Give my respects to all the folks.

Yours, Jake

1. The manufacture of flintlocks had ended roughly 20 years prior to the start of the Civil War, but they were still in use at the outbreak of the war. As soon as was possible, both Union and Confederates replaced them with more modern percussion arms. (Jack Coggins, *Arms and Equipment of the Civil War*, page 31)

Jacob's Furlough

Special Order   Headquarters 1st Regiment
No. 34   Keokuk May 25/61

To all whom it may concern

The bearer J.B. Ritner, a private of Cap. Wise's[1] Company 1st Regiment Iowa Vol aged 33 years 5 ft. 9 in. high, dark complected—eyes dark brown—hair dark,—rather heavy set,—whiskers & mustache—by profession a farmer, born in Pa. and enlisted at Mt. Pleasant in the State of Iowa April 30th, 1861, to serve for the period of three months, is hereby permitted to go to Mt. Pleasant in the Co. of Henry in State of Iowa, he having received a furlough from the 26th of May, till the 30th of May inst., at which period he will rejoin his camp at Keokuk, or wherever it may be—or be considered a deserter. Given under my hand at Keokuk this 25th day of May 1861.

Recommended by   Approved
S. M. Wise Capt. of   J. F. Bates[2]
Company F.   Col

1. 40-year-old Samuel M. Wise served as Captain of Company F, and later as Major of the 17th Iowa Infantry.

2. The Colonel of the 1st Iowa was 30-year-old John F. Bates, whose apparent military ability was limited to having "a gifted way of leading a squad of men up to a bar and shouting in a hoarse baritone, 'Whiskey for six.' " Before the war, he had been an insurance agent, a real estate agent, and a local politician. (Eugene F. Ware, *The Lyon Campaign and History of the 1st Iowa Infantry*, page 306)

Historical Sketch—1st Iowa Infantry

May 23rd, 1861, the regiment received arms and accoutrements, and on May 28th—the tents and camp equipage having arrived—went into its first camp. Previous to that date, it had been quartered in buildings.

The short time that intervened before the regiment was engaged in active service was utilized to the utmost. The Field, Staff and Line officers—with a few notable exceptions–were taking their first lessons in the art of war, and in the study of the rules and regulations for a gov-

ernment of the United States Army, of which the regiment was now a part, and found little time for rest or recreation. Company and battalion drills were in progress many hours each day, and far into the night the officers were engaged in the study of the movements, the manual of arms, and the rules of discipline, so necessary to be learned and taught to the men under their command. How well these lessons were learned in so short a time was demonstrated in the brief but severe campaign in which the regiment was soon called to participate under the leadership of that thoroughly trained and gallant officer, Brigadier General Nathaniel Lyon, of the regular army. (Roster and Record of Iowa Soldiers in the War of the Rebellion; *Published under the authority of the Iowa General Assembly*).

Keokuk, Iowa
May 31, 1861

Dear Wife,

I received your letter today at 10 o'clock, had just time to read it twice, and then go to drill. I have a few minutes before supper to write you a few lines. I think you must have had the blues when you wrote it—had 'em bad. You never told me whether you were all well or not, or did not say a word about the children. Keep a stiff upper lip and remember that I love you and think of you all the time. Indeed I think of you more and miss you more than I thought I would. I wonder whether the bugger catch you at night—whether there has been any storm? Does the water come in the cellar yet?

We are grinding away about as usual here, drilling and being drilled, &c. We have not gone into camp yet, don't know when we will, maybe tomorrow. I guess the guns that came are not for us, but for the home guards. In fact we don't know anything about anything, we just go and drill when we are ordered to, go to meals when we are told to, go to bed when we are ordered to, get up when the drum beats, and don't ask no questions of nobody about nothing, and so keep out of trouble.

I went to hear Oscian E. Dodge sing last night did not get back till 10 o'clock and have to stand guard for it tonight. I don't care though, it paid. I got a good laugh for the first time since I have been here.

Dudley and Foster were down here yesterday to see us. None of our folks were at the station to see me except Hen[1] and Pete[1] and Spence[1]. I did not get to see Mrs. Hen[1]. I don't think I can get away to go to see you. The Captain says I would have to get leave from the Colonel. None of our company have been away except officers. I want very much to see you and have a good hug and kiss, and if you cannot come, I will try to go up there if we stay here long— but we may go any time, so you and Father[2] or Billy[2] had better put old Prince in a buggy and come down. You can come in a day and it will not cost much. Stop at the Simpson House. I like to have forgot to say what I commenced to write about. I left Car's[2] certificate with Alvah[2]. I would have been better, I suppose, to have left it with you, but I was leaving some other papers with him, and gave him that among the rest. Tom[2] has the McClure note and has had for more than a year . . . Kiss all the children for me and when you pray remember

Jake

1. Henry, age 29; Peter, age 16; and Spencer, age 11 were Jacob's brothers. Mrs. Hen was Jacob's sister-in-law, Henry Ritner's wife.

2. Emeline's father was Samuel E. Bereman, age 57. Billy, age 26; Alvah, age 32; and Tom, age 28, were Emeline's brothers. Car was Caroline Freeman, Emeline's sister, age 24.

Camp Ellsworth[1], Near Keokuk Iowa
June 5, 1861

Dear Wife,

There is a parcel of the Mt. Pleasant folks down here and I have a chance to send you a letter tomorrow without pay, so I thought I would write you another letter. I do like to write to you and am glad that I can commune with you in that way. I am going to write to you every chance. And you must write to me; it seems like about a month since I saw you. If I don't get a letter tomorrow, I expect I will get the blues.

A lot of folks came down from Mt. Pleasant yesterday and brought us three wagonloads of provisions. Such a time of joy and rejoicing, yelling, you never heard. Almost every man got a box of pies, cakes, and goodies of all kinds. Till and I stood round with our hands in our pockets and wished it was us. If we had been so fortunate as to have any friends or relations in Mt. Pleasant, I expect we would have got something too. But Bill McClure and Ad

Roads sent Whippo's[2] boys a box of cakes and crackers, a can of butter and a can of blackberries and they divided with us. We have changed our way of cooking since I wrote to you on Sunday. At first we had one cook to every three tents, and each mess eat their own grub in their tent and washed their own dishes. Now we have a long table fixed up outside and all eat together. We have five cooks for the whole company, and they cook it all together and put each man's mess on his plate and then we march up and each one eats his pile and then quits. If any one has anything extra sent by his friends they keep it in their tents and eat it wherever they feel like it. I like this plan better than the first, as it does not mess up the tent so much. We would get along pretty well now if we had plenty of good water, and I guess we will get used to that pretty soon. We had a big shower of rain yesterday, and wind among it, it blew down some of the tents—it did not wet ours much.

We had a fine regimental parade yesterday afternoon; they marched around the parade ground a while and then went down to town to salute Governor Kirkwood. They sent me out to help to build a bridge and I did not get to go. I was glad of it afterward, too, for it rained while they were down town and the whole regiment got ducked and came back wet all over, muddy up to the knees—good joke on the mud. We are proud of our flag—I think it is the nicest one on the grounds—the only one that has a bird on it. The ladies of Mt. Pleasant sent a cake for each man; each cake had the name of a lady on it. We fell into line just before dinner. The Captain walked along the line and each man put his hand in the poke and drew a cake, to see who he would get. I got Miss Josephine McDowell; what are you going to do about it?

You must be getting ready to come down to see me. I do wish I could see you every week and be a soldier too; it would be so sweet, wouldn't it. There are lots of ladies here every day; the omnibuses run from town here all the time, and all the fine ladies and gents come to see the dress parade at 6 o'clock each evening. Mrs. George Stone[3] has been here for some time; sometimes she stays all night in the camp. They all wear gray dresses like yours. Write me another letter Sunday and tell me you love me, and put a kiss in it. You are my sweet wife—take care of our babies and believe I always love you. (kiss)

Jake

1. At the commencement of the Civil War, the U.S. War Department instructed Governor Kirkwood to open a training

camp at Keokuk, located in the southeast corner of Iowa, which became Camp Ellsworth. (Don Elder, *A Damned Iowa Greyhound*, page 183).

2. The Whippo boys were Jonathan and Jacob. Emeline's brother, Jont Bereman, was married to their sister, Amanda Whippo, who died in 1854.

3. The first lieutenant of Jacob's Company F was George Augustus Stone, who would later serve as Jacob's colonel in the 25th Iowa Infantry, and subsequently rise to the rank of brevet brigadier general.

• The June 1, 1861 edition of the Mount Pleasant *Home Journal* contained the following advertisements, both of which indicated that some people were taking this conflict lightly.

New Music, New Music
I wish I was in Dixie's Land, A new and popular Song for the Piano, for sale at the
CITY BOOK STORE.

UNIONISTS AND
Secessionists!
FARMERS
AND FELLOW CITIZENS!
If You Want To Buy
New Goods,
Cheap Goods,
Plain Goods,
Fancy Goods,
Or
Any Kind Of Goods,
Why Go To
McLeran & Gill's
And You Will Be Accommodated
With Anything In The
Dry Goods Line.

Headquarters of 1st Regiment Iowa Volunteers
Camp Ellsworth, Near Keokuk, Iowa
Saturday, June 8, 1861

Dear Emeline,

I am sorry I have not time to write you a long letter as you requested, but will write as much as I can. I wrote you a letter a few days ago and sent it up yesterday. I would have written another and sent it today only Strang said some of you were coming down yesterday and I was in hopes it was you. Ol[1] and Theo Schreiner[2] got here all right, a good while before night, but I did not get your letter till after dark. I was very glad to get it then. I would rather have a letter from my sweet little Emeline than to see everybody else in Mt. Pleasant. The provision was very welcome. All the boys bragged on your cake and I ate a big piece myself because I knew you made it.

This morning about 8 o'clock Hen[1] and his wife and Susanah[1] and Jud[1] got here. They came in a two-horse wagon and brought us a lot of good things. They have gone down to town a little while to see Jim[1], and I can write to you while they are gone. They are going to go part of the way home this evening. Zan[1] must be at her school Monday and Pap is going to start for Pella [Iowa] on Monday. They started in the evening and came part of the way and then started early in the morning and had a pleasant ride. I think you and Billy had better do the same way. It would not cost much to stay all night if you had your own provision—perhaps nothing. I am sorry to hear the baby has been cross. I hope she will not be sick. You must take good care of her. She is a sweet little baby, isn't it? Zan wants to know what you call her. I told Zan her name was Eveline[3].

You must come down to see me the last of next week, won't you? I don't think the baby will mind it much and I don't think the other children will be much trouble. It would be a nice ride for you. I don't want you to be cooped up there at home all the time. I am sorry I have to write to you with a pencil, but I have to write on a book on my knee and cannot use a pen. They have got back from town and I guess I will not get time to write any more today. We have a dress parade this evening. You must excuse this bungling letter and I will write you a better one in a day or two. Fix us up a lot of good pickles and bring them along, and tell Ma to send us some butter. You did not send me any kiss in your letter, and I am going to keep mine till you come down, and then you may have lots of them.

Write to me the first of the week and tell me when you are coming. This isn't half as good a letter as the one you wrote me, but if you will excuse me this time I will try again.

Yours forever, Jake

1. Samuel Oliver "Ol" Bereman, was Emeline's brother, age 20. Susannah Ritner, age 21, nicknamed "Zan," was Jacob's sister. Hen and Judson Ritner were Jacob's brothers. Judson later served with Jacob in Company B of the 25th Iowa Infantry. Jim Freeman was the husband of Caroline (Car) Bereman. Jim also later served with Jacob in Company B of the 25th Iowa Infantry.

2. Ol's friend Theodore M. Schreiner, age 18, was swept up in the patriotic fever and soon enlisted in the 6th Iowa Infantry. He paid the price for patriotism. He was captured at Shiloh, in April 1862 and died in a Confederate prison camp on September 25, 1862.

3. "Eveline," Jacob and Emeline's daughter, born February 16, 1861, was still without a name almost four months after birth. "Eveline" eventually became Katherine, nicknamed Kittie.

[Mt. Pleasant, Iowa]
June the 10th, 1861
Monday night 9 o'clock

Dear Jake,

Ol came home this evening about sundown and brought me two letters. I need not tell you that I was glad. I went out to meet him, and told him to hand them out the first thing. Well, I have read them both twice, and feel much sadder than I have felt for some time. For the last two days I have been <u>elevated</u> with the hope that you would perhaps be at home before your time was out, <u>because</u>, you know they want to ascertain how many will go for three years, and I supposed they would send back all those that wouldn't enlist again, and I thought <u>you</u> would be one, of course. But what must I infer from your letters—You say "But I am in for it now, and want to see the rebels cleaned out, and want to help to do it." Now this cleaning out of rebels will not be done in your three months, and how can you help unless you stay longer—But haven't I got your promise in black and white that you will come home at the end of three months. (certain) (Now Sir, remember it.) You say, "When I get home from this trip I shall never leave you again." If you do not keep the first promise, can I trust that you will keep the last? I would suffer anything rather see you dishonored, but who would think it "sneak or cowardly" to return to a family of little children, when there is enough without you. I have heard several say they knew <u>Jake</u> wouldn't stay. I tell them "no, <u>he is</u> coming home by all means."—Excuse me for such horrible imaginations. You did not say once that you weren't going to come home.—But, but, I feel as if you were thinking it.

Your Father and Mother took dinner with us today on their road to Pella. We acted as though nothing had even occurred between us. I mean to treat her with all the respect that a daughter should treat her mother, and try, by the help of the higher power, to forget the past. You know it has been deeply seated, but I think I can overcome it . . .

I expect Billy would rather be there on a week day to see the drill. But we can't go sooner than that, and could go the first of next week, for I want to be here when Pop comes back . . .

Love, Em (kiss)

Don't think I have been scolding, for I haven't at all, but <u>surely will</u> if you have any idea of staying longer than I expect. We are all well. I have a slight headache. The children always ask, "did Pa say anything about us?"

Historical Sketch—1st Iowa Infantry

The regiment left Keokuk, Iowa on the 3rd day of June, 1861, and was transported by boat down the Mississippi to Hannibal, Missouri, thence by rail to Macon City and Renic. From there they marched across country to Boonville, a distance of fifty-eight miles, in less than two and one-half days, an extraordinary march for these men fresh from their Iowa homes, and not inured to the hardships of a soldier's life. (*Roster and Record of Iowa Soldiers in the War of the Rebellion*; Published under the authority of the Iowa General Assembly)

Editor's Notes:

At the outset of the Civil War, the border states of Delaware, Maryland, Kentucky and Missouri were in the most precarious of situations. Not only was there the possibility of being invaded by either Northern or Southern forces, but the issues that were separating the country were also erupting within these states. Neither the North nor the South wanted to be the first to offend any states' sovereignty by sending troops across their borders.

Slavery was legal in those border states, but was not as important to the economies as compared to the states of the deep south. Within each of the states, there were many who wanted to protect the right to hold slaves and to secede from the Union, but there were also many who opposed slavery and wished to remain within the Union.

Such was Missouri. Governor Claiborne Fox Jackson argued for his state to secede, but others, including Missouri Congressman Francis Blair, Jr., pressed for the state to remain in the Union. Blair was from a prominent Union family—his brother Montgomery was the Postmaster General in Lincoln's cabinet. Governor Jackson brought about a state convention on secession, but Unionist convention delegates successfully defeated the motion.

The Missourians sympathetic to secession had organized a military compound, called Camp Jackson, in honor of Governor Jackson, for the Missouri State Guard. At first, the camp was declared to be a training ground for soldiers to protect Missouri, but the State Guard finally indicated their intentions by raising the Confederate Flag over the fort. In response to this threat, Captain Nathaniel Lyon raided Camp Jackson on May 10, 1861 and captured the 635 Missouri militiamen inside. Lyon then marched his prisoners through St. Louis, where large crowds of citizens gathered, many in protest of Lyon's treatment of these Missouri citizens. Also in attendance at this march were William T. Sherman, his son, and his in-laws.

Unfortunately, someone in the unruly crowd fired a shot at the pro-Union Home Guards who were marching their prisoners through the streets of St. Louis. The Home Guards fired back into the crowd, and in the melee 28 people were killed. The next day, the prisoners were released on parole, but only after each took an oath pledging allegiance to the United States and promised not to take up arms against the Union. All but one prisoner agreed to this. Captain Lyon took this process seriously; violation of this parole could mean death if one of these soldiers were captured again, taking up arms against the United States. (See Jacob's letter of June 22, 1861).

On June 11, there was an important meeting of four men at

Planter's House in St. Louis. This meeting had been arranged by a group called the Conditional Unionists, who firmly felt that war could be averted if the two sides would talk to each other. Attending were Governor Jackson and former Governor Sterling Price representing the secessionists, and Congressman Blair and Captain Lyon representing the Union. Lyon had allowed Sterling Price into the Union-controlled city for this meeting with a "safe conduct" permit.

Jackson quickly presented his proposal, which included protection of all citizens equally, disbanding both the pro-Confederate Missouri State Guard and the pro-Union Home Guard, and also included the provision that the Federal troops commanded by Lyon could not go beyond their current positions within the state of Missouri. This final provision, limiting Federal troop movements in Federal lands, outraged Lyon who stated that this was "outside the bounds of reason," and at the conclusion of this contentious meeting, he declared "This means war!" and had his men escort Jackson and Price out of the city. Jackson retreated to Jefferson City, the capital of Missouri.

Lyon, who was soon promoted to brigadier general, then marched to Jefferson City, and chased Claib Jackson out of town. Jackson retreated to Boonville with Lyon in pursuit. After a brief skirmish at Boonville, Jackson retreated again. At this point, additional forces were sent to Lyon, including the 1st Iowa. (William Riley Brooksher, *Bloody Hill—The Civil War Battle of Wilson's Creek*, pages 41-80).

Hannibal, Missouri
June 14, 1861

Dear Emeline,

I did not expect when I last wrote you that I would write my next letter from here. Everything here is hurry and confusion and we have orders for the first battalion of each regiment (1st & 2nd) to be ready to march on a scouting expedition in one hour, and I thought I would write you a few lines before we start. We are to take three days' provisions. Don't know where we are going. We did not know anything about it till yesterday morning, when we got orders to be ready to march by 2 o'clock. The word came to Keokuk about midnight and Colonel Curtis[1] had his regiment on the way by sun up. We had to break up camp, and have all our baggage hauled to the river and did not get started from camp till 5. We embarked the whole regiment on the Steamboat Jennie Dean just after sundown and arrived here at 12 last night. They marched the whole regiment into the depot, and every man lay down in his tracks with his gun in his hand and slept till morning. I slept first-rate.

They are calling Company F to fall in. I must stop. It rather spoiled your visit, didn't it. Well, never mind, you need not rear up so about me going for three years[1]. I never thought of such a thing. But you may expect to hear of somebody being cleaned out suddenly. I must go.

Your Jake

Address to Hannibal

1. Colonel Samuel Ryan Curtis commanded the 2nd Iowa Infantry, a regiment mustered for a full three-year term, as opposed to the 1st Iowa's 100-day term. Curtis, a Congressman before the war, rose to Major General of volunteers during the conflict in various commands in the Union Army. His greatest accomplishment was his victory at the Battle of at Pea Ridge in Arkansas in March 1862.

Historical Sketch—1st Iowa Infantry

The regiment joined General Lyon's little army at Boonville, Missouri, on the 21st day of June. (*Roster and Record of Iowa Soldiers in the War of the Rebellion*; Published under the authority of the Iowa General Assembly)

Boonville, Missouri
June 22, 1861
On Board the Steamboat *White Cloud*

Dear Friends,

I have but a few minutes in which to write, and in order to save time and money I will write one letter for all. We cannot trust anything to the mail here, but there is a boat going from here to St. Louis this morning, by which we can send letters. I suppose you are all pretty well posted as to what we did, &c. Up to the time we left Macon City, Missouri. How did you like our paper? We left that place last Tuesday at noon on the North Missouri railroad and went down to Renic, Missouri, 40 miles. We heard before we got to Renic that we would have a fight there, but when we came in sight it was diverting to see the way they run, men on horseback going at full speed in every direction and women with their children in their arms running and screaming. There were a lot of cavalry there on their way home from the defeat at this place (of which more hereafter) who had just sat down to a good dinner. They left their rations and broke for the timber. We searched the principal hotel and found a large secession flag with a rattlesnake on it. We sent down the road 3 miles and got an American flag which had been taken down once by the rebels, and raised it on a nice pole, and had another good speech from O'Conner.

Till and about 100 others under Captain Mason[1] of Company C went on to Sturgeon, Missouri, 10 miles, where they had burned a bridge road. The inhabitants nearly all fled at their approach. They took 3 prisoners and raised a flag. We then made preparations to march 40 miles across the country to this place. I went out with Captain Wise's squad (10 men) and impressed two teams to haul our baggage and tents. Each company had to provide two or three teams. We took everything we came to for several miles around.

That night, about 9 o'clock, George Stone[2] went out with a squad of 15, of which I was one, to search a house for arms and ammunition. We surrounded the house and woke them up. They were somewhat astonished when they found out who we were and what we came for, but offered no resistance. There were 6 men and 5 women in the house. We searched the house and everything about the premises but found nothing. When we had got back about a mile we were suddenly arrested by seeing a squad of men 4 or 5 rods to the left of the road. We heard them cock their guns. They ordered us to halt. We formed a line, cocked our guns, and expected a general pitch in immediately, supposing they were Missourians who had found we were out, and intended to cut us off from camp. Each party thought the other an enemy and some were considerably excited on both sides, but none thought of running. George had presence of mind enough to order no one to fire till we found out who they were. He went out alone towards them and found them to be a squad of 32 men from Company C on the same errand that we were. If it had not been for Stone, it would have been a bad affair.

Well, the next morning we commenced the famous march. We came pretty near giving out the first day; it was very hot, and the road through the timber, and water very scarce. We had to go till 3 o'clock without dinner, then marched 4 miles to a place called Bunker Hill, and camped—that is, lay down on our arms without pitching the tents. Next morning we started at 3 o'clock and went 10 miles before breakfast, to a town called Fayette. It is a very pretty town of about 300 inhabitants. The rebels there did not run much, but stood and gritted their teeth at us, but did not attempt to interrupt us. We found some good Union men here too; one of them, the circuit judge of the county, gave us 5 beeves for nothing, which was a great treat, as it was the first beef we had had since we left Keokuk. We ate dinner at noon, and started at 4 o'clock and marched till 11 that night. We had nothing for supper but beef which we broiled on the coals. I stood guard that night from 1 o'clock till morning. Yesterday morning we had nothing for breakfast till we got to this place, which was about 10 o'clock.

Two steamboats of the largest size were lying on the other side waiting to bring us over. It was noon when we got all our baggage on board and got over.

General Lyon says we marched at least 60 miles the way we came and that we beat the famous march of the 7th Regiment of New York[3]. We had to carry our guns, 40 rounds of cartridges, a change of clothes and our blankets, and were very scarce of food and water. We passed only one stream of running water on the route, and slept in the open air with our clothes and arms all on, as it was reported all along the road that the rebels were gathering to meet us, and we did not know what minute we might be attacked. I have not told you near all about the march, but I suppose you will hear it all, and more too. There is a set of poppycocks in our company that thought they were suffering martyrdom all the way, and were continually growling and cursing the officers. I have no doubt but that everything was done for us that could be under the circumstances, and that we suffered nothing more than might have been expected, but some are not satisfied unless they can ride in the cars and have more to eat than they had at home. Such men are a disgrace to the company; it is disgusting to hear them talk, but enough of this.

I think we have done more good since we left Macon than if we had fought and won a battle. Our character and mission has been entirely misunderstood. They told us all along the road that (they thought) we were coming to steal everything we could find, run off the Negroes, ravish the women, &c, and they had always heard in advance that we had done so at the last town. So the whole countryside was filled with consternation (a regiment of soldiers with muskets and bayonets and 25 or 30 teams does make a pretty fierce appearance going through a country). I do not think there was a cent's worth of private property taken on the road without pay. We never went into a house without being invited. Several runaway Negroes came into camp, but the Colonel sent them back; and by this means we created quite a revolution in public sentiment, and encouraged the Union men greatly. Though they always fled at first, when they found that we were behaving like gentlemen, they would return and be friendly. I think the rebels are the most dastardly cowards that ever were made. There was not a gun fired at us in the whole march; the fight, like the "milk sickness" in Indiana, was always 10 miles ahead. I believe we have not lost a man out of our regiment yet, though some have come pretty near killing themselves by accidentally discharging their own guns.

As to this place I have not seen much of it yet. They say it has about 6,000 inhabitants, and is 170 miles above St. Louis. General Lyon is here, also Colonel F. P. Blair with his regiment. There are about 2,500 soldiers here, including 300 regulars belonging to the light artillery; they have several cannons. The soldiers are nearly all quartered on 7 large steamboats that are anchored just below the town. Our regiment has two. We are not allowed to go on shore without permission. The cooks do the cooking on shore and carry it on board to eat.

They are waiting for another regiment to arrive from St. Louis and then we are going up to Lexington, where General Pearce[4] is encamped with 1,000 troops. If we don't get a fight there we will have to give it up altogether, I reckon. General Lyon had a fight a few miles below here last Monday[5], where the rebels attacked them in the rear. Lyon had one regiment, the rebels from 3,000 to 4,000. The rebels ran after the first two or three fires. Claib Jackson took three of the best companies on board a steamboat and escaped up the river, and left the rest to their fate. Two men were killed on our side and about a dozen wounded. Nothing certain is known about the number killed on the other side; they say they lost only four, but some of the men told me that they counted 40 dead bodies and supposed there was a great many more.

They took 100 rebel prisoners, among whom they found 8 that had taken the oath at St. Louis when Camp Jackson was taken; they were taken out and shot the next morning.[6] They took, besides 400 stand of arms, two cannons, all the tents, &c, several hundred pairs of shoes, and large amounts of ammunition, and provision enough for a regiment for ten days. We have been using some of it since we came. The most that escaped crossed the river here on two ferry-boats and went out the road that we came in. We found horses 5 miles from here that had been killed by running; if we had been there then to have intercepted them on the other side, it would have been a good thing.

It is reported now that there was a battle yesterday up at Arrow Rock and another rebel battery taken, but there are so many reports going that we can not believe anything; every ten minutes there is some story going round about a battle or an army of rebels or something of that kind, and it is impossible to find out the truth about anything. We have not seen a paper since we left Keokuk and do not know a thing about what they are doing in Virginia or any-place else. We sometimes see a paper that is published out here, but they have no news from the east.

I must stop for the present. I have written this in a great hurry in order to be in time for the boat, and I don't know but it is gone now. Write to me immediately, direct to me at Boonville, Missouri, Company F, Care of Colonel Bates, 1st Iowa Regiment.

Yours, &c, Jake

N.B.[7] We had to leave Buffington[8] at Macon sick. The rest are all able to travel.

P.S., the opinion of the company on the cavalry question is somewhat modified![9]

1. Captain Alexander Mason of Company C, age 42, of Muscatine was described by Eugene Ware as a "brave man and a very capable officer." He was to be the only officer from the 1st Iowa Infantry to die at the Battle of Wilson's Creek. (Eugene F. Ware, *The Lyon Campaign and History of the 1st Iowa Infantry*, page 338).

2. First Lieutenant George Stone of Company F, of the 1st Iowa Infantry, had been a banker in Mt. Pleasant before the war.

3. General Nathan Lyon referred to the 1st Iowa as his "Iowa Greyhounds" as a token of his admiration for their ability to march long distances. Once, the "Iowa Greyhounds" marched 48 miles in a 24-hour period.

4. Jacob's report on the location of Confederate General Nicholas Bartlett Pearce was incorrect. Pearce, a West Point graduate and

frontier veteran, was still in Arkansas at this time organizing his troops. He would later participate with Confederate General McCulloch in the upcoming Battle of Wilson's Creek opposing General Lyon and the 1st Iowa in August 1861. In September 1861, Pearce's troops unanimously voted not to enter Confederate service because they would be transferred to General Hardee instead of remaining with McCulloch. General Pearce then marched those troops back to Arkansas and disbanded them. (William Riley Brooksher, *Bloody Hill*, page 94; Stewart Sifakis, *Who Was Who In The Confederacy*, page 218).

5. Jacob is referring to what became known as the "Boonville Races."

6. Captured prisoners were frequently paroled during the Civil War. Actual terms of parole varied. Usually a paroled prisoner signed an oath to return to his home and not to bear arms against the opposing army unless he was formally exchanged. The penalty for parole violation could be death, as was the case for these eight Confederates who had been captured a second time.

7. N.B. stands for Note Bien, similar to P.S.

8. Risen S. Buffington, who had enlisted as a fifer, mustered out with the rest of the regiment August 21, 1861.

9. Throughout the war, generals would debate the effectiveness and best purpose of cavalry, but apparently the infantrymen discussed the same issue. Cavalry worked well for information gathering and quick strikes, but were not always satisfactory in battle.

Boonville, Missouri
June 22, 1861

Dear Emeline,

I have just written a long letter in great haste, I want you to read it and then let Billy and Father, Tom, Al, and Billy McClure read it, but don't lose it, and now I want to write some to you, yes, just for my sweet wife. I have been wanting to write to you for several days but had had no chance. Some of the boys wrote yesterday evening and sent them down on a boat that went last night, but I had to stand guard night before last and was so tired that I could not write. We are very much crowded on the boat and not much chance to write. I slept on the hurricane deck last night—slept first-rate. It was the first time since we left Keokuk that we slept without our arms at our side. I have not heard a word from you since we left Keokuk. How I would like to get a letter from you. I do want to know how you are getting along, whether Billy is gone yet, about the children, and everything else. I know that you have written to me but if the letter went to Macon City I do not expect that I will ever get it, as nothing comes across from there without being searched, though the post master there is a Republican and may send them round some other way. You must write to me often anyhow, perhaps I will get some of them. I have just spent the last dime I had for three postage stamps and I will send them all to you.

You need not be uneasy about me going into the army for three years. I have come to the unanimous conclusion that I can do all my fighting in about three months. I don't remember what I said in that letter that made you so spunky, but I certainly had no intention of leaving you for three years. No indeed, I love you too well to do so for any person or anything, especially for such a life as we lead here. You may expect to see me home and get forty thousand kisses just as soon after my time is out as I can get there. And then you will see if I ever leave you again. I do wish I could have seen you again before we left Keokuk, but it will soon be over. I am not afraid of getting sick; my health is first-rate. I am more afraid that you or some of the children will get sick. You must take good care of them and tell them Pa loves them and is coming home to see them and stay all the time. How I would like to see Tommy. I believe there is a boat just going to start.

Good-bye, Your Jake

Direct to J.B. Ritner, Company F, 1st Regiment, Iowa Volunteers
Care General Lyon, 1st Brigade, Missouri

Camp Near Boonville, Missouri
June 27, 1861

Dear Emeline,

I am going to write you a short letter this morning before break-fast. I expect you are not up yet. I think I see you taking such a good nap in that nice room, with our baby. It rained here this morning, but we all had to stir out early to get ready to leave here. We are under orders to be ready to march at an hours' notice, but don't know certain when or where we will go, though we all expect to go south towards Arkansas. The officers have brought 100 teams and wagons and a good many loose horses and mules[1], and they are evidently preparing for a long march somewhere.

We got our pay from the state yesterday evening; we got $7.70 apiece. It came just in good time as I was clear out. It is all State Bank of Iowa money and I do not know whether we can use it here without submitting to a shave[2]. Frank Bowman was accidentally shot in the leg yesterday by a musket. One of our boys had left it standing in his tent with a cap on, it fell down and went off. He is going back to Mt. Pleasant the first chance. John B. Shaw and Parker are going along. I will send this letter by them. I am also going to send you $5 of my money, to pay for what I took when I was at home last. If I keep it here I will spend it some way or other, and I expect you need it worse than I do. I want you to use it to buy clothes for yourself and the children, if you need them, or let Father take it and buy some pigs. You must tell Father to get you some money from the county.

Till was sick all last night and puked a good deal. The doctor has not been around yet but I don't think there is very much the matter. We got tired of living on hard crackers and fat meat and he and I went up to town evening and ate two cherry pies and some cakes. I expect that made him sick. There are lots of fruit here of all kinds. Cherries are $.75 per bushel; the apple and peach trees are loaded—some apples are ripe. Harvest commenced about a week ago.

Don't you think? I have not got any letter from you yet. I do want one so much. It seems like it has been a year since I heard from you. I would give all the money I get for one of your sweet letters. I do not blame you for I know you have written, but I have not got it. I suppose you have got the one I wrote last Saturday on the boat. I wrote the last part of it in such a hurry that I do not expect you could read it. While I was writing the last part of it George Stone said to have my letters directed to J.B. Ritner, Company F, 1st Iowa Regiment, care of General Lyon's Brigade of Missouri. Direct in that way and maybe I will get it.

We moved into camp on the bluff below Boonville last Monday. It is a very nice place for a camp. They are building a battery here to defend the river.

It is breakfast time now and I must quit. It looks now like it would be a wet day, and I do not think we will start.

Noon—the men are nearly ready to start, and I must put up this letter. I have bought a yard of merino from one of the soldiers. I think it is good. I got it for a bit a yard. Make a dress of it, for yourself, or a parcel for the children, and help them to remember me and the war. Tell the children about me—do not let them forget me. I told Parker to go and see you and tell you all the news.

Your Jake

1.   Private Eugene F. Ware of the 1st Iowa Infantry provided the following description of the Missouri mule: "There is no animal on earth like the Missouri mule. He has no superior, no equal. His strength is superflous [sic] and inexhaustible. He will pull until he drops. He enjoys profanity, likes a joke, and is good judge of men." (Eugene. F. Ware, *The Lyon Campaign and History of the 1st Iowa Infantry*, page 162)

2.   Jacob suspected that he would not be able to have his State Bank of Iowa paper money accepted at full value. At this time, the Federal Government was not printing paper money because of the bad experience of it dating back to the Revolutionary War.

Alas! The Vanity of All Mortal Hopes and Calculations

Going Down to "Dixie"
July 3, 1861

Dear Emeline,

Left the camp at Boonville and started southwest. Don't know where we are going or when we will get there. I did not feel much like traveling, had been sick and eaten nothing for four days, felt very weak, but I was determined not be left behind—carried musket and cartridge box, canteen and haversack. Started at 10 o'clock and went 13 miles by 4; just about winked out but made the connection, camped among the brush and slept without tents.

July 4th—Up at 3 o'clock, had breakfast; started at 5. Just before marching I had the good fortune to be promoted—was appointed to drive the team with the Colonel's baggage—bully for me. I have the best mule team[1] in the train and not a very heavy load and get along fine—except to drive it clear through. Think this is one "Fourth" that I will remember. It will do to tell about.

Some of the men wanted General Lyon to fire a salute with the cannon in the morning, but he said he "had often saved his bacon by taking care of the last old cartridge and he would keep his powder for equally patriotic and more useful purposes"—"sound!" And yet there was a good deal of similarity between our celebration and others which I have attended. The main part of all of them is a long, dusty, tiresome march, or "procession" and we beat anything in that line I ever saw. 1st—two companies of artillery with four cannons, 2nd—General Lyon on a gray stallion, with his staff, and ten dragoons[2] for a body guard; 3rd—3,000 men with muskets, most of them with havelocks[3] on, which makes them look, from a distance, just like a drove of sheep; 4th—150 wagons, altogether making quite a grand sight, and then we had quite a picnic, in fact we "picked" more or less all day at some hard biscuit we had along.

We made about 16 miles and camped on Shave-Tail Creek at 2 o'clock. We had a cup of coffee, a cracker, and piece of fat meat for dinner. But then we are going to have beef for supper and breakfast, and all feel patriotic. We have to stay here tonight on account of water—there is plenty here with the creek and three good springs.

The road today had been very rough and rocky, with good springs every few miles, but as the men were seldom allowed to stop and drink, a good many gave out. I passed hundreds lying beside the road, most of them were only tired, but I saw some that were sun struck and seemed to be dying, with no one near them. The hospital wagons were on the rear of the train, and they would have to lie some time before they could be taken up. Such sights rather took the romance out of the "excursion" but I suppose it will be nothing when we get used to it. We passed several large plantations today—the Negroes were all at work as if it was the "Fourth"—all fudge about it being a holiday for them.

I forgot one thing yesterday. We had an eight inch howitzer at Boonville which the General wanted to bring along. They hitched 10 horses to it, but they stalled and balked and broke things generally. The general stormed and swore and cursed everybody to kingdom come, but it was no go, we had to leave it.

July 5th—Alas! The vanity of all mortal hopes and calculations, at least all expectations of taking it easy in the army. I was congratulating myself yesterday on my good luck in getting to drive a team. But I find that one of my mules is the wildest thing in six states. I had rather fight two seceshers[4] every morning before breakfast than bridle that mule[5]. We threw away all the tents this morning except six to each company. It rained about 10 o'clock and we camped at noon. Everybody was as wet as they could ring, but in a good humor.

6th—Started at 5 o'clock as usual, road mostly over a rolling prairie, very thinly settled. It has been a very hot day and a good many gave out. We made 20 miles by 2 o'clock and camped. There was a secession store which they had locked up, but the soldiers broke it open and cleaned it out.

7th—I suppose if we had been at home today it would have been Sunday, but here it was just like any other day. We traveled 20 miles and camped on Grand River, a stream somewhat larger than Crooked Creek, and very high and rapid now. We have to ferry it and have nothing but a little flat boat which can only take one team at a time. They will ferry all night. We were joined this evening by General Sturgis'[6] Brigade from Kansas. He has 2,700 men, including 4 company of cavalry; they have 6 pieces of artillery with them. I understand that we are all going to march together under General Lyon to attack somebody someplace, don't know where. I suppose we are after Claib Jackson. We are now 25 miles from Boonville, which is good marching for 3 days. The men would have stood it very well if they had not walked so fast and camped later, but there is a rivalry between the two regiments to see which can run the other down. Whichever one gets in the lead tries to run off from the other. There is no doubt but that our regiment has stood it so far much better than the other, which is F. P. Blair's crack regiment.

Yours forever, Your Jake

1.   On June 23, Union Quartermaster Justus McKinstry, at odds with Lyon over his habit of ignoring supply regulations, found an opportunity to strike back at him. McKinstry appropriated the supply wagons that Captain Thomas W. Sweeney had acquired, dismissed the mule team drivers, and then resigned. Lyon then had to search Boonville for mule teams, wagons, and teamsters. Jacob was one of those that had volunteered to take the place of the departed teamsters. (William Riley Brooksher, *Bloody Hill*, page 104).

2.   The ten dragoons would have been Prussian soldiers dressed in ornamental uniforms.

3.   Havelocks were a white cloth covering for caps, with a two-foot flap hanging over the neck. They were worn by both Union and Confederate soldiers as a protection from the sun's heat. Havelocks became very popular during the summer of 1861, but were not used much after that year. Besides keeping the sun off

the neck, the havelocks would keep in the heat. Havelocks had several other uses, including straining coffee and drying dishes in camp. They were named after General Henry Havelock of the British Army who was distinguished in the Indian Mutiny in 1857. (Museum of the Confederacy, New Orleans, Louisiana)

4. Secesh, short for secessionist, was a nickname for Confederates.

5. A mule is a cross between a male donkey and a female horse. Mules are an unnatural species, in that they are concocted by man—almost all male mules are sterile, so the species is only continued through planned breeding. The purpose of this breeding is to produce an animal that combines the strength of a horse (a large animal) with the strength of a donkey (endurance and surefootedness).

6. Major S. D. Sturgis had come to join Lyon from Fort Leavenworth, Kansas with approximately 2,200 men.

Camp on Grand River
Missouri, July 8, 1861

Dear Emeline,

I have just discovered that there will be a chance to send a letter back now in a few minutes. I have not got any letter from you yet, but will write anyway, since we left Keokuk. Oh! How I would like to get a letter. I think it is strange I do not, as a good many others have received letters since then. Some have got them since we left Boonville. I can only hope that you and the children are all well. You may look for me and all the rest of us home just as soon after our time is out as we can get there, though we are all willing to serve the time out.

There is a great deal of talk among the men about the way Parker[1] backed out; it is considered rather a sneaking trick.

I was not well when we left Boonville. I had the diarrhea and had eaten nothing for four days, but I said nothing about it for fear they would leave me behind. I am getting better now and think I will soon be well. I get to ride most of the time. Till and Whippo's boys are well and get along very well.

It will take all day tomorrow to get the army across the river, but I understand that as fast as they get across they go on to the Osage, which is 18 miles farther, and cross it and wait there till all are across. It is a very hot, mean place here and we want to get away. I expect our regiment will cross tonight.

I must stop for fear I lose my chance to send this. I will write to you every time I have an opportunity to send a letter, though I may not have another for a month . . . I want you to have me a nice white shirt and good dinner ready when I get home.

Yours forever, Your Jake (kiss)

1. In Jacob's June 27 letter he mentioned that Parker and John B. Shaw accompanied the wounded Frank Bowman back to Mt. Pleasant.

Historical Sketch—1st Iowa Infantry

Here [camp on the Grand River] the regiment remained until July 13th and on that day, took up the line of march with the other troops composing General Lyon's command. From this date to the close of its term of service, the history of the regiment is identified with that of the little army commanded by General Lyon, on the march, the skirmish line, in camp and bivouac, and in battle. (*Roster and Record of Iowa Soldiers in the War of the Rebellion*; Published under the authority of the Iowa General Assembly).

This Is The Poorest, Rockiest, Meanest, Most God-Forsaken Country I Ever Saw

Camp of Brigade of Missouri
Near Springfield, Missouri
July 17, 1861

Dear Emeline,

I am going to write you another letter, but I do not know whether you will ever get it. I found out accidentally, at Grand River, that the officers were going to send an express back with letters, and that they did not intend to let the men know anything about it, for fear he would be overloaded. So I wrote you one in a hurry and slipped it in among theirs without their knowing it. Did you get it? They say there is a regular mail to Springfield, and I was in great hopes that all the letters you have written to me would be forwarded on there and I would get them, but I was entirely disappointed. Isn't it too bad. I have not heard a word from you directly or indirectly since we left Keokuk! I would give everything I have for a letter from you. I am so anxious to know how you get along, where you are living, whether Billy and Tom are gone, what the children do and say, and all about everything. We hardly ever get a paper or hear any news from the east that is reliable. I got a copy of the president's message yesterday. I want you to save all the papers you can get till I come home—they will all be new to me.

We left Boonville the 3rd of July and arrived at this camp last Saturday. We are about 12 miles from Springfield, northwest. It is reported that we will stay here some time, perhaps two or three weeks. This is as near the town as they could find a good place to camp. We are camped on a high prairie where there is plenty of grass and near several large springs that afford an abundance of good water.

Major Sturgis' command is also here, and we make altogether 6,000 men, and 1,000 mules and horses. It is about 100 miles in a straight line from Boonville to Springfield, Missouri but we traveled 175 to get here. Jackson had destroyed the ferries and bridges on the direct route, and we had to go out of the way to get across the Grand and Osage Rivers. Our officers say we made as good marching as was ever done considering the character of the roads and the length of the train. We made one forced march that I think would be hard to beat.

Last Wednesday night we crossed the Osage, did not all get over till after midnight. General Lyon heard in the night that General Sigel was defeated by Claib Jackson[1], and that he was retreating toward Springfield, pursued by Jackson. Lyon determined to go to his relief, it was 75 miles to Springfield. We started by 3 o'clock, rested two hours, and went 20 miles. The regiments camped at 2 o'clock in the morning, but the train did not get in until after sun up. I drove all night over the roughest roads I ever saw. I drove up hills a mile long where the road was nothing but a mass of rock— in fact this is the poorest, rockiest, meanest, most God-forsaken country I ever saw, very few inhabitants, and but little timber, but plenty of good springs. We had some very hot weather on the road, but it has not been so hot here as I have seen it in Iowa. The folks who live round here say this is the highest part of the Ozark mountains. I do not see any signs of mountains, but we are certainly on very high ground.

We are about as far south as Cairo, Illinois and the weather at night especially is cool. Till and I slept in the wagon last night with three blankets over us and were cold, and the mountain cactus is abundant on the high rocky points. We are not troubled by flies or mosquitoes.

I forget to say that after we made the forced march, the general learned that Jackson was defeated instead of Sigel[2], and that the troops had arrived at Springfield from the east. The general makes his headquarters at Springfield. Most of our officers have been down there. They say it is generally believed there that Jackson lost 1,181 men killed, but I suppose you will know the particulars before we will. Part of the Kansas Regiment went out last night, and captured and disarmed a company of 100 secessionists. Claib Jackson has gone off toward Arkansas; we may follow him in a few days, and we may stay here until our time is out.

Our commissary department has just about dried up. They cut down our rations one-third several days ago, and yesterday they cut down the bread three-fourths—that is, instead of six crackers per day, we get one and a half. We get very little coffee, no sugar, but the usual amount of beef. The natives round here bring in a good deal of provision, but sell it scandalous high. We have spent nearly all our money, and are going to commence stealing pretty soon unless we are fed better. I think we will be. General Lyon is running three or four threshing machines, and two steam mills at Springfield, and having the flour baked as fast as possible. We can get plenty of blackberries within two miles of the camp, but can get no sweetening. Apples and peaches are very plenty, but not ripe.

I think you may look for us home when the time is out, or soon after. We may have to stay here till the 14th of August, and go home afterward. If we go no further we will have 100 miles to march to a railroad. General Lyon says that our regiment is the best drilled, best behaved, and the best travelers in the brigade, and that it is a pity we are only in for three months. As far as the marching is concerned I am satisfied that we can beat them badly[3]; five men fall out of F. P. Blair's regiment every day to one of ours.

The men are all in favor of going home when the time is out, though a great many will enlist again if they get a chance, but very few will do so before going home.

I believe I have told you all the news. Till and Whippo's boys are well and getting along first-rate. If you get this letter in good time, write to me and direct to me at Springfield, Missouri, same Company F, 1st I.S.V., care Colonel Bates, please forward . . .

Yours forever, Your Jake

1. Jacob is referring to the Battle of Carthage, where Confederate Claiborne Fox Jackson did defeat Union General Franz Sigel, another German-born General, who fled to Springfield.

2. This restated story of the Battle of Carthage, where Sigel defeated Jackson, was not true.

3. The marching song of the 1st Iowa Infantry, as printed in the September 28, 1861 *Home Journal*:

The Happy Land of Canaan
War Song of the Iowa 1st

I'm almost ninety-nine and shall remember well the time
When this country was invaded by Great Britain–ha, ha!
But freedom's noble sons with the brave Geo. Washington,
Made 'em get from this happy land of Canaan.
[Chorus:]
Oh, oh, oh, ha, ha, ha, ha, ha, ha!
The day of the Pentecost is coming, ha, ha
Oh, it's never mind the weather,
But get over double trouble,
For we're bound for the happy land of Canaan.
Now I'll bring my rhyme down to the present time
Once more we are threatened by invasion, ha, ha!
Jeff Davis and his clan say they can take Washington,
And bust up this happy land of Canaan.
Chorus.
But Lincoln he is there, you'll bet he'll take good care
To maul all the traitors in the Union, ha, ha!
The secessionists will turn pale, for he'll ride them on a rail!
Clean out his happy land of Canaan.
Chorus.
I suppose you all do know, that not many days ago,
When a swarm of traitors was a buzzing in Camp Jackson, ha, ha!
But one day while at their lunch, Uncle Sam surrounded the bunch,
And he drove 'em from this happy land of Canaan.
Chorus.
Then up with the glorious flag, and down with secession rags,
Let the scream of the eagle be the Union, ha, ha!
God bless the whole caboodle, hail Columbia, Yankee Doodle,
Hurrah for the happy land of Canaan.
Chorus.

Camp at Pond Springs, Missouri
July 27, 1861

Dear Emeline,

This is Saturday evening and I have been thinking all day what a long letter I would write to you tomorrow, but a messenger just now came into camp with orders from General Lyon to Colonel Bates. And the captain just now came around and told us all to be ready to march at a moment's notice. It is generally believed that we are going south to try once more to get a fight with Claib Jackson. This came rather unexpectedly to us, as it had been reported in camp for two or three days that we would start any minute. I will write as long as I can and then quit.

I wrote to you from our camp 12 miles northwest of Springfield. We stayed there a week and moved here a week ago today. This is 15 miles from the other camp and 25 miles west of Springfield. There are between 2,000 and 3,000 encamped here now, quite a large number at Springfield, and one regiment 15 miles west of here. It is reported that Jackson is coming to attack us. We hope it is so, but think it is too good to be true.

I was very unwell the day I wrote the last letter and for several days after. I never had the diarrhea[1] so bad in my life. It was made worse by not being able to get anything wholesome to eat. I would have given anything almost for a little toasted bread or thickened milk, but could not get. I am well enough now except that I am very weak in the legs. I do not believe that I could walk two miles, but if we have to march I can drive my team and shall get along very well unless we have to run and then I shall make a poor hand.

Don't you think we had a big time in camp day before yesterday. Our commissary came in from St. Louis and it was reported that he had 1,000 letters for our regiment. It raised quite an excitement among the men. I expected to make a big haul, of course. Well, I did. I got one letter from you dated June 19, the first one you wrote after we left Keokuk, and one from Ike[2] dated June 23rd. I was very glad to get your letter if it was old. I read it over three times. It did me a great deal of good.

I am very glad that Billy did not go with the cavalry for three years. The regular army is the last place, as at present constituted, for any person to be who has any intelligence or self-respect. They are treated worse than the mules. I have seen many of them tied up and whipped like brutes for trifling offenses[3]. I would sacrifice anything, even life itself for the good of country if it was absolutely necessary, but nothing else would ever induce me to join the regular army. Tom and McClure being officers may get along better, but they will have a hard time.

We have been living on very short rations for two weeks. For two days we got nothing but beef[4] and coffee without sugar; now we get 1½ cracker[5] apiece per day and 1½ pint corn meal. This would do if we had any grease or milk to eat it with, but we have not; we make mush and eat it so, without anything with it except beef. We have had so much beef and no way to cook it except boil it that we are all sick and tired of it, and would like to have some fat pork again.

Our commissary brought havelocks for some of the companies, but not for us. He brought no money or clothes. We are the most ragged set of men I ever saw; some are nearly naked. We expect to get our new uniforms at St. Louis on our way home. I have seen a specimen of it—it is very nice.

If I can find out in time where we are going or when I will let you know before I seal this letter. It is about 8 days' march from here to the nearest railroad station. I suppose it would take us about 10 days to go to St. Louis, though we might do it in less time if it was necessary.

Sunday Noon—Well we have not moved from here yet, and I don't see any signs of our going soon. I think the report of our going south after Claib Jackson was a false alarm. I think we will remain here until we start home, which will be about Wednesday or Thursday. I think we will be at home about the 20th of August or at least by the first of September. I don't expect it will be worth while for you to write me any more. I hope I will get some of the letters you have written on the way home. Till says to tell the folks that he is all right but has no time to write. He is boss cook now which is a very responsible position and keeps him very busy. I don't know whether you have any money yet from the county or not, but I want you to tell Father to get you some more. If there are plenty of blackberries there you must get some jugs and put up some.

Tell the children that I am coming home before long, and I am going to bring them something. Till got a letter from Ada the other day.She said our baby had blue eyes, and that its name was Minnie[6]— is that so? I will write to you again when we get started home.

Yours forever, Your Jake

1. During the war, diarrhea accounted for over 44,000 deaths in the Union Army.

2. Isaac Ritner, age 24, was Jacob's brother. Isaac later served in the 33rd Iowa Infantry.

3. Jacob is contrasting the Regular army to the Volunteer army. Although Billy Bereman did not enlist in the Regular army cavalry, he did enlist in the 4th Iowa Cavalry with his brother Ol. Early in July, the 1st Iowa surrounded a soldier of the Regular army who had been "bucked and gagged" for some minor offense, and threatened to untie him. At one point, about a dozen soldiers in the Regular army, with bayonets fixed, approached the 1st Iowa to warn them off. (Eugene F. Ware, *The Lyon Campaign and History of the 1st Iowa Infantry*, page 152).

4. Some time around July 20, the 1st Iowa was given a "fly-blown, putrid quarter of beef" that had been rejected by the Regular army. Initially the 1st Iowa "raised hell," then, turning anger to humor, buried the putrid beef with full military honors.

5. Crackers were also referred to as hard tack.

6. This is a reference to Jacob's and Emeline's daughter Kittie, still unnamed at age five months.

• This was the last letter that Jacob wrote while in the First Iowa Infantry. In August, General Lyon and his Union troops continued to engage the Confederates, with skirmishes at Dug Spring on August 2, McCullah's store on August 3, and Battle of Wilson's Creek on August 10.

The Battle of Wilson's Creek

General Lyon found himself deep into Missouri, outnumbered by Price and McCulloch, his Confederate opponents, two to one. He considered a withdrawal but thought he would improve his chances for a successful retreat by first attacking his enemy.

One of his generals presented a plan where the Union Army would separate into two forces and assault the enemy in a "concentric surprise." This proposal violated military principle by dividing a smaller army against a larger foe, but Lyon accepted the strategy over the objections of the other Union generals.

On August 10, General Sigel, the author of the "concentric surprise," attacked from the south, but after a confusing charge, withdrew his troops back to Springfield, leaving Lyon without the support he was expecting.

The 1st Iowa and Jacob were in the center of Lyon's attack from the north where they engaged the Confederates on Oak Hill, later renamed Bloody Hill. During the battle, Lyon was wounded in several places and had his horse shot out from under him. He mounted another horse, was struck by another bullet, then tumbled off his horse and died. The fighting continued until Lyon's second in command, Major Sturgis, ordered a retreat. Losses were about 1,200 on both sides, but Confederates claimed a victory because they remained on the battlefield. From a broader perspective Lyon's attack at the Battle of Wilson's Creek helped keep Missouri in the Union by purchasing time for the Union to gather powerful forces in the state.

Jacob's Company F suffered casualties in this battle, including one of the Whippo boys that Jacob frequently mentioned in his letters. The following poem eulogized Corporal Jonathan R. Whippo, who was shot in the head and killed instantly:

J. R. WHIPPO
Fell August 10th, at the battle of Springfield . . .
Yes many a mothers darling son,
Comes home no more—the murderous fray
Was pitiless: Their young lives were
Their country's; on that fearful day . . .
We scarcely name one, from the whole
But bless the graves that cover all.
A loyal Band—unparalleled,
In their most consecrated fall.
Two brothers went—brave—noble—true
Now greets but one, the mother's view . . .
Thy death young Whippo, binds the chain
That brings us peace and hope again.

—L. A. F.
[Mrs. Lydia A. Fowler] Mt. Pleasant, Sept. 1st, 1861
Home Journal, September 7, 1861

(The Roster Report incorrectly listed Jonathan Whippo as having survived the war.)

Historical Sketch—1st Iowa Infantry

The day the gallant Lyon gave up his life on the battlefield of Springfield, Missouri, August 10, 1861, practically ended the active military history of the First Iowa Infantry. A few days later, the regiment proceeded to St. Louis, where it was mustered out of the service on the 21st day of August, 1861. The subjoined summary of casualties shows a loss of over 17 percent of its total number at muster in, and is convincing evidence of its arduous service in the field, which lasted less than two months. The loss of the regiment at Wilson's Creek was 13 killed, 141 wounded and 4 missing, and constituted by far the greatest part of its total loss during the campaign.

The history of the service of this regiment reveals the fact that a very large number of the officers and enlisted men of the regiment re-enlisted as fast as opportunity was offered in the Iowa regiments which were subsequently organized, and that many received commissions. Some of these officers attained high rank before the close of the war, and all reflected honor upon their State by their heroism in the numerous battles in which they were engaged . . .

To the dead and the living of this splendid regiment—Iowa's first contribution to the Grand Army of the Republic—the compiler of this sketch makes a soldier's salute, before . . . recording the history of the long line of Iowa regiments that followed it. In nearly every other Iowa regiment, one or more representatives of the First Iowa Infantry found opportunity to lengthen the record of patriotic service to his country.

SUMMARY OF CASUALTIES:
Total Enrollment: 959
Killed: 13
Wounded: 141
Died of Disease: 7
Died of Wounds: 5
Missing in Action: 4

(Roster and Record of Iowa Soldiers in the War of the Rebellion; *Published under the authority of the Iowa General Assembly).*

- Jacob returned to Mt. Pleasant, where he soon began his efforts as a recruiting officer. Eventually he re-enlisted and was mustered in as First Lieutenant of Company B, 25th Iowa Infantry.

Chapter Three
The Vicksburg Campaign

Historical Sketch—25th Iowa Infantry

The Twenty-Fifth Regiment was organized under the proclamation of President Lincoln, dated July 2, 1862. The ten companies composing it were ordered into quarters by Governor Kirkwood, on dates ranging from August 2 to September 1, 1862 . . . The commander of the regiment, Colonel George A. Stone, had won honor and distinction in his previous service as First Lieutenant of Company F, First Iowa Infantry and, later, as Major of the Fourth Iowa Cavalry. Under the instruction of this very capable and energetic officer, the regiment improved to the utmost in the time it remained in rendezvous. By the time it left the state, it had acquired a fair knowledge of the drill and discipline so essential to effective service in the field.

Early in November, the regiment proceeded to St. Louis, and thence down the Mississippi River to Helena, Arkansas, where it went into camp. During its stay at Helena, detachments from the regiment accompanied reconnoitering expeditions to White River and elsewhere, but the record does not show that these expeditions encountered any considerable force of the enemy. The regiment was assigned to the Second Brigade of the First Division, Fifteenth Army Corps[1]. Brigadier General Charles Hovey[2] led the brigade, while Brigadier General Frederick Steele[2] commanded the division. (Roster and Record of Iowa Soldiers in the War of the Rebellion; *Published under the authority of the Iowa General Assembly)*

1. The 15th Army Corps was formally created in early January 1863, with General Sherman as commander. The Army of the Tennessee, commanded by General Grant, would include the 15th Army Corps, the 13th Army Corps, commanded by General McClernand, and the 17th Army Corps, commanded by General McPherson.

2. Brigadier General Charles Edward Hovey had been a teacher from Illinois, and at the outbreak of the Civil War, organized a regiment of professors and students. Brigadier General Frederick Steele, the former Colonel of the 8th Iowa, was a native New Yorker and graduate of West Point. Steele had

fought at Wilson's Creek as a captain. (Stewart Sifakis, *Who Was Who In The Union*, page 202, 389).

• Union forces, led by General Grant as Commander of the Army of the Tennessee, were on their way to Vicksburg, Mississippi, located on high bluffs overlooking the Mississippi River. Early in the war, the Federals recognized the importance of controlling the Mississippi River– accomplishing this would cut off the western states from the Confederacy and open trade routes down the Mississippi for the Union.

As Grant stated in his Memoirs:
Vicksburg was important to the enemy because it occupied the first high ground coming close to the river below Memphis. From there a railroad runs east, connecting with other roads leading to all points of the Southern States. A railroad also starts from the opposite side of the river, extending west as far as Shreveport, Louisiana. Vicksburg was the only channel. . . connecting the parts of the Confederacy divided by the Mississippi. So long as it was held by the enemy, the free navigation of the river was prevented. Hence its importance.

From Emeline's Mother to Emeline's Father

[Mt. Pleasant, Iowa]
Aug 10, 1862

Dear Husband,
We have been looking for a letter from you for two weeks and received none. I have commenced to write again. Maybe you are sick and can't write. If so, get somebody to write me. I want to hear from you were much and more than that. We want you to come home and that soon. We are all in excitement here again. There never was such a time before. I thought I wouldn't hurry you home before your time was out, although, I wished you were home many times, especially at this time.

I suppose you have heard of the 300,000 volunteers called for and 300,000 to be done after. All the loyal men are determined not to be drafted. They are enlisting so there will not be many to be drafted and all the disloyal will be left at home . . . 8 or 18 left already. The disloyal ones are getting to be very bold.

Roderick[1] was getting up a company. Sent a recruiting officer to Rome [Iowa]. They threatened to hang him, saying there were men in Mt. Pleasant have promised to help them to hang all the abolitionists. Three of them have been taken and sent to Alton[2] . . .

Jim[3] was sworn in yesterday. Till is to stay with Car if he is not drafted. Jont[4] is to be down tomorrow to be sworn in. I don't know what will become of Sarah[4].They moved down Thursday. She was crying all the time. Says she can't stay at home and her father and mother are such hardheaded Democrats, they don't think Jont ought to go so she can't stay there.

Pro Smith[5] is captain of a company. Jake[6] is lieutenant. Their company is nearly full. They expect to start next week. Roderick's is full. There are four more companies making up here. Em expected Car today with her. She don't know what to do and what will we do. Till is going to leave in a day or two . . .

We are in an awful fix here. We heard Tom[7] had resigned but can't hear from him. Jake says he has resigned to get to be Maj. General . . . Al[8] hasn't got his discharge yet. He is in a fret. He wants a place in [with] some of the new recruits . . . What is left are for going into home guard. They have 40 muskets. I shall be so uneasy till you get home. So much more traveling more than when you left. I wish you were home tonight. I would have one night's rest. I always feel safe when you are home. We got a letter from Billy[9] and Ol[9] last week. They went at Helena. Billy said Oliver was complaining, but he was well.

Your affectionate wife,

E. H. Bereman

I have three nice apples of our tree saving for you. Zan Ritner is crazy. They have taken her to the Asylum[10]. Sarah is not well yet, but is better . . . Give my love to your folks . . . Going to have lots of watermelons and sweet potatoes, but how can we enjoy them when we know there are so many suffering ones.

1. Second Lieutenant Simon F. Roderick had served with Jacob in Company F of the 1st Iowa Infantry. He recruited a company of men and led them as captain in the 19th Iowa Infantry. 206 men of that regiment, including Roderick and his older brother Daniel, were captured at the Battle of Stirling's Plantation in September 1863. Roderick eventually was exchanged and returned to his regiment, where he was promoted to major.

2. Alton, Illinois, on the Mississippi River, housed a Union prison camp where Samuel E. Bereman worked as a guard as part of the 37th Iowa Infantry. The 37th Iowa frequently went by the nickname "the Greybeards" because the initial enlistment was from men too old for normal service.

3. Jim Freeman, their son-in-law, was married to their daughter Caroline (Car). Jim enlisted in Company B of the 25th Iowa Infantry with Jacob.

4. Jonathan (Jont) Slaughter Bereman was their son, who had enlisted in Company B of the 25th Iowa Infantry with Jacob. Sarah Fleming was Jont Bereman's second wife. Sarah's parents did not approve of the war nor Jont going to war and would not let Sarah live with them while Jont was away.

5. Pro Smith was Professor John Allison Smith, Captain of Company B of the 25th Iowa Infantry at its formation. Professor Smith was the Superintendent of Public Schools in Mt. Pleasant at the time of his enlistment. At age 47, Smith was one of the oldest members of the regiment. Quartermaster Frederick J. Clarke, age 54, and Lieutenant Alexander Lee, age 48, may have been the only men older than Captain Smith in the regiment. Clarke later resigned his position and Lee died of disease. (Mt. Pleasant *Home Journal*, January 31, 1863).

6. Jacob Ritner, age 34, their son-in-law, was First Lieutenant of Company B of the 25th Iowa Infantry and Emeline's husband.

7. Their son, Thomas Bereman, resigned as Second Lieutenant of the 1st Iowa Cavalry on September 3, 1862. He later re-entered in the 1st Iowa Cavalry, being appointed Captain on May 7, 1863, and Major on February 15, 1865.

8. Another son, Captain Alvah Bereman of the 18th Infantry, Regular Army, had been wounded at the Battle of Shiloh. Alvah was anxious to resign his position in the Regular Army so that he could take a position in the Volunteer Army (Alvah's Obituary).

9. Their sons Billy Bereman and Samuel Oliver "Ol" Bereman were both in the 4th Iowa Cavalry.

10. The Iowa Hospital for the Insane opened in Mt. Pleasant in March 1861.

From Samuel E. Bereman, Emeline's Father

[Fragment—August 1862]
[Dear Em,]

But I think I hear you say that if a bear had come along when he and little Johnny were sleeping, there would be danger of his devouring those two little boys. Now look here, everybody has to die and I believe everybody dies when their time comes and everybody dies when God's time for them to die comes and not before. If God has anything to do with it, numbering our days here on earth, no bear or Secesh or anything in the world can shorten our time one minute. I think that there are too many Christians like us poor Infidels. They are not afraid to die. One, but they don't want to die yet. They are afraid God will not watch them close enough, and let things die before their time comes, or let some Secesh kill them, which would be just as bad. The Christian says, "Thy will be done" and if it is thy will that a secesh should kill me, Why, amen, not that I will submit to it because I can't help it, but I am actually willing to be disposed of as thou Lord seest fit. . . And if a bear had eaten up little Johnny and his brother, God would still take care of him or them.

Emeline, these reflections are the result of my most serious and honest thoughts. You know that the preachers are frequently arguing their persons to read and investigate and hunt for the truth and then when their same persons differ with them in coming to conclusions, they are denounced as infidel and dangerous persons sometimes.

Well, now do think I had actually forgotten myself and was writing along as though you would be at home alive and well when this reaches Mount Pleasant. What strange beings we are, that is myself, I would not insinuate that anybody else is strange or odd by any means. How wonderful and strange are the ways of Providence. Who would have thought last May the 7th when I left home that my family would all be murdered by the ruthless hand of rebellion and I alone left.

Well, I think I will winter at Pike's Peak and then go to Cal or Oregon or Washington. Wonder what I will follow for living there? No trade, no talents, no money, no nothing except old Prince. My land here not worth anything and my home at Mount Pleasant by this time is confiscated to pay for my abolitionism.

I am bereaved above measure surely. Oh is there any God? And where is He and does He care and does He pay any attention to what is going on, or has He just started this machine and gone to take a nap and left things to chance?

Wonder if my boys won't all be killed in the army or will He take care of them till their time comes to die? O, this horrid notion that people have of things happening by chance. This widespread infidelity of denying that God governs all things. That nothing takes place contrary to his will and good pleasure. Of denying that God had any use for sin and the Devil. Do you suppose there ever would have been any Devil if God had not had the use for him? Does the Devil exist merely by God's permission or in spite of him, or does God have any further use for the old fellow and therefore sustains him by his almighty? However, I say that the Devil without God's sustaining power would hop into oblivion and forgetfulness in a moment. God governs is the motto that should be on the banner of every Christian. What idea or truth once heartily embraced acts as an anchor to the soul. God governs. "My father is at the helm" was the reply of a lad on board a vessel that was about to go down, when he was asked why he was not alarmed. Recollect that our having confidence in God does not prevent us from dying when He sees fit to take us away, but it takes away that fear or dread of dying, or as Paul says, it takes away the sting of death. That is why it is represented as an anchor. It helps one from being topped about from that hath that torment.

You recollect an argument Jake and I had at your house once in December on the use of Prayer. He argued that a Christian could have it to rain in a dry time by asking God to send a shower or to have it stop raining and the sun shine out just by praying for it. I suppose he has seen the fallacy of that argument by this time. If his position was correct, why did not he or some other good man or woman have this war stopped long ago, or have it stopped now?

The advantage that the Christian has over one who is not a Christian is simply this. The Christian has love, peace, joy, &c. And the unbeliever has fear, doubt and no anchor. Hark! What was that I heard? I thought I heard somebody say that all this was cold comfort. Well, I cannot afford anything better from my shop. When I give you the best I have on hand you should not grumble. You know I am not like anyone else and do not peddle in all the trash that is in the merchantmen because it is popular . . .

They thought it would not do to contradict what they saw in a Methodist preacher. Their preacher last Sunday told them they were not at liberty to criticize his sermon as they were to criticize a political or war speech. They were bound to hear him and take it for truth just as old Pap Burnette said up in Jefferson once.

That is just what the Roman Catholic Priest tells his dedicated followers and they have to sit mum. I am like old Sam Howe. I liken my Liberty too well for that. I must be think for myself and if I think differently from the preacher, I want the liberty to say so if I want to. That's all.

Pop goes the weasel.

From Emeline to Her Father, S. E. Bereman

[Mt. Pleasant, Iowa]
August the 15th, 1862

Dear Father,

I sit down to write you a few lines in great haste to tell you that we all want you to come home immediately. Everybody is going to war, and you must come home to stay with us poor women. Jake, Jim, and Jont are all going, and maybe Alvah. Till is going to stay with Car (provided he is not drafted) so Ma is left alone and I am alone and I don't know what will become of the Sarahs[1]. Sarah Jont can go to her Father's but she doesn't want to. Jont is going to rent his farm out and she talks some of living with the renters. I suppose you have heard long before this of the call for 300,000 volunteers, and for another 300,000 to be drafted. Well there are so many volunteers, that they think there will be no need of drafting in this county. It is perfectly astonishing to see how the men do rush to the call of the president. There are about five companies making up here in town. Two are full and have been waiting for further orders for some days. Trenton, Marshall, and Jefferson have turned out. Don't you think old Hiram Nosler is going, and Billy Degroodt, and Bill Harlan and a host of others from around there. Professor Smith and Jake got up a Co. together, the Professor is Capt. And Jake 1st Lieutenant, and the Trenton boys elected Sam Steele 2nd Lieut. ("What wooden officers you say") They are ready to go into camp. I expect Jim Freeman will be Orderly Sergeant. He got the nomination for that at the Trenton meeting. He ran for 2nd Lieut., but Sam beat him. (They haven't elected but the three yet) Roderick has a full Co. and old Ollie Lee the tavern keeper has one most full and so has Jim Spearman. Dick Brown is trying to raise one, says he has 60 men don't know whether it is so or not. So you see they will take all the Union men off and leave the secesh here to play hob and burn up the town and you must come home and be a home guard, and help defend the country, and let that farm alone for awhile or everything will go to sticks yet. I feel as though everybody must do something. Jake has got to get me a gun before he leaves, and I will try to use it, if there is any necessity for it here at home.

Now we soon to know whether you are coming home or not (right soon I mean) because we don't know how to get along without you. Sit right down and write us a letter just as soon as you get this and tell us you are coming. We haven't had a letter from you for four weeks I believe. In your last you talked of going to Pikes Peak, don't go, for pity sake, for it won't pay. I heard Ma saying she had $7.00 of your money saving for you to come home or if you need it, don't wait for it, but come home on credit and paying your way afterward. Write soon and come bring the letter. All well, but Lulie's eyes. She is most blind. <u>Nothing more</u>

E.R.B. Ritner [Emeline Ramsey
Bereman Ritner]

1. The family would refer to the various Sarah's by attaching the name of the particular Sarah's husband, as in Sarah Alvah and Sarah Jont.

Letters Beginning with the 25th Iowa Infantry
With General U. S. Grant and the Army of the Tennessee

Camp Near Helena, Arkansas
2nd Division, 2 Brigade,
November 16, 1862

Dear Emeline,

This is Sunday night, 8 o'clock, and I have just got time to sit down and write you a few lines. I have no ink and have to take a pencil. Billy and Jont have been in our tent all evening just now. It has been raining hard ever since dark. I wonder how it is at Mt. Pleasant, and what my sweet Emeline is doing? I expect the children are all in bed and you are sitting up trying to write me a letter. No, I expect you are in bed too, and taking a good sleep, without thinking about Jake, but maybe you are sick or some of the children, or somebody is there and you are all sitting around the stove talking, or perhaps you are down at Ma's or someplace. I wish I knew all about it. Won't you write and tell me. Do, my sweet dear. There were a lot of letters that came today for our company, but none for me, but I expect to get one by the next mail, as I have got none yet since we left home. Billy and Ol, got one today from Sarah. But I must begin and tell you about our travels, and where we got to.

Well, I wrote to you just before we got to Memphis. We got there at 10 o'clock Thursday and stayed till the next morning, and then started again for Helena, Arkansas. Memphis is quite a large place and there is a good deal of business done there, mostly in army stores, though a good deal of cotton is coming in now. They said 1,000 bales the day we were there. I saw several wagons loaded with cotton bales on the bottom and covered with corn fodder and wood, &c, so as to pass the rebel pickets and spies.

We got to Helena by 2 o'clock, and then marched out back of the town about 3 miles and camped, or rather stayed right beside the 4th Cavalry, for we had no tents. We found the 4th all right, and very glad to see us. We had a perfect camp meeting. I ate supper with Josh Gardner[1] and all our company got their supper with the 4th. I got my breakfast at Dr. McClure's[2]. Billy & Ol and all the rest of the Boys are well and look first-rate and just as natural as life.

We had to leave Jim Freeman, Jeffrey[3], Jim Stockton[3], and two Fleagles[3] at Helena in the Hospital. They are all pretty sick. Ol and I went down yesterday to see them. I think Jim is a little better, but he is pretty low. He has a good place and is well taken care of, but

I want to send one of our own men down to wait on him as soon as I can. Billy was down to see him today.

Our regiment moved yesterday evening about ½ mile further west. We are camped right in the woods. The timber is very large and heavy. Right in our camp it is nearly all Beech, Poplar, Sassafras, Gum, &c. We got our tents last night and today I rolled up my sleeves and worked hard all day to get them fixed up. The tents our men got are not like anything I ever saw before; they are nothing but a square sheet of tow cloth with buttons and button-holes on the sides. We fastened six or eight together, and cut forks and poles, and got them up in the best shape we could, but they leak tonight. They are calculated for every man to carry his own tent and pole on his back. The officers got wall tents with a fly, but only one to each company. We got ours up all right just in time for the rain, and we got Joe (that is our Negro) to carry in a big pile of leaves to make a bed. Captain Smith thought it was a splendid arrangement and was going to have a nice sleep tonight. He has been in two hours, but every time he gets to sleep, a bullfrog jumps on to the bed and scares him out. There are half a dozen in here now, jumping around. The captain is getting disgusted with the whole thing and had concluded not to sleep any.

Steele[4] is officer of the guard. There are five regiments camped close here, 3 of infantry and 2 cavalry, composing the 2 brigades— Colonel Vandever[5] commanding. About every third man you meet is a Negro, every mess in the 4th Cavalry has a Negro cook, and the officers two or three apiece. Our captain got one today for our mess; don't know much about him yet, but I think he will do very well. The Secesh are thick around here; they fire on our pickets almost every day. Only day before yesterday they killed seven. No forage trains go out without an escort of four or five hundred men and two or three cannons. Billy was out with a party yesterday and they got 114 loads of corn. Colonel Stone with four companies of our regiment and detachment from most of the other regiments here, 8,000 in all, started on an expedition down to the River yesterday. Some say to Vicksburg, others to Little Rock, no one knows where. 10,000 passed down today from Memphis, so I suppose something is to be "did" some place.

I believe I have told you about all I know. It is 10 o'clock and still raining like fury and the bullfrogs are getting thicker, and I must quit and go to bed. I don't think any four-legged animal will keep me awake.

What did you do with the cow? Did you get the kitchen papered—have you got that wood yet—are the apples all gone? What is Al doing? Does Lib know where Ike is? Are Lulie's eyes still getting better? Do you take the *Hawkeye*[6]? What does Thomas say? How is Kitty[7] and all the rest of you—and what are you all doing? And do you ever think about me? I know you are in bed sleeping by this time and don't hear a word I say. If I was there I would jump in and give you a good hug and kiss and wake you up.

Your own, Jake

1. Second Lieutenant Josh Gardner of the 4th Iowa Cavalry was a carpenter who built the Finley Chapel in Trenton, Iowa in 1856. (*The History of Henry County, Iowa*, page 54).

2. Dr. Andrew W. McClure of Mt. Pleasant was the surgeon of the 4th Iowa Cavalry.

3. Francis and John Jeffrey were both privates in Company B. John was later wounded near Vicksburg. Jim Stockton was a corporal who returned to see further action. William Fleagle returned to service but his brother Jacob died of disease a few days after Jacob wrote this letter.

4. Samuel L. Steele was the Second Lieutenant of Company B.

5. William Vandever was Colonel of the 9th Iowa Infantry. Vandever became a Brigadier General and later Brevet Major General, based on service during Sherman's March to the Sea. When the Civil War broke out, he was a member of Congress from Iowa, where he had served two terms. After the war, he moved to California where he again served in Congress, representing the Sixth Congressional District of California for two terms.

6. The *Burlington Hawkeye* was a local Iowa newspaper frequently read by the Iowa troops.

7. Kitty was Jacob's and Emeline's daughter, age 1, born in February 1861 and who remained unnamed in Jacob's earlier letters while with the 1st Iowa Infantry.

***I Don't Swear Nor Smoke Nor Drink Whiskey and I Ain't
Going To, For the Sake of My Sweet Emeline and the Babies***

Camp Near Helena, Arkansas
November 23, 1862

Dear Emeline,

It is Saturday night again and I have set down to write you
another letter. What are you doing, I wonder? Come and sit down
on my lap and let us have a talk—come right along now. I want to
tell you something. There now, ain't you sweet? If I had you in my
arms again I would kiss you a thousand times. I have just been
looking at your picture and I just know it is the prettiest thing that
ever was. Be still now!! You ain't going to get away yet. If you
wasn't such good stuff I believe I would scold you a little. But you
are my own sweet dear and I can't . . .

We have been hard at work here since I last wrote you, cleaning
off the camp, &c. Steele and I cut and split Beech logs and built an
addition to our tent for a sleeping apartment. "Joe" (that's our
Negro) daubed it up tight and I jayhawked a bushel of yams yesterday and a pig, so we live in style.

I have been as well as ever I was all the time. Jud is well too.
Jim is getting well fast. I was down and stayed all night with him
Thursday night. All that ails him now is that he cannot get enough
to eat. I bought him can of oysters and got a woman to cook for
him. I think he will be able to come to camp in a few days, though
he cannot walk but a few steps at a time yet. He was very sick and
made a narrow escape, but there is no danger now, if he doesn't eat
too much. One of our men, Jacob Fleagle, died in the Hospital a
few days ago. Jim Stockton has got about well and has come out to
camp. He is staying with Bob at the 4th Cavalry for a few days. Ol
and Billy are both well and hearty. Ol and "Jake" (that is their
Negro) are company cooks; they have an oven. I went by there the
other evening and Ol had about 40 pies fresh-baked for sale on his
own hook. They were made of dried apples and the best I have seen
since I left home. He bakes some almost every day and sells them
at 10 and 15 cents apiece.

The expedition that went down the river got back yesterday.
They tried to go up White River, stuck on a sand bar, fizzled out,
and came back without accomplishing anything. I have been out on
picket guard one night and two days with 60 men from our company. It rained all night and we had a bad time of it. My line was

about two miles long and ran across an old cotton plantation that was grown up in cockleburs as high as my head. I had to go the whole length of the line twice by myself after dark. I fell into a well, and into several ditches and got in the Burs, but didn't see any Secesh. The pickets extend all around the town and camp and they allow no citizen to pass in or out.

I went out yesterday with a forage train. We have 120 wagons, 300 infantry, and 800 cavalry. We went about 15 miles and got all the wagons loaded with corn. We also got several hogs and lots of potatoes and yams and chickens. On the way home we found the Secesh had got in behind us and torn up a bridge. We expected to get a fight there. I was ordered to take Company B across and skirmish in the woods while they fixed the bridge. We went out some distance but saw no one. There are plenty of Secesh round here and it is not safe to go outside the guard lines without a strong force. Two or three of our men were a short distance beyond the lines night before last and two were taken prisoners. They belonged to the Burlington Company.

But I expect you will go to sleep reading this dry letter. Just wait till I get one from you to pattern after and then I will do my best. I don't swear nor smoke nor drink whiskey and I ain't going to, for the sake of my sweet Emeline and the babies.

Your own, Jake

Camp Near Helena, Arkansas
November 25, 1862

Dear Emeline,

Well, dear, I have been sitting here in the back room of our tent trying to get to write you another letter, but Josh is here talking and gassing and I can't get to write. I wrote to you night before last. But How White[1] got here today and brought me a letter from you. I was so glad—it was the first word I had heard from you since I left home . . . I love you dearly and love to sit down and write to you. I don't care a cent about writing to anyone else. I wrote to you at St. Louis before we left, I put another letter on a steamboat that was going up, I mailed another at Memphis, and this will be three since I came to this camp. I'm afraid I scolded a little in my last letter because I had not got any letter from you; I am sorry for it and will take it all back . . . Now Captain Smith got a letter today by mail that was dated the

19th inst., ten days later than yours. But this will do for the subject. I do not deserve to get a letter from you at all, though I try to. And it does me so much good to get one or to get out your picture and look at it. I just know it is the prettiest thing in this camp. Do you ever wear that pin? Or look at my picture and think of me?

I do not know what to say about the cow. But you must get things fixed some way so you will not be bothered, so no matter what it costs. I won't have any such doings. Can't you make Tom find out whose cow it is that is so bad, and make them keep her up? He might attend to it for you, I think. What is he doing—does he ever come to see you?

Well, I don't hardly know what I'm writing about. Everybody is talking here and making a noise and I want to sit down and have a talk with you all by ourselves—don't you wish we could? You wish I would come home, do you? I would like to first rate, and I expect I will be nearly dead to see you before I get a chance to go home. There is not much chance for an officer to get away from here now. Josh has been trying to get a leave of absence for some time, but he has about given it up. Some say Colonel Porter[2] has resigned and is going home, others say he is arrested and will be court-martialed and discharged.

We have not seen or heard anything of the payments yet—don't know when the paymaster is coming. I wish he would hurry up for I am clear strapped—haven't got more than a dollar left. We have to buy everything we eat here, and almost everything is very high, but we have a pretty good supply on hand now. And I guess there is no danger of us starving. I am as well as common, I believe. Everybody says I look slim and bad like I had been sick, but there is nothing the matter with me that I know of except hard work. Jim is getting better as fast as could be expected. He can walk to the door and look out. I have not been to see him since I last wrote to you, but I hear from him every day. Tell Mrs. Taylor that Frank[3] is well, doing finely. He plays in the B Band now at Dress Parade. A good many of the men are sick. The water here is very poor, and we are furnished flour in place of bread, and we have no way to bake it. We are going to build an oven and bake our own bread.

Well, I guess I must quit for this time and I will write again next Sunday. I hope I will get another from you before that time. I am officer of the guard tomorrow, and must sleep tonight, so I can sit up tomorrow night. Good night, sweet dear. Kiss all the babies for me.

Your own, Jake

1. Corporal James H. "How" White, age 24, was in Company B with Jacob. He had served with Jacob in Company F of the 1st Iowa Infantry.

2. Fifty-three-year-old Asbury B. Porter, former Major of the 1st Iowa Infantry, was Colonel of the 4th Iowa Cavalry with Billy and Ol Bereman. Although he had been in the command structure of the 1st Iowa Infantry at Wilson's Creek, many of the soldiers felt that the ten companies of the 1st Iowa had operated independently of any central command during that engagement. Porter formally resigned his position as Colonel of the 4th Iowa Cavalry on March 19, 1863. (Eugene F. Ware, *The Lyon Campaign and History of the 1st Iowa Infantry*, page 332).

3. Benjamin Frank Taylor, age 20, of Mt. Pleasant, enlisted as a drummer.

• The November 29, 1862, *Home Journal* included a report by Alvah Bereman, Emeline's brother, who was the Draft Commissioner of Henry County. Henry County's quota was 1,372 and the number enrolled to date was 1,233. The draft was scheduled for January 1, 1863, and any township that had met its quota would not be subject to the draft. Alvah offered flexibility to the new enrollees, stating: "Men are permitted to enlist in any old regiment, to be mustered out when the time of such regiment expires."

Kit Says Pa Has 'Gone Way Down Dichie'

[Mt. Pleasant, Iowa]
Thursday night
November the 27th, 1862

Dear Jake,

I received a letter from you today written at Helena. I had been looking for it for several days. Yesterday I went up to the office to get it but was disappointed. I inquired around and nobody had heard from you since you left Memphis. I began to get the blues, but they were all scattered today by the arrival of a good letter. Tom brought it out. It found me with my hands all greasy and salty for I had just finished salting away the meat. We got the pig killed yesterday and they brought it home today so Lib and I went to work and cut it up ourselves. (don't you laugh) We done it up just right. We just had to do it. There was not a man on the hill that we could get. Morley had gone to the country to work and Tom is always dressed up so I don't like to ask him to do such things. Well, we had got it nearly all salted when here comes Dave & John Alters and Ike and Berton with a hind quarter of a beef. So you see we have lots of meat on hand after doing without for so long. I wish you were here to help eat it . . .

It has been trying to snow all day, so I am afraid the children will freeze unless it gets warmer I think I will not go.—I believe I am getting the sore eyes, one of them was very sore this morning and swelled, to night. I can hardly see. Nellie & Kittie had a short spell of the same kind, but they are well now.

We are all well. Lulie's eyes are about the same as when I wrote you last. I understand there has been several cases of smallpox in town. Mrs. Cripland is pretty bad with them and several of the Cole family have been exposed. So it is likely to spread. I intend to have the children vaccinated as soon as I can get the "stuff" and I want you to be vaccinated if you have not been since you started. There might be a danger of you taking the smallpox. This is Thanksgiving day. There was a Union meeting at the Congregational Church. Tonight the Episcopalians have a supper at the Union Hall— Tomorrow the sisters of the Baptist Church meet at Sister Gunn's to help her sew. Going to have two sewing machines there (I am not going) . . . I must quit, write soon dear & let me know how you do.

Your wife, Em

Kit says Pa has 'gone way down dichie.' Ike's Co went into Barracks at St. Louis last Saturday. This is Nellie's birthday. She wondered if Pa wouldn't send her something. Al is grinding away in his office. We are looking for Father this week.

Headquarters Army in the Field
November 30, 1862

Dear Wife:
This is Sunday again and I will commence another letter to you . . . I did not bring my memorandum book along and will write you an account of the expedition so far, and you must keep it to refer to.

Thursday (the 27th) we started from camp near Helena at daylight, with 250 picked men from our regiment under command of Lieutenant Colonel Brydolf[1]. I have command of 50 men detailed from Companies B & G. Lieutenant Steele is along. Captain Smith stayed at camp. The expedition consisting of 10,000 men, including a strong force of cavalry, embarked on 16 steamboats and drifted down the river 10 miles to a place called Delta, where we landed and camped for the night[2]. The next morning early we started out east through Mississippi. We have quite a long train, 100 rounds of ammunition to each man, and 14 days rations. So I expect if we do not get whipped or scared we will be gone some time. The general impression is that we are going to destroy the Railroad between Corinth[3] and Vicksburg, to prevent the retreat of Price[3] from Rosecrans[3], and help bag the old Rebel.

The country was very flat and the heaviest timber I ever saw had all been overflowed. The high water marks on the trees [as seen from the steamboats] were from 3 to 30 feet high. We did not see a foot of land for 20 or 25 miles that does not overflow. Here and there a large plantation with a levee around it. The cypress swamps are a grand sight—trees almost as thick as they can stand, and from 60 to 80 feet without a limb.

The road was pretty good, but would be impossible after a rain. We made 23 miles the first day; the men had three days' rations and overcoats and blankets in their knapsacks and got very tired. We stopped about two hours after dark and Whippo and I went one and a half miles through a canebrake to a swamp for water. Yesterday we struck the Gold Water River about noon and followed it down to the mouth where it emptied into the "Hatchee." The cavalry had a skirmish here Thursday evening—killed 2 and took 6 prisoners. We have a pontoon bridge across the Hatchee, one we brought along. The Secesh have 2,000 Negroes at work on the other side, falling trees in the road. The prisoners say they have 15,000 men out at the railroad, and that we will never get back to the River. We don't know how it will be but are all anxious to try it on. All we are afraid of is that General Hovey[2] will back out without a fight. Most of the cavalry and a large part of the infantry went over the river yesterday and this morning and we are waiting here for something to turn up. It is now past noon and we are laying around here spoiling for a fight.

I don't know what regiments are along except that the 4th, 28th, 26th, 31st, and 25th Iowa, and part of the 4th Iowa Cavalry are here. Billy and Ol did not come. It is cloudy now and I believe it is going to rain tonight—if it does we will have had a bad time, as we have no tents at all. I must quit till after dinner and then perhaps I may write more.

Well, I have had my dinner. I had sassafras tea, bear-meat, and hard crackers. There are plenty of bears round here. A man who lives here killed two day before yesterday, and I got some of the meat. I am just writing this because I have nothing else to do. If you have nothing else to do when you get it, perhaps you will read it.

I like soldiering a great deal better than I did the other time. This is a very interesting country. I see new and strange sights every day, and then there is quite a difference between being an officer and a private. My health is first-rate. My feet nearly gave out the first day, and I am a little stiff today, but I am not afraid but that I can stand it as long as anybody else. We have lots of fun one way or another. I believe my company is the liveliest and spunkiest in the regiment.

Bill White and Wils Payne[4] can beat anything stealing in the whole army. Bill White especially. He can Jay-Hawk as much as the whole company can eat, and not be missed from the ranks. This is the greatest country for honey and yams I ever saw—we get all we can eat. There has been soldiers camping here for two days, right around a house. We thought of course everything was taken that was worth anything. But Bill brought in two or three loads of honey, coffee, tobacco, &c. He got a lot of old love-letters, books, and a looking glass, though there was a guard in the house. We had lots of fun with the letters.

I guess I will dry up for the present and write to you some more in a few days. I wish I could hear from you and know that you and the children were all well.

Your own, Jake

1. Swedish native Lt. Colonel Fabian Brydolf, age 43, of Burlington resigned his position on June 8, 1863.

2. Jacob is describing an eastward expedition led by Brigadier General Alvin P. Hovey aimed at Grenada, located in Mississippi about midway between Vicksburg and Corinth. The Union intent was to embarrass the Confederates and possibly destroy railroads and bridges supporting Confederate supply lines. Although much of what they destroyed was quickly rebuilt, this thrust did cause the Confederates to abandon their Tallahatchie line and withdraw 50 miles to the Yalobusha. (Edwin Bearss, The Campaign for Vicksburg, Volume I, pages 77—109).

3. Union General Rosecrans had defeated Confederates Sterling Price and Earl Van Dorn at Corinth, Mississippi on October 3-4, 1862. Price was still operating in northern Mississippi.

4. Jacob is probably referring to William H. White of the 4th Iowa
   Cavalry. Charles W. "Wils" Payne, age 22, of Mt. Pleasant, was
   a sergeant in Company B of the 25th Iowa Infantry. Wils' parents had emigrated to Iowa from Virginia in 1836 in covered
   wagons with their four daughters. At that time, Iowa was part of
   Michigan Territory. In 1837 Wils' parents built a log cabin
   where Wils was born in 1840, the first white child born in Henry
   County. (Portrait and Biographical Album of Henry County,
   1888, page 474).

Camp Near Helena, Arkansas
December 2, 1862

Dear Emeline,

Well, dear this is Thursday and I have sat down to write you
another letter . . . it is raining today and we can't do much, and
whenever I have a little time to sit down and write to my own, dear
sweet wife [I will do so]. I know you love me, and I love so much
to get a letter from you—you do not know how much good it does
me. I am sure that if I did not get to come home for 20 years I would
love you all the better and write to you all the time. I will never forget my sweet wife, and the time you promised to be mine, and the
time you were made mine, and I yours. I often think of these things
down here. And I hope it will not be long before I can come home
to see you, if not to stay, but there is no prospect at present. I think
it very doubtful if I can get to come before the war is over.

We have very strict regulations in our regiment, and are all kept
hard at work all the time, when the weather is good. We have to
recite to the Colonel twice a day, and have company drill, battalion
drill and dress parade every day, besides police guard, picket guard,
and forage parties and fatigue parties of various kinds.

I caught a bad cold on the expedition to Mississippi and have
not been very well since—had nothing here I could eat. But the
Colonel came very near putting me under arrest this morning for
not going out on a company drill. I got mad, and got well. We sent
to town today and got some potatoes and dried peaches, and I will
be all right now. Jim is getting along very well; he is able to drill
some now. Jud is not very well today, but went out foraging. Ol was
over here last night; he and Billy are both well.

You would like to see our tent and the "addition," would you?
Well, it is raining and a gloomy day, but I wish you could put your
dear sweet face in here just now, somebody would get kissed very

quick. And then I will tell you what you would see. You would see a fireplace with a good fire on one side of the front tent, that keeps everything dry and comfortable, and Steele and I sitting by it, writing. The mess chest in the middle of the tent, three stools, and a long bench on one side, and a barrel with meat in it on the other side, and a long board on the barrel to set things on and a pile of wood in the corner, a rack fixed up at one end to hang swords, haversacks, cap, pistols, &c on; then in the "addition" we have a bunk on one side for the captain and one on the other for Steele and me. The trunks, &c under the beds; two shelves between the beds to lay books on and put the looking glass on if we had one. In one corner is a pile of guns and cartridge boxes belonging to sick men. I believe that is about the amount of our possessions here. Come right in and sit down by me. You may have the captain's stool, as he is gone foraging. Oh, that won't do?—Well, you may sit on my lap! I know that is what you want.

You will not see "Joe," poor fellow; he took sick one night while we were gone, and died the next morning. That is while Steele and I were gone on the expedition. He was a good honest fellow and I was sorry to lose him. But Steele and I brought one home along with us to take his place. He has a wife and five children; we brought the whole family along, and they have built a real "Uncle Tom's Cabin" close to our tent and they are going to cook and wash for us. She is a good washerwoman and he is a real smart, intelligent man, and a good cook. He is half white, has blue eyes and his name is "Jim." He is clean, and a rouser to work. Now I will tell you how and where we got him and his family.

We camped one night about dark on the way back from the Tallahatchie, on a cotton plantation. The owner was there, but no Negroes or mules, but after dark one of the Company B found a little "darkie" about ten years old out in the cotton field. We brought him in, and he told us that he was nearly starved and frozen. He said his master had chained two of his Negro men out in the cane break to keep them from going off with us, and that the mules were tied out the same place. He said that he and the other Negroes, mostly women and children, 25 in number, had been driven out into a swamp about two miles, and made to stay there for fear we would take them along. We determined to investigate the matter. A squad went to each place.

We found the two men handcuffed and tied with a log chain, in the cane break, and the other lot in a swamp where the water was half-knee deep in the shallow places. They had been in this condition for forty-eight hours without <u>fire</u> or <u>food</u>. They were the most miserable looking lot I ever saw. They had scarcely any clothing at all, ragged, dirty and bare-footed; it had snowed that morning and that night it froze hard. So I think you will not blame us for taking pity on them. I wouldn't see a dog treated so. It made an abolitionist out of Wils Payne and several other Democrats. We brought the whole lot along, and the mules and wagon too, and burned the cotton gin, and would have shot the owner if we had been allowed. "Jim" is one of the men who was chained. He is going to put a shingle roof on the "addition" and put the fly back on the other tent.

Well, here it is Sunday morning again and I haven't got this letter done yet. Well, in the first place I made a mistake at the start— it was <u>Friday</u> instead of Thursday that I commenced it. I intended to finish that night, but it was very wet and dark, and the forage train had been attacked that day. So Company B was ordered out on extra picket guard that night. I did not get any sleep and did not feel like writing yesterday. I got a letter from you last Tuesday and was very glad to hear that you were well and had gone to Des Moines County. Your letter was only 5 days coming and such a good letter I never saw before. How I wish I was there to eat dinner with you today. I can't eat anything here. I don't expect I will ever taste coffee again till I get you to make me some. I can't drink it here, and the water is poor.

I am so glad you and the children are well provided for. Just have a hot buck-wheat ready for me when I come. You did just right to buy your dresses. I want you to use just as much money as you need to keep yourself and the children nice and comfortable. I don't allow any of you to go ragged or cold, and shan't like it if you do.

I like your plan about the cow first-rate—it is better than to sell her. I think I see you and Lib cutting up the hog. A great cut, I reckon. You didn't say who killed it, or how much it weighed.

I sold the corn at Jefferson to Tom Stockton. We have not been paid yet and I have been strapped for some time, but I think we will be paid soon, or I would have you send me $10, but I guess we can make shift without, as the payments will certainly come before long. And then I am going to send you some pictures.

Everybody says I look so poor and dried up you would not know me, but you would, wouldn't you?

I am so glad that old tooth has quit hurting you; the next time I would go right up and have it pulled out. Hildreth owes you 25 cents anyhow. Jim and I and Billy and Ol are talking about getting you and Car & Ma to send us a box full of something to eat, such as canned fruit and pickles, butter, &c. Steele's folks and Mrs. Smith would help if they knew of it. If you have a chance to get them I wish you would send me a box of Old Man Payne's pills. I think I am a little Dyspeptic. Perhaps you can send them by some of our men who are coming down soon. I got a letter yesterday from Al. He says Father[1] is at home, but doesn't say anything about you. I guess he doesn't care much, do you? Little "Black eyes" wondered if I would send her something on her birthday. I did not think of it in time or I would have. I will next time. You must be certain to make "Santa Claus" fill all stockings clear full at Christmas. I will bring them all something when I come. I hope Lulie will get her eyes well by that time. Don't you think I have written about enough for once? You will get tired reading this . . .

Your own, Jake

I haven't said near all I want to nor answered all your questions; never mind. I will write again soon. Tell Tom and Al that they must come to you for the news. Tell "Josey" to be a good boy, and not hurt Kitty or make her cry. He must be Pa's good little boy, till I come home.

1. Emeline's father, Samuel E. Bereman, age 57, had been mustered into service November 5, 1862 but may have been home on temporary leave.

[Mt. Pleasant, Iowa]
December the 3rd, 1862

Dear Jacob,

This is Wednesday night. I received a letter from you today. You said that it was the fifth you had written and had received none from me, that is strange!! . . .

Don't call that sour picture pretty any more. I wish you had a nice pretty picture to look at. I would get another if I could make it any better looking, but it's no use. It will look like the original. I have the nice one. You don't know how pretty it does look, I mean that handsome, sweet, noble face that I pin on my bosom. Oh keep it pure and let it not be marred by any evil thoughts or feelings.

Keep yourself unspotted from all the wickedness that surrounds you. Keep a clear conscience of all those little sins that tend to make a person feel miserable, and then your nobleness will shine out more & more through you countenance and everybody will <u>see</u> that the inside man is <u>good</u> just by looking at the outward. (I will any how) . . .

How I would like to be down there and see your camp, especially your tent and addition, the "sleeping apartment" made of Beech logs. I should like to see all of Co. B very much. Give my respects to Captain Smith & Lieutenant Steele & Sergeant Gardener, and all the rest. Tell me what kind of fruit or vegetable "yours" are and what is the meaning of the term "Jay-hawking." (It is a short method of spelling hook isn't it. Better look out.)

We were all glad to hear that Jim was getting well hope he won't eat so much and get sick again . . . I am sorry you are all in such a secesh country, when it is so dangerous to be on picket guard. I can't bear to hear of the poor fellows being shot down while standing out alone in the dark. You must be careful when you are out and not come across any of the mean rebels and look out for the <u>wells</u>. How did you get out for pity sake? I would like to see Billy and Ol. Tell Ol to bake me a nice pie and send it up. Wonder if he puts any shortening in or sweetening. It is nine o'clock, the children are all in bed asleep. You must write them a letter some day. They want to know what you say about them. Don't say you haven't got any letter from me again as I will come down and bring you one.

I don't see how you get along without money as you spent the most of what you took away in St Louis. How do you get something to eat? I wish you could be here to dinner Sunday and eat buckwheats and honey & beef gravy. I should think it was pay day again by this time. Goodbye and don't forget to write often. I am afraid that you will be sent out on a scout and won't get my letters when they do come. Don't go out scouting. It's too dangerous. It's nobody but the citizens around there that shoot federals and destroy bridges. Why don't you take every one of them and hang one every time one of our men is shot? They will soon quit it. Good bye dear Jake.

Yours, Em

Give my respects to "Joe." Tell him I would like to see him. Wonder if he is much black? Have him show himself around and take good care of you or I shan't like him. Is there any women down there, and what do they look like? I suppose they are all secesh and not worth seeing. Don't eat anything cooked by the secesh, it might be poison.

[Mt. Pleasant, Iowa]
December 12, 1862

Dear Jake,

Where are you tonight, and what are you doing? Oh I would so like to know. I have got the blues most horribly tonight and the wind is blowing a perfect streak. Your old canteen is bumping & banging against the wall in the porch, trying to keep time with the howling of the wind, and the dismal patter of the rain. Oh how gloomy everything seems tonight! How I wish you were with us to chase away the melancholys, but where are you tonight and what are you doing . . .

I heard today that you & Steele with 20 from your Co and 20 from each Co. in your Reg't. had gone out on some expedition. Didn't hear what for or where you were going or anything more about it, but it must be so, or I would have got that letter, which I waited for before writing this, and perhaps I have been keeping you waiting for a letter (if you have got back) which I hope you have by this time. I <u>do hate</u> that scouting business. I wish you didn't have to go. Yet I suppose it is somebody's business, and your turn must come around but I hope it won't be often. News came day before yesterday that was a big battle in Ark., in which 600 of our men were killed, among whom was Lieutenant Colonel McFarland. Poor Mc. He has given himself as sacrifice for his country. It was a glorious deed, but yet how sad, to think he should be called to leave his little family and friends, and to face death in such a manner just for the meanness of Old Jeff Davis and his followers. Yet his case is only one among thousands. Oh how I would like to wipe out rebeldom at one blow, and send all the poor soldiers home to their families.– And poor Mrs. Mc. How I do pity her. She has been sick a long time, and had just got able to be up a little. I know it will almost kill her. We have got no particulars of the battle yet. Don't know who else is killed. We understand the 19th & 20th were engaged, & the first Cavalry so Jim and Archie Campbell both were there.

Well, what do you think? The smallpox is all over town nearly. As it is something so near like it that the Doctors can hardly decide what it is. Mrs. Cripland (the Cripland that died out of your Co.) was one of the first that took it. She was very bad with it. At first the Doctor said it was not smallpox & there were several exposed to it and there after awhile he pronounced it part the puss smallpox and then again it was something else, so the people got careless about it, and it had spread to quite a number of families in different parts of the town. I never saw such careless people in my life. The schools are all going on yet the same as ever and vaccination is no preventive the Doctors say. So you see it will be thick all over town in a short time. It won't help it now, it is bound to spread the way it has got started. There had been so many exposed. Mr. Haynes in the Post office died with it yesterday. I understand he took sick in the office and was carried home. So you see there will be a chance for somebody to take it. If it is not the smallpox it is something about as bad, and it should not have spread so. Lib stopped school today but we are bound to go to the post office. Now how will we keep from it?—The children are all well. I have an ugly headache once in a while otherwise I am well . . .

Your mother told me to tell you to take good care of Jud. And I want you to quit looking so slim jawed. If you are such, you must own up, and don't kill yourself with work. Let the rest do something . . . Remember us and write often & take good care of that soul of yours as well as the body. I will pray for you that you may be spared through all dangers & return to us again.

Farewell dear,

Your own Em

The Great Expedition Down the River

Camp Near Helena, Arkansas
December 19, 1862

Dear Emeline,

I believe it is about time I would write you another letter and I will commence it tonight. I do like to sit down and write to you, and would do so oftener if I had time . . . I have not been very well for a week or so, but am now about as well as usual. I caught a cold on the expedition and had no appetite for a while. I got some corn meal and made some corn bread today—it was first-rate. Wouldn't you like to have some of it? I expect you would laugh to see me cook and wash dishes, but I have to do it.

We have orders to break up camp here and go down the River. We expect to start in a day or two—don't know where we are going, most likely to Vicksburg. Our Negro "Jim" that I told you about in my last letter would like to go along, but could not leave his family. So he has found another place and moved to town. So we have to cook for ourselves until we can find another "darkie." Jim is determined to go north as soon as he gets money enough, and I want him to go to Mt. Pleasant. I gave him directions how to get there and told him to call and see you. If he comes you must use him well. I thought perhaps we could get him on our farm up in Jefferson.

We have had marching orders for several days and are ready to start at any time. Our teams and part of our plunder are on board the boat now. We are going in the great expedition down the river. One hundred steamboats are on the way down from St. Louis and there are 20 here. It will make a grand sight. We are only allowed to take six teams to the regiment, and most of our men have boxed up their dress coats and sent them home. I had to send my gray coat home. I put it in a trunk directed to W.A. Saunders[1]. You will have to get it and pay your share of the expense. None of the officers are allowed trunks. I just hit it by buying a handtrunk at St. Louis; it holds my things nicely. The line officers are allowed nothing but "shelter tents" like the men, and they must carry them. Most of the soldiers here are going—don't know just how many. The 4th Cavalry are not going. "Jim" and I were there last night. The boys are both well and would like to go along. There are several of our men that we will have to leave behind, Nelson[2], Banks[2], Scott[3], Ross[4], Poucher[2], Randles[4], McGill[5], and a few others. Jud is not well and I am afraid we will have to leave him here.

Lyman Fluke[6] shot himself last night while on picket guard. Some say he was drunk at the time. The ball entered his right breast one inch from the right nipple and went nearly through his body. I think it impossible for him to recover though he is still living. The rebels still fire on our pickets occasionally, but there has been no one hurt for a week or so.

I got a letter from Alvah the other day. He said Father was at home. I hope you had a good time. Have your eyes got well yet? I am afraid they are worse than you let on. Lize wrote to Jud that one of them was very bad; I do hope they won't be bad. You did not tell me what they all said down at home. What did "old Bets" say? Write and tell me all about it—don't say "Oh, I don't know." I want you to pack up and go to Jefferson and stay two weeks and visit all round, and don't stick there at home and pout, and never go anyplace. You have no cow now and can go as well as not. Dress yourself and the children up warm and start.

We have not seen anything of the paymaster here yet, but we hear he will be around after New Years. And I guess we can stand it that long now. I want you to use just as much money as you need—that is what I left it for. I wish you would take the bank book to the bank and have them post it up and tell me how much money we have there, and when I send mine home, I will tell you what to do with it. I am afraid it will be a good while before I can send you another letter, but I shall keep writing and you will get them sometime. We are in the 2nd Brigade commanded by Colonel Williamson[7] of the Iowa 4th Infantry, First Division commanded by General Steele. You may see something in the papers about us.

I think you asked me in one of your letters if I ever saw any <u>women</u> down here, and what they look like? There now, you aren't afraid I will see anybody prettier than you are, are you? You needn't be uneasy. You know I have somebody's picture along with me, and I carry it in my pocket too, and look at it every day. Well we hardly ever see a woman of any kind about here, and those we see are not very attractive. I believe there has not been a white woman in Camp since we came here except Mrs. Stone and Mrs. Wittenmeyer[8]. And there are very few about Helena. The Negroes are all common field hands, or nearly all, very dirty, ragged, and ignorant, both men and women. There isn't a woman in all this country or any other as pretty and sweet as my dear little wife at home. And I am going to love you better and be a better man when I come back than ever before.

It is getting late and I must quit. I suppose it will be after Christmas before you get this. I hope you will have a good time. I wish I could slip in on you and get your Christmas gift. What would you give me? I would like to have some of your dinner. We did not think last Christmas that we would be this far apart by this time. I wonder what will happen this year. Take good care of the children and tell me what they all say and do, and if they are good. Does Joe ever cry? How are Lulie's eyes? Who pulls Kit's hair <u>now</u>? Is Nellie in school? Get a big sheet of paper like this and write it full. Give my love to Ma and all the rest.

Your own, Jake

1. William A. Saunders was a brother of Presley Saunders, pioneer and founder of Mt. Pleasant. William had come to Mt. Pleasant in 1845 and operated a store that sold "a full assortment of Dry Goods, Notions, Groceries, etc., which they offer to their friends and the public generally." (*The History of Henry County, Iowa*, page 191; *Home Journal* April 16, 1864).

2. John Nelson was discharged for disabilities February 19, 1863. John Banks and Hiram Poucher were both discharged for disabilities April 14, 1863.

3. Soloman Scott deserted from a hospital on August 1, 1863 in St. Louis—a further report stated that he died November 18, 1863 in Tullahoma, Tennessee.

4. Luther Randles, George and Thomas Ross, all of Mt. Pleasant, all survived the war.

5. James McGill of Mt. Pleasant died of disease May 18, 1863 at Young's Point, Louisiana.

6. Sergeant Lyman Fluke of the 4th Iowa Cavalry had also been a member of the 1st Iowa Infantry, Company F, with Jacob. Lyman died the day Jacob wrote this letter.

7. The change in brigade structure that Jacob is discussing did not take place immediately. The 25th Iowa remained in the brigade commanded by General Hovey for the Battle of Chickasaw Bayou.

8. Mrs. Annie E. Wittenmeyer of Keokuk was head of the Iowa Sanitary Agency, referred to nationally as the Sanitary Commission. These commissions were set up by private individuals, and would arrange Sanitary Fairs to collect supplies to take to the Union troops. Nurses would often accompany the Sanitary Commission on trips to the troops as well. Originally the Sanitary Commission was called the Commission of Inquiry and Advice in Respect of the Sanitary Interests of the United States Force. Mrs. Mary Stone was the wife of Colonel George Stone and daughter of the Quartermaster Frederick Clarke of the 25th Iowa Infantry. Mrs. Stone was probably part of the Iowa Sanitary Agency. (Darryl Lyman, *Civil War Wordbook*, page 145; *The History of Henry County, Iowa*, page 150).

Historical Sketch—25th Iowa Infantry

On the 22nd of December, 1862, the regiment embarked on trans-
ports and moved down the Mississippi with forces under command of
General Sherman, to participate in that notable but unsuccessful
movement against Vicksburg, by way of Chickasaw Bayou. The 25th
Iowa lost one man killed, seven wounded and two captured or miss-
ing. (Roster and Record of Iowa Soldiers in the War of the Rebellion;
Published under the authority of the Iowa General Assembly)

On Board the Steamer *John J. Roe*[1]
Helena, Arkansas
December 22, 1862

Dear Emeline,

I wrote you a letter a few days ago, and as we are just starting away, I will drop you a few lines more if I have time. We are on board the boat and expecting to leave every minute. We left camp yesterday (Sunday) about 2 o'clock, and came down here and lay around in the mud till midnight, when we got on board the boat. There are a large number of boats here loaded with soldiers—don't know how many. A great many had already gone down and more are coming from above all the time. There is a tremendous army going down the river for something and I expect something will be done down there soon. I think we will whip the rebels yet before spring. Jim and I ate dinner with Billy and Ol yesterday; they are both well but are not going. They all want to go and I wish they could. I am as well as usual and think I shall stand the trip first-rate. Jud is not well and I think we shall have to leave him here, though he wants to go and is on the boat now. I got a letter from you dated the 13th, on Saturday; I wish I had been there to keep you company when it was raining and blowing. You must not get lonesome and get the blues. Whenever you get that way take your pen and sit down and talk to me, and write talk sweet and cheerful like you used to do when you were sitting on my knee in the big rocking chair, and that will scare it away. It does so with me, anyhow.

I am uneasy about the small-pox up there. I am so afraid our children will get it. You must not let them go to Morley's nor let them come to our house, as they are sure to run around and get it if anyone does. I wish you would take all the children and go right off up to Jefferson and stay two or three weeks till it is over. You have no cow or pigs and could do it as well as not. Lib, could get along or stay with Sarah till you come back. When you get up there, go to Stockton's, Payne's, Black's, Josh's, McClure's, and every place else. Till can take you around some. Get up and start now.

We have not been paid yet. We were in great hopes we would be before we left here, as we heard the paymaster was coming, but I guess we will have to leave without. They charge 75 cents per meal on this boat, and that is more money than I have. But I will make out some way—all the other officers are in the same fix. If we should not be paid until after the 1st of January and then paid all that is coming, I will have pretty near $300, to send home. I think it would be safe to lend the money to Alvah if he wants it; and you may do so. Let him have what you have to spare, but be sure to <u>keep enough for yourself</u>. I will try to write to Tom before long and tell him about the Campbell matter. I don't think he could settle with the Judge. I got a letter from Zan yesterday; they were all well. You may address your letters just as you have been doing for the present. I shall keep writing to you whether I can send them or not, and tell you all about our expedition.

Well, dear I must stop for this time. I expect we will be on our way down the river in a short time. Boats are continually leaving and passing down loaded with soldiers; there are 1,500 on this boat besides horses and mules for 3 regiments. I want you to pray for your Jake, and I know you will. I don't swear nor drink nor smoke one bit, and don't intend to. If I was ever tempted to do anything mean or bad, I would think of my dear little wife at home and <u>our</u> children . . . Eat some New Year's dinner for me.

Your own, Jake

1. The 25th Iowa was on the steamer *John J. Roe*, headed to Chickasaw Bayou under the command of General Sherman. The *John J. Roe* later sank near New Madrid, Missouri in August or September of 1864. (Charles and Kay Gibson, *Dictionary of Transports and Combatant Vessels, Steam and Sail, Employed by the Union Army, 1861-1868*, page 180)

Steamer *John J. Roe*
December 25, 1862

Dear Wife,

Well, dear, it is Christmas and I am on board this old boat. Landed at Milliken's Bend in Louisiana 22 miles above Vicksburg by land, and have just been on shore taking a walk and saw the rebel pickets. Now where are you and what are you doing? I would like so well to know. Where were we last Christmas and what did we do? I have been trying to think, but can't make it out. I know we were together someplace and I hope we will be again next Christmas. It seems so strange that I should be away down here 1,300 miles from you. What did the children find in their stockings? I lay awake two or three hours this morning thinking of them and wishing I could see them.

What kind of weather have you got up there? Cold as Greenland, I expect. We have had the nicest weather I ever saw since we have been on the trip. Very warm and pleasant and no rain. Yesterday and today it is quite comfortable sitting round without any coat on. Our whole regiment is quartered on the hurricane deck of the boat and we have not needed any fire. The officers sleep in the cabin. Last night it was too warm to sleep with any cover. The men eat raw bacon and hard bread. And the officers eat whatever they can get—whenever they can find any. If we had the money we would get meals on the boat for 50 cents. I am going to try to make a raise of a ticket for dinner, being it is Christmas.

I do not know exactly how many men there are in the expedition, but it is on a grand scale. There are not less than 60,000— some say 80,000[1]. It is a grand sight to see the fleet steaming down the river, one boat behind the other as far as you can see. I have seen as many as 50 at one time, all loaded with soldiers. This morning about 4 o'clock I had the most magnificent sight I ever beheld. Our boat was the hindermost one in the fleet yesterday and we ran all night and this morning before daylight we passed the whole fleet, tied up at this point, and landed below them. There were more than 100 boats, all with their head and rear lights burning. As we passed by it made a sight I shall never forget. I don't know when we shall leave here or go on shore, or when I shall get a chance to send this letter back. There is an order prohibiting the writing of anything that would give information to the enemy if it should fall into their hands.

December 26, 1862 [same letter]
Camp on the Yazoo, Mississippi

I wrote you some yesterday. We were then at Milliken's Bend. We left there in the afternoon and came down to the mouth of Yazoo, which is about ten or twelve miles above Vicksburg. We

landed on the Louisiana side and sent out a detachment to destroy
the railroad which runs west from Vicksburg. They accomplished
their purpose and returned in safety.

This morning at 8 o'clock the fleet commenced moving up the
Yazoo, which is a narrow but deep stream. The banks are covered
with a very thick growth of timber and underbrush of all kinds—
swamp and cane breaks, and the trees are covered with a kind of
moss which grows all over the trees and hangs down almost to the
ground. It is of a kind of gray color, and looks very curious and
makes it impossible to see any distance although there are no
leaves on the trees. We went up the river about eight to twelve
miles, and have landed now and are going to take it on foot the rest
of the way. There are some strong forts and batteries just above on
the river which we must take before we can get Vicksburg, which I
suppose is what we are after.

The fighting has already commenced; there was pretty heavy
cannonading up the river this afternoon and our force had already
taken one fort. One Illinois Regiment lost about 40 men. That is all
the particulars I have and everything is hurry and bustle, landing
the troops and getting the baggage and artillery on shore. We are
camped in a large cornfield close to the river. Regiment after regiment is constantly marching by in different directions, and cavalry
and batteries rushing from one point to another. We do not know
what minute we will be ordered to march ourselves. So you see we
are getting into war in earnest, which is just what we want. The
men are all in good spirits and keen to start at any time. And if we
get a chance I think the 25th will give a good account of itself. I
think Company B will do to tie to anyhow. I hope we won't go to
entrenching and take the posts by "regular approaches,"
McClellan[2] fashion. But Colonel Stone says that is the order and
we will commence in the morning. I must close this now, so as to
get it mailed tonight, as I hear our postmaster is going back on the
first boat. Kiss all the children for me and don't let them forget me.
And think of me sometimes yourself. I know you do and that
knowledge makes me happy.

Your own, Jake

1. The actual size of the force commanded by General William T.
    Sherman was closer to 30,000. (Jim Miles, *A River Unvexed*,
    page 249)

2. General George McClellan was Commander-In-Chief of the

Union Army, the Union's highest-ranking general, from November 1861 to March 1862, and personally led the Army of the Potomac until November 1862. Abraham Lincoln relieved him as Commander-In-Chief, partly because of his cautious nature in directing military operations. Lincoln said of McClellan, "he's got the slows."

The Battle of Chickasaw Bayou

On December 29, 1862, General Sherman, in his first independent command, led a Union attack at Chickasaw Bayou, located five miles northeast of Vicksburg. The land of Chickasaw Bayou was bordered by Chickasaw Bluffs and the Yazoo River, leaving very few dry spots for Union troop movements, and these dry spots were in range of Confederate artillery fire. Adding to the misery on both sides, a horrible rain storm drenched the area. During the fighting, the terrain forced attacking Federals into a "funnel effect" that put many Union troops in a concentrated area that was easily shelled by the Confederates. In some places, the Confederates were able to shoot straight down on the Union troops. Many of the wounded men fell on their faces and were unable to turn over, drowning in the mud, while others died from exposure in the cold, heavy rain.

During the failed Union assaults, the Union lost more than 1,700 men, compared to Confederate casualties of only 200. Atypical of

Civil War commanders, General Sherman accepted the blame for the defeat, telling Grant "I assume all responsibility and attach fault to no one." (Jim Miles, A River Unvexed, *page 279)*

Letter From Jacob's father, Henry A. Ritner—God's War

[Fragment]
[January 1, 1863]
[Dear Jacob,]

. . . but I think there will be a change before long and that change will bring a <u>crisis</u> . . .

My opinion of the war is that it is an abolition war got up for the purpose of abolishing slavery and that God is its author[1,2]. [That] the Republicans did not make it the whole course of the administration gives such a charge the lie[3]. The abolitionists did not make the war for they were too few and dispersed to effect any thing and they always prayed and laboured for a peaceful abolition of slavery, and the South makes no such charge against them. The South did bring on the war, but only instrumentally after they were deprived of their reason, for while they could reason, they must have known that if they succeeded they would be worse off even with regard to the security of their slaves than they were before; indeed all their calculations show that their leaders had lost the power to reason correctly and therefore only brought on the war as instruments in the hands of a just God, that they might eat the fruit of their own doings. It is therefore as I said before, God's war, and the object is to abolish slavery and punish the nation for its sins, especially that of slavery and to install the black man in to his natural and inalienable rights, and the sooner the government [and] the army recognize this aspect and act upon it the sooner we will have peace. [That] will be our punishment and the more complete and glorious will be our triumph. But if we as a nation refuse to acknowledge the rights of the black man then it may cost us our national existence.

I said there might be a rebellion in the north against the administration. There is such a thing in embryo not only in New York but all over the north. Even in our own township there have been several meetings of the Democrats to get up an influence in favour of <u>compelling</u> the administration to stop fighting and offer terms of peace to the rebels, and they boast that Lincoln will not be president six months longer unless he stops the war. But in New York they have been completely foiled . . . I regard these however as omens of good, but certainly more depends on the success of the army this winter than on any other thing, and in this regard it looks as if God was using the elements against us. I hope that soon the government and the army will soon put themselves on the side of right and I shall hope even in the darkness.

Your father, H. A. Ritner

1. Jacob's father, Henry A. Ritner, may have been making reference to God hardening the heart of the Pharaoh as in Exodus IV, 21—"And the Lord said unto Moses: 'When thou goest back into Egypt, see that thou do before Pharaoh all the wonders which I have put in thy hand; but I will harden his heart, and he will not let the people go.' " When the Divine came to Pharaoh and said, "Set the slaves free," Pharaoh's response was "I will not." On the face of it, this seems to say that God is causing Pharaoh to do evil, while presumably an omnipotent God would cause him to do good. Another interpretation of this Biblical passage is that God was not purposefully making Pharaoh sinful, but was hardening his heart so as to trigger other events. (Dr. J. H. Hertz, C. H. Late Chief Rabbi of the British Empire, *The Pentateuch and Haftorahs*, Hebrew Text, English Translation and Commentary, pages 220-221)

2. Parson Brownlow of Tennessee, a pro-Union man who strangely supported slavery, had similar views as Jacob's father, except that he thought it was the devil that provoked the Southern leaders, rather than God. "Three years ago, when influenced by the devil, and in this madness they [Jeff. Davis and the leading Rebels of the South] fired upon Fort Sumter, they shot slavery out of every State in the Confederacy. They can not now Shoot it back if they would. The slave property of the South was safe under the Constitution and in the Union—it was safe no where else—and the Abolitionists of the North never could have disturbed it, had the owners of such property behaved themselves, and stayed in the Union." (Mt. Pleasant *Home Journal*, May 14, 1864). Although Henry A. Ritner was an abolitionist and Parson Brownlow a supporter of slavery, both felt that the abolitionists by themselves were not strong enough to bring an end to slavery. Both felt that a spiritual force (either God or the devil) had caused the Southern leaders to lose their ability to reason, which provoked the war that would terminate the institution of slavery.

3. Henry Ritner was criticizing the initial Lincoln administration position that the war was not meant to free the slaves, but only meant to preserve the Union.

The Battle of Chickasaw Bayou

Army Before Vicksburg
January 1, 1863

Dear Emeline,

I wrote to you last Friday evening in haste and this is the first chance I have had to write a word since. We have been fighting a good part of the time since, and I have not seen any of our baggage or anything but what I carried on my back since. I borrowed this sheet from another officer and will try to give you an account of what we have been doing since I last wrote. I told you then that we had run up the Yazoo River a short distance and landed. Well, it rained all that night, and early the next morning we were ordered back on the boat in great haste, and after a great deal of "strategy" we got on board and started by noon, and went up the river about 4 miles and went on shore. Our brigade was formed with the 25th in front and we skirmished a while through a field of cockle burrs, but found no rebels. We then marched out through the woods about 4 miles when we came upon the enemy just before dark and had right sharp firing for some time. They retreated and we lay down in line of battle without any fires and slept till morning. The brigade is now commanded by General Hovey. He complimented our regiment very highly on their conduct under fire.

The next morning, Sunday, we advanced a half mile and found the rebels in a strong position in front. They were fortified on high bluffs that extend along the river, three or four miles back and out of reach of the gun boats. They commenced at daylight to throw shells among us. We got two batteries up and returned the compliment. We lay there under fire all that day. The cannonading was tremendous on both sides. Shells burst among us continually, though none of our regiment were actually engaged except Company B.

Our position was in thick timbers between a bayou on our right, and a swamp on our left; the regiment reaching clear across. Company B was sent out on a small strip of dry land in the swamp to the left of our regiment and the batteries, to protect them from sharp shooters who were posted behind a fence about 600 or 700 yard distance. I was out there three or four hours, and it was the hottest place I ever was in. We protected ourselves as much as possible behind trees and logs. And the bullets flew thick all around us; if one of us showed ourselves from behind a tree, he was sure to have half a dozen shots fired at him. There was hardly a man but made a narrow escape. I lay flat on the ground and was shot at several times, but did not get touched.

Corporal Isaac Yount[1] of our company was killed, shot through the heart. He never spoke after he was hit. The company feels his loss very much; he was one of the nicest young men we had. William Harlan[2] was wounded slightly in the thigh. The regiment lost some 8 to 10 wounded. There was some talk of making a bayonet charge on their position in the evening, but it would have been an unjustifiable exposure of the men. They had two strong forts on the hill, and masked batteries and rifle pits under them, and the passage across the swamp at the base of the hill was only wide enough to be crossed in columns of platoons. We concluded that it was useless to make an attack at that point.

And after dark we went back to the river and in the morning (Monday) went down the river about one mile and then landed again. I forgot to say that on Saturday evening and all day Sunday there was heavy cannonading and musketry both on our right and left. On our right the battle was very close and very severe. Our men made several charges and drove the enemy back two miles; we could hear the men yell when the rebels run. The musketry was awful all day and a great many were killed and wounded—don't know how many. It was the right Division of our army, commanded by General Morgan[3]. He succeeded in driving the enemy out of two or three positions and reached the foot of the hill at one place.

Our brigade marched out there in the morning. There was hard fighting all day. Our men made two attempts to storm the hills and were repulsed. About 3 o'clock our regiment was again marched up under fire and fully expected to have to make a charge, but after laying there till after dark we were ordered to get picks and spades and throw up a breastworks[4] in front of our line. And you had better believe we had a time of it! The rain just poured down all night. We worked nearly all night, two hours on and two off, in mud and water up the knees, and built a breastwork 500 yards long, 10 feet thick, and 4 feet high, and built the front up with timber which we had to cut and carry in the dark. The rebels threw shells at us every few minutes, but we could always see the flash in time to lay down in the ditch before the ball came. Park Morehouse was slightly wounded by a piece of a shell.

Tuesday there was no fighting on either side; both sides were occupied in bringing up heavy guns and moving troops. Yesterday was all quiet on both sides, all day. We could see the rebels plainly planting batteries on the hills. Last night after dark our division (Steele's) lighted our camp fires and then with trailed arms and without noise left our camp and went back to the river and on board some boats.

We were then told that there were 7 forts or batteries 4 miles up the river that we had to take by storm this morning before light. The General showed us a map of the position and told us that the program was for Commander Foote⁵ with the whole gunboat fleet to shell the position for two hours, commencing at 4 o'clock. He said he could throw 1,400 shells per hour, and at that point the hills come close to the river. At the same time General Morgan was to open with all his heavy guns, and General Sherman down at the City, and give them such a New Year serenade as they never had before. When the forts had been shelled sufficiently we were to land and charge in three columns, our brigade in the center, and the 76th Ohio in front, and the 25th Iowa next, in columns of companies. The men were to throw away blankets and overcoats and charge with no <u>loads</u> in their guns. But daylight came and no fight. It is now 3 o'clock and we are still lying on the boats. No firing today and I have not learned why the movement does not take place.

Captain Smith is sick; he is on some of the boats. I heard yesterday evening he was better. Freeman is not very well again. I think he will have to stay behind if we move soon; he caught cold the night we worked in the ditch. Lieutenant Steele and myself are both well. I have not time to particularize but tell the folks that all except those I have named are well. A few have the diarrhea but none seriously. They are all in good spirits and if we get into a fight I think they will do their duty as a general thing. I am sorry to say there are a few I cannot depend upon. I have written this in so much of a hurry that I don't expect you can understand it. I have no doubt but we will take Vicksburg, but it may be a long job. I think our Generals are all prudent men and will not expose us unnecessarily.

It does very well for a man at home to turn up his nose at ditches and picks and spades, but to a man brought up before cannon and sharp shooters they become a good institution. I have not said the half I could but must stop for the present. I have got no letter from you yet. I have never felt the least fear yet or any presentiment that I would not get back to see you. I want you to remember me and love me and pray for me, and I will write to you every chance, but you must not be uneasy if you do not get a letter for some time, as but few boats get up the river now. Take good care of yourself and the children.

Your own, Jake

This had been a very dry New Years; we left all our baggage, mess chests and cooking utensils, &c, where we first landed and have not seen them since. We eat hard crackers and raw bacon. The quartermaster sometimes sends us out cooked rations from where we left the baggage. What did you do today? I have not heard from Helena since we came here. It is rumored that both General Grant[6] and General Banks[7] are coming to our help, but I suppose you know more about it than we do. We get no papers or news of any kind except rumors. The weather is very warm today. I will write to Tom the first chance I get. I can't carry paper.

1.   Nineteen-year-old Corporal Isaac Yount, a former student of Captain Smith, was killed in the Battle of Chickasaw Bayou. His older brother, Thomas, was with him in Company B and, as reported by Chaplain T. E. Corkhill,

> On the evening before the battle he had said to his brother, who is a member of the same company: "If it shall be my fate to fall in the coming struggle, or at any other time during this war, I shall try to meet it calmly and with a spirit of resignation I have never felt before. I shall do my duty under every circumstance, hoping that all will be well."
> When he had fallen, he was taken by his brother and several others to the rear, but his wound was mortal, and in about twenty minutes a lifeless corpse was all that was left of one of our bravest and best soldiers. A narrow grave was dug upon the field, and

Calmly yet sadly we laid him down,
From the field of his fame fresh and gory;
We traced not a line, we raised not a stone,
But we left him alone in his glory.
The Rebels may speak of the spirit that's gone,
And o'er his cold ashes upbraid him,–
But little he'll reck if they let him sleep on
In the grave where his comrades have laid him.

(as published in the January 31, 1863 *Home Journal*)

2. Private William C. Harlan survived this wound, and was later promoted to corporal and then sergeant, but was discharged for disabilities almost a year later on December 30, 1863.

3. General George Washington Morgan had served in the Regular Army as a Colonel of the 15th Infantry in the war with Mexico, and had been wounded at Churubusco. Due to problems with Sherman, his health, and his opposition to the Union changing its purpose of the war, General Morgan resigned his position in June 1863. (Stewart Sifakis, *Who Was Who In The Union*, page 278)

4. A breastwork was a chest-high protective earthwork, or mound, over which a soldier could fire. The term had been used since the 1600s. (Daryl Lyman, *Civil War Wordbook*, page 28)

5. Commander Andrew Hull Foote, nicknamed the "Gunboat Commodore," had worked closely with General Grant in several previous military engagements, including Forts Henry and Donelson on the Tennessee and Cumberland Rivers. Foote's previous sea service had included fighting pirates off Sumatra and battling the Chinese near Canton. At the time Jacob wrote this, Foote was not participating in the attack, but suffering from wounds he had received in previous engagements. Foote would die in June 1863 of Bright's disease. (Stewart Sifakis, *Who Was Who In The Union*, page 139)

6. Although General Grant commanded the Vicksburg campaign, he had not yet journeyed down the Mississippi River. However, he was now in a hurry to get to Vicksburg to prevent McClernand from taking command, who had sought this authority from his friend, Abraham Lincoln. McClernand, an Illinois Congressman before the war, had petitioned Abraham Lincoln for command of the entire Union Vicksburg operation, but through maneuvering, Grant had been able to retain his command. When McClernand did arrive near Vicksburg, Sherman's forces were split into two corps and placed under McClernand's command. Sherman was subordinate to McClernand and commanded the 15th Army Corps while General G. W. Morgan commanded the 13th Army Corps.

7. Part of the plan for concentration of men was to include General Nathaniel P. Banks moving his troops north, coming up river from New Orleans.

• On January 1, 1863, Abraham Lincoln's Emancipation Proclamation, in the eyes of the Union, freed the slaves in the lands still under Confederate control. The most immediate impact on Jacob was that the Union Army would now enlist black soldiers. Some in the Union Army, both enlisted men and officers, opposed this move, but others openly supported Lincoln's decree.

Historical Sketch—25th Iowa Infantry

Returning from the Battle of Chickasaw Bayou, the regiment, with its brigade and division, comprising part of the Fifteenth Army Corps, under command of Major General Sherman, with the Thirteenth Army Corps, commanded by Major General Morgan, both reporting to Major General McClernand, moved up the Mississippi River to Arkansas Post. (Roster and Record of Iowa Soldiers in the War of the Rebellion; *Published under the authority of the Iowa General Assembly).*

On The Way to Arkansas Post

On Board the Steamer *Continental*
At Milliken's Bend, January 3, 1863

Dear Emeline,

I wrote you a letter day before yesterday and I have just now heard that there will be a chance to send letters back this afternoon at 4 o'clock, so I will write a few more lines in haste. I am as well as usual. I will not undertake at present to tell you any more about what happened before I wrote last, though there is a great deal more I could say. You read the letter I wrote New Years first and you will have some kind of an idea of what we did up to that time.

That night at midnight we dropped down the river a few miles to where the baggage was left and were ordered to go on board the *Continental* and take all our baggage along. We worked hard all night getting changed from one boat to the other and getting things on board. At daylight it became evident that we were about to "change our base of operations." The whole army and everything that belonged to it was on board of the boats. About noon we started and the whole fleet steamed out of the Yazoo River in as gallant a style as we had steamed in.

We are now about 15 miles above the mouth of the Yazoo on the opposite side of what is called "Milliken's Bend." We are still on the boats, but I think we are going to land here and wait for reinforcements. It rained all night last night and all day so far. We have not got any letters yet, and have not seen the paymaster[1] either. But I think there will be communication up the river now. And I want you to write me a letter whenever you get this and send me ten dollars in it. I don't know when we will be paid and I am tired of being out of money and sponging on others.

. . . I think about you all the time, and wonder how you are getting along and what you and the children are doing. I would so like to see you all again. Wouldn't it be nice to be there in our nice quiet home with you and the children, in place of here in the wet and noise and confusion, eating hard crackers and raw meat. And yet I would rather stay here another six months than to go back without taking Vicksburg. I hope we will never leave here till we take it, which I believe will be done as soon as Grant or Banks come up to help us. We had to fall back because they did not get here in time.

Jim is better, Jont is well, and stands it first-rate. There are several of the boys not very well at present, but none of them dangerous. The captain is some better.

Well, dear, I must quit for the present. You must remember me and love me, won't you? I carry your pretty picture with me every place I go, and look at it every day. I think of you and love you dearly all the time, and Lulie and Nellie and Tommy & Kit—the dear little things, what do they do and say? And are they good children? Write me two sheets and tell me about them. Tell them Pa loves them and is coming home to see them and they must be good.

Your own, Jake

1. On December 31, 1862, a paymaster in the Union Army, Isaac M. Cook, was arrested in Cincinnati for default of $233,000, which he had lost to gamblers. Fortunately, he had been a conscientious bookkeeper, allowing for the simultaneous arrests of professional card players in Cairo, Springfield, Columbus, Chicago, and Cleveland. (*Burlington Hawkeye*, January 3, 1863 and January 10, 1863)

[Mt. Pleasant, Iowa]
January the 5th, 1863
Monday night

Dear Jake:

I started you a letter last Monday morning by Tom Allen. I believe I told you in that that I had not got a letter from you for twelve days. Well the next day I got one. It was the next one you wrote after you got back from the expedition, and told about your Negro "Jim." Well, today I got two more after looking anxiously for them all week. Your last, the one I got last Tuesday, was 15 days on the road. It was mailed at Memphis the 24th nine days after you finished it. Your letters are generally about five days getting to Memphis. But to yours of today, we heard last week that you were gone, or about to go. So I was sure I would get another. I knew you would write to me just before starting if you had time and so you did. But Oh! The suspense of waiting till I get another. When <u>can</u> <u>you</u> write again?? Not until the <u>battle</u> is over, and then yes, you will be saved. I feel as though you would surely be, yet you may not. Oh! I <u>will not</u> think of it, I <u>will</u> have hope. And I pray that you may not have a broken limb, or bloody wound about you any place, but that you will be saved entirely. But it is all over now, whatever it is, is done, and we shall not hear the particulars for so long.

Today's *Hawkeye* gives an account of the attack on Vicksburg. It speaks of Gen. Steele's division having some bloody fighting in turning the enemies left. So I know that you must be there, as you told me you were under him. I hope you will succeed in taking the place and routing the mean rebels. Now mind! If you are wounded and can't do anything for a while you must be sure and come home. I can't help but feel that you are safe, but I dreamed the other night that you were at home sick, and that you had gone crazy and come very near killing me in one of your crazy spells, but that is all non-sense. You know my dreams never amount to much . . .

You said I must go to Jefferson and stay two or three weeks. I should have gone two weeks ago, but couldn't get there at all. There has been no chance for some time and now I will not go, for the smallpox has spread so, that I know the people up there wouldn't thank me for coming. I understand they are very much frightened about it. I don't think I have been exposed to it at all, but I know they will be afraid to have me come right from the midst of it, among them. And it might be possible that we have been exposed on the streets, for we are bound to go to the post office, smallpox or not. So you see we might take it right up to them which I would not do for anything. But we have all been vaccinated and it took first rate. So I don't feel afraid of it much. If we should take it at all, it would be very light. Some have had it that were vaccinated and did-n't go to bed. But I will tell you, it has spread from one end of the town to the other. I never heard of measles or whooping cough spreading to such an extent, and it is all the Doctors fault. They said it was not smallpox and that vaccination would do no good. So the people got careless about it, as it didn't seem to be very dangerous at first, but it has got to be more serious. There has been some very bad cases, but not many deaths. Crane's family have it. I understand that Mrs. Crane is very sick with it. . . Mary Morley had it but she didn't miss a meals victuals. I don't think our children will get it. I don't let them go any place only to Ma's, not even to Morleys. So you see I can't go to Jefferson under circumstances though I was nearly sick to go . . . The people won't come to town from there on account of the smallpox and mud. It has been raining till the roads have got very bad . . .

Give my respects to Jim and Jont and all the rest. They are not forgotten at home. Haven't see Sarah Jont since you went away. We have the cow yet. She gives enough milk and butter to do us, so I guess we will keep her! We are out of fodder. I shall have to turn out and hunt some. Christmas it rained all day. We were down to Ma's. New Years day Tom bought a turkey and brought it here for me to cook. So they all came up and eat dinner. When we sit down to dinner we all wished you & Jim & Jont & Billy & Ol were here to help eat. Ma thought she could do without any dinner if she could see you all eat. I hope you will all be here next new years' day; Good bye. Write soon. If I could only get a letter every day I believe I would be satisfied.

E.R.B.R. [Emeline Ramsey
Bereman Ritner]

I Am Beginning to Lose a Great Deal of
My Respect for the Big-Bugs in Our Army

Steamer *Continental*
Wednesday, January 7, 1863

Dear Emeline,

I wrote you a letter on New Years Day and one since, and having nothing else to do today I will write another. I have no news at all to tell, but will try to say something that will be worth reading—don't know yet what it will be. But there is no way in which I can spend time so pleasantly as in writing to you. It drives away the blues and I forget to be lonesome. I am afraid you get very lonesome sometimes, do you? I wish I knew. I am afraid no one pays any attention to you or cares anything about how you get along. This troubles me more than anything else. Well, I will be at home again some of these days, and then I will stay right there with you. I am not going to leave my sweet wife again for anything. Ah, but you say, you said that once before; well, I will stick to it this time. I am not tired of the army, nor sorry I volunteered this time. But I am tired of the way we are treated and of the conduct of our leading men. But I know I would have been a great deal more dissatisfied if I had remained at home.

I believe I wrote to you last Sunday. After I had finished the letter we got a mail and I got a letter from you and one from Henry, and one from Pap and Zan. Yesterday we got another large mail, but I got nothing. The rebels took one mail boat on its way down and I expect they got some of my letters. I am going to commence numbering mine since January first. So you can tell when you get them all. You do the same with yours. Four of the boys were left sick at Mt. Pleasant, and James Stockton[1] who was left sick at Helena came down on the boat with the mail yesterday. Stockton says the box you sent to us got to Helena the day after New Years, and the boys ate it all up. He says it had been opened; everything was smashed up. It makes me provoked that I did not get any. It would have done me good to have seen it, if I hadn't eat a bite. I do want some of your nice cooking so much, and I know you put in something for me.

We have been on the way up the river since last Friday and have got to Gain's Landing, where we have been for nearly two days, and don't know when we shall leave. We are taking on wood here, of which there is an immense quantity, but it is back from ½ to 1 mile from the river, and the soldiers have to carry it up.

We are on the *Continental*, one of the largest boats on the river, and the Flagboat of our Division. We have on board General Steele and staff, General C. E. Hovey and staff, and General F. P. Blair[2] and staff. And we have the poorest accommodations we have ever had on a boat, and we have steamboated a good deal since we left home. We thought at first it was a big thing to get on the same boat with a Major General but the staff officers and hangers-on occupy all the rooms and we have to lay on the floor. And we have no money to buy meals or anything and have to work all night sometimes getting wood on board. We have 200 cord on this boat.

Still my health is good, and it will be all right in the end, as I will have more money left when I get home. I thought when I commenced this I would take my time and write as good a letter as I could, but they are talking about closing the mail and I must be in a hurry. It is still not known (to us) where we are going[3]. Some say up the Arkansas River, others that we go to Memphis. I suppose we will all find out some time.

The letter I got from you was written on the 18th. I believe you said you had a headache and were nearly sick. I do wish you could get clear of that old headache. I am so afraid you will get clear down sick and then what will become of the children? You said you were talking of going up to Car's to stay over Christmas. I hope you got to go and had a good time. You did not say whether Nellie was up there yet or not. Or anything about the children except that you had not named the youngest yet. I haven't got any name to send. Haven't seen a woman or seen the name of one since we have been down here. The whole country on both sides of the river is deserted, even by the Negroes, who have been driven off. I want you to tell me all about our babies, the next time you write. I think of them a great deal. I want to know if they ever talk about Pa, and what they do. Did you get the little sled for Tommy? How are Lulie's eyes? Have you got good warm clothes for them all? What kind of weather is it up there? Have you got plenty of wood, and who cuts it up?

The weather here is very nice and warm except when it rains, never had more than a light frost, and in the middle of the day the flies bite. Tell me how Ma and Sarah get along. I would like to see them first-rate. I must write Ma a letter if I ever get time. I hear that Alvah has moved into his fine house. Tom wrote to Jim, said Al paid all down but about 2,000. Do you know anything about our house—was anything done at Court? I suppose you will have to get Tom to pay our tax. Don't pay on the house and lot till the title is fixed.

I am beginning to lose a great deal of my respect for the Big-bugs in our army. They all or very nearly all drink and gamble and swear. And an officer who does not mix in with them is considered "Old Fogy." For my part I would rather have a clean conscience and my own self-respect, and the approbation and love of a sweet wife at home, than to be a toady to any Brigadier or Major General. I am certain that when it comes to fighting I can act as bravely and command a company as well as any of them, and better than most of them. But I despise to be ordered round by men who drink and carouse all night as our big-bugs do on the boat. General Hovey[2] is pretty much of a gentleman, I think. But Steele[2] and Blair[2] are supercilious aristocrats, who will not even condescend to speak to a "Volunteer Officer[4]."

Jim is not very well yet, but is getting better. Frank Taylor is well. Tell his mother that he gets along first-rate. He seems to enjoy the life here as well as anyone in the company. Jont stands it first-rate. He makes a good soldier. So does Billy DeGroodt. I did not get the paper you said you sent. Send me more. They sell papers here at 25 cents apiece and it is very hard to get anything to read. We have not found out yet why we retreated from Vicksburg. I hope we will go back there before long, and take the mean Secession hole. I would like to start back right away and stay there till we took it. General McClernand[3] I believe has command here now. But I must stop. Direct as usual.

Your own, Jake

I am out of stamps and money and will have to get the Major to frank[5] this and you can pay there. I wrote to Tom a few days ago, but was in so much hurry and confusion that I expect there was not much sense in it. Jud is still in the hospital at Helena, but is better; he can walk around.

1. Jim Stockton, age 19, was from Trenton, Iowa.

2. Steele commanded the Fourth Division; Blair and Hovey commanded brigades reporting to Steele. Steele reported to Sherman, who reported to McClernand, who reported to Grant, commander of the Army of the Tennessee. Jacob was in Hovey's brigade.

3. McClernand, Sherman, and the troops were on their way to Arkansas Post, up the Arkansas River.

4. Jacob was an officer in the Volunteer Army, as opposed to the Regular Army, and was among those to whom Steele and Blair would not condescend to speak. Later Jacob was able strike up a conversation with General Osterhaus; Jacob probably had made an effort to have a casual conversation with Steele or Blair.

5. When Jacob uses the phrase "to frank this letter" he meant that Emeline would have to pay the postage when she received the letter. (Roger Durham letters)

The Battle of Arkansas Post

By January 10, McClernand's 30,000 troops had Fort Hindman, located at Arkansas Post, under siege. After two days of fighting and at a cost of a thousand Union casualties, the Confederates surrendered. Confederate casualties were only 140 killed and wounded, but 4,791 Confederate troops were captured. Naval bombardments had hit the fort hard during the assault. Everyone involved in the battle considered it a major victory for the Union, but not an offset to the Union defeat at Chickasaw Bayou.

No. 4—January 13, 1863
On The Battle Field of Arkansas Post

Dear Emeline,

I sit down to write you a few lines in great haste. I have been through another battle and came out all right, did not get a scratch though I was in the thickest of the fight from first to last. I have not time to give you a detailed account of the whole thing now, nor do I suppose it would be interesting to you. We came up the Arkansas River to this point last Friday, landed after dark, and I stood picket guard all night, which was very dark and rainy. We were in gun shot of the rebel pickets and exchanged shots with them occasionally, but no one was hurt.

The next day (Saturday) our Division marched all day through brush and swamps where the mud and water was shoe mouth deep all over the ground and sometimes knee deep, to get a position in rear of the enemy. We finally came to a swamp that was perfectly impassable, and had to go back to the river, which we reached about dark. Without waiting long enough to get supper we started on another route to get the same object, and after traveling through mud and water without any road till 2 o'clock in the morning we came onto the main camp of the enemy, and found it entirely deserted, they having all retreated in great haste inside of their breast works. We found a large amount of clothing, arms, cooking utensils, cornmeal and beef and bacon, &c. My feet were wet and I was as near given out as I ever was. My back was so lame I could hardly walk. I got no sleep that night, as we did not dare to make fires, not knowing but the rebels were in the brush close at hand.

When daylight came Sunday morning we found them behind their works, one and a half miles in front of us. It took till 1 o'clock to get our artillery in position and the "ball opened" along the whole line and from the gunboats and the roar of cannon for half an hour was awful; it shook the ground for miles. Then a charge was made by the infantry with a yell along the whole line, which was a mile and a half long. We were on the extreme right, the 76th Ohio in front, and the 25th Iowa next. The ground was covered with an abatis[1] of brush and fallen timber that was almost impassable, but we got up to within 200 or 300 yards of the breast works. We lay down as we had been previously ordered to do. We soon silenced all the cannons, shooting all the horses and men that showed themselves.

Then the next brigade that came up were to go into the works, but they broke and ran back right over us. But I have not time to give all the particulars. As we came up the bullets came like hail, mixed with grape canister and shells. It actually seemed that there was not one foot of ground that was not struck by a bullet. Company B did finely—went up in good order and did good fighting till 4 o'clock, when the White flag was raised and we took the whole thing prisoners, about 5,000 men and a large amount of arms and ammunition.

Captain Smith was sick on the boat. He has resigned and is going home. I suppose I am captain now. We had one man killed, G.W. Calhoun; and Sergeant Baron Crane and Harvey Millhone were wounded. I had 56 men in the fight.

Jim was sick at the boat. Jont made a narrow escape but was not hurt. I was on different parts of the field and saw men shot down by my side, but God in mercy brought me safely out. I hope I am grateful to Him for His great care . . . We are camped now in the rebel quarters. We are destroying the works and will leave soon now.

Your own, Jake

I am all right now but very tired. I will write again in a day or two.

1. An abatis was an arrangement of felled trees, with the branches facing outward from the defending position to impede the advancing enemy.

•   One of the Union casualties at Arkansas Post was Brigadier General Charles Edward Hovey, who despite having his arm mangled from an exploding shell, continued to command his brigade. Hovey survived his wound and continued to serve the Union Army, being awarded a rank of Brevet Major General for his actions at Arkansas Post. (Edwin Bearss, *The Vicksburg Campaign* Volume I, page 381; Stewart Sifakis, *Who Was Who In The Union*, page 202)

- One casualty of the 25th Iowa was their adjutant, Kirkwood Clark, the nephew and adopted son of Iowa Governor Kirkwood. Clark may have survived if he had allowed the amputation of his leg, but he had refused this operation. (See the resolutions of honor passed by the 25th Iowa concerning the death of Adjutant Kirkwood Clark, following Jacob's letter of April 4, 1863) (*Burlington Hawkeye*, February 26, 1863)

I Walked Over the Battlefield After the Fight

No. 5—Napoleon, Arkansas[1]
January 15, 1863

Dear Emeline,

I wrote you a short letter a few days ago and promised to write another soon. And so I guess I will do it tonight. I told you something about the battle in my other letter and I wrote a long one to Alvah today and tried to tell him all about it. You must get that letter and read it and that will save me from writing the same thing twice. I don't suppose you will care very much anyhow about hearing of so much fighting and killing folks. But that is the way things go in war.

I think the 25th has got into the business pretty lively for a new regiment. We have seen very hard service since we left Helena and the regiment is very much reduced.

Out of 960 men that we had at Camp McKeen, we cannot muster now more than 400 men for duty. I have the largest company, and report only 51 men fit for duty. I told you I never was so tired and exhausted as I was Sunday night and Monday and the men were perfectly prostrated with fatigue and hunger. The weather has been the worst I ever saw. Night before last and yesterday it rained as hard as it could pour down and the men got wet to the skin. Last night and today it snowed and there is now 3 or 4 inches of snow on the ground. I never felt so bad in my life as I did today, to see the men huddled on the boat, crouching and shivering without being able to get to the fire.

I walked over the battle field after the fight and saw the dead and dying, some places lying almost in heaps and some scattered round in almost all kinds of shapes, limbs torn off and bodies mangled in almost every manner, and was comparatively unmoved, because I knew they went down willingly in a good cause. But when I saw the men today exposed to the storm and could do nothing for them I had to go to my room and "take a cry." We have a large cabin on the boat with two stoves, large enough to accommodate half the regiment. But General Steele will allow no enlisted men to come into it, nor to occupy staterooms, but Steele [Company B's 2nd Lieutenant Samuel Steele] and I did take two into ours last night in spite of him. But I am getting ahead of my story.

I believe I told you in my last letter that we were quartered in the rebel camp. Well, we were ordered to leave there and go on board the boats that evening and burn the quarters as we left. We did not get started till this morning, and got down to Napoleon on the Mississippi at the mouth of the Arkansas River just at dark. We have orders that the men might go on shore and make fires on the banks and cook but must not leave the bank. But I took Company B right up to the town and back one street from the river and put them into a brick house that has two large fire places, and told them to stay there till morning. And they shall stay there or there will be another battle right here. I feel very well myself now. I believe that I can stand it, if I do not have to fight more than once in two weeks, which I think is often enough for a man's health.

I don't know but I think the whole army will land here and camp a while to recruit[2]. We were in hopes we would get to go up to Helena or Memphis, but I think now we will stop here till we get a good ready and then go down and try Vicksburg again. I am in hopes we will get paid off here; that would do the men more good than anything else.

Captain Smith is very sick and has resigned and is going home. I borrowed some money of him long ago and got a pair of boots of him, so I owe him ten dollars, which I want you to pay him when he gets there, if you have it to spare. If not, wait till I send you some. He promised to go and see you when he gets home and tell you all about things down here. He is a very good man and I think a great deal of him, but he would never do for a soldier.

Jim was not in the fight; he started and would have gone if I had not ordered him back. That march the night before the fight would have killed him. He is better now and I think will soon be well. I am going to have him appointed 2nd Lieutenant if I can, but I can't tell yet how it will be.

Wils Payne volunteered to carry the National colors in the fight, and is praised by everyone for his bravery. He is one of the best men we have, and does more for me than any other man I have.

When we march he always carries our coffee pot and frying pan and cooks for us. I don't see how we could do without him. I have not heard anything from Billy and Ol or Jud since I wrote to you. I must write to them tomorrow.

I believe I told you once that they got the box of things you sent, and that we never got a bite. I was spited; I would just like to see something again that you had cooked. I don't expect that we will ever get anything that was in the box . . .

Mrs. Wittenmeyer came down here just before we started up the White River and brought a boat load of things for the sick and wounded soldiers, and some to sell to the well ones. I got a barrel of kraut, a box of butter, and a box of eggs for our company on credit; it did us a great deal of good. You ought to have seen me eat kraut out of the barrel. I suppose I ate about a gallon. Jont was in the fight and fought like a hero; he gets along first-rate. Baron Crane is sick and on the hospital boat. There are none of our men here that are very sick, none of them dangerous. Well, dear, I must quit for this time; it is time to go to bed. Tell me what kind of weather you had about the 15th. Give my love to Ma and tell her I often think of her and would like to hear from her. I wish she would write me a letter.

Your own, Jake

1. Napoleon, Arkansas, once a thriving river town, disappeared after the war. (Correspondence with Ann Crane Farrier)

2. With the Emancipation Proclamation now in effect, Grant's Army of the Tennessee began to recruit Negroes for the Union Army.

No. 6—Camp Near Vicksburg
January 24, 1863

Dear Emeline,

I wrote you a letter a week ago last Friday and gave an account of the fight at "Arkansas Post," and that we had them go back to Napoleon. I was out of humor then and felt a good deal down at the heel, and have felt so ever since till within a day or two. I have got on land once more with the company, and we all feel better, though the company is very much reduced; we can only report about 45 for duty[1] and that is better than any other company in the regiment can do. We did not get to stay long at Napoleon.

I took possession of the whole brick house that I told you about, and had the company all right, but on Sunday at noon we were ordered on board the boat again and we have been nearly a week coming down here and getting on shore. This is late Saturday night. We landed here yesterday evening. We are in plain sight of Vicksburg, on the opposite side of the river. It seems to be about the size of Burlington and built on pretty much the same kind of a place, high bluffs above and below the town; looks like a pretty hard place to take, but I believe we can take it. We are camped on the side of the levee as near the city as it is safe to go with steamboats. We are at work finishing the canal that Butler commenced last summer[2]. It is about one and a quarter miles long. They are digging all along and will soon have it done, I think as the river is rising very fast. The rebels throw shells at them but do not hurt anybody.

Our regiment has not worked any yet, but I suppose it will be our turn to work or fight one, tomorrow, as it is Sunday. And we are sure to have something to do every Sunday. That is one reason I thought I had better write to you tonight. And another is that I got a letter from you today, the first I have had for a long, long time— I don't know how long. This one was No. 9, written on the 14th inst. and the last one I got before was written on the 18th of December, 1862! We got three mails that did not bring anything for me, and I got clear out of patience and concluded I wouldn't write any more till I got one. The last one I got before this said you were talking about going up to Car's on Christmas. But I never heard whether you went or not, nor what you did on Christmas or New Years. I wish I knew. Tom Allen[3] has not got here yet with that letter. I suppose he is at Helena. This makes 6 I have written to you since New Years, most of them great long ones too. I want you to get some big paper like this and write me a long letter so they will last longer when I do get one. I always get them read through before I get started hardly. You did not tell me anything about Ma or Tom and Anna or Al, nor whether you had plenty of wood &c. When I sit down to write to you I always have so much to say I don't have time to write half of it.

I guess you have "not seen Captain Smith about town" yet. He resigned some time ago and has not been with the company at all since the day before New Years. But he is still here and waiting for a chance to go home, has been sick on the hospital boat most of the time. I think he will get off in a day or two now, as most of the boats are going up to St. Louis for provisions. I suppose I will be captain as soon as his resignation is accepted, and Steele 1st Lieutenant. I don't know who will be 2nd Lieutenant. I think it will be Whippo or Freeman. We are talking about having an election some day soon. Jim has not had a letter from Car since two weeks before we left Helena. What is she about? You must tell all you know about her when you write. He is afraid from what you said that "Fredie" has the small-pox. I am glad you all got vaccinated in time and hope you are safe. I was vaccinated about three weeks ago, but it did not take.

One of the men (Robert Hite[4]), one of those who came down from Mt. Pleasant this winter, was taken very sick at the "Post," and we put him on a hospital boat. On the way down they found out that he had small-pox and they laid him out on the guard in the cold and snow and he remained there all night and was nearly frozen in the morning. When I found it out I had him carried to our quarters and taken care of. He was broken out very thick all over. I don't know whether it will spread in the company or not. I fear it will. I had to leave Hite at Napoleon. I left his brother[4] and William Tedrow[4] to take care of him, but there were no soldiers left there and I expect the guerrillas would get them as soon as we were out of sight, but I suppose they would parole them. It was a hard case but I couldn't help it. They were all first-rate boys.

The 11th Iowa is a few miles up the river from here. Harry Holloway and Arch Campbell were here yesterday and ate dinner with us. They both look well and hearty and seem to enjoy soldiering. I saw Bub Turney and Mart Stubbs and Will Wade; they belong to the same company[5] and are all well. I have seen Joe Black[6] several times—he is as big and fat as you please and I think is a good officer.

I think from what you said about the battle of Vicksburg that you did not know much about it. We got some *Home Journal*s today and the account in that is the biggest lie I ever saw. I suppose though by this time you have got the true account. If you have all my letters you know about all I can tell. You will find that the 25th [Iowa] was in the fight. I have learned lately that the Generals opened some of the letters that were written down there. I don't know whether they opened any of yours or not. If they did I don't think they found anything "contraband" in them.

I got a letter from Pap[7] today, but it was written January 1st and he did not say anything about coming after Jud[8]. I have not had a letter from Jud since we left Helena, which is five weeks ago today.

I doubt if he could get him if he did come, but I wish he would come on down here. I would like to see him. I think Jud must be about well by this time. You and he both talk about its being <u>muddy</u> up there. Now, that must be a joke. I never saw any mud in Iowa— it never gets muddy there. If you want to see mud come to Louisiana and camp in a swamp. And then you might talk about seeing mud!! The driest place I could find to sleep last night the mud was four inches deep.

There are hundreds of teams all around here sticking fast. The only way to transport anything is on the backs of men and mules— wagoning is played out. I suppose all the people in the North and all the newspapers will be raising a great "Hue and cry" before long and want to know what McClernand or Grant is about. "Why doesn't he move" "Onward to Vicksburg!" But I tell you that if there is going to be much of a fight the men must rest first. I never saw men so used up, discouraged, and run down. A great many would actually delight in an opportunity to give themselves up to the rebels and get paroled. The whole army has been on the boats nearly all the time for five weeks; during all of that time the men have had no chance to wash or cook, and have become dirty, lousy, and sick. And I hope we will be allowed to rest two weeks, and then we can make a good fight if necessary.

But if it keeps on raining as it has done since we got here we will get mired in the mud.

Well, I must quit for the present. I will write again the first opportunity . . . I still have your picture to look at. I carry it in my pocket all the time and look at your pretty, sweet face every day . . . Kiss the children for me, and give my love to Ma, and all the folks and tell them I won't write to any of them till they write to me.

Jake

1. Company B had approximately 100 men when it was mustered on August 13, 1862, compared to the 45 that it now had.

2. Jacob is describing what became known as "Grant's Canal," as a means to safely bypass Vicksburg. Vicksburg was located high on the bluffs on a winding part of the Mississippi River, which allowed the Confederates to easily fire down upon Union ships with artillery. If Vicksburg could have been safely bypassed via "Grant's Canal," the importance of Vicksburg to the Confederacy would have been greatly diminished and Union forces could have gained control of the Mississippi River without actually capturing Vicksburg.

Unfortunately for the Union, after much effort, the canal plan failed. Before the canal was finished, heavy rains caused the water level on the Mississippi River to rise and wash out the canal. Ultimately, none of the four Union efforts to dig canals in the area surrounding Vicksburg succeeded.

Although not successful in changing the course of the Mississippi River in 1863, approximately 20 years after the Civil War the channel of the Mississippi River did change and followed the course of Grant's Canal. Vicksburg is no longer on the main channel of the Mississippi River.

3. Tom Allen, age 21, was a private in Company B. He died of disease July 1, 1863 on the Hospital Boat *R.C. Wood.*

4. Robert Hite was taken prisoner January 11, 1863 at Arkansas Post along with Nathan Hite and William Tedrow. They were paroled January 21, 1863 and rejoined Company B on March 2, 1863.

5. Sergeant Harrison Holloway, age 25, Archibald Campbell, age 19, Darius "Bub" Turney, age 19, Martin Stubbs, age 28, and William Wade, age 21 were in Company G of the 11th Iowa Infantry. The 11th Iowa had participated at Shiloh in April 1862, and was now part of the 17th Army Corps commanded by McPherson.

6. Captain Joe Black was with Company K of the 55th Illinois. Black, from Abingdon, Illinois and two others rotated the position of Major of the 55th Illinois. Abingdon is 30 miles east of Burlington, Iowa and it is possible that Jacob and Joe met in Burlington. (*The Story of the Fifty-Fifth Regiment Illinois Volunteer Infantry*, pages 161, 214, 512)

7. This is the letter written January 1, 1863, where Henry Ritner discusses the war being fought under God's authority.

8. Judson Ritner was Jacob's brother, who was with him in Company B. Judson was severely ailing.

No. 7—Camp Before Vicksburg
February 1, 1863

Dear Wife,
    This is Sunday again . . . I wrote you last Sunday and told you I was not very well. I have been getting worse ever since till now I am

hardly able to walk around. I am bilious and have the jaundice a little. I have no appetite to eat anything I can get here. I got a letter from you day before yesterday. It was written on the 22nd and had $10.00 in it. I was very glad to get it. It came though very quick. I think there will be no delay now any more, and you will get your letters regularly and I will get mine. I do hope so. Nothing does me so much good as to get a letter from you. I am going to get well now. I can get some little notions to eat with the money, and that is what I need more than anything else. I see by the last papers that the money had been furnished to pay us off, so I expect we will soon have plenty. If they pay up to the 1st of January I will get about $340.

I have nothing new to tell you at all. Nothing of importance has transpired here since I last wrote. We are still lying here before the city; there has been no fighting of any consequence. We have moved our camp twice a short distance, and have been at work building corduroy[1] roads over the swamps round here. Some are repairing the levee, and some working on the ditch[2]. I think that ditch is going to turn out to be a great humbug. I don't know whether they depend much on it or not. I don't believe they will ever turn the river, nor get boats through the ditch. I can't tell anything about the plan of attack or when it will be made, but I think likely we will be here a month yet, perhaps more.

I suppose you know all about our first trip down here, if you got four letters in one day, and read them all, and then wrote to me, I don't think you did much else. I suppose you have got another lot by this time from the "Post[3]." I can think I see you sitting there in the rocking chair reading my letters. As you say it would be so nice for me to be there with you. I wish I could have you to cook for me a few days. I want some of your nice victuals more than anything else.

I have been thinking that perhaps I might get leave to go home for a few days, after we take Vicksburg, but I don't know as there will be any chance. I won't resign or leave the company unless I see my life depends upon it. I suppose you will see Captain Smith before you get this, as he started home last Tuesday; he said he would call to see you right away. He will tell you all the news. He will be a great "lion" about town, I suppose. He was the most homesick man I ever saw. I can't say just what I think of him, so I will say nothing. He went away without leave and I expect will get into trouble.

General Grant[4] is here now, in command, and has issued an order that there shall be no more resignations accepted or leaves of absence granted to anyone, but I think that will only last till after the fight here. I am <u>so provoked</u> that I did not get anything out of that box. I never got the letter or the book or anything at all. Tom Allen has not got here yet—don't know where he is. I have never heard from Billy or Ol or Jud since we left Helena. I don't see why they don't write. I'll never write to them till they do.

I am glad the cow does so well—she is a good cow and you must feed her well. If you do not she will die off in the spring. You must make Morley have that wood hauled up right away for fear there should come a big storm and catch you out of wood. You will have cold weather there yet before spring.

I am glad to hear that Lulie's eyes are getting better. I hope they will get clear well. You must get the sled for Tommy yet, if it snows. I hope his arm has got well by this time so he can haul in wood. I think Nellie had quite a visit. I expect she got home sick and was glad to get back to see Ma. I would just like to be there to hear "Kitty" talk. I expect she can make it rattle by this time. I think you might find her some better name by this time. Well, I do wish this was over so I could come home and stay with you all once more. I hope it won't last much longer. You must excuse this measly letter this time. I will feel better by next Sunday and write you a better letter, see if I don't. Our preacher has gone home and we have no meetings any more. I wish I could go to church with you once more. It would be so nice. I think a great many times that if I ever get back I will appreciate the privilege of going with you to a good meeting more than I ever did. I hope you go every chance. Jim got a letter from Car. She told about the meeting there. She wrote about <u>twice</u> as much as you do. Now I want two sheets the next time. Give my love to Ma. I hope Sal did not have the small-pox.

Your own, Jake

1. Corduroy roads were built using logs spaced periodically to give support to the road.

2. See references to Grant's Canal following Jacob's letter of January 24, 1863.

3. Arkansas Post.

4. General Grant, who commanded the Army of the Tennessee, arrived at Milliken's Bend, Louisiana, on January 29 and personally took control of the Vicksburg campaign.

[Mt. Pleasant, Iowa]
February the 5th, 1863, No. 5

Dear Jake,
   This is Thursday again, my writing day. I got a letter from you on last Saturday dated the 15th of Jan, I believe you were then at Napoleon. You thought you would stay there awhile and rest, but it seems there is no rest for you. I understand that you are all at Vicksburg again. I know you will all be worn out entirely. And then what a siege before you the taking of, or the attempt, to take Vicksburg again. I suppose it will all be over when you get this. Either this Victory or defeat. Oh how I do pray that it may be the former, and that you may be spared to tell of the great success to the Union cause. I feel so uneasy whenever I hear of the commencement of a battle, especially that at Vicksburg, for it is so well fortified that we will have to lose a great many men before we can take it. Somehow I feel that you will not be hurt, but I may be mistaken, if you should be wounded, I hope you will try very hard to come home. You will get well so much quicker. I should be very sorry to see you hurt but I would so like to wait on you awhile if you were sick.
   Captain Smith got home Tuesday I believe. I haven't seen him yet. Don't know whether he is much sick or not. Are you Captain or not? If so, were you appointed or elected. I think your men have confidence enough in you to make you Captain, if it were left to them. Frank Taylor wrote to his folks that you was the best hearted fellow in the world. I am so glad, if you have gained their esteem, and hope you will keep it if you can do it by fair means.
   Were you acquainted with Captain Rector[1] of the Fourth Cavalry? He was promoted to Major some time after he was in the service. Well his body was brought home last week a corpse. He died at the hospital, after an illness of only a few days. His family knew nothing of it till his body came . . .
   I have got all my wood hauled in at last. When they corded it up it made near 4½ cords, and cost $12.00. John Brummet is cutting it up which will cost $4.80 that is quite a sum for wood isn't it. I set down the cost of everything I get. You would think it quite a formidable sum if you should see it. Indeed it costs more to live than I had any idea of.—I have the hardest kind of a cold and so have all the children every one of them. Nellie & Kittie are almost sick with theirs and so am I. All have a sore throat with it. I got a bottle

of expectorant but it doesn't seem to do much good. We are having some real winter just now. It turned cold Saturday night & has been as cold as Greenland ever since. You want to know what kind of weather we had the 15th. Well, it was windy and disagreeable & the next day was the coldest day we had this winter and very windy.

I would send you the *Home Journal* if it was any account but there is never anything in it worth reading hardly. The Secesh in the north are splitting the country to pieces, or trying to. I shouldn't be a bit surprised if we should have war at home before another year . . .

Be sure and tell me whether you get all my letters or not. Haven't seen Car or Sara Jont for about 3 months. Guess they are afraid to come to town. Plenty of smallpox yet. The Doctor said Tom had it. He is well now. Eliza is here yet. Sallie got a letter from Ol Tuesday. He said Jud was getting well & that Ike had just got there.

Em Ritner

1. Fourth Iowa Cavalry Major Benjamin Rector of Sidney was taken prisoner October 11, 1862 and exchanged on October 29, 1862. He died of disease January 21, 1863 in Helena, Arkansas.

No. 8—Camp Before Vicksburg
February 8, 1863

Dear Emeline,

. . . I wrote you a letter last Sunday, but I felt so bad I expect there was no sense in it, and it would give you the blues. I got worse after that, so I could not get out of the tent for a few days. But I am getting well now as fast as I could expect. I feel first-rate except that I am still very weak. I have been walking round for a few days, and have a good appetite. The only danger is that I will eat too much, or eat something I ought not to. I don't believe I would have got well at all if I had not got that ten dollars from you. I think it will last till the paymaster comes around. But everything is very dear here and many things that I would like to have cannot be had at all.

I have to pay 50 cents per pound for butter, cheese 50 cents, canned fruit $1.25 per quart, potatoes $3.50 per bushel, dried fruit and eggs not be had, pickles .50 cents per dozen. I paid fifty cents for an old rooster and have been eating at him for nearly a week—

don't know what I will do when he is all gone. I don't expect I can get another chicken in the whole country.

The men have all been very good to me and do everything they can. I like them all first-rate. I suppose you will have seen Captain Smith before this and he will tell you all about matters and things down here better than I can write it. It is a pretty hard place, and I think will be unhealthy as soon as the weather begins to get warm. It has been very wet, cold and disagreeable since we have been here. The ground is very low and flat. The water in the river is even with the banks and on a level with the ground we camp on, but the levee is very strong in most places and about 15 feet high, but there is a break in it about 5 miles from here where the water runs through as large as Skunk River and we expect to be drowned out and have to go on board the boats before long.

We all dread the boats more than anything else. But General Grant says he has his plans all laid to take Vicksburg and he is bound to do it with the loss of but very few men. So perhaps we will be camped over on the hills before long. Nothing of interest has transpired here since I last wrote. The health of the army is improving very slowly. We report about 250 men for duty in our regiment. Dr. Marsh[1] has resigned and is going home first chance. A great many officers are resigning, or trying to. I would like very much to go home a few days and see you all, but I don't intend to resign. I started out with Company B and I intend to see it through and go home when they do, if I live. The army here is not very enthusiastic—on the contrary a great many are discouraged and homesick.

What disheartens us more than anything else is that we learn from the papers that the North is becoming divided. The cowardly, sneaking, traitorous Democrats are throwing off the cloak and taking sides openly with the rebels, and are in favor of disunion!! If such men ever get their just deserts this side of hell I shall doubt the Justice of the Almighty. We can fight the rebels and are willing to do it, and can whip them without their help, if the black-hearted rascals would only be still at home, and not take sides with the enemy. I had just as lief fight such men in Iowa as in Mississippi.

I was very glad to hear that you are all well. I hope you will have a good time at the meeting. I am glad that you can go and leave the children. I think it is very smart in them to be able to stay by themselves; they must be getting sharp. I have not had a chance to go to meeting since I left Helena. Our preacher has gone home and I expect we won't have any more meetings here at all. I have often thought that if I ever get home I would like so well to go to church again. I think I can appreciate the privilege now. I try to do as near right as I can in this hard place. I do not think I am any worse than when I started, pretty much the same old sort. I don't feel the least desire or temptation to indulge in drinking whiskey, swearing and playing cards. In fact I see enough of them every day to disgust anyone of good sense and manners.

Joe Black is camped close here. He was here and talked till midnight last night[2]. He is acting Major of the 55th Illinois. I think he is a first-rate officer and quite a gentleman. He indulges in none of the bad habits common to officers.

The 15th is a few miles above here. I have seen Charlie Cady and Rogers and several more of the Danville boys; they are all well and hearty, except one who has the small-pox. I saw Perry Vanwinkle[3] the other day. I had not heard he was here. He was well. Freeman is perfectly well and hearty.

We had an election for officers the other day and Sergeant Yount[4] was elected and Jim did not run. Yount beat Whippo by 5 votes. I was very sorry for it. They elected me Captain by acclamation, and Stecle 1st Lieutenant in the same way. Jont has been quite unwell for some time; he has got very poor and looks bad, but is getting better now.

You need not be uneasy about the "expense" of keeping the family. I want you to spend all you need to make you comfortable, and am glad you have it there to spend. I suppose if Eliza is there to board off of you for two or three weeks it will take that much more. I hope you will succeed in getting corn and flour. Be sure to feed the cow well, no matter what it costs. And be certain to have enough to last till grass comes. Get some bran if you can. You must make them get all that wood hauled right away, so it can be measured before it is cut.

I can't resign my guardianship unless I was there to settle and make Crawford pay over as fast as he can. I hear that money is plenty there and property high. I want Tom and Alvah both to go to work and sell that 50 acres of ours up in Jefferson if they can. Take $500 and as much more as they can get. I do not think it will pay us to keep it and repair it up. If they can get enough down to make it safe with a mortgage it will be all right. I have not heard or seen Tom Allen yet. I have not heard from Jud either, or Ike[5.] I don't see why some of them don't write to me. I hear that Ike is in Helena.

I have seen some men here who know Jim, and saw him not

long ago in Tennessee. You must excuse my scribbling this time, dear, I am very weak yet, but I will be well by next Sunday, see if I don't. I hope Tom did not have the small-pox. I wish he would write to me if he is able.

Your own, Jake

1. Dr. William Marsh, age 46, resigned on February 7, 1863, as Surgeon of the 25th Iowa Infantry. Assistant Surgeon Henry Farr, age 34, was promoted to Surgeon, and Hospital Steward Charles Marsh, age 21, was promoted to Assistant Surgeon.

2. As to Joseph Black and Jacob's probable conversation that kept them up until midnight, the Colonel of the 55th Illinois, David Stuart, had just resigned that position while he awaited his confirmation as brigadier general. On January 27, a commission came from the Governor of Illinois, which carried the official promotion of Lieutenant Colonel Oscar Malmborg to Colonel. The men of the 55th Illinois had hoped that the position of Colonel would go to Major William Sanger, who had been acting as an aide to General Sherman. Malmborg was so unpopular with the men of the 55th that nearly every officer had signed a petition protesting the promotion. (*The Story of the Fifty-Fifth Regiment Illinois Volunteer Infantry*, pages 161, 214-215, 512)

3. Charlie Cady and Newton Rogers were from Company E of the 15th Iowa Infantry. Perry Van Winkle was a private in the 11th Iowa Infantry.

4. Twenty-three-year-old Thomas Yount was officially promoted from Second Sergeant to First Sergeant on June 11, 1863. Yount had been wounded at Arkansas Post, where his younger brother Isaac was killed.

5. Jud and Ike were Jacob's brothers. Jud was in Company B with Jacob, but had been sick and away from the company. Ike was in the 33rd Iowa Infantry.

No. 9—Young's Point, Louisiana
February 15, 1863

Dear Emeline,

This is Sunday again and I must write you another letter. I haven't got any news to tell though. We are here in "status quo" and expect to remain so for some time, or longer. I complained of not being very well in my last two letters. Well, I am complaining now, of being some better. I am not right well yet, but I think I am coming to, and if I could only get another <u>chicken</u> I would be all right. It makes me mad to think I can't get even an old rooster for love or money, and I want it so bad. I have tried to get the boys to steal me one, and they would do it if there was any to be had. You will cook me one when I get home, won't you? You must set the old hens and raise a lot by that time. I think I will be home about the time they are big enough to eat.

I got a letter from you yesterday, dated February 5th. Your letters come very regular here lately. I always get one about the last of the week. I was sorry to hear that you all had bad colds. You must get to work and cure them up <u>right away</u>. If Expectorant won't do, try something else. If you should take the small-pox or sore throat, cold would make it so much the worse. I hope there won't be any of you to get the small-pox, but I am very uneasy about it, and look to hear by every letter that you or some of the children have it. One of the men got a letter yesterday which said that Caroline Freeman had the small-pox. I do not believe it, neither does Jim, but we are anxious to hear about it. If Till was worth a copper cent, I think he might write to some of us once in a while, but he won't do it. I am glad you have got the wood all hauled and are getting it cut up. Never mind the cost—I want you to have plenty of good wood and think that pile will last till I get home!!

I believe from the way you write you kind of wish I <u>would</u> get sick or get wounded a <u>little</u>—just so I could come home don't you? Now ain't you bad! Well, the Lord knows I would like to go home for a while and see you all first-rate, but I do not want to go sick or crippled. You need not flatter yourself about me getting home that way anyhow—that is played out. There is a hospital at Memphis expressly for sick and wounded officers, and I would be sent there and you would have to come down and wait on me. How would you like that? This is a very sickly place and I may get sick if we stay here till the weather gets hot. But I think the chance to get wounded is rather small.

General Grant says he has his plans for taking the city all laid, and that he will take it with the loss of very few men. I don't know what the plan is, but I don't think it will be executed very soon.

They have gone to work at last to widen the canal in earnest and make it of some account; they are going to make it 80 feet wide. Our Brigade has been assigned about 150 feet to dig out, and tomorrow that space is to be divided among the different regiments of the brigade, so each one will have to do its own share and no more. I am appointed to see that our regiment has a fair shake in the division. They have closed up both ends and drawn the water out as much as possible, and given up the idea of its <u>washing</u> out; it will take us two or three weeks to dig it out, I think.

I suppose the attack will not be made till that is done. We had the biggest rain here last night I ever saw—I never heard such thunder and lightening in my life. Everything is flooded with water. Shouldn't wonder if we would be drowned out of here before long. Most of the sick men are getting better. We now report 50 men for duty but we are a good deal the strongest company in the regiment. I was glad to hear that Captain Smith had got home, but was surprised that he had not been to see you. He promised me certain he would go and see you right away. Between you and me, there is a great deal more blarney about him than I like. The men are all well pleased to be rid of him. They made fun of him all the time. I am acting Captain. No appointment will be made till Captain Smith's resignation is heard from. He left here without leave and I should not be surprised if he would be cashiered and discharged dishonorably. He was not half as sick as I was when he went away. There is not one in the company now but would rather have me for Captain than him. And I will get the appointment as soon as Smith is out of the way.

John Orr[1] has resigned and has gone home. So has Joe Black[2], I hear. Well, the men all say I must stick to them and I will. I hear that Josh has gone home—is that so? Well, Jud and Tom Allen and 10 others of our men who were at Helena got here day before yesterday. Tom Allen brought the letter you gave him. It was very good—if it was old it hadn't spoiled. I did not get the letter or anything else you sent in the box. Jud is about as well as ever. He thinks Ike will be down here before long.

I want you to tell Tom and Al to make a strong effort to sell that land or trade it for good notes. I think it might bring $600, but sell for $500 rather than miss. Has anything been done yet about the title to the house and lot? Several of the men who came down from Helena are still sick and I will try to get some of them discharged.

We have not seen the paymaster yet—guess he has resigned. There will soon be two month's pay due us. We don't know anything definite yet about when we will get it. Tell me all about what the children do and say. I lay awake most half of every night and think of you and them. You must not let them forget me. I would like to hear Kitty talk. You must get them all some good shoes and cure their colds. Jont is getting well very fast. Jim is perfectly well. Give my respects to Ma and Sarah and tell Tom and Al I have quit looking for letters from them.

Your own, Jake

1. John Orr, age 45, First Lieutenant of Company I of the 25th Iowa Infantry, was wounded January 11, 1863, at Arkansas Post. He resigned his position January 21, 1863.

2. Captain Joseph Black of the 55th Illinois, along with five other officers of the 55th Illinois, resigned to protest the promotion of Oscar Malborg to Colonel, whose manners and temper had lost him the respect of others in the regiment. (*The Story of the Fifty-Fifth Regiment Illinois Volunteer Infantry*, pages 161, 214-215, 512)

No. 10—Young's Point, Louisiana
February 22, 1863

Dear Emeline,

This is Sunday again . . . I have no news to tell—nothing unusual occurred last week. We just live along in about the same old way. I suppose we are getting a good ready to take Vicksburg. It is reported that the bombardment will commence in earnest in a few days—some say tomorrow is the time set. But I don't think we know anything about it.

There was heavy firing from the gun-boats today at noon, which created some excitement at first, but it turned out to be blank cartridges fired in honor of Washington's birthday. About an hour afterward there was very heavy and very rapid firing up at the mouth of Yazoo. They seemed to be shooting balls and fighting in earnest. Some think it was caused by a rebel gun-boat trying to come out of the river. Can't find out certain yet. Night before last there was heavy cannonading on the river just below here.

Some say that the ram, Queen of the West[1], that ran the blockade, has been captured by the rebels. It does not receive much credit. One of our mortar boats has been lying below the upper end of the canal for several days, engaged in throwing shells into the city. It was in good range; some of the shells (220 pounders) went clear over the hill back of the town, most of them burst among the buildings. We cannot tell whether much damage has been done. I do not think that all that has been done yet has injured the rebels much. But I think a good deal has been done in the way of getting ready, more perhaps than most persons here are aware.

I am beginning to think they will make something out of the canal yet. They have stopped the water out at both ends, and then drained out all they could, and have a large steam pump rigged to pump out the balance. They have also divided the work of enlarging it among the different brigades and regiments according to the number of men reported for duty in each regiment. And as there is considerable emulation among the regiments to see which will get done first, I think the work will be done in about two weeks. Our regiment works 40 men a day. And besides that two companies have to stand grand guard every 5 days, so that $\frac{1}{5}$ of the regiment is on guard all the time. Yet our work is not much; we are having an easy time, as far as that is concerned, but the weather is very bad. I believe it has rained every day and night but one since last Sunday. Still the health of the men is steadily improving, as well as their courage; they begin to look and feel much better. Some have the blues yet and a few are really sick.

Jim Stockton is pretty sick. I do not think he is dangerous if properly treated. We do the best we can for him—he has the diarrhea again. Jont is going around and will soon be able for duty again. Frank Taylor is pretty sick with fever; he is in the hospital and everything done that can be here. Jim is all right. Baron Crane was appointed Sergeant Major the other day. And then I had Freeman appointed 1st Sergeant in his place. So he has got the place he wanted at first. I think he will do first-rate. I made How White a Sergeant and Bill Harlan and David Coiner Corporals.

I am still getting better but am very weak yet. I got an old rooster and an old hen about a week ago. I lived on the rooster all last week and killed the hen today. I have had her tied under the bed, feeding her, and she is real fat. I paid one dollar for them. I haven't got much more money and the paymaster has not come yet. There will be two months more pay due us next Saturday. I am going to make out payrolls again this week. And then if they pay up all that is coming we will get a pretty good pile.

I have not got any letter from you since I wrote last. I expect you sent it by Corkhill[2] and he has not got here yet. We are anxious for him to get here as we think he will bring us lots of nice things. I got a letter from Captain Smith; he said you had been to see him, and were well. I don't suppose you would ever have seen him if you had not gone there, for all he promised so much. His sickness in my opinion was all "in your eye." His resignation has not been accepted yet, and I can hear nothing from it. Lieutenant Thompson[3] of New London got back here last Sunday; he is going to try to resign again. Jud is still well; he got a letter from home today. I got a letter from Ike, dated January 31st! I have not heard from Billy and Ol nor Tom or Al. I have not written to them and I ain't going to. I will write to Father some day soon. Well, I believe I have told you all the news I can think of.

I think I will get two of my men discharged and send them home (Gregg & Eyre[4]). If they go I will send an overcoat that I found near the battlefield at Arkansas Post. It is a first-rate one but I won't need it here. It is cold enough to make it pleasant to sit by a fire sometimes, but we would call it May weather in Iowa. The bull-frogs and birds have been singing this long time and some of the trees are beginning to put out leaves. I will send you a specimen of moss that grows on the branches of trees down here. It hangs down all over the trees, sometimes two or three yards or more long and looks very odd—it makes a good bed to sleep on.

I expect it is as cold as blazes up there. I wonder how you all get along. I wish I could just peep in some evening and see. How do you all sleep and where, and do you keep warm? Who gets up to make the fire? I guess you don't get out very early these cold mornings. Don't you wish you had me there to make fires and feed the cow? Who dresses all them young ones? Can Tom put on his pants and shoes? I guess he can't run to Pa every morning now to get dressed. Who pulls Kit's nose and red hair? I wonder if she has forgotten me. I want you to write me all about them and everything else. How do you like the sewing machine by this time? What all did Captain Smith say and do when he got home.

Have you got plenty of corn and fodder for the cow? You must keep her fat. I am going to live on milk and chicken gravy when I get home. I am still uneasy about the small-pox. I do hope you will all escape that and all other diseases. I think you had better send Lulie and Nellie to Howe[5] if he is teaching, and have them start as soon as you can. I want them to be smart girls and see how much they will learn by the time I come home. I must stop. I believe this is a very dull letter anyhow—what do you think? The drums are beating for Dress Parade. Company B is still the largest in the regiment for duty, 50.

Your own, Jake

1. On February 2, 1863, the Queen of the West successfully passed the Vicksburg batteries. The Queen of the West was struck 12 times, but never seriously. For the next 12 days, the ship continued successful operations on the Mississippi River and Red River until she went aground under heavy fire. The Confederates took control of the ship after it had been abandoned by the Union sailors, then used the Queen of the West against the Union to sink the USS Indianola. In April 1863 the ship was destroyed on the Atchafalaya River by Union vessels. (Charles Dana Gibson and E. Kay Gibson, *The Army's Navy Series-Dictionary of Transports and Combat Vessels Steam and Sail Employed by the Union Army 1861-1868*, page 264)

2. The Chaplain of the 25th Iowa Infantry, Thomas E. Corkhill, age 41, a resident of Mt. Pleasant, had been born in England. Corkhill was also a Minister for the Wayland Methodist Church for 1861-1863. (*The History of Henry County, Iowa*, Volume I, page 78)

3. The First Lieutenant of Company K was John Thompson, age 44. He lived in New London, Iowa, and had been born in Ireland.

4. Robert Gregg, age 35, died of disease April 11, 1863 at Young's Point, Louisiana. John Eyre, age 39, of Salem, survived the war.

5. Samuel Howe, a former high school teacher of William Tecumseh Sherman, ran Howe's Academy in Mt. Pleasant. Jacob and Emeline both attended Howe's Academy. See additional comments regarding Professor Howe in the Appendix.

No. 11—Young's Point, Louisiana
March 1, 1863

Dear Emeline,

This is the day to write you another letter, but I came pretty near getting the blues and not writing. It is two weeks today since I got a letter from you, just think of it. What made me think more strange of it, your letters have been coming very regularly for several weeks. I most always got one on Saturday or Sunday. But this evening I got one so you see I am all right again. I was very uneasy. I just expected that you all had the small-pox, or something else. The letter I got was dated February 23rd, so you see it came in a week. We were all sorry to hear that Corkhill was sick. We were all looking for him anxiously, knowing he would bring us lots of news and good things. I hope he will soon get well or that you will be able to send the things down by someone else. That will do us all so much good. I suppose Captain Smith will bring them if he comes. I have heard nothing from his resignation yet. The company will be very much disappointed if he comes back to stay . . .

I have not got much news to write to you. My health is improving very slowly but surely, I think. When I get that box of canned fruit I think I will be all right, as that is just what I need. And I think you are so good and thoughtful for sending them. I hope I will have better luck than I had the other time. I have a pretty good appetite now, but have to be very careful what I eat. I gain strength very slowly. I knock around camp, go on guard every fifth day, and do all that any of the officers do. But at the same time I could not march more than five miles in a day.

I have been very busy for a few days making out muster and pay rolls again, besides several other rolls have to be made out the first of each month. It is quite a long tedious job to get them all up right. We have not been paid yet!! I suppose you are tired hearing that by this time, but not more so than I am of writing it. I don't know yet when we will get it. But the paymaster is here—there is no humbug about that this time, for I have seen him with my own mortal eyes. And he has our payrolls now. He will only pay to the 31st of October, so we will not get much this time. But he told me they would keep right on paying till they get caught up.

I cannot get a discharge for the man I spoke of in my other letter[1]. The health of the army is still improving rapidly.

We are at work in good earnest on the canal now; about half the available force is to be called out every day hereafter. So we will have more work to do hereafter till we get it finished. I don't know how long it will take. The river is very high, and still rising, and the water is very much in the way of working. The men have to work in mud and water knee deep. I was on picket guard last Thursday and it rained all day just as hard as it could pour down. I never saw such a rain. Since then the weather has been clear and pleasant, like summer.

I don't know what kind of weather you are having up there, but I suppose it will soon be time to make garden. You must get Palmer or someone else to fix up the fence so there will be no danger of anything breaking in—have him get some lumber if necessary. If the title was fixed I would have a new fence all around it. You must have the currant bushes planted out, where we talked about (where the onions were) and take up about half the gooseberry bushes and plant them in the row of apple trees along the east fence. Get some-one to plow the lot and have it planted as soon as the ground is fit. I want to see what a nice garden you will have when I get home. Don't you wish you had me there to hoe and plant it for you? I do, I am sure—it would be so nice to go out and work a little while you got me a nice breakfast, in place of having to get up here and get my own breakfast, and then not have anything I can eat.

Jim is as hearty as you please. I believe I told you he is the 1st Sergeant now. He does very well in his new place. Jont looks very slim yet but has a good appetite and is getting along fine. You must stop and tell Mrs. Taylor that Frank has been sick for some time. He had the typhoid fever[2]. He is in the hospital and has a cot to lay on, and every attention that can be rendered here so he is pretty comfortable. He is not dangerous at all, but it will be some time before he is able for duty. He got two letters today, and was glad to hear that his folks were going to send him some things.

I have been writing all day at rolls and am tired, so I believe I will stop and save the rest for an answer to that long letter of yours when it comes. I suppose you told me all about the meeting. I hope it did you a great deal of good. I would like to be there and go with you. I don't think Ma[3] had better go to St. Louis. I hope she won't. I would like first-rate to have her stay with you, if it was not for Manda. It would not do to have her and our own children together. Could not Manda go and stay with Car and nurse Fred? I hope if Ma does go down there she won't stay long. I got a letter from Tom today. I will answer it in a day or two. Kiss the children all for me, and tell them to be good children till I come home. I am going to come back someday and bring them something. They must not for-get about Pa. You won't, will you?

Your own Jake

1. Jacob was not able to get a discharge for Robert Gregg, who died of disease April 11, 1863.

2. Typhoid fever is caused by the bacterium Salmonella typhi, and is passed between people by contaminated food or water. Symptoms include fever, headaches, abdominal pain, diarrhea, and delirium. In some cases the bacterium can cause open sores in the intestines, which can be fatal.

3. Emeline's mother, Eleanor Ellis Bereman, was planning to go to St. Louis to work as a nurse.

The Death of Jacob's Father

> The Burlington *Hawkeye*, February 24, 1863
>
> FATAL ACCIDENT.—The train from the West last night, ran over and instantly killed Mr. Henry A. Ritner, of Danville township. The accident occurred this side of Middletown station. The deceased was walking on the side of the track. Just as the train was about to pass him, he stepped upon the track, apparently with the intention of crossing to the other side.– Miscalculating the distance of the train from him or its speed, he was struck by the engine and instantly killed, the body being shockingly mangled. No blame can properly attach to anyone upon the train, as the deceased stepped up on the track and was killed at almost the same instant of time. The train was stopped and the body carried back to Middletown.
>
> The deceased was about 55 years of age—an old and highly respected citizen of Des Moines County, having a large circle of friends and acquaintances. He was a son of Gov. Ritner, of Pennsylvania.

Camp at Mouth of the Yazoo
March 10, 1863

Dear Emeline,
This is Tuesday morning and I have not written to you since last Sunday week! . . . We have heard nothing of Captain Smith or Chaplain Corkhill or Lewis Hilleary except that they were coming down. But that is not the reason I did not write sooner. Last Sunday in the forenoon I went down to the boats to see T. H. Stanton of Washington, who is here as a paymaster. He was out paying off a regiment and I did not get to see him.
When I got back to camp we had orders to move immediately. We pulled up stakes and moved up the river about two miles, which took till after dark; and then yesterday we were busy all day fixing up our tents and getting thing arranged about the camp, so I had no time to write. The reason we moved in such a hurry was because the levee across the upper end of the canal broke Friday night during a very heavy rain and let the water into the canal before we

were ready for it, and they were afraid we would be drowned out. There was a break in the levee of the canal just opposite of the center of the 25th Iowa which let the water out on our side. The work on the canal had been going on finely for about a week. There was a good moon and we worked day and night without any intermission. I worked there with our company from Thursday morning till Friday morning. And the whole thing would have been done in a few days if the water had not broken in. I don't know now whether it will ever be finished. I will try to make a kind of a map of the place we are in on the last page—perhaps you can understand it better by that.

We have not been paid off yet. You are getting tired of hearing that, I expect! We are getting out of patience waiting for it. The paymasters are thick down here now and one of them promised to come and pay us this afternoon but we don't look for him anymore. We shan't think he is coming till we see him.

I heard the sad news about the accident to Father on the 4th inst. I got it first from a letter Mr. Hebard wrote to his son, but it came in the *Hawkeye* the same day. I never heard anything so shocking in my life. I did not know what to do at first. I thought I must go home for a few days anyhow, but soon found that was utterly impossible. I then thought I could get detailed to take the money home when we are paid off. But Colonel Stone says it cannot be done. I have been waiting anxiously ever since I heard of it, to get a letter from you or some of the folks at home to tell me all about it. I suppose you went down, did you? I don't see what they will do down there now unless Henry will come back and manage things. I hope he will. If he had died at home of sickness I would not have minded it so much, but the way he was taken away is too awful almost to bear. It seems that it is not only in the army that we are exposed to sudden death, but we are exposed to it at home as well as here. I hope we will all be able to say The Lord's will be done, and that we may be as well prepared for our final end as I have no doubt he was.

My health at present is very good, my appetite is first-rate; I can eat everything I come to <u>except</u> pork and crackers and coffee and tea, and that is the most we can get here. Jud is well but looks slim yet. Jont is getting well, but gains strength slowly. Jim is all right. He gives very good satisfaction as 1st Sergeant.

Company B is still the crack company in the regiment. I always have more men for duty and less sick men and the neatest quarters of anyone in the regiment. The men will all be very much disappointed if Captain Smith comes back to stay. They make fun of him all the time—call him "our old lady" &c.

I think there will be an attack on Vicksburg before long. There was heavy firing by the gun-boats last night from 1 to 3 o'clock, don't know what was the matter, but from the movements all around I think there will be a fight before long. We are getting impatient at the delay. I believe the 25th would fight as well now as it ever did. I believe it is the strongest new regiment in the army. I mean we have less sick men.

The most I fear is that a few of the officers and some of the men are "copper-heads[1]." I believe they are doing the country more harm both North and South than all the rebels. But I believe I wrote you some of my politics not long ago and will not trouble you anymore at present.

I expect you will laugh at my great map. You must remember that the space between the river and levee is now covered with water. The water is about six feet higher inside of the levee than the land outside. If the <u>canal</u> levee had been finished before the water got in we would have been all right, as the water could not have got the camps, which were thick north of the railroad and all along the river. There are still a good many trees and stumps in the canal so I doubt if it will be of any account, as I learn they do not intend to stop it at the upper end again. There had been but very little <u>digging</u> done to the canal. The soldiers were throwing up the levee and the Negroes and pioneers were taking out trees and stumps. I suppose they intended for the dredge boats to do the digging. There are two at work between the river and levee.

Well, I think when you study that map right well you will know a good deal about war; if you can't understand it, let me know. I do wish I could get to go home for a few days to see you all, but I guess there is no chance. I have just been notified by Colonel Stone that the paymaster will be here to pay us tomorrow. I will only get pay for one month and four days this time, but I will send some home by Hilleary if he gets here. I think we will get more soon, but I owe some, and must keep enough to be sure not be caught out again. It seems so long, dear, since I got a letter from you. I can't hardly wait. Your letters do me so much good. I keep your sweet picture in my pocket and kiss it every day. I love you just as well as ever and better too. Good-bye, dear, don't forget your Jake.

Your own Jake

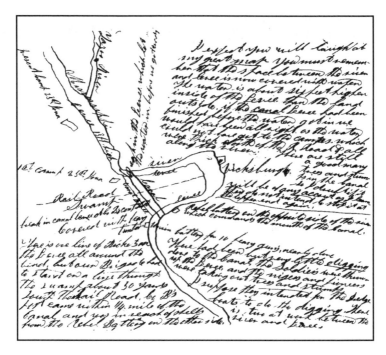

Jacob's map of "Grant's Canal"

There is one line of pickets on the levee all around the bend, but our brigade had to stand on a line through the swamp about 50 yards south of the railroad. Company B's post came within one-fourth mile of the canal, and was in reach of shells from the rebel battery on the other side.

1. A copperhead was a Northerner opposed to the war. The copperheads would sometimes signify their support by wearing an Indian Head penny on their hats, hence copper-head. The most notorious copperhead was Clement Vallandigham, a Democratic Congressman from Ohio. The word "copperhead" had been used in the United States with several meanings—as the name of a poisonous snake since 1775, a disliked person or group of people since the early 1800s, and a faction of the Pennsylvania Democratic Party in the 1840s. The reference of a copperhead as a Northern supporter of the Confederacy began in July 1861, and the copper cent badge was used beginning in 1862. (Darryl Lyman, *Civil War Wordbook*, page 47)

From Henry Ritner, Jacob's brother, to Jacob
A Dark Cloud Gathering in the Western Horizon
. . . Which Indicated Evil

Leesburg, Ohio
March 12, 1863

Dear Brother;

I received your very acceptable letter of February 28th this morning and with pleasure improve the present opportunity to send you a few lines. You say you are rather suspicious that you wrote last, but it is not so. It has been a long time since I have received a letter from you, but I wrote immediately after I got one the same with Judson[1]. I have written to all three of you since you have. I suppose you have heard before this of the death of Father and the circumstances. He was walking home from Burlington on the track and was run over and killed instantly. He had been making preparations for sending a box of provisions down to you and had concluded to go down with it himself and was going home to make arrangements for that purpose and was just suddenly taken off. It is a severe blow on the family at home to be best deprived of a father so much needed at present . . .

I got a letter from Isaac[1] this morning. Also he is on a transport at the mouth of the Yazoo River but expected to go back to Helena in a few days. He was well and hearty. I suppose you get some discouraging news from some of the Northern traders. But, things up here are not as bad as you might think, for there was a dark cloud gathering in the western horizon about the whole ages which indicated evil. But, it all passed away as the dew of the morning, and all is now calm and serene . . .

Although there are traitors among us yet, there has a great [change] taken place in the last few weeks for the better. There have immense war meetings been held in Cincinnati, Indianapolis, in New York, Iowa and a great many places, all of which were most intensely enthusiastic for the prosecution of the war. And there are no fears now but what you will be fully sustained by the great masses of the north. There will be no difficulty about the operation of the conscript if it is only put in operation. I am in hopes the Pres will call out not less than six hundred thousand in the next month. There is strong belief here that if the thing is pushed on with vigor and energy, the thing can be dried up during the summer. There is a great reaction in England[2] in our favor so there will be no trouble from that country. The French[3] are getting awfully used up in Mexico, so I think that will take their attention for awhile. They also have a revolt in China, so think there will be no danger from her. Things look more favorable for our cause at present than any time during the war. But, I shall have to stop.

I hardly know where to direct this letter, but I guess I will direct it to Young's Point [Louisiana]. I would send you a Cincinnati Gazette if I thought you would get them. Please write soon. Victoria sends her love.

Your brother, Henry[1]

1. Judson, Isaac, and Henry were Jacob's brothers.

2. England was dependent upon Southern cotton, and for that reason many feared England would enter the war in support of the Confederacy. The English populace was strongly against slavery and did not want to support the Confederacy. Now with the Emancipation Proclamation, at least a partial end of slavery was a stated goal of the North.

3. In 1862, the French landed in Mexico under the orders of Napoleon III to collect debts from the Mexican government. They quickly captured Mexico City. In 1864, under French administration, Maximilian, the Archduke of Austria, became Emperor of Mexico. After the Civil War, the U. S. Government enforced the Monroe Doctrine, and in 1866 and 1867 the French were forced to withdraw their troops. The Mexicans then captured Maximilian and executed him.

[Mt. Pleasant, Iowa]
March 12, 1863

Dear Jake:

I wrote you day before yesterday and told you all the news. Captain Smith came out that afternoon and told me that he was going down this week . . .

I was glad to hear that you was most well. Hope that you will not get sick any more. I was also much diverted at the idea of tying an old hen under the bed to fatten her. I imagine she felt herself quite comfortable under the protection of the Union Army. Wonder if she laid any "Union eggs"? I expect if you had Ol there to hunt the nest, he would find one. I haven't set any yet but will as soon as it gets warm enough and I shall feed them good and make them grow fast, if you are coming home as soon as they are big enough to eat. We had one for dinner yesterday and one the day before . . .

Also Tom Stockton, he is on the Jury, (this is court week) and came out to get his dinner. It is the first time he has been here since you left. I told him about Jim being sick. He was uneasy about him. He said I should tell you, that if he died, you must send his body home. You needn't mind what it cost. Said you must send him by all means.

I guess our boxes will go this time. They are packed, and will start today. Hope you will be certain to get them. You must think of me when you eat them. I wrote a great long letter (3 sheets full) to accompany the box, but concluded we couldn't send the box. So I started the letter by a Mr. Gaily that belongs to Spearman's Co. His wife told me last night at church, that he was still in Keokuk & didn't know when he would go on. I'm afraid you will never get it. In that I told you all about what was in the box; but I will tell you again.

Ma sent a can to Jim & one to Jont. I think their names are scratched on the out side of the cans. Mrs. McClure sent a can to Jake Whippo and one to Jim Stockton. Their names are on the can too. The rest I sent you . . .

I put in a can of tomatoes pickles. But I expect they will be spoilt, for they have been packed nearly three weeks. I sent it up to Taylor's store, and hated to bring it home and unpack them thinking I would have a chance to send them some time. The edibles are to be sent in the care of Mrs. Wittenmeyer and will cost nothing and won't be opened. If Captain Smith should be separated from her, I fear she will take them to the hospital, and you won't get them. That would be too bad. Mr. Taylor came over to see what you said about Frank. He is very uneasy about him.

We are all well, none of us took the small pox that I know of. Tom and the rest of them have been full of sores and they look like the smallpox, but wasn't sick and didn't have any chance to take it so I guess it wasn't that—. . . Excuse this, and write often. I must hurry and go up to Captain Smith before he leaves.

Good bye, Em

I haven't heard from Danville since your Father died.

But Why Can't A Person Be Either A Man Or A Monkey?

Young's Point, Louisiana
March 15, 1863

Dear Emeline,

This is Sunday again and as it is raining I will have a chance to write you a letter. We are still camped at the same place. I think it likely that we will remain here till everything is ready for a grand combined attack on Vicksburg, which I think will take place before very long. I think that two-thirds of the army has left here. I don't know where they have gone, but regiments and batteries are continually going on board of boats and leaving for parts unknown. I think our division will remain to make the attack from this side.

I have not got any letter from you since the one you wrote about the accident to Father. I have been waiting very patiently for that big letter you tell about; I think it must be a rouser, as you say it is "too large to send by mail." I hope it gets here before it spoils. We have not seen anything of Captain Smith yet. We hear so many reports that we don't know what to believe. Some say he is coming, others that he ain't. Some say that he will bring the boxes with things for the company. But some say that the things have all been unpacked and taken home. I don't understand why they should have done that if anyone is coming down.

Esq. Perry and Hillearys[1] got here yesterday; <u>they</u> brought their things through all right, and the Burlington Companies have everything nice you could think of. They got a six-mule load to each company. Edward Hebard got the box his father sent all right. But we had bad luck with ours as usual. Perry says that it was directed to Helena and that they put it off there! So I suppose none of us will ever see it. Isaac is not at Helena now, his regiment has gone down to Yazoo Pass[2]. I felt a great deal of interest in the box, both because we needed what was in it, and because it was connected with the last act of kindness Father ever did for any of us. I don't see why they directed it to Helena. Hilleary thinks it was not and that Perry put it off by mistake, but it is gone for good, anyhow.

We have been paid off, <u>at last</u>. We were paid last Wednesday, 11th inst. up to the 31st of October, 1862. The privates got about $80 apiece. I got $122.30. I have sent home $75.00, which leaves me about $35 after paying my debts. The company altogether sent $539.80. We sent it by F. J. Clark[3] and it will be deposited in Saunders Bank. You can take your bank book up there and let them credit $75.00 on it. I think we will be paid again next week, up to the 31st of December, when we will be able to send home a good deal more.

There has been a good deal of excitement in camp for a few days about the report that we are only nine month's men, and will be mustered out on the 27th of June[4]. I understand that Alvah[5] has given it as his opinion that such is the case. I hope the war will be over by that time and that we all get to go home. But I don't believe the report and hope it is not true. I am very tired of the war, and want to go home very much. But I enlisted to fight the war through, and I want to finish the job before I quit. I am disgusted with and ashamed of men who enlisted with the fair understanding that they were to serve for 3 years and now rejoice at a quibble that promises to let them out at nine months. I enlisted for the <u>war</u>. I think it very likely that if I was discharged now, I should go into the service again. I have always felt that war was not my calling, and I think I miss my family and friends and the comforts of home as much as anyone that ever volunteered. But why can't a person be either a <u>man</u> or a monkey? We know that we must all make sacrifices to save our country from this wicked rebellion, and it would be criminal at this critical time to deprive the government of 300,000 men who have been drilled and disciplined and have their places filled with <u>conscripts</u>. I say again, I hope we may be mustered out before the 1st of June, but <u>never</u> until this unholy rebellion is put down, and the last traitor, both North and South, brought to condign punishment. Company B and the 25th Iowa with a few cooper-head exceptions are all right and in favor of fighting the war through.

The health of our regiment has improved wonderfully since we came here. We are now the strongest new regiment in this corps, if not the strongest of all. And Company "B" is the crack company in the regiment. We always have more men on duty, more on drill, and on dress parade than any other company. Then we have more "snap" and "git-up" than any other company. We drill 4 hours a day, and pitch horse-shoes and play ball[6] between times. I make all the men keep themselves and their clothes clean, and their quarters well policed. Which is the main reason we have so few sick men. Spearman has lost 12 men by sickness, I think. I have lost only 8— Nathaniel Beeb, and Alfred Johnson[7] (step-son to Old Man Harlan) have died lately. Most company commanders allow their men to lay round in their tents, in dirt and filth till they nearly rot. You may think it strange, but <u>many</u> of them will do just that way if allowed; I make my men all get up and dust around, and take exercise, and they soon get well. You need not tell anybody that I said so, but I do not believe there is a Commander in the regiment more popular with his men than I am. My health at present is very good, and I think I will get along now fine. Jud and Jont are all well.

If you see Mrs. Taylor, tell her that Frank is on the hospital boat sick, about two miles above here. I was up to see him yesterday. He has the typhoid fever and is pretty low, but the Dr. thinks he is not dangerous. I got his money and took it to him. I do not think they need to be uneasy about him as he is beginning to improve.

We are drawing new clothing now, and I have more work to do than 4 men ought to do. There are more rolls and reports and returns to make than you every heard of. I often work till midnight and then get up at 4 o'clock. Well, I guess I must stop for this time. Tell me how you get along making garden. How does the cow look? Did Ma[8] go to St. Louis? I hope she did not. Are you most ready to start Lulie and Nellie to school? Tommy must be a good boy and take care of Kitty. I <u>do wish I could</u> come home a few days and see you all. Though we are many miles apart I feel that you are as near and dear to me as ever, my own sweet wife whom I will never dishonor or forsake; if I had a chance I would get some pictures.

Your own, Jake

1. Mr. R. Perry and J. & A. Hilleary were members of the Iowa Sanitary Agency, who had brought supplies down to the troops from Mt. Pleasant. The 25th Iowa Infantry passed a resolution expressing thanks to these gentlemen:

   > *Resolved*, That our thanks without number, are due Messrs. Perry and J. & A. Hilleary, for the faithful manner in which they discharged the onerous duties of guarding and protecting the contributions on their passage through shoals and breakers, in the shape of *Red tape*, custom house officers, Provost Marshals, Memphis thieves, and steamboat sharpers and the numberless obstacles, which beset the path of anything soldier bound. (Resolution dated March 21, 1863; Burlington *Hawkeye*, April 4, 1863)

2. Jacob's brother Isaac Ritner, as part of the 33rd Iowa Infantry, participated in the Yazoo Pass Expedition, which lasted from February 3 through April 10, 1863. The purpose of this expedition was to explore alternate routes to Vicksburg.

The Confederates opposing the Yazoo Pass Expedition at one point sank a vessel in the Tallahatchee River, the U.S. ship previously known as the *Star of the West*. This was the ship that had received the first shots from the South Carolina State Militia in 1861. The troops aboard the *Star of the West* were commanded by Charles Robert Woods, who was attempting to bring supplies to besieged Fort Sumter when cannon fire forced the ship to give up that effort. Confederates later captured the *Star of the West* in Indianola, Texas, renamed her the *CSS St. Phillips*, and brought her north for operations around Vicksburg.

See Jacob's letter of August 10, 1864, for additional comments about Charles Robert Woods, who, at that time, commanded Jacob's division. (Stewart Sifakis, *Who Was Who In The Union*, page 464; Charles Dana Gibson and E. Kay Gibson, *Dictionary of Transports and Combatant Vessels Steam and Sail Employed by the Union Army 1861-1868*, page 300; Edwin Bearss, *The Vicksburg Campaign* Vol. I, pages 506-507)

3. Frederick J. Clarke, age 54, was the Quartermaster of the 25th Iowa Infantry, and the father-in-law of Colonel George Stone. He officially resigned his position July 22, 1863.

4. This rumor of the soldier's being "only nine month's men" was not true. The 25th Iowa remained in service until the end of the war.

5. Alvah Bereman was Emeline's brother and the Draft Officer of Henry County, who may have been expected to have had an official position on whether the 25th Iowa was soon to be released from service.

6. The Union soldiers frequently played baseball during their free time.

7. Nathaniel Bebb died February 18, 1863, on the hospital boat City of Memphis. Alfred Johnson died of disease March 12, 1863, on the hospital boat at Young's Point, Louisiana.

8. Emeline's mother did go to St. Louis to work as a nurse for sick and wounded Union soldiers.

From Emeline's Mother to Emeline's Father

[Mt. Pleasant, Iowa]
March 15, 1863

Dear Husband,

This is Sunday night again and I am seated maybe for the last time to write to you . . .

The smallpox has broken out afresh. Several new cases have occurred and some deaths. On Harmos have a child buried with it yesterday. All his family have had it. We have all escaped it so far and are enjoying good health except myself. I have been feeling very feeble for some times since I have concluded to go to see you so soon. I feel better. It is because I want to see you so bad.

The folks here say St. Louis is a sickly place and that I will get sick. Tom says I will be sure to get sick. It is such a dirty place. Well, I am bound to try it if I get money enough after selling my hogs and lugging a few things we had to have (everything is so dear). I have but three dollars left . . .

Alvah procured a divorce last week for a woman on the grounds that her husband was a secesh. They quarreled about it. She wouldn't give up, so he turned in and whipped her so that ended the dispute. He employed Dean to plead his case.

I expect to do a good deal of work on our place this spring planting grapevines, cherry trees and peach trees and trimming our other trees but don't know what about it now. It has been nice spring weather for several days. The blue birds have been singing. Our Bees are not doing much. Jake's old stand is entirely about stoned to death. The winter has been too warm for them. I took out more than a quart of dead, dead bees from under the last year's swarm. Some of them are alive. Our stand seems to be doing very well, good many bees flying out. I think they will do well if the moth could be kept out this summer.

Em got a letter from Jake yesterday. Said his health was improving. Jont looked pretty slim, but was able for duty again. They were working on the canal in the mud and water up to their knees poor fellows. How can they keep well? I must not let my thoughts dwell upon suffering soldiers. It is too much for me. I will tell you all when I come. Goodbye, my dear husband.

E. H. Bereman

To Emeline's Father

Youngs Point, Louisiana
March 16, 1863

Mr. S. E. Bereman

Dear Sir,

I recd. yours of the second inst. a few days ago and take the first chance I have had to answer . . .

I suppose you have heard before that my father was run over by the cars and killed Feb 23 between Burlington and Middletown. He had been to Burlington to take down the box, to send letters and was walking back to the track when he was run over and instantly killed. I never heard anything so shocking in my life. I tried to get to go home for a few days, but couldn't do it. Captain Smith has not come back yet. I don't know whether he will or not. We have been paid off up to the 3rd of October, 1862 and I expect to be paid again this week up to the 3rd of December. The health of the Regt. has improved a great deal since we first landed here. There are not many sick now except those that have been sent up the river. Nathaniel Bebb of my company, died Feb 18 and Alfred Johnson died March 12 on the hospital boat here which makes three that have died out of the company. I report 70 men for duty and have the largest and best company in the Regiment. I always face more men for duty on drill and dress parade than any company. We have more snap and git up than the next. I suppose it is all owing to the remarkable efficiency of the commission officers.

. . . Jont was quite sick for awhile and looks very slim yet, but I think he will soon be all right. We have not taken Vicksburg yet. We have been waiting to get a good ready. I think there will be a grand combined attack made that won't leave a great lot of the damn secesh hold.

About two-thirds of the army have gone on boats and left here within a short time. I don't know where they have gone, but they will turn up someplace at the right time. I think our division will be left to make the attack on this side when everything is ready. . .

The water broke into the canal before we got ready for it and I don't know whether it will ever be finished now or not. The trees and stumps were not all out yet and can't be got out now. So, I think the thing is likely to fizzle yet, but they are still at work next to dredge boats deepening it. We were working on it day and night and would soon have had it done if the water had not broke in.

It is all Humbug about my resigning. I don't intend to go home until Company B goes. I would not take a discharge now if it was offered me. I would like first rate to go home for a few days & see the folks and kill a few Copperheads, but I enlisted to help fight this war through and I want to finish the job now while I am at it. I have not heard from home for a week. Our letters do not come very regularly, but we generally get them all. Yours was about ten days on the way. I hope the Fourth[1] will flourish finally under its new officers and that you will not have to stay at Helena during the war. I reckon you are still baking bread and pies and don't care whether the war runs or not. I hope you will both have a good time and that we may all meet safe at home someday when we will have a good time generally. Write again and I will answer. My respects to Billy. Tell him to write.

Jake

1. This is a reference to the 4th Iowa Cavalry that included Emeline's brothers and Samuel Bereman's sons Billy and Ol. Several officers of the 4th Iowa Cavalry had recently resigned, including Colonel Asbury Porter.

Young's Point, Louisiana
March 20, 1863

Dear Emeline,

This is only Friday evening but as I received a letter from you yesterday for the first time in about two weeks, and as Hillearys are going up the river tomorrow and will take a letter, so I believe I will write you a few lines in a hurry at any rate. The letter I got yesterday was dated March 10th, the one you wrote when Car was there. The one you sent by Gailey has not got here yet. You had better not send any more letters by soldiers coming down. They are always a great deal longer getting here than they would be by mail . . .

We have boxed up all our overcoats and some other things and are going to send them up by Hillearys. They will be sent to W. A. Saunders to be distributed. I sent home a fine officers overcoat that I found at Arkansas Post. It has got very dusty and dirty lying around in the tent. You must brush it up and keep it nice till I get home, when it will be a good thing. I also sent a copy of Webster's Unabridged Dictionary, a book I have always wanted, but never was able to get, till I "confiscated" this one at Napoleon. I found it in the house we occupied while there. You can learn to spell while I am gone if you get that—though I believe you can beat me at that now. I would like to keep it here, as we use it a good deal, but we have no way to carry it. I also sent two pairs of woolen socks which are so badly torn I can't wear them anymore. They are too hot for the summer anyhow. I sent one pair of drawers and one shirt that I shall not need anymore this summer. Just fix them up and keep them all right till I get back. I believe Jud had his overcoat directed to you too. You will have to pay your share of the expense.

My health at present is first-rate. I can't drink tea or coffee or eat pork, but the river water is first-rate and we get plenty of good light bread now from our bakery, and we can buy dried fruit, molasses, and pickles and kraut, fish, &c, from the commissary. Can't get any potatoes or butter, still we get along very well now. I wish I had thought in time to write to you to send me a bottle or can of horseradish! Captain Smith has not got here yet, but we expect him in a few days. The men will be very much disappointed if he comes to stay, and it will be a great bore to most. I don't believe he will stay long if he can help it.

We have not been paid the second time yet. The paymaster has gone off up the river—don't know when he will be back. The weather has got pretty hot here. We sweat some days sitting in the tent doing nothing, but I have not suffered from the heat yet. It has not rained much lately and the health of the regiment is still improving—there are very few sick now. You can tell Morley that it is all a lie about this regiment being all secesh. There may be a few who have been tampered with by Northern copper-heads, but the great majority of them are as loyal as ever and in favor of fighting the war through all hazards, cost what time and money it may. They are all anxious for a fight and when the time comes will show that they have not forgotten the duty they owe their beloved State and Country. I don't believe the 25th will ever bring disgrace on the fair name of Iowa. Some may have written home very discouraging letters about the time we first got here, when we were nearly all sick, and knee-deep in mud. But neither Bill Willeford nor anyone else would express such sentiments now.

I am glad you got the pigs from Ma. You must keep corn on hand and feed them well. You think I must be chicken hungry, do you? Well, I am, or have been. You may raise as many as you please this summer. I guess they won't trouble me much. I told you in one of my other letters what I thought you had better do with the lots. I do not think it would be best to rent them out, if you can get anyone to plow them and plant them. You must get someone to fix up the fence so it will be safe—get some more lumber if necessary. If the title was settled once I would have a new fence all around. Did you ever say anything to Al about attending to it? I wrote about it once before.

You want to know what makes me talk about coming home. Why, because I expect to go home some of these days. I told you in my last letter about the three months idea. But I think this rebellion will be crushed out before next fall and we will all get home. Jont is not very well. I don't know what is the matter with him—he mopes around and "doesn't say nothing to nobody," doesn't eat anything, and looks very slim. Freeman is well. He got a letter from Car yesterday.

They have been fighting up the Yazoo[1], and part of Bank's fleet[2] has come up from below, and I still think that there will soon be such an attack made on the city as will not leave a grease spot of rebel hole. We are anxious for the fight to come off. And yet I do not want them to make it till we are perfectly ready. I was glad to hear that you were all well. You do not know how anxious I am about you sometimes. I am afraid some of you will get sick. How I would like to go home a few days and see you all. I think you will find this letter awfully mixed up. I have written it in a great hurry . . . Remember that I am your Jake and that I love you more dearly than ever, my own dearest, sweetest little wife.

Your loving husband, Jake

1. Jacob is referring to the Yazoo Pass Expedition, an expedition led by Brigadier General Isaac Quinby that was searching for alternate routes to Vicksburg. Jacob's brother Isaac was part of this expedition. (Edwin Bearss, *The Vicksburg Campaign*, Vol. I, pages 479-591)

2. General Banks was now leading a campaign against Port Hudson, south of Vicksburg.

Young's Point, Louisiana,
March 30, 1863

Dear Emeline,
This is Monday morning; I did not get time to write yesterday.

Captain Smith got here about noon, and we all had such a big time unpacking boxes and what we had all got that there was not time to do anything else. He got everything here all right so far as I know—nearly everyone in the company got something. And we had a big feast and a great time generally. It did us all as much good as anything else to know that we were not forgotten by the friends at home, and to see and eat something that had been cooked and fixed up by the dear loved ones we left at home. You want to know how my box looked; well, it looked all right. I can tell you I would not take $25 for it. Just because my sweet wife, everything tastes better than anything we can get here. Everything was all right except the tomato pickles; they had come unsealed and some of the juice had run out, and there was some mold on top, but after taking that off, the rest were very good. I like the shirt first-rate—it was just what I needed. I guess I will not <u>sell</u> it <u>soon</u>. I would not give it for two others, because <u>you</u> made it, Dear. You need not to send the dried apples, since you had to buy them, as since we have money we can buy both peaches and apples from the government at 7 cents per pound, which is cheaper than you can get them. They are very nice, though and I shall think of you whenever I eat any of them. The dried beef is very nice. There was ½ bushel of nice potatoes in the large box directed to me, which I got.

Lieutenant Steele got a big lot of things—3 or 4 pieces of dried beef, and the captain brought some, so we have 25 or 30 pounds. Steele got a cheese that Mrs. Black made; no one likes it but me and I think it is first-rate. He got a gallon of molasses, a jar of pickles, lots of cake, popcorn, candy, apple butter, &c, and Wils Payne got a box and as he is in our mess, you see we have lots of good things to eat. Yes, Steele got a lot of good butter. Everything kept first-rate.

Frank Taylor was gone up the river to the hospital, but I don't know whether to Memphis or St. Louis. The captain brought me two letters from you; which was a great treat, I can tell you. I didn't hardly know which to attend to first, the letter or the box, but concluded to read the letters first. He got the big one from Gailey. It had not spoiled a bit . . . The captain also brought me a first-rate letter from Ma. I must write to her some of these days. She is the best Ma that ever was. Did she take Manda[1] along to St. Louis? You never told me. I wish Ma would stay with you and let Manda live with Car, or someplace where there are not so many children. I don't know what you will do if Lib goes away. I don't think Sal will get into the Union School and then you will be out entirely.

She would be next to nobody anyhow. You would have one more to wait on and cook for. It troubles me a great deal to know what you had better do—perhaps you can hear of some good girl who wants to go to school, that you can get. I don't want you to stay by yourself. I do not think you are extravagant with your money at all. I want my dear wife and family to be comfortable.

I wish you had paid Captain Smith the $10. He is here strapped and in debt, and hinting around about it. I shall pay him here as we shall soon be paid again. He is going to resign and go home if he can. I hope he will soon get off. I think Tom Stockton ought to pay you what he owes. I want the farm sold if we can get $600 dollars for it. I don't care what Tom Stockton says, if we cannot get that I think we had better take $500. Tell Tom and Alvah to <u>go ahead and sell it</u>. I wrote to Tom some time ago about the Campbell matter. I think he will understand it, and find that we do not owe them anything. If their money can be lent at six percent on good security you may do. I am like you, I think if we lose the house in town we will be about broke, and I want to be getting all the money together we can so as to buy another place. But we will talk about that when I get home, won't we. I guess we will get along some way if we never do get rich.

I see by the *Hawkeye* that administrators have been appointed for father's estate. Give our note and the Campbell note to Tom and tell him to file them as claims against the estate, or we will never get anything. If you have got anything on either of them since I came away, have it credited first. There are some things that need my personal attention, but I suppose they will have to wait. I told you in one letter before what I thought you had better do with the garden. I think you had better find some darkie to plant and hoe it. I don't want you to hoe it all yourself. If you can you ought to get the stable fixed if it can be done so that the pigs can run inside. I was sorry to hear that Kitty had the sore throat. I hope the little dear has got well. I was glad to hear that the rest are all well.

My health at present is first-rate. Jim is still well. Jont is not very donkey, but is improving slowly. We have had some very warm weather here—the trees are all green with leaves. One of the men brought me a nice nosegay of locust and other blossoms yesterday. But night before last we had the awfulest storm of wind and rain you ever saw and it blew all night. I thought it would blow every tent away. I thought about you and how scared you would be if it would storm so up there. I hope it won't ever. Yesterday and today it has been real cold; a fire feels good.

I told you in my last letter that we had boxed up our overcoats and sent them home. We afterwards made up the money and paid the freight in advance, so you will have nothing to pay there. I hope they will get through safe. I would not take a pretty thing for my coat and book. I got a letter from Al the same day I got yours, and have written him a long one in reply. It is not worth while for me to try to tell you any war news; you will hear it all by the papers before a letter could get there. We look to them for the news ourselves. We are still in camp at the same place waiting for the attack on the city to come off, but when that will be we don't know, anymore than we did a month ago.

Jake Whippo has been quite sick with the fever, but is getting better. The regiment is in first-rate condition. I don't care who says to the contrary. The men got more to eat and better than we got at Camp McKean from the government. They all look stout and hearty, and I have heard several of my men say that they weigh more than they ever did. I told Captain Spearman what you said about Bill Willeford's letter. He told Bill about it and Bill said it was a lie, that he never wrote any such thing. Bill has written home to his brother to break Joe Morley's mouth for lying about him. But there are some secesh in this regiment—more than I thought there was. We tried to pass some Union Resolutions. Company B voted 69 for them, 1 against, and 6 did not vote. While Spearman's Company and two or three others voted them down. I was greatly surprised and disgusted at the result. But I expect that you are tired of this long letter. No, I know you ain't either. I never get one from half long enough. There are forty things I would ask you about if I could only get a pass to go home and stay with you some night— don't you wish I could? Tell me if you got the money all right that I sent by Clark. . .

                    Your own, Jake

Remember the 3rd of April[2], won't you, Dear. Tell me whether you thought about it or not. I am going to celebrate it some way. I hope we may never be separated again when the dear anniversary comes round.

1. Nineteen-year-old Amanda Eleanor Whippo Bereman was the daughter of Jont Bereman and his first wife, Amanda Whippo. Manda's mother died shortly after childbirth and several years later Jont had married a second time, to Sarah Fleming.

2.   April 3 was Emeline and Jacob's twelfth anniversary.

•   On March 29, 1863, the southward movement of McClernand's
     13th Army Corps and Major General James McPherson's 17th
     Army Corps commenced. As part of Grant's plan, the 15th
     Army Corps began an expedition to Greenville, Mississippi,
     north of Vicksburg on the Mississippi River to confuse the
     Confederates. Sherman assigned the Greenville Expedition to
     General Frederick Steele's division, which included the 25th
     Iowa and Jacob. Steele's opponent in this effort was
     Confederate Lt. Colonel Samuel Ferguson. (Edwin Bearss, *The
     Vicksburg Campaign,* Volume II, pages 107-128).

     Sherman's instructions to Steele stated that "If the planters
     remain at home and behave themselves, molest them as little as
     possible, but if the planters abandon their plantations you may
     infer they are hostile, and can take their cattle, hogs, corn, or
     anything you need. Cotton which is clearly private property
     should not be molested, but cotton marked "C.S.A" should be
     brought away or burned. Also all provisions which are needed
     by us or might be used by the army in Vicksburg, unless need-
     ed by peaceful inhabitants, should be brought away, used by
     your men, or destroyed." (Edwin Bearss, *The Vicksburg
     Campaign,* Volume II, pages 107-108)

Letters Describing General Steele's Greenville Expedition

Camp at Young's Point, Louisiana
April 1, 1863

Dear Emeline,
     This is Wednesday evening and I write you a few lines in haste
to let you know that we have orders to be prepared to go on board
transports immediately. Steele's whole division is going. We got
the order yesterday evening, and expect to go on board tomorrow
morning early, but do not know certain. It is too bad, isn't it to have
to leave just now when we have so many good thing to eat that we
can't take along. We are living here like kings, just think, we have
lots of first-rate butter, lots of canned fruit, apple butter, potatoes
and onions fried in butter, honey, cheese, dried fruit, and pound and
fruit cake, pickles, molasses, &c. But I suppose we will have to
travel and leave them. We are to take fifteen days' rations. But it
will be hard bread and bacon so it can be packed on mules. We are
not allowed to take any wagons at all, but the rations are to be

packed on mules. I don't know where we are going—but it looks to me like we were going to travel through <u>swamp</u>.

We will leave the camp, baggage and tents here in care of a guard. I shall leave ten or twelve men who are not very well. Captain Smith is to stay in command of the camp. I think a good deal of our provision will be good yet when we come back. I expect we will have a pretty rough time. No one can take any baggage except what he carries himself.

Neither Jont nor Jake Whippo are able to go along, but they are both getting better and are able to be around.

Captain Smith, I think, will put off handing in his resignation till we come back.

The weather here has been quite cool for a few days. There was white frost both yesterday and this morning.

I shall try to take some paper along and write to you if I get a chance. I will not close this letter till I know just when we are going to start. I have not the least idea where we are going, or what is going to be done. I will tell you all about it when we get back. The men are all keen to start. I will take 58 men from Company B. There will be about 500 from the regiment in all. We have not heard of the paymaster for some time. Guess we won't now till we get back. But I will stop for the present and finish this when we get more orders. They may be countermanded yet.

Thursday morning—Dear Wife, I have just time to say that we are ordered to start in 1 hour (or at 10 o'clock). We got a mail this morning and I got a letter from you dated March 25th. I have not time to answer it now. I can write no more at present. You must not get the blues, dear, if you do not hear from me for some time. I shall write the first chance.

Yours forever, Jake

When Treason Lifts Its Hydra Head

Steamer *Emma No. 2*
April 4, 1863

Dear Emeline,

This is Saturday morning and I will write you a few lines in great haste, not knowing when I may have another opportunity. . ..
We got on board the Steamer *Emma No. 2* and the fleet, consisting of twelve boats and carrying Steele's Division started up the river

a little before sundown. In the morning we found ourselves about 120 miles above Vicksburg. The cavalry were sent out to scout and all the troops were landed and ready to march at a moment's notice. But the scouts, after scouting the country for several miles, reported no sign of an enemy. We got a quantity of mules, chickens, &c, and all went on board the boats at night. At three o'clock this morning we moved ten or twelve miles further up the river and landed again on the Mississippi side[1]. The cavalry are again out scouting. The infantry have not yet landed, but if there is anything found to fight, we will. We will immediately go on shore and pitch in. That is all that has come of the expedition so far. We have had a very fine time so far—the weather has been splendid.

There are some nice places along the river. They look quite different now to what they did before the leaves came out. Where we stopped yesterday there was quite a fine plantation. A large gang of Negroes, men and women, were plowing when we came in sight. They all wanted to come on board and go with us but were not allowed to do so.[2] It looked hard to go away and leave them when they begged so earnestly to be taken along. There are two as fine residences close to where we are now as I ever saw. One is brick and the other frame and they are equal to the best in all Mt. Pleasant. I went out to look at them early this morning. I never had a more pleasant walk. The sun was just rising clear and beautiful, the air fine and invigorating. The trees are all out in full foliage and full of birds, the grass is green, the white clover is in blossom. At the farthest place I saw the most splendid flower garden I ever saw. I gathered a few which I will send to you in remembrance of the third day of April. When you look at them you will think of me and that time, won't you? I sat on the levee all afternoon yesterday with all my traps on and ready to start, and thought about you and the time we were married and the pleasant life we have had together ever since. It made me almost wish I was at home. I do wish it. And I would be there if I could go honorably.

Well, the regiment has just been ordered on shore and I expect that I have to stop before I get this done. If we march out into the country here we may have a skirmish with the rebels, as there are some guerrillas about here who fire on boats. I have not got your last letter along and I read it in such a hurry just before we started that I almost forget what was in it. I am sorry you could not get Ma's cow home. I think it would pay well to keep her. You can do as you please about Mrs. Kibby's furniture—if you think you need it, buy it. I think you must be very sharp to know my letter when you see it in the *Home Journal*. We got the paper down here, and when I read the article I fancied I had seen it before, myself. I didn't think of its being printed or I would have written something more sensible. I understand that Uncle Jake has put part of one of my letters in the *Hawkeye*[3], but I have not seen it. I have written several letters to folks in Henry County a good deal stronger than Tom's, but did not intend they should be printed.

The 25th never marched out of camp in better spirits than they did on Thursday. We turned a lot more men than any other regiment in the whole division—500. And Company B is the largest company in the division. I have brought 61 sound men, and left several for camp guard.

I am ashamed and disgusted at the vote in our regiment on the resolutions[4]. But am proud of the record of Company B—we came out ahead, as usual. We have only one vote against them, and that was W. H. Mason of Mt. Pleasant, who is considered the "lousy calf" of the company anyhow. Six were present and did not vote. I have no doubt whatever but that if they had been read to the regiment on dress parade and a vote taken immediately, as was done in other regiments, they would have been adopted without a dissenting vote. But in order to have a fair expression, we read them to the men on Friday and took the vote on Monday.

A great many voted against them merely because they thought they were something gotten up by the commissioned officers, and they could spite them by voting them down. While a great many more have got the notion in their heads that we were only nine month men. And they thought that by voting for the last resolution they bound themselves for three years. They thought there were some trick in it. And they were such ignorant numbskulls that it could not be got out of their heads. Another thing is the influence that has been exerted both from home and from those present. The result is regarded here as a very fair index to the politics of the commissioned officers in each command. The resolutions were adopted with great unanimity by the officers, but it cannot be denied that the conversation of some of them heretofore, has not been calculated to inspire the men with confidence in the administration. They have also misrepresented the objects of the war and the intentions of the government. All of which they would like to take back now.

I don't think we have a man or an officer who would not make a good fight today against the rebels. Now I know you think this is very dry—what do you care for such stuff? Well, I haven't got time to write to anyone else, and you may show this last part to Tom, so that he can correct any false impressions that may get afloat, especially about Company B. I want our record kept straight in Henry County.

My flowers look <u>very nice</u> this morning. I hope they will still smell sweet when you get them. Keep on writing as usual. I hope we will soon get back to camp to eat the rest of our goodies. The blackberries were very nice. I have not opened the plums. We have not got the box that was sent from Des Moines [County].

Your own, Jake

I have forgotten to number lately, but I write one every week, two this week, but I think there will be no difficulty now—they may be a few days late sometimes.

1. As reported in the May 5, 1863, *Burlington Hawkeye*, the 25th Iowa Infantry landed on the celebrated "Fanny Bullit Plantation" located about 25 miles south of Greenville, on April 3.

2. At this point, Steele was not enlisting Negroes into Union military service, but this soon changed.

3. The March 21, 1863, edition of the *Burlington Hawkeye* had an article entitled "Extracts from a Letter Written by a Member of the 25th Infantry." The letter is unsigned but the writing is unmistakably Jacob's. In the letter, he discusses work on the canal and copperheads: ("I don't see why you don't go to killing off the Copperheads forthwith.") The letter also included the declaration "I know I would love to be at home as well as any man, and long for the war to close, so that I can return.– But rather than submit to a dishonorable peace, or acknowledge ourselves whipped, I will stay here *till I rot in these swamps*."

4. During the Civil War, communities and regiments frequently passed resolutions, which were mostly forms of declarations of support for the continued war effort and to praise individuals. The following set of resolutions was published in the April 7, 1863, *Hawkeye*, honoring adjutant Kirkwood Clark, the nephew and adopted son of Iowa Governor Kirkwood, who had been wounded at Arkansas Post.

Camp of 25th Iowa Vol. Inf'try
Young's Point, La., March 14, 1863.

WHEREAS, We have heard with deep and heart-felt sorrow of the death of Lieut. S. K. Clark, Adjutant of this Regiment, at St. Louis, February 20th, 1863, therefore be it

Resolved, That while we recognize in the God of Battle a power more potent than the Surgeons skill, or the nurses of solitude, and while we acknowledge the supreme wisdom of our Great Commander, we deeply feel the loss of one so brave, so generous, so patriotic as our late companion-in-arms, Adjutant S. K. Clark.

Resolved, That in his former service as 2nd Lieut. in the 4th Iowa Cavalry, and his services since as Adjutant of the 25th Iowa Infantry against the enemies of the Union he has evinced that chivalrous, patriotic and honorable spirit which can animate none other than a genuine lover of his country and its cause.

Resolved, That in times like these when treason lifts its hydra head in the midst of our homes and threatens alike in front and rear, our sorrow at the death of such a man is deepened and intensified, feeling as we do that his loss is almost irreparable . . .

Jno. N. Bell, Chairman,
A. J. Withrow,
J. B. Ritner

J. G. NEWBOLD, Chairman
Sam. W. Snow, Sec'y.

In the 1870s, Captain Newbold served the state of Iowa as Governor for one term.

Greenville, Mississippi
April 12, 1863

Dear Emeline,

This is Sunday afternoon, and as I have a little time I will use it writing you a letter. I believe I wrote to you a week ago yesterday and sent you some flowers in it—did you ever get them? I expect there was part of that letter you would not understand—that about the resolutions. I supposed the secretary had sent them on for publication before we started, but find he has not done so yet—though several copies have been sent home by the men—and you will get to see them. Two companies voted against them. I have carried this sheet of paper in my pocket with your picture ever since we started and it is not fit to write on now.

I will try to give you some account of our expedition. The men who own the two fine places I spoke of in my last letter are brothers, by the name of Worthington, from Kentucky. I had a long talk with one of them. He is strong secesh. Finding no way to get back into the country from there, we started up the river again in the afternoon, and stopped at this place in the evening. Sunday morning we landed and started on a tramp through the country. Got five miles to Black Bayou and camped for the night to rebuild a bridge that had been destroyed by the rebels.

The next morning we crossed and in two miles further reached Deer Creek, which is a very fine stream, thirty or forty yards wide and very deep. We followed it down all that day and the next. It runs through a very rich country. Large plantations with splendid residences surrounded with nice shady groves and gardens filled with all kinds of flowers and fruit trees. The houses are generally one story with a wide porch or "veranda" all around. And on every plantation is a little village of Negro quarters, sometimes containing nearly 100 cabins and making a town as large as Trenton or Marshall. There is also on every plantation a cotton gin of some kind, generally steam, and they mostly have a grist mill and a sawmill connected with them, making quite a large building. In fact, it is the real "South" just as we have all read about many a time.

There had been a bridge across the creek about ever mile, as the planters generally own on both sides, but they put the most of their Negroes and all their best stock across and burned all the bridges in advance of us. The weather and roads were fine—we might have taken wagons along as well as not. There was a band of rebels in front of us about 1,500 strong, as near as we could find out. They had four small cannons. We came in sight of them two or three times and had a small skirmish, but they always run before we got close enough to hurt anyone. The last we saw of them was the evening of the third day they fired on us with their cannons. We formed two brigades in line of battle and marched across a plantation for two miles, in great hope that we would find them. But they crossed the creek and burned the bridge.

General Steele had orders not to go more than six days at one time from the boats, so we started back the next morning. We nearly laid the country waste along the road—burned most of the cotton gins, and a large amount of cotton, corn, bacon, &c, intended for the rebels army at Vicksburg. We brought in a large drove of fat cattle, besides what we got all the chickens, geese, ducks and turkeys we could eat, and at one place we found 300 or 400 bushels of sweet potatoes that were real good yet. We got more Negroes and mules than you could "shake a stick at." Most of the Negroes are women and children, miserable, dirty, ragged creatures. I don't know what will become of them. I think the general will send them up the river. There was no effort made to bring them along—they would come. They made rafts of rails and crossed the creek.

We got back here Friday evening and got a mail the first thing. I got your letter dated April 1st. I was very glad to get it and hear that you were all well. I gave out on the march the second and third day, but since then I stood it first-rate. I believe I could march a month now. Jud got the bilious fever and had to be hauled most of the time; he is sick yet. I am afraid he will have another spell of sickness. The men were all tired and foot sore when we got back here, and were in hopes we would be taken right back to camp. But it is reported now that we are not going back, at least not at present. Perhaps the camp will be moved up here. I want to go back to eat my plums and the rest of the goodies you sent me. I hope we get them before they spoil. I have never heard of the box that our folks sent. I got Hilleary to stop and inquire and send it down, but it didn't come. I am in hopes that Isaac was there and got it.

I hope you did get to go to Jefferson and that you had a good time. I am glad you went to the "concert." I don't want you to stay at home all the time and never see anything. You must go around and get acquainted. You must go to the "Soldiers' Aid Society." That is a good place to get acquainted with the town folks. And you are just as good as any of them, and better too. You are smarter and better looking than any of them, and you need not be afraid to go. Of course you must go to the donation at Gunn's. They couldn't have a donation party without you. I have thought many times that I would bring you down to see this country when the war is over. It would be so nice to travel here with you along, when there is no danger of being shot at. I would like to have you come down now and see us if it was possible, but it ain't. Several officers came down with Captain Smith and tried to bring their wives along, but the women were all stopped at Memphis. Never mind, I hope the war will soon be over and then I will come to see you. I am glad that you got Ma's cow at last. I hope she will soon get so she will come up. If not you have plenty of girls to send after her.

. . . Tell Kitty I will bring her a candy baby when I come home. Why don't you say something about Nellie and Tommy—do they grow any? I would like so much to see them all, and you too. I lay awake half the night sometimes thinking about you all. Last night it rained from dark till midnight as hard as it could pour down and the wind blew hard. I had no tent but lay on a board with an oilcloth over me and kept pretty dry. But I thought it was not quite so pleasant as to be at home in a good bed. I believe the longer I am away the more I think about you all and the better I love you.

I believe I have answered everything in your letter. I don't know when I will get to write again unless they take us back to camp as I have no more paper along and none can be had here. I think we will go soon or have the camp moved up here, as none of us has a change of clothes along and are very much in need of some. But it is generally thought we will take another scout before we go back. I will write the first chance . . . I expect you can't read this scribbling. I am writing it on a cracker box.

Your own, Jake

The Death of Judson Ritner, Jacob's Brother

Greenville, Mississippi
April 17, 1863

Dear Emeline,

This is Friday and . . . as you talked about having the blues because you did not get a letter for ten days, I will try to start this two days before the time I generally write, so it will be sure to get there in good time. You must not get the "blues," dear, if you do not get letters just at the time. I always write but we have no regular mail, and they send mail up the river just when there happens to be a boat going. Sometimes the mail lays here for three or four days, which accounts for the delay. But now when I come to think of it again I can't tell certain when I did write last or what I wrote about. My mind is so confused I cannot remember anything, but I am pretty certain I wrote since I got the letter in which Tommy had been sick and you did not get to go to Jefferson.

I have bad news to tell you this time and something I will remember without any effort—Judson died yesterday. I think I told you before that he was sick. I got him on board the Steamboat Nevada which is lying here, and put him in a stateroom. He had been bilious for some time, and threw up his medicine. The doctor thought he was going to have the bilious fever but did not think he was very bad, and I never thought about him being so dangerous. Indeed, he was not, till a short time before he died he took a congestive chill. We did everything we could but the medicine had no effect, and he lasted but a short time. Poor boy, his soldiering in this world is over, and he has gone where there are no more wars or fighting. I never felt so bad hardly, about anything in my life. It was so hard to have to see him die and be buried away here in this hostile country, so far from home and friends. I shall feel a great deal more lonesome now that he is gone. He died about 5 o'clock in the morning, and we buried him at 5 in the evening. It did seem so hard, I hardly knew what to do, and then this morning I had to write to Mother and tell her, and that was almost as hard. It will be a terrible blow to them all at home. May God who tempers the wind to the shorn lamb, enable us all to bear this new affliction with fortitude and resignation to his will who doeth all things well.

My health at present is pretty good. I am trying to take as good care of myself as I can. We have not got any tents or mess chests here (though we have sent for them). So I have been eating and sleeping on the boat a good part of the time when we are out scouting. This costs a good deal more, but is better than to risk getting sick. We had ten days' rations issued to us and I suppose it will be that long at least before we go back to camp. We are all anxious to get there.

. . . I believe I wrote you last on last Sunday and told you what we had done up to that time. Well, we were roused up at midnight that night and ordered to be ready to march at 3 o'clock. We got up and got ready, and waited till nearly daylight before we got started. We were ordered to leave blankets and knapsacks and take one day's rations. General Steele thought he could get across a swamp and surround and capture a lot of rebels. But it began to rain soon after daylight and rained steady all day. We got out eight miles and stuck in the mud—the artillery could not near get through. So we had to come back. We got a lot of mules and Negroes and a drove of sheep.

Since then we have been hauling in lots of cotton. The Negroes tell us where it is hid out in the cane breaks. We got quite a lot of it. We also get mules and Negroes every day. We have sent off one steamboat load of cattle, two of mules, and have five or six hundred Negroes, and more coming every day. We put them into quarters on a plantation near here and issue rations to them, women and children and all. They are organizing all the able-bodied men into military companies and Colonel Shepherd[1] of the 3rd Missouri drills them—they learn very fast. They are going to organize two regiments of Negroes at Helena and we are recruiting for them. Our regiment has not been out since last Monday, but some go every day, and I expect we will have to take another turn in a day or two.

The soldiers have all got to be in favor of setting the Negroes free, and arming them too. They see that this is the quickest way to end the war, and that is what they all want. Although this is the universal sentiment as far as I know, yet there is just as much prejudice against them as there ever was. There is always someone trying to abuse, insult, and impose upon them. I have a great deal more respect for a Negro than for anyone who will misuse them. I hope some plan will be found to end the war before long, so that I can get to go home.

I was not at home the other night when you dreamed I was. But I have often dreamed I was at home. I am going to try to get a short leave of absence and go home a few days sometime this summer. I don't know as I shall succeed. But I think if we get Vicksburg once there will be a chance to get some furloughs. It would be so nice to be at home a week or two, wouldn't it? I shall try to come, but you must not be too much disappointed if I do not get to go. I have the best company in the regiments and the largest and am always on hand for every duty. But I am not as popular with our officers as those who swear, drink, and play cards half the time. I do none of these things and they think I am "old fogie." But I don't care for that. I preserve my own respect and that of my men. And more than that I retain the love and respect of a dear, sweet wife at home, which I value more highly than the smiles and favors of all the Colonels and Generals in the army. You do not know what a great comfort it is to me to think that I have a dear wife at home who loves and thinks of me. I have thought many times what a great blessing it is to have a sweet, dear wife at home, although we are separated by so great a distance. It gives dignity to a man's character, elevates his thoughts and affections, enables him to overcome temptation, and makes him feel that he has something worth living and striving for. I never thought how good you were till I have been away so long.

You seem to think I would not like it because you say you spend $25 per month. I shall be very well satisfied if you can get along on that much. It will take that to keep me this year at least, but then we will have about $800 of my wages left. My salary to August 13th will be about $1,400. Most of the officers spend all theirs as fast as they make. But I want to save all I can for you and the children. I hope you have got the fence fixed and the garden plowed before this time. You must make whoever plows it take great care not to hurt the trees. You must get some "darkie" to plow and hoe it for you.

I hope you did get a letter that day you wrote. What do you think of my coat and book? How did you get along at the Aid Society? I want you to go every week. When you get that fine furniture you must have one at our house. Freeman is well. I want you to get ready again and go up there and stay a week. I have not heard a word from Jont since we left camp. We have sent for some clothes and tents and the payrolls, but they have not come yet. We expect our mess chests too; Crane went after them.

I expect you get awful tired reading my long, dull letters, don't you? I can always find plenty to say when I am writing to you, and fill the sheet, no matter how large it is. You write me some big ones and pay me back.

I think there is something going to be done at Vicksburg soon. *Boats* loaded with soldiers have been going down by here ever since we have been here. There must be more soldiers there now than there has ever been before. I think Isaac has gone down. But I must stop. You will never get this read.

Your own Jake

1. Colonel Isaac Fitzgerald Shepherd of the 3rd Missouri was Harvard graduate, educator, journalist and Massachusetts legislator. Early in the Civil War, he moved to Missouri to support his abolitionist views. He later became Colonel of the 1st Mississippi African Descent and then commanded the African Brigade, District of Northeastern Louisiana, Army of the Tennessee. After the war he became a diplomat to China. (Stewart Sifakis, *Who Was Who In The Union*, page 364)

Greenville, Mississippi
April 22, 1863

Dear Emeline,

This is Wednesday evening and I think I will write you another letter. I got the one you wrote at Car's, day before yesterday . . . That was such a good letter you wrote to me. I wish you would write to me two every week. I know you wrote lots, the best that was written around that table that night. I can see you all sitting around there, writing. I know just how you look—you see I have your picture yet. What have you done with mine? If I ever get a chance I will send you another. I expect you wouldn't know me now, I am so poor and dried up, and sunburned, and bald-headed, I expect you would laugh at it. I wish I could step in some time when you were not looking for me. What would you do? I guess you would know me. And I believe there is one sweet little woman at home that will always love and stand by me, if I should return ever so much broken down by disease, or crippled by wounds. I tell you it is a great comfort to me to know this. I am very glad you got to go to Jefferson. I hope you got to go all around and did not go home till you got ready . . . I hope you got to go to Payne's, and told them how much I think of Wils; he still cooks for us. I don't see what we would do without him.

I told you before that we had been ordered away without any tents or baggage of any kind. The weather most of the time has been very fine, but is has rained all night several times and we were very much exposed. But we have sent down to camp and got our mess boxes and a few tents for each company. The colonel lets me sleep on the boat Nevada which lays close to camp, which suits me first-rate, as it don't cost anything. The captain sent me that can of plums; we have been eating at them—I tell you they are real nice, just as good as when they were put up. I never see them without thinking of you. Is there going to be any strawberries? If there is you must put up some for me.

There was a boat passed up from below just now, and brought the news that General Grant intended to be in Vicksburg by Sunday at noon. I don't know whether there is anything in it or not. But he is running the blockade and crossing troops below. I don't want them to take it till we get back[1]. I want to be there myself when that fight comes off. We have done nothing but lay here since I last wrote to you.

It is not necessary to march through the country to get Negroes—they come in by scores, as fast as we can provide for them. There are fifteen hundred or two thousand here now, the most of them women and children. The men [Negroes] are driven away [by the Rebels] or taken to the rebel army. We have two steam mills at work grinding corn, and providing for all that come. They are organizing all the able-bodied men [Negroes] into military companies; several hundred are enrolled already. They expect to organize two or three [Negro] regiments here. This plan has become very popular with the soldiers— they are all in favor of it now. They see that the sooner the slaves are taken away from the rebels, the sooner the war will be over and the sooner they will get to go home. You can't convince a soldier that a Negro is too good to carry a gun and knapsack, when they have to do it themselves. I suppose our copper-head secesh friends in the North will be very much shocked at this, and raise a great howl. Well, if they don't like it let them enlist, and take the Negro's place. It makes no difference to me. I had just as lief one should be shot at as the other [Rebels and copperheads].

Adjutant General Thomas[2] is expected here to organize the regiments. And General Steele issued an order the other day that all persons who desired to be 1st Sergeants or commissioned officers in any of the Negro regiments should apply in writing immediately. There was a great rush of applications from every regiment, some 40 or 50 from the 25th. There is a committee of three appointed to examine all applicants. They have been in session several days and I understand they are very strict. They will have none but the best of officers, six of Company B applied, Freeman for one—what do you think of that? I expect he will be appointed captain of a "colored" company. Sergeant Garvin has applied and Corporal Morton, Jerome Bowman and Tom Joliff[3]. If they all get their places I will lose some of my best men. None have been examined from this regiment yet. But I have no doubt some of them will get places. I had a great mind to apply for a field office myself. What would you had said if I had, and got to be colonel or major? But the men were all so opposed to my leaving that I concluded that Company B was good enough for me. What do you think?

I am certainly very much obliged to Mr. Palmer for fixing the fence. He is a gentleman and a patriot. I hope you will succeed as well in getting someone to plow the lot. I have such a mean pen I expect you can't read this scribbling.

You must write to me often, I feel so lonesome here now that

Jud is gone, and I don't care for anybody's letters but yours. I do dread to hear from home. They depended on him so much since Father is gone. I don't know what they will do. I pray God to give them strength to bear this new affliction. Jont and Whippo were getting along fine the last I heard. I hope we will all get to go back there soon, but don't know. The paymaster has not got here yet. Write soon. Tell the children I said they must be good.

Your own Jake

1. General Grant began the movement of the 13th and 17th Army Corps below Vicksburg in late March. During this early movement, Sherman's 15th Army Corps remained north of Vicksburg. Jacob was still on the Greenville Expedition north of Vicksburg when he wrote this letter. The main purpose of the Greenville Expedition was to distract the Confederates.

   Grant's plan was that the Union forces would leave their supply base and forage off the land as they moved south of Vicksburg, then northeast to Jackson, Mississippi, and then due west to attack Vicksburg all on firm land.

2. Adjutant General Lorenzo Thomas had came from Washington with authority to organize Negro regiments to be commanded by white officers. General Grant then directed General Steele to recruit Negro males of military age for service in the Union Army. Grant's directive had surprised Steele, since it represented a distinct change in policy of the Army of the Tennessee. The actual process of choosing these white officers was quite selective. Of the first 120 applicants, only about 40 were accepted. (Edwin Bearss, *The Vicksburg Campaign*, Volume II, page 117; Dudley Taylor Cornish, *The Sable Arm: Black Troops in the Union Army 1861-1865*, pages 204-207)

3. All these men mentioned remained in the 25th Iowa Infantry and did not join colored regiments. However, several men of the 25th Iowa Infantry did join colored regiments: James Spencer, John G. Smith, David Miller, Henry Chatterton, Clarence Lemen, James Vincent, and Abial Wintz.

Milliken's Bend, Louisiana
April 29, 1863

Dear Emeline,

This is Tuesday and . . . I have no news to write in particular except that we were paid off day before yesterday up to the 28th of

February. I got $446.00. I wanted to send $400 home but Captain Smith figured up me in his debt again about ten dollars, so I will send $380. I will not need all I have kept unless I should get a chance to go home before we are paid again and then I will need it all. Captain Smith expects to start home in a few days; his resignation is not accepted yet, but I have no doubt it will be shortly. He only presented it yesterday. If he gets off soon we will all send our money by him. This company will send about $4,300. You can take the bank book up again and have ours credited, as you did before. We will be mustered for pay again tomorrow.

. . . It seems a month since I heard from you. When I last wrote to you we were at Greenville, 120 miles above here. The next day after I wrote we were ordered to start at ten o'clock a.m. on a 6 day scout after Negroes. We got ready and started, went about a mile, and found the whole division turned out and maneuvering round in a large field as if they were going to have inspection or review, finally formed a hollow square 3 or 4 regiments deep around about 4 acres, then stacked arms and broke ranks and had a grand mass meeting in the center.

It was the best meeting I ever attended. General Steele made the first speech and a better or more patriotic speech I never heard. He came out heartily and boldly in favor of the policy of the administration in freeing and arming the Negroes—he said all slaves should be encouraged to come within our lines and be well treated and provided for. And every soldier or officer who refused to obey the orders of the president[1] in this matter would be promptly punished. He raised himself very much in my estimation. I have always considered him rather too pro slavery and too much disposed to protect rebel property. But he said "we had treated them as erring brethren long enough—that we had carried on the war as though we were afraid somebody would get hurt, but the time had come to throw away gloves and use every means in our power to crush the 'infernal rebellion.' "

Speeches were then made by many other officers, all on the same subject. Every regiment was represented. And the sentiment was universally in favor of the new policy[1]. Some had always approved it, others declared that if it had been adopted a year or more ago they would have opposed it, but now supported it heartily, and there was not the least murmur of disapprobation among the soldiers. The most radical[2] sentiments received the loudest cheers. Some of the speakers were so affected by the sublimity and importance of the occasion and

the subject they could hardly speak. I never saw more enthusiasm
and unanimity in any meeting, or heard more eloquent and patriotic
speeches. It was good to be there. The army <u>now</u> is all right—there
is no mistake about that. I have [yet] to hear of the first man that is
opposed to arming and freeing the Negroes.

But enough of this. We didn't "scout" but went back to camp,
put on our best clothes, and went to see General Steele on the *J.C.
Swan*, were introduced, &c. And on Friday evening were ordered
on the boats and Saturday morning we found ourselves back at
Young's Point. We were all very glad to get back, found everything
all right, and were in hopes that we would get to stay there a while
and rest. But no, Sunday morning we had to break up camp and
move the whole thing up to Milliken's Bend, 12 miles.

We all went to work in good earnest and fixed up our camp here
thinking we would certainly stay here a short time. But yesterday
we got orders to move, and the regiment has now gone to
Richmond, about 15 miles west of here, to guard a bridge. The 30th
Missouri is ordered to the same place. I had to help Captain Smith
fix up his accounts and some other business to attend to, so I did
not go out today. We did not have teams enough to take all the
tents, so I kept ours. I will go out tomorrow. Several "divisions"
have gone to Carthage, Louisiana (the road runs through
Richmond), but the soldiers are still camped thick for miles up and
down the river here. I think the plan is now to cross below
Vicksburg, and attack it from that direction[3].

I believe I have told you all that has happened down here since
I last wrote. Jont is still sick. He walks around most of the time,
says he is not much sick, but never speaks unless he is spoken to;
he does not eat anything hardly, and looks very slim. I think he is
improving slowly. Jim is as well as usual. I told you about him and
others applying for commissions in the Negro regiments. We have
been moving about so much that they have never been examined
yet, but I have no doubt some of them will get appointments. The
men in this company are very sorry now they did not vote for Jim
for 2nd Lieutenant. They want to have a new election; if they do he
will get nearly ever vote, I think. But I don't know whether it would
do any good—that depends on the Colonel.

I got a letter from Tom and one from Father a week or so ago, I
thought I would answer them both before this time, but I just
haven't got time. You must tell Tom the news when you get this.
My business got clear behind while we were gone, and it will take

some time to catch up. I have muster and payrolls to make. All the monthly reports and my quarterly return of clothing, &c, is not made yet, because Captain Smith had never made his. He doesn't know the first thing about doing the business of the company, and I have always had it to do. The G.Q.M.[4] is issuing clothing every chance, and that is always a troublesome job.

Tom said that Eng. Crawford had paid him a little on that Judgment and said he could not pay any more till fall. Now I want Tom to tell him that unless he pays up <u>all</u> the interest due (at compound interest) he will proceed to sell the farm. <u>I won't wait till fall</u>, that is played out. It is none of Crawford's business what I want with the money, or whether I need it or not. I have waited long enough, and he can get the money if he wants to. And he must pay it now. Tell Tom that T. H. Stanton was one of the paymasters who were down here. I saw him several times. He is in good health and seems to like his business first-rate. I am glad to hear that Tom has a prospect of getting to be captain in the 1st [Iowa] Cavalry—hope he will succeed. I got the letters just now, but neither one from you. One was from Ike he is well and still at Helena. No letters or papers came from above Memphis; they say the rebels have blockaded the river again above there and the mail can't come down. I hope it is not so, for I shall get the blues if I don't get a letter soon.

It is reported this evening at Steele's Headquarters there was a severe battle today in the vicinity of Carthage—result not known. They are preparing some more boats to run the blockade here. We have a new canal on foot now, across from "Duck Point[5]." I think it is the best chance of any that has been projected yet. One small steamboat and several flatboats have been though it; the river is falling very fast or it would be available now. It commences a little on this side of Young's Point and connects with a bayou that runs into the Mississippi, I believe.

There is no use trying to hide it, for you will know it anyhow by reading this dull letter—I have not been very well for a day or two. I had a very bad headache yesterday and today I have the diarrhea and feel weak and stupid, which is the reason I write such a stupid letter. I ate nothing from yesterday noon till this evening, when I went to a boat and got my supper and feel a good deal better. I was not able to go with the regiment today, but will go in the ambulance tomorrow. I think I will be all right in a day or two.

Mrs. Major Bell Reynolds[6] of Illinois and her husband were at the table where I ate this evening. She looks more like a nice sen-

sible woman than a major. But I must stop. Write often and soon;
direct as usual.

Yours forever, Your own Jake

I think I will send home by Captain Smith some little things
belonging to Judson. They are not of much value, but perhaps our
folks would like to have them. You can give them to them when
you have a chance.

1. By the "orders of the president" and the "new policy," Jacob
   was referring to the Emancipation Proclamation. The subject
   and policy they are discussing involved freeing and arming the
   Negroes.

2. During the Civil War period, a "radical" Republican was a
   member of that political party who was strongly in favor of the
   abolition of slavery. The moderate Republicans were more concerned about preservation of the Union and viewed the abolition of slavery as a secondary issue. Jacob's reference to the
   "most radical sentiments" would have been the strongest views
   towards freeing the slaves and enlisting them into the army.

3. Jacob's understanding of Grant's strategy toward capturing
   Vicksburg is mostly correct. The Union Army was going south
   of Vicksburg, and then would travel northeast toward Jackson,
   the capital of Mississippi, and then straight west to Vicksburg.

4. G.Q.M. was the General Quarter Master. Quartermasters were in
   charge of providing food and supplies to the men in the field. The
   field organization of the Union Army had a Regimental
   Quartermaster for each regiment, with the rank of first lieutenant;
   a Quartermaster for each brigade, with the rank of captain;
   Divisional Quartermaster with a rank of major; Chief
   Quartermaster with rank of lieutenant colonel for each corps; and
   a Chief Quartermaster with rank of colonel for an army. (Jack
   Coggins, *Arms and Equipment of the Civil War*, pages 120-121)

5. The canal at Duckport Landing connected the Mississippi
   River with Walnut Bayou. Grant believed that a canal from
   Duckport to Walnut Creek to Roundaway Bayou and Bayou
   Vidal to the river south of Vicksburg might offer safe passage
   around Vicksburg, but lower water levels prevented the success
   of this plan. Previously, the Mississippi River had risen and
   washed out Grant's Canal, but now the water was receding to
   previous levels.

6. Major Belle Reynolds was a nurse attached to the 17th Illinois. Belle Reynolds' husband, Lieutenant Reynolds, was General McClernand's *aide-de-camp*. During these engagements around Vicksburg, Belle was quartered with McClernand's new wife. (Stewart Sifakis, *Who Was Who In The Union*, page 331)

• With Porter's successful run past Vicksburg, Sherman's 15th Army Corps moved south of Vicksburg to Hard Times Landing. McClernand's 13th Army Corps and McPherson's 17th Army Corps had already traveled south and commenced action at Port Gibson and Grand Gulf.

[Mt. Pleasant, Iowa]
May the 6th, 1863

Dear Jake:

This is Wednesday night again, my regular time for writing to you, although I don't always write at regular times, as you have found out . . .

I am glad the Colonel let you sleep on the boat. It would be so much better than sleeping on the ground in the open air. You must try and take good care of your health, cost what it will. I just feel that all the poor soldiers who do not die or get killed will be so broken down in health that they will never recover. You needn't be afraid that I won't know you. If you are "poor" and "dried up" and "sunburnt" or "bald headed" I guess you couldn't slip in here and scare me, and make me think that you was a "man." I shall know the crook of your nose anyhow. Oh, how wish you would come in some time. I hardly know what I should do. I should be so glad and the children too. They want to see you so bad . . .

I do hope you can get to come home sometime before long. You want to know what I have done with your picture. Well, I have worn it so much that I have broken the pin off. I shall take it up tomorrow and get it fixed . . .

I forgot to tell before that I had got a sample of your rations. Mr. Lee sent home a parcel of stuff in his box of clothes that he said the soldiers had to eat. Mrs. Lee sent me some of it. One mess was potatoes mashed and crumbled fine and dried. The other was a mixture of pumpkin and forty-one other things mixed it up in a dish. The awfulest looking stuff I ever saw. I wondered that the government would feed men on such stuff. It was hardly fit for hogs. I said I knew you didn't eat any of it and I don't believe you do. You would be very near starvation if you did.—I also forgot to tell you that I got your flowers all right. They had not lost their sweetness nor color much. I think a good deal of them, put them away in my Bible and think of you whenever I see them. You must send me something again. Anything that you can get in a letter. I shall prize it very much.

I believe told you that I didn't get to Paynes or Blacks, while at Jefferson. I wanted to go very much but couldn't walk with Kittie, I told Gardeners how much you thought of Wils. They said he thought a good deal of you. I think you did right in not leaving Co. B. They wanted you to stay. I am sure if I were you I would rather command your Co. then a whole regiment of Blacks. I should be afraid of them. I wish you would not think about it. Perhaps you will get to be Captain of your own company and also will do very well with it.

I didn't get that Kibbie furniture. I had told Frances McClure about it and while I was gone to Jefferson, she went down and bought it and hauled it home without saying anything to me about it. Wasn't that a trick? She says now that I can have it if I want after she had paid for it and took it home. She said she thought I talked like I didn't want it. I told her, if I had a house to put it in I should buy it. I intended to all the time if you thought best. It was a very cheap bargain and she knew it. And everybody else thought so too. Many was at the better of it with her, but would a very mean trick to serve a friend as she terms me. I was really provoked but concluded to let her keep them. Perhaps it was all for the best as I had no place to keep them. I don't care so much about them but didn't want to be treated so—.

We have got our garden plowed and planted. Mr. Yager plowed it. He charged $1.25. Lib and I planted the corn & potatoes ourselves. We didn't know where to find anybody to do it for us so pitched in and planted it ourselves. I believe I told you that we had four little pigs, . . . very nice little fat things. I guess it will pay to keep them.

The children are all well. Lulie's eyes a little better. I am washing a blue mineral in them.—As it is the post office time I must quit. Oh yes, Mrs. Taylor told me the other day that she wanted you to send Frank's things home if you could. Very safe way sending them so they would be there to come. She says Frank told her so much about his knapsack that all she would to see it. Send it for her if you can by some reliable person. They feel so bad about him.

Your Em

I dreamed last night that you were home.

Hard Times Landing, Louisiana
May 7, 1863

Dear Emeline,

I sit down this evening to write you a few lines to let you know where and how we are. We got to this place about 4 o'clock this evening. We are some 60 miles from Milliken's Bend by land, and about 40, I think, from Vicksburg—on the river at the point where the troops embark to cross to Port Gibson. The whole army is crossing over by this now and I never saw such a movement. The whole road from here to the bend is crowded with soldiers, teams, and artillery. And they are crossing the river just as fast as the transports can carry them.

The last time I wrote to you I was at the Bend and the regiment had gone out to Richmond, Louisiana 10 miles from the river. I was not very well then, or for a few days afterward, but since I have been on this march my health had improved and I now feel first-rate. The doctor recommended me to stay at Richmond, but I told him I would try it and go as far as I could. I am glad now I came along. We expected that we went to Richmond to stay there some time and guard the place and went to work and fixed up a nice camp. We hardly got fixed when we were ordered away. We had to leave all our tents and baggage almost again and our mess box. We have only one baggage wagon to the regiment. Money does no good down here. There is nothing to buy at all. I eat hard bread and bacon.

The 4th [Iowa] Cavalry have just got here. Ol was in here just now; he and Billy are both well and look hearty. They are going on across the river today. The news from the front is that our forces are driving the rebels back—have got about 20 miles from the river, and the orders are to send on the troops and supplies as fast as possible. No baggage or tents is allowed to cross—not even for field officers. All the teams haul rations and ammunition. I think that Vicksburg will be taken before you get this letter, or we will be badly whipped.

I do not know when we will cross. We are detailed to remain here in command of this place and regulate the crossing of troops and teams till Frank Blair's Division comes up, when he will relieve us and we will go on to the front and rejoin our brigade. This may be in a day or two, as Blair is now on the road from the Bend.

We passed the 11th and 18th Iowa camped 3 miles on this side of Richmond. I saw Archey Campbell, Harry Holloway, Bub Turney, and all the boys that I was acquainted with. I saw Charles Cady and Rogers, who are in the 15th. They are all in good health and looking well. They expect to come on down and cross the river in a few days. We met two guards of secesh prisoners marching back to the Bend—some five or six hundred altogether.

If I had time and a place to write I would like to write you a long letter and tell you all about the country down here, but the pencil is so poor and I have so little time, I must make it short . . .

Billy brought me the testament you sent me last winter in the box. It is almost spoiled but I read what you wrote in it. You are a dear, good wife, and I will try to do as you tell me. But I trust more to your prayers and the goodness of God than anything I can do. I have not much time to read anything, but I will read that testament every chance . . .

Your own, Jake

I expect Lulie and Nellie are going to school by this time. You must not let them forget me. Tell them I said they must be good girls. Tommy must take care of Kitty. I expect he is a great big boy by this time. How I wish I could see you all.

[Mt. Pleasant, Iowa]
May the 14th, 1863

Dear Jake:
    . . . We are all well except Tommie. He has been complaining for a week or so, has a very bad cough . . . He mopes around and looks real bad. He groans in his sleep and makes such a fuss I don't know what to do with him. Tonight he has the earache. I must go to town in the morning and get a bottle of expectorant for him. I wish you were at home to tell me how to doctor him. He went to bed before sundown this evening, a half an hour ago. He called me in there and told me that "he coughed himself to death" awhile ago.

We had been moving things around considerable this spring, you would hardly know it, I guess. We have a bed in the parlor for the company bed and took the old bed cradle out in the kitchen. Lib

& Sallie sleep in our room upstairs and Lulie & Nellie sleep in the other. Tom and I and Kittie sleep in the bedroom downstairs. Wish you were here to keep off the "boogers" though I am not half so big a coward as I used to be . . . I believe I told you that Tom was going to war. Well, he had got his commission and expects to start next Monday week I believe. Annie is going to Dr. Holme's to live.—. . . We have got the garden all made. I have some corn up and potatoes, beans, radishes as I expect you think that it . . .

Em

[Mt. Pleasant, Iowa]
May the 22nd, 1863

Dear Jacob:
   I have had no letter from you since last Monday week till today. I received the one you wrote at "Hard Times Landing." I was quite uneasy about you what you said in your last that you was not well. I hope you will take good care of yourself and not get down. Don't go when you are not able to. You might just as well lay by and rest as anybody when you are sick. I am glad to hear, though, that you are better again. Hope you won't get sick anymore,—I should have written this sooner but have been sick myself about a week. Been in bed most of the time till today. I have been sitting up about half of the day. Dr. Marsh came out to see me three times.
   My disease principally was the "piles." I never had such a time in my life. You know I used to have them pretty bad sometimes, but never had such a time as this. I believe I should have gone crazy if I hadn't got relief. I took them bad on Saturday night, didn't sleep a bit. Sunday I walked the floor and rolled and trembled all day in perfect misery. About sundown I sent for Mrs. Morley but she didn't know what to do for me. So she sent Morley for some medicine. It didn't do me any good scarcely and Monday morning I sent for the doctor to come out. He came three days hand running. I am considerably better now but, Oh dear, I did suffer dreadfully. It took me down so that I could hardly walk across the floor. I am very weak yet. My hand is so weak I can hardly write. I haven't slept any hardly except one night for a while for a whole week. Hope I won't have it any more so bad, though I am not cured yet by a good deal.
   Tom and Annie staid here all night last night. They broke up house keeping yesterday. Stored part of their things up our stairs. Tom expects to start next Monday. Annie will go to Dr. Holmes

next week . . . I wish Tom and Annie wouldn't go away . . .

Old Captain Smith hasn't made his appearance yet. What has come of him? Tom Stockton sent me $20 the other day on that debt he owed. Said when he found out how much it was, he would send the rest of it if there was any more. The old farm isn't rented yet this year at all, so I suppose it will all go to sticks or weeds. I must quit for I am so tired. I hope I will feel better next time I write. I don't like to be sick when you aren't here to pity me. I haven't anybody to complain to. If I could see you coming I would get well immediately.—I expect you can't read this scribbling. My hand shakes so. Write as often as you can. I will try and not get the blues if I don't get a letter every week . . . The children are all well except Tommy's cough. It is better.

Good bye, dear, Your Em

Vicksburg

To reach Vicksburg, Grant and his armies were forced to fight five battles in Mississippi—Port Gibson on May 1; Raymond on May 12; Jackson on May 14; Champion Hill on May 16; and the Black River Bridge on May 17. All were Union victories.

On May 19th, the day after arriving at Vicksburg, Grant began movements to probe Confederate defenses, which resulted in Union losses of 950 men with only limited Confederate losses.

On May 22nd, Union forces attempted another assault on Vicksburg, also unsuccessful, suffering losses of 3,200 men. After this second unsuccessful attack, Grant realized that direct assaults would continue to result in disproportionate Union casualties, and that a siege of Vicksburg was necessary. When the siege began, Grant had about 31,000 soldiers, but with the arrival of reinforcements this number soon grew to 50,000.

The Failed Union Assault of May 22, 1863
The Death of Sergeant James Freeman, Car's Husband

Vicksburg
May 23, 1863

Dear Emeline,

How glad I am that I can again sit down and write you a few lines. And I know that you will be glad to hear from me, as it has been a long time since I had a chance to write or send a letter. I have not time to write much now, but can say that through the mercy of God I am alive and well, for which I have great reason to be thankful. I cannot tell you all that has happened since I last wrote at Hard Times Landing. We left Grand Gulf on the 11th inst. in charge of a train of 200 wagons. We got to Clinton, 10 miles this side of Jackson, on the 16th. Finding it had been taken by our advance, we turned back toward Vicksburg. We reached the rebel lines and commenced skirmishing on Monday evening, the 18th, and the battle has been going on with more or less violence ever since. We have gained a good deal of ground, having driven the rebels back about two miles. But their present position is a very strong one, and one they must hold or surrender the city, as we have them completely surrounded.

Yesterday was a terrible day; I pray to God I may never see such another. An effort was made to advance our whole line and storm the enemy's works; charges were made at three points, and as far as I know at present we were repulsed at all of them. Steele's Division with the 25th Iowa in front—on the right, next to the river. I cannot give you particulars of the battle now. I do not suppose you would care to hear it. The fighting on both sides was desperate. It is said by those who pretend to know that it was the hardest fight of the war. I thought we had to work at the "Post[1]," but that was a mere nothing to this. The mortars and some of the gun-boats were at work at the same time—and artillery and musketry firing—I never heard. The hills shook to the foundations. The slaughter—for I can call it nothing else—was terrible, on our side. We lost a great many men and officers.

I must now tell you what I have been putting off all along—Company B lost one man killed—and that was Sergeant Freeman[2]. He was just as good and brave a soldier as ever enlisted. He fell within less than 50 yards of the breastworks where it was almost certain death to go. Car, what will she do? I have been thinking all day that I must write to her. But I have concluded that I can't do it. I want you and Tom to go up there as soon as you get this and tell her. You can break the news to her so much better than I can. And save me the task of writing the sad news to her. You will do this for me, won't you, dear? It will be a great relief to me. He was shot through the hips and lower part of the bowels, and may have lived some time, but the place was exposed to such a raking fire of the enemy that we could not go to him till after dark, when he was found dead. He was very popular with the company and they all mourn his loss very much. But that does no good now.

Four others of our company were wounded, 3 slightly, but one—
Swinford[3]—I fear mortally. Captain Spearman[4], I think, is mortally
wounded. I don't know how many were lost in the regiment. But not
so many as in the regiments that followed us. As the enemy had not
time to mass his troops in front of us until we were over the most
exposed places and reached the foot of the hill on which they were
posted and where they could not reach us with their fire.

I have not got a letter from you since the 20th of April, at
Greenville. The mail is here someplace, but nothing is thought of
now but to fight till we take the city, which we will certainly do;
but how long it will take or how many more lives it will cost I cannot tell. I do not think there will be any more charges made, like
those of yesterday. <u>The men cannot be made to do it</u>. And it is not
necessary. We have the place <u>completely surrounded</u> and get <u>our</u>
supplies easily by hauling a few miles from the Yazoo. I have heard
since I began this that no letters are allowed to go up the river at
present. So there is no knowing when you will get it. The 4th
Cavalry is here. I see Billy and Ol every day or two. Gardner[5] got
here last Sunday. He brought a letter from Car to them, date May
3rd; I read it. It is no use to tell you not to be uneasy. I know I am
exposed to danger, but you must hope for the best and bear what
comes with fortitude and resignation. I hope and expect to live to
see you all again. If not, may God protect and sustain you, and
bring us to meet where there is no war.

Jake

There has been no hard fighting today but the artillery and the
sharp shooters keep up the firing.

1. Jacob is referring to the Battle of Arkansas Post, which occurred
   January 10-11, 1863.

2. Sergeant James Freeman of Company B was the husband of
   Emeline's sister Caroline.

3. Richard Swinford, age 19, was severely wounded in the May 22,
   1863, assault on Vicksburg and died of those wounds on July 5,
   1863. He is buried in the National Cemetery at Vicksburg,
   Section G, grave 1247, close to where he was wounded.

4. Captain James Spearman of Company H was severely wounded, but survived. He was discharged from the army May 2,
   1864, for disability.

5.   Josh Gardner was Jacob's carpenter friend.

Vicksburg
May 24, 1863

I wrote one sheet to you yesterday. But as this is Sunday and I can't send this away now I will write some more. We got two mails last night. I got no letter in the first one, and was very much discouraged, I assure you. But we soon got another and I got one dated May 6th, which did me a great deal of good . . . As you say nothing about Judson's death, I suppose you had not heard it yet, or perhaps you wrote about that in a former letter that has not come. There is very little fighting going on today. Our mortars and artillery and sharp shooters keep up the firing at intervals. But the rebels do not reply except by an occasional shot from their sharp shooters. I do not know whether they are running out of ammunition—or only "remembering the Sabbath Day to keep it holy," but I think the former, as their firing was very slack all day yesterday compared to what it had been before.

This is the seventh day of the fight. It is surprising how soon one will become indifferent to the roar of artillery and the whistling of bullets. Where I sat when I wrote yesterday and where I am now, we are out of sight of the rebels, but their shells and musket balls come over the bluff right among us, and every once in a while a man is killed or wounded, but the regiment is posted here in the rear of the 1st Missouri battery which is on the bluff just above us. Here we must stay till we are ordered away. We have all got so we do not notice it unless the balls come thick as hail. We cook and eat and sleep here under the fire of the enemy just as if a great battle was not all the time in progress. The first time we were engaged in the fight was Tuesday afternoon, when we were ordered up over the bluff to act as sharp shooters. We remained till our ammunition was all exhausted and were then relieved by the 76th Ohio. We occupied rifle pits from which the rebels had retreated, and very few were hurt on our side. (We just now got another small mail, but nothing for me.)

Our division went into the fight at 11 o'clock on Friday with about 6,000 men and lost about 800 or 900 in killed and wounded[1]. It was an awful slaughter. I hope never to see the likes again. The dead and wounded lay thick in places. But if Sergeant Freeman had only come off safe I should not mind it so much. He was such a faithful soldier, always ready for duty. He and I marched side by side at least 150 miles since the first of May, through dust, rain and mud, day and night; and wherever he was wanted he was sure to be found. Our men then went to Jackson[2], sacked and burned the whole town, and came back loaded with spoils. Our regiment cleaned out some stores in Clinton as we came through. Freeman had a nice little box with some trinkets in it that I will send or bring to Car if I can possibly take care of it till I get a chance. He had 11 or 12 dollars in money and I can sell some of his things for something. I do pity poor Caroline. I know it will nearly kill her.

I never saw such hills and hollows as there are here. It beats Missouri all to pieces. We have had plenty to eat for 2 or 3 days, but on the march we were short of rations—sometimes only one cracker a day. I was hungry for 3 or 4 days; but my health and appetite are first-rate. I have not seen a tent or a blanket for a week. We sleep on our arms, in line of battle. The weather is very hot and sultry. But the health of the men is good. I must stop for the present—perhaps I will write more before I get a chance to send this away.

I have no doubt but you do write "regular," dear. But the letters do not get here. I hope they will come yet, if not I will make you tell me what was in them when I come home. You think you would know the "crook of my nose," do you? I am not so certain of it if you could see me now. I expect I am the dirtiest fellow you ever saw. I have been sleeping on the ground and traveling through mud and dust alternately for two weeks without a change of clothes, and you may be sure I look pretty hard. I hope I will be able to slip in on you some day, when no one is there, as Nellie says, just to see what you would do. I want to see the dear children so bad and hug and kiss them all. What does Tommy do and say? I often think of him. I hope he will never have to be a soldier. We will all have a good time when I get home, won't we.

I was glad to hear that you had the garden plowed and planted. I think you and Lib must have had a hard job. I wish you could have got some one to do it for you. I did not know before that you had 4 little pigs. You must take good care of them. I think that was a mean trick in Frances, but it was just like her. I wish you had got it, but I wouldn't have anything to do with it, or Frances either now.

This is a secesh pencil and so mean I can hardly write with it at all. I don't expect you will be able to read this by the time it gets there. You must not look too strongly for me to go home this summer. I will if I can, but it is uncertain whether I can or not. You must not be disappointed if I can't come. I wish this battle was over once, so we could attend to something else.

Jake

1. On the May 19 assault on Vicksburg, the Army of the Tennessee reported 157 killed, 777 wounded, and 8 missing. Confederate loss reports were incomplete. Casualties from the May 22 assault for the Union were 502 killed, 2,550 wounded, and 147 missing. Confederate loss reports were incomplete. (Edwin Bearss, *The Vicksburg Campaign*, Volume III pages 773-780, 862-873)

2. Jacob is referring the capture of Jackson, the capital of Mississippi.

Near Vicksburg
May 30, 1863

Dear Emeline,

I have got a pen and ink this time and will try to write you a long letter if I am not interrupted. I got a letter from you yesterday dated May 22nd. I was very sorry to hear that you were sick. I do hope that you are clear well by this time. I do wish I could be there to pity you and take care of you and have you cured right up. I am very anxious to get another letter. I want to hear how you are, I am more uneasy about you or some of the children getting sick than about myself. It is always a great comfort to get a letter and hear that you are "all well." But you must always tell me just how you are. I was glad to hear that Tommy was getting better of his cough. Never mind, I hope that I will get home someday yet to take care of you when you get sick. But poor Caroline—what will become of her—I think of her nearly all the time. I hope God will give her strength to bear her great affliction. I believe she is a true Christian and knows where to go for help. She used to write such good letters to Freeman. He used to let me read some of them. I thought by the way she wrote sometimes she hardly expected to ever see him again. I miss him a great deal here—it seems like the company is half broken up since he is gone. You must go and see Car if you have not done so, and comfort her all you can. I do hope Ma will go home. She would be so much company to her and you both. My health is still good, but a good many of the men are getting sick, mostly "ague!" and diarrhea.

The siege of Vicksburg is still going on and I do not know how much longer it will last. Our situation here is very unhealthy, but I believe we will get out of it before long. The country is the roughest and most broken I ever saw. I never did see such hills and hollows and gorges and washes—and we have to keep in the deep hollows and rifle pits. As sure as one of us shows his head over a hill or above a rifle pit, he is shot at. Ditto—the rebels. We are from 50 to 300 yards apart and shoot at each other every chance in day time and dig rifle pits at night. The weather is very hot and sultry, especially in the deep ravines, and the water is poor and scarce. We have not got our works completed quite to the river yet, and have to depend on small springs among the hills.

Our regiment has moved since I last wrote, and is now on the extreme right of our line, and has been for 3 or 4 days. The right of the regiment is within about 50 yards of the river, a short distance below the bend, and is near the first water battery, which we are going to capture some of these nights. Company B, is posted on a high hill near a large white house, where we have a splendid view of the river—can see our boats at Young's Point. It is also the best position for sharp shooting on the whole line. I have had some good pits dug there and keep one-third of the company in them all the time. We have to "run a blockade" of two or three rods to get on the hill, but none of us have been hurt yet, which I am certain is more than the rebels can say.

We had a fine view of the gun-boat fight the other day—our boat[2] came down the river in gallant style and was opened upon by all the rebel batteries on the river. She fought gallantly for a short time, but was soon disabled and turned just at the right of our regiment and went up the river a short distance and sunk in shallow water. We can see the wreck from here.

I go on picket guard ever other night. I was out night before last and had quite a long talk "across the hollow" with the rebels in their works. We jawed each other till 11 o'clock[3]. They taunted us about "Joe Hooker[4]"—they have a report, which they all believe, that General Lee is in possession of Arlington Heights. They also made fun of our gun boat[2]. But I matched them by asking them when they got their last mail. And what is the "Capital of Mississippi"? That got them down. They were anxious to know what we had done with Vallandigham[5]. I told them we had sent him to Ft. Warren[6]. They said he "was all right"—we must take good care of him—several of them said they were going to have him for

their next president. Good joke on the copper-heads of the North.
One fellow said his name was Jacob Phelps and he used to work at
Parks livery stable at Mt. Pleasant. Another said he was Dr. Elliott
from Cleveland, Ohio and would fight us till "hell froze over."

George Barrett of St. Louis who used to go to school to Howe
was "conscripted" at Memphis last summer and deserted from
them last Tuesday night. He escaped by swimming the river. He
went to Young's Point and says the rebels are short of both ammu-
nitions and rations and must soon surrender. They did not know
what had become of Barrett till we told them. One fellow tried to
make us a speech. He said they had nothing against the North-
West[7]—did not want to fight us—but the Yankees. If we would go
home they would give us the free navigation of the river[8], &c. I told
him we did not ask them to give us the river—we were going to
take it—that we would have the free navigation of the river and not
go home either till we got ready. So you see we talk friendly at
night and shoot at each other all day.

We do not expect to make any more charges, but to take the
place by a regular siege. We are advancing on the lines slowly but
surely. They expect General Johnston[9] to come to their relief and
attack up in the rear with a large force. But General Blair[10] has
been sent back to meet and whip him, and when the rebels hear that
he has done so (as I have no doubt he will) they will surrender. I
wish the thing was over—it has lasted so long that it has ceased to
be interesting. Our batteries throw shot and shell into their works
from morning till night. They do not reply with artillery at all, but
a ball from sharp shooters whistles over our heads or drops among
us occasionally, but altogether it is getting to be decidedly dull.
They won't show fight but are saving all their ammunition in hopes
we will make another charge. That cannot be done at this point, as
the hills are so high and steep a man could not climb them if there
was no one to oppose him. The mortar boats make night hideous to
the rebels, but it is a splendid sight to us to see the huge shells fly
through the air and burst over the city with a noise that shakes the
hills to the very foundations.[11]

But I expect you are tired of this kind of news. Well, we have
nothing else to talk about down here. When I get home I will have
a great many things to tell you, for all I write so much. I am glad
to hear that Lulie and Nellie are going to school. I hope they will
try to learn and see how smart they will be when I come home.
They must mind the teacher and be good girls in school.

I do wish you had a pony. I am sorry you have so much trouble to get your things home. I guess I will buy you a horse and buggy. I am glad to hear that there is a good prospect for crops and plenty of fruit. If I don't get home you must put up lots to send to me. Plums and blackberries are ripe here now, but not very plenty. How do my chickens get along? I haven't had a taste of one hardly for two months. But mess chests and baggage are at the Yazoo Landing and will be up here tonight, then we will get along much better. Our bakery is here too—we got light bread this morning. I thought I would tell you how we have been living, and how dirty and greasy we are; but if I did you would not believe it, so I shan't try. I have got all your letters now except for the first one you wrote after you were up to Cars about the 21st of April. I hope it will get along some of these days.

You must take good care of yourself, dear; it makes me feel so bad to hear that you are sick and me not there. As soon as we take this place I will try to let you know about the tenth of what month I will be home. You dear, sweet wife—I hope the Lord will spare me to love and comfort you many years after this wicked and causeless war shall be over. Billy and Ol are both well; they are gone on a five days' scout to Jackson[12]. I have not seen Jont since we left the bend. I hear he is not much better. Write soon and a long letter too.

Your own, Jake

1. Malaria was referred to as "ague," "autumnal fever," "chills and fever," or the "shakes." It was thought that malaria was caused by "bad air" from swamps but its real transmission was caused by mosquitoes. Doctors would frequently treat malaria using quinine, but it was frequently in low supply, and doctors would not know the proper dosage. (Thomas P. Lowry, M.D., *The Story the Soldiers Wouldn't Tell–Sex in the Civil War*, page 101)

2. On May 27 the Union gun-boat *Cincinnati*, protected by logs and bails of hay, engaged several Confederate batteries toward the northern part of Vicksburg. The logs and bails of hay provided insufficient protection to the *Cincinnati*, which went down with her flag nailed to the stump of a mast. (*Vicksburg, Official National Park Handbook*, page 54)

3. During the siege of Vicksburg, the Union and Confederate pickets would frequently agree to a truce during their night watch, which allowed for extended conversations such as this one.

4. This insult was most likely regarding the Battle of

Chancellorsville, May 1-5, 1863, where Confederate General Robert E. Lee and the Army of Northern Virginia defeated Major General Joseph Hooker and the much larger Army of the Potomac.

5. Ohioan Clement L. Vallandigham was a well-known Northern peace advocate and had been a member of Congress. By 1863, he had been voted out of office but was running for governor in Ohio. On May 1, 1863, Vallandigham made a speech claiming that the war could easily be concluded by negotiation, or by accepting the French offer to mediate between the North and the South. For this he was accused of violating Order No. 38, issued by Union General Burnside, which stated that the "habit of declaring sympathies for the enemy would no longer be tolerated." Vallandigham was placed under military arrest, denied habeas corpus, and was tried and convicted by a military commission. Lincoln feared that Vallandigham would become a martyr for his cause and commuted Vallandigham's sentence from imprisonment to banishment to Confederate lands. Vallandigham went south, but Jefferson Davis did not want him either. Vallandigham then fled to Canada, where he ran for governor of Ohio in abstentia. In 1864, he returned to Ohio and helped draft the Democratic platform as part of McClellan's candidacy for president.

6. Ft. Warren was a Union prison located in Boston, Massachusetts. (J. G. Randall & David Donald, *The Civil War and Reconstruction*, page 337)

7. In this reference, the Northwest meant the states of Ohio, Indiana, Michigan, Illinois, Iowa, Wisconsin and Minnesota. As the United States had become sectionalized, the Northwest was distinct from the Northeast; rebels referred to residents of the latter as Yankees. One of the causes of friction between the North and the South were tariffs that protected manufacturing, primarily located in the Northeast.

8. Jacob is referring to the Mississippi River, which provided transportation vital to the economy of the Northwest. The Confederate government had proposed the same terms as the picket.

9. This is a reference to Confederate General Joseph E. Johnston. A false hope of the Confederates defending Vicksburg was that Johnston would break the siege and free them.

10. Union General Francis Blair had taken a large force to the "Mechanicsburg Corridor" with the dual purpose of devastating the area between the Yazoo and Big Black Rivers and combating

Johnston if necessary. This force included Billy and Ol
Bereman of the 4th Iowa Cavalry. (Edwin Bearss, *The Vicksburg
Campaign*, Volume III, pages 995-1006) See footnote 12.

11. During the siege, Jacob and the 25th Iowa Infantry were located north of Vicksburg, right on the Mississippi River, so that
they could easily view the Union gunboats' fire.

12. Contrary to Jacob's comment that Billy and Ol both were well,
twenty-eight-year-old First Sergeant Billy Bereman had been
severely wounded near Mechanicsburg on May 29.

Grant Said I Was A Pretty Good Engineer

[Fragment – No Date
Must be Vicksburg, June 1863]

I wrote a letter to Father and Ma, telling them of the death of
Freeman. But I expect Ma had started home before they got it. I
received a good long letter from Ma the day before yesterday. I am
glad she has gone home; she will be so much company for you and
Car. Tell her I am ashamed I did not write to her sooner and oftener. But if she knew how much we have been away from our baggage and how little time I have to write she should not blame me.
I do not write to anyone but you now. I have not seen Jont since
we left the Bend, May 1st. But I hear he is a little better, but still
weak. I must try to have him sent home as soon as I get time.

The whole army here is very glad to learn, through <u>Northern</u>
papers and letters that Grant has taken Vicksburg!!![1] The news
gives great satisfaction. It is somewhat amusing though, that
while you were rejoicing and speechifying over the victory, having your one-horse cannons out, and your great illuminations,
&c, that we were at the same time pounding away at the everlast-
ing hills and infernal forts with a hundred cannons, and didn't
know they had surrendered! It was a good joke on us!! This is the
19th day of the fight and we haven't taken it yet, but we expect
everyday we will.

I don't think they can hold out much longer. We are gaining
ground on them all the time. We dig in the night and shoot in the
daytime. As we advance our pickets they fall back. But the last
two nights they have fired on our working parties, but didn't hurt
anyone. We have got our rifle pits within 50 yards of their two

upper batteries on the river – the ones that do the most damage to gun-boats. I think we will drive them out in a day or two. Our line is about 9 miles long, and we can throw shells all over the enclosed space. We have them in the bull-pen and keep the ball hot day and night. Our regiment occupies the same position as when I wrote you last. We have got a ten pound parrot[2] gun mounted on our hill, and annoy them a great deal. Very few have been hurt on our side this week. We have [to know where] to dodge and where to stand up, and so keep pretty well concealed. We make small port-holes in the breastwork to shoot through, but the rebels fix in the same way, and it is seldom we get a fair shot. But if a man on either side shows his head he is certain to be shot at. But there is no real safety anyplace. They shoot very carelessly.

We got our mess box and book-box and wall-tent a few days ago. We and most of the other officers, put up our tents at a spring about 300 yards in the rear of our works. We come down one at a time to eat and sleep but one stays at the rifle pits all the time. Spent balls and pieces of shells fall here pretty thick, and every once in a while someone is wounded, but we are so used to it that we do not mind them much. It is astonishing how soon we become accustomed to such things. I do not know much about what is going on at other points in our line. We hear a great many reports but nothing reliable. Every regiment is assigned to duty at some place, and there are very strict orders to prevent officers or men from straggling about.

It is reported that a rebel officer came over last night, and says the rebels are living on pea meal, and will either break out or surrender in three days. I would like to see them try to break out – they would have a good time getting through. They played us a sharp trick last Sunday night, when they slipped up the river in skiffs and burned the gun-boat they had disabled a few days before. They won't catch us napping again.

Generals Grant, Sherman, and Steele[3] were all three up on our hill today. Grant said I was pretty good engineer but did not make my works strong enough. The rebels will find it pretty strong if they try to run us off there.

The Barrett I spoke of in my last letter is a man that used to be a painter in Mt. Pleasant . . . The weather is still very hot and sultry and dry. You must excuse my poor writing and not show this letter to anyone.

                    Your ever faithful, Jake

Mrs. Stone has been here for two or three days and is going to stay, I guess. Now, bad as I want to see you I would not let you come here. Everybody talks about her and thinks he ought to send her right home, if she hasn't sense enough to go. They have a tent back about a mile and he stays there with her most of the time in place of attending to his business. It causes a great deal of dissatisfaction.

1. As of June 1863, the Union Army had <u>not</u> captured Vicksburg. The following erroneous article appeared in the May 25, 1863, issue of the *Burlington Hawkeye*.

BY TELEGRAPH
GREAT VICTORY IN
MISSISSIPPI.

JOHNSON OUT-GENERALED.

THE REBELS BADLY WHIPPED.

VICKSBURG AND ALL ITS
FORTIFICATIONS TAKEN.

Fifty-Seven Pieces of Artillery
and Many Prisoners Taken.

---

2. The parrot gun, named for its inventor, was rifled artillery with a three inch shell. The length of the tube was 74 inches and the 10 pound parrot weighed 899 pounds. (Jack Coggins, *Arms and Equipment of the Civil War*, page 77)

3. Steele commanded the 1st Division in the 15th Army Corps, reporting to Sherman who commanded the 15th Army Corps, reporting to Grant who commanded the Army of the Tennessee.

• On June 12, 1863, the 25th Iowa Infantry formally promoted Jacob to Captain of Company B.

[Mt. Pleasant, Iowa]
Tuesday night
June the 9th, 1863

Dear Jacob,
    I have just returned from Jefferson today where I have been

since Friday evening, the day that I got your letter informing us of the death of Freeman. Oh, what a blow it was to us all, especially Car. For a few days she was a perfect picture of despair. It seemed as though it would almost kill her. I got your letter about noon . . .

As soon as I got dinner over, I went up town and happened to find Tom Stockton down with the buggy. I got in with him and went right up, but oh, what a task to tell her. I feel that I wasn't the person to do it, but it was as I hoped – she had heard it when I got there. Several of the neighbors were there trying to comfort her. Till had been to Marshall that afternoon and heard it read from a letter. He came by for some of the women to go over and tell her. She took if very hard when they told her, but she could hardly believe it till I got there, then she knew it was true and she commenced screaming, and it seems as though she would go into a fit. She looked so pitiful. I felt so bad for her. Everybody pities her so much. I brought her home with me. She couldn't stay there by herself till she would get over it some. Everybody feels so bad about Jim. It seemed to be a terrible blow to all. Oh, you don't know how much trouble and anxiety of mine we have all had within the past two weeks. The suspense was almost past enduring sometimes. It was so long before we could get any news at all.

I was so glad to get your letter and I am so thankful that my lot is not as Car's. But I keep thinking what if it should be so. How could I bear it? I had been very anxious often after I got that letter thinking. Today I got another dated the 30th. I was glad to hear of your safety and health but can't feel easy till that terrible time is over at Vicksburg. When will it be? How I do hope you will succeed in taking it. I feel afraid when I hear of the reported reinforcements the rebels are having. Everybody is confidant that it will be ours before long, but if it should not be, what a disappointment and what a loss of life for nothing. What great courage it will give to the Copperheads. I will try and hope for the best and shall expect you home whenever that battle is over.

We are all well once more. I have got to feeling pretty well again. Hope I shall stay so. I guess Car will stay down here till Ma comes home, which I think will be some time next week and we have written for her to come immediately. She has gone from St. Louis out into Missouri scouting around with the graybeards, grounding bridges. I feel real provoked to think she has not come home and take care of her house and trying to be some comfort to us in our affliction. Got a letter from them yesterday. Father says he can't drive her home. She says she likes it first rate and thinks she will stay till grapes are ripe and then over a great plenty of them. But I think she will come right home when she gets our letters.

I suppose Captain Spearman got home today. The *Hawkeye* said he had arrived at Burlington. Nothing of Captain Smith yet. Why won't he express the money? Tom has been gone for two weeks. Annie starts to Dr. Holmes yesterday morning.

I must <u>tell</u> you that I have the poorest luck in all creation in raising chickens or making gardens. I have about a dozen young chickens. They wouldn't hatch and the pigs caught some of the old hens and ate them. The chickens eat up the garden. I tried to shut them in the stable but couldn't do it. It has been so dry that the stuff would grow hardly. It is perfectly dusty out there. The cut worms are thick. Take it all together, I have real bad luck. I have a mind to eat up what hens we have and not bother with them. It is half past ten o'clock. I must quit.

If it wasn't so late I would write another half sheet, but I guess we're going to write again in a few days. Zan is here yet. There are only five women about the house now. What would you do with so many if you were me?

What became of the 4th Cavalry? Had to cut their way through 5 regiments of Secesh and come out with the loss of 190 men. Is it so? We are feeling uneasy about them.

Tommy says that anybody shoots Pa, they had better look out. He (Tom) will shoot them. I should have written this sooner if I hadn't gone to Jefferson. Hope you will get it in time. Tom Stockton had sold out and is going to Missouri to live. Good bye, dear.

Em

The Death of Jacob Whippo, the Second Son

[Mt. Pleasant, Iowa]
Monday, June the 15th, 1863

Dear Jake,

How do you do today? How I would like to see you. I am afraid you are burning up with the heat away down there, as it is hot enough here for any white person to stand. It has been very warm for the last four or five days. The only hot weather we have had. It has been quite cool all Spring but very dry. Everything seems to be dried up just now, as we have had no rain at all, for more than two weeks, and it was very dry before that. It is very discouraging for farmers. The gardens are doing no good. We can't get cabbage plants to stay at all hardly. The cut worms and dry weather together just kill them as fast as we can plant them. There is nothing for the cows to eat scarcely. The grass all over the prairie is dried up. The ground is almost bare. I don't know what to do with them. The new one that we got from the farm is such a poor shab side thing. I am afraid she will die. She is so poor that I am ashamed of her (paid $22 for her too).

Zan has gone home. I am afraid she is not altogether well. She acts very strange sometimes. I rather think, though they didn't say that they want me to keep her up home till she gets better. Your mother thinks she could get medicine from Dr. Patterson and take it here. I don't feel as though I could keep her. It seems to me that I have enough to think of and troubles me now without such an addition. What do you think about it? Perhaps it is my duty, but I don't feel that she would be any better here than at home, as company don't seem to do her any good. She is so very gloomy that she makes me feel bad whenever I am with her. When she was here she would watch me all the time and follow me around and tell me how mean she was and sigh and groan till she really gives me the blues. I tried to comfort her and cheer her up, and make her be lively, but it done no good. I do believe it is partly her own fault. She don't try to shake off the blues, but just allows herself to think, and study and mount some up or stir around but just seems determined to go into the melancholys. I don't know what I shall do if they want me to take her. I don't see how I can. She will be such a charge –.

We are all well. I am not stout by a good deal but am able to travel around. This hot weather takes me down. I am so needy about you, am afraid you will get sick if you have to stay there much longer. How I wish you could take Old Vicksburgh and just get out of that hot hollows. Will it ever be? Oh, how glad everybody would be to hear for certain that Vicksburgh was taken. We have had that news here several times but always know to be false till the people put no confidence in telegraphs & reports anymore. What jubilee then would be all over the land if it should be taken. Everybody is so anxious about it, but it would be sad rejoicing to a great many, that have given their dearest friends to purchase it. Oh, what more will it cost? It pains my heart to think of it. I pray God that it cost no more precious lives, as there seem to be enough sacrifice already.

We had news a few days ago that Jake Whippo was killed[1]. Is it so? His father was down here Saturday to inquire about it. Jim

Pollock wrote it home. Mr. Whippo don't hardly believe it but I feel as though it was so.

We all heard that Billy was wounded 3 or 4 days ago but can't get any of the particulars. Colonel Swan wrote to his wife that he thought he was mortally wounded. Poor Billy – he is one of the best of brothers. I feel that we ought to get him home some way, but there is nobody to go but Alvah and he seems to be too busy. How I wish we could hear from him. Why don't we get a letter from Ol or somebody about him? I never saw such a time as this. We can't get the news at all about anything, till a two or three weeks after it has happened. I look for a letter from you today certain, and then I will hear all. Your dear good letters. How I do love to get them. What if I should never get another? Poor Car. She says she has got her last one.

Em

1. Jake Whippo, Third Sergeant of Company B, was killed in action, June 1, 1863, at Vicksburg.

The Death of James Stockton, the Son of a Friend

Rear of Vicksburg
June 15, 1863

My Dear Wife,

I sent you a few lines a few days ago by Prof. Smith, and promised to write more soon, so I will try to do it today. I am in good health at present. I was quite sick when I wrote to you by Smith and for two or three days after. But I am as well as usual now.

I got a letter from you dated June 2nd a few days ago. I was very glad to hear that you had got about well. It had been so long since I got a letter that I was afraid you were real sick – too sick to write, and was very anxious to <u>hear</u> from you. You say you are very anxious about me, and did not know whether to write or not. I know it is a very trying time to you, dear, especially when the fight lasts so long. I cannot tell you, there is no danger and that you need not be uneasy. But you must hope for the best, and try to look on the bright side, as I do. If trouble comes, it will come soon enough without being waited for.

It seems like I have bad news to tell you in nearly every letter. James Stockton was killed yesterday morning. He was shot through the breast by a musket ball. He lived about thirty minutes only, after he was struck. He was one of the bravest and most daring men in the company. He did not fear anything. We all mourn his loss. But another one of Company B has fallen at his post, while fighting bravely to crush this most wicked rebellion and to uphold the honor of the old stars and stripes, and preserve the integrity of that glorious union which was handed down to us, cemented by the blood of our forefathers. Whose turn it will be next, God only knows. Another one of our men, William H. Denny, died here of dysentery, night before last. So we are fast dropping off. Company B is no longer the largest in the regiment. But what are left of us are all in good spirits, and willing to fight all summer rather than not take Vicksburg.

I believe there is nothing new to tell you about the progress of the siege. There is a great deal that I could tell you, but it is not worthwhile to begin to write it. Our position is about the same it has been for two or three weeks. The rebels occupy about the same ground they did at first. But we are gradually closing up the space between. We have silenced some of their batteries, and planted new ones of our own. They have not fired a cannon on our part of the line for three or four days[1]. There is considerable firing between sharp-shooters in the morning and late in the evening. In the middle of the day it is too hot to do anything, but we have to remain in the pits and watch. Our battcries throw shells at intervals all through the day and night. We have working parties at night to dig new rifle pits and strengthen the old ones. And that is the program, day after day.

The general opinion is that they will not hold out many days longer. I am satisfied they are nearly out of provision. I do not think there is any danger of an attack on our rear. We have received large reinforcements from the North and could whip 100,000 on the rear, besides leaving enough here to hold those in the city. You need not doubt but that the victory will be on our side. We are certain to take the place – there aren't men enough in the Southern Confederacy to save it now. For we are as strongly fortified as the rebels are. But how long it will take or what it will yet cost, the future must tell. If we have to lie in these rifle pits another month, we will lose as many men by sickness as would by a <u>charge</u>. I do wish it was over. Our regiment has been under fire and fighting everyday for the last month – it will be a month the 18th, while not half the regiments here have fired a gun at all. Although the firing has not been very brisk of late, yet there is a continual <u>excitement</u> and strain on the nerves, which will wear out any set of men in that length of time.

I have not heard from Ol since I wrote to you last; Charles Cady was here to see me the other day. He says Jim Ritner is here, around on the left, and that he is well and hearty. I have not seen him yet. I have heard that Jont is to be discharged and sent home. I hope it is so. I have been trying to have him brought over here, so that I could see to him myself. But it is impossible to get anything done now. I think I will try to go to Young's Point myself in a few days, to see about him. I sent his descriptive list a few days ago, and am in hopes he will get off up the river. I suppose you will see Prof. Smith before you get this, and hear all the news and get the money. I am captain in earnest now, and have two good lieutenants to help me do the work, I think I can get along easier now.

One of our company, Mr. Abraham Hollems, has been promoted to Chaplain of this regiment in place of Corkhill². He is a first-rate man, but not very much of a preacher. A great many black coat, kid glove gents from the North had applied for the place, but the Colonel preferred to recommend a <u>soldier</u>, and I think he did right.

I hope that Ma is at home before this time. And that Car will come down and live with her. I think Car would not be so lonesome there. Tell Ma I will write to her if I ever get the time.

You said that some of our folks had been up and brought you some things, and a new cow and a calf. You said you had asked me about the cow in one of your letters. If you did I never got the letter at all. I never knew or heard a word about it till now. But it is all right. I am glad you got the cow. But I do think the price extravagant. You say that Mother wants to know if I will not take less than 10% on the note. I think if cows are worth $22 they can afford to take less. I would rather have the money than 6%. But I cannot tell from this distance what is best. You had better tell them that I said it had better stand as it is till I come home, or till I see if I can get home this summer, and then we will make arrangements about it. And if they would rather pay it off it will be all right, though I do not ask or expect it.

I have not had a letter from any of them for a long time. I don't see why they don't write. I hope Kitty has got well by this time – you must take good care of the little dear. How I would like to see her and all the rest of you. I suppose Tommy has got well, as you don't say anything about him. I expect he is so big I won't know him. I hope he is a good boy. Lulie and Nellie must be smart girls at school and at home too. Tell them I want to see them and would like to have one of them here to get me a drink and to keep the flies and mosquitoes off me when I am sick.

Your own, Jake

. . . I worked all day yesterday getting a metallic case for Stockton and sealing it up. It was quite a job. The case cost $93. Stockton made me promise to send James home if he should get killed or die, and I did the best I could. I hope the corpse will keep well, but the weather is so hot I think that is doubtful.

1. The Confederates were limiting their cannon fire because they were becoming short on ammunition.

2. The 25th Iowa promoted Abraham Hollems, age 45, to Regimental Chaplain on June 8, 1863, replacing the 41 year old Englishman Thomas Corkhill, who resigned April 28.

[Mt. Pleasant, Iowa]
June the 25th, 1863

Dear Husband,

I haven't received a letter from you since yesterday week and I am very anxious to hear from you, you may be sure. Captain Smith arrived home last Saturday on the __ o'clock train and was so driven as to come out and see me in the afternoon of the same day, but he didn't bring me any letter. He said he thought that you wrote one for me but didn't know where was the envelope. But when we came to open it, there was nothing for me. I haven't seen or heard of any since. Do I suppose he didn't bring any? I was somewhat disappointed but I know you must have been hurried and hadn't time to write, but I am expecting one every day by mail as it is high time I had one.

I hardly know when I wrote you last or what I wrote. I have been about half sick and had so much to think about that I can't remember anything any more. If you would only take Vicksburg and I could hear that you were all safe and well, I think I would come to my senses again. Oh, the suspense and great anxiety a person feels, that has a dear friend in such a dangerous place. I do hope you will take all the care of yourself that is possible. I keep thinking what if you should meet the same fate of poor Jake

Whippo. How could I bear it? What a stroke it was to his Father and Mother to have a second son taken from them in that way. Oh, the horror and trouble that is spreading all over the country, <u>when will it end</u>? How we will all appreciate peaceable times if we should ever again be so fortunate as to have peace. And how we <u>Dear</u> will appreciate each other's society more than ever if we shall be permitted to meet here on earth again. Let us pray that we may, for how <u>can</u> I live without you, and train up these little children in the right way? What would become of us? I have always said that I would die first, and I may. The All-wise knows what is best for us both. We <u>may</u> spend many happy hours together but let us be prepared for whatever comes. Are we ready? Go, if called and are we prepared to give each other up if necessary? I don't feel prepared for either, are you? Oh, let us give ourselves unto the hands of the Lord and be willing to let him do what seems best to him. Above all, let us be ready to meet each other in the better land, if not in this.

Car seemed to be better reconciled than I expected. She would be, though she feels very bad. She says sometimes she thinks she <u>can't</u> give him up, and that she must see him again. Poor Car, her grief is great. She went home day before yesterday, took Lulie with her. She thought she would stay till Ma comes home and took her with her, but I guess Ma has gone to see Billy. We haven't heard from her lately. Got a letter from Ol yesterday, said Billy wasn't dangerous, that he has had been sent to St. Louis. I suppose Ma is there with him. I think she might write.

The children are all well. I believe there is no news from home to tell you. I took Lulie & Nellie and went to the show. We went with Alvah's but he got a free ticket and took us all in for nothing. It was a great sight to the children.

Yes, Tom Stockton told me to tell you again that if anything happens to Jim, you must take care of him. If he is killed, you must send his body home, if possible. No difference about the expense. He said he would pay all costs.

I shall look for you home some before long. According to the Signs, you will have to come about the <u>first</u> of the month instead of the 10th, now as things have changed, but come some time. It's no difference, when you do you get here. The girls are hurrying me. They are ready to go to school and post office. I got no letter today. I'm most blue. Write often and I will. Good bye, dear.

Your Own, Em

The Death of Josh Gardner, the Carpenter
The Death of Frank Taylor, the Drummer
All the Best Friends I Had Here Have Been Killed Or Died

Rear of Vicksburg, Mississippi
June 26, 1863

Dear Wife,

I wrote you a letter a few days ago, but as I know you are anxious to hear from me often, I will try to write again today. I love to sit down to write to you – would do it oftener if I had time. I don't write to anyone except you, and no one writes to me but you. I think I have not got a letter for five weeks from anyone else. Well, I don't care, do you? I think Alvah[1] might take a little more interest in his friends in the army than he does. He has owed me a letter for three months at least. But I suppose he is so busy with his great legal business that he scarcely ever thinks of us away here in the army. I have no idea that he does. He has never written to me yet except when he wanted me to attend to some law business here for him, which I did as well as I could. I am sure I did not serve him so when he was away, and you may tell him so if you like. Till has owed me a letter for three months or more. And Tom has never answered that letter, part of which he printed, and never will, I reckon, I have not heard a word from any of our folks in Des Moines County since the 26th of May.

So you see there is nobody cares for me but you. And as all the best friends I had here have been killed or died, I don't know what I should do if it were not for getting a dear good letter from you once in a while. Even Lieutenant Gardner[2], whom I got to see occasionally, was mortally wounded a few days ago. I suppose you got Ol's letter to Sallie which will tell you all about the fight the 4th Cavalry were in and I need not repeat it. But Wils Payne went to see Lieutenant Gardner yesterday and found him still alive and some better. He was sensible but unable to talk. He was on board a hospital boat and going to start home – he may live to get there, and may possibly recover. I do hope he will at least live to get home. His body will be sent home at any rate. Now you must not think I have got the blues, for so long as I know you love me and think about me, and write to me, I don't care for anyone else.

I feel very well today, but I have had three chills in the last three days; I haven't taken any medicine for it yet. There is a great deal of ague in the regiment and no medicine at present.

I got a pass last Sunday and went over to Young's Point to see if I could find Jont and do anything for him. I found that he had been gone up the river two days. He went to St. Louis. I hope that if Ma is not gone home by the time he gets there she will find him and get leave to take him home. He started on the 19th inst. If I could have had him brought over here or could have gone to him in time, I think I could have had him discharged. I hope he will soon get it anyhow. But I can do nothing for him now.

The two days I was gone over there and yesterday when I went to the Landing and to the Division Hospital are the only three days I have not been under fire and had bullets and sometimes shells flying around me since the 16th of May. I have become so accustomed to it that I don't mind it much. Our mortar and siege guns throw shells into the city every night and frequently there is brisk musketry firing on some parts of the line. But it does not interfere with my sleeping unless our company is ordered out.

We are still gaining slowly on the rebels; we have got possession of their work in two or three places, which gives us quite an advantage. We are getting up more siege guns and planting new batteries. We shelled them from all the guns yesterday afternoon and blew up two of their forts that we had undermined. We are all confident that they cannot hold out many days longer. We are not in the least uneasy about Johnston attacking us in the rear. We wish he would. It is reported that he has now crossed Black River with 60,000 men. Sherman has gone back to meet him with a strong force. We are all confident that he can defeat any force they can bring.

We are all anxious to hear the news from Pennsylvania. The last we got was rather alarming. The rebs had got into Pennsylvania[3] and Harrisburg and Philadelphia were in danger. I hope we will not lose there all that we gain here. There is sharp firing on both since just now and the bullets from the rebels whistle over our tent thick. The weather is still very hot and dry.

I got a letter from you today. I was glad to get it. We had had two mails before and I didn't get any. This was dated the 15th and I was very glad to hear that you were all well. I am really sorry that your garden does so poorly; I hope it will rain yet and you will have plenty of everything. I am sorry Nellie and Lulie could not go to the show. I will take them to see one when I go home. I am glad to hear that they are learning to read so fast. I think they are real smart. They must be good girls at school and on the way to school, and never do anything that their Ma or the teacher tells them not to.

Then they must learn to wash the dishes and sweep the floor, and to sew and knit, and sing. I think you might take Tommy to Sunday School; it is too bad to make him stay home all the time. He must get very lonesome when the girls are gone to school all the time. I expect he has got to be a great big boy by this time. I wish I could get home and see you all, and I will if possible, but I think it somewhat doubtful if I can, even after the fight is over. So you must not be disappointed if you do not see me soon. I know that I deserve to go as much as any officer in the regiment.

I think you had better get some bran and feed the new cow, and water her well; if she is worth $22 she is worth feeding and it will not do to let her die. I wonder that they could ask such a price. I do not think it is your duty to keep Susan[4]. You certainly have enough to attend to without, and I have a family of my own to support, and a very hard way to earn the money to do it with. I think we have earned all we have very dearly. The state has provided an institution for such cases as hers. They helped her once. I think they should send her there immediately.

You have no doubt heard before this that it is so that Whippo is killed, and James Stockton. That neighborhood seems to be very unfortunate. Billy[5] is better and will get well. He has gone to St. Louis. I hope he will be allowed to go home. Ol[5] was here day before yesterday. He is now detailed as orderly to General Sherman, which is a very good position, and a good thing for him. He will not have so much to do now nor be exposed to so much danger.

I got a letter from Ma dated about the 1st of May. She said she was going to start home in a day or two and I was surprised to hear that she had gone with the regiment.

I have just heard that we are to be paid off tomorrow. We will get two months' pay. I suppose we will send it to Saunders' Bank again, but I think I shall advise them not to publish the amount each one sends. I will have to commence tomorrow to make a new set of payrolls, and quarterly returns and reports, and will be very busy for some time without having anything to do with the fight.

I am glad there is going to be plenty of blackberries. You must get some. I do hope it will not be long before I can sit down and eat some of your good cooking. It will cost $100 to make the trip, but I won't stop for that. You must write every chance, and write long letters.

Your own, Jake

I do not remember that I ever sent Mr. Taylor a copy of Frank's[6] final statement. I will enclose it in this and you may hand it to them. It may be of some use. When I come to think of it again, I have sent a final statement to Mr. Taylor.

1. Alvah Bereman, whom Jacob accused of lack of interest in the war effort, was an older brother of Emeline. He had been the Prosecuting Attorney for Henry County and served in the Iowa State Legislature. He had also served as Mayor of Mt. Pleasant for a period in the 1850s. Previously he had served as a Captain of the Regular Army 18th Infantry, but resigned this commission because of a leg wound received at Shiloh. Despite Jacob's insinuations, in 1864 the Governor of Iowa appointed Alvah Colonel of the 45th Iowa Infantry.

2. This is a reference to carpenter Joshua Gardner, Second Lieutenant of Company K of the 4th Iowa Cavalry who had spent time talking to Jacob in Jacob's tent on November 25, 1862. He had been mortally wounded June 23, 1863, at Bear Creek, Mississippi and died of those wounds on June 30, 1863, in Memphis, Tennessee.

3. As Confederate General Robert E. Lee and the rebel army crossed into Pennsylvania, many thought their target might be Harrisburg, the capital of Pennsylvania, or Philadelphia. Instead, the battle was fought at Gettsyburg, Pennsylvania, during July 1-3, 1863, the last few days of the siege of Vicksburg.

4. Susannah Ritner was Jacob's sister, who previously had been admitted to the State Insane Asylum located in Mt. Pleasant. Jacob is suggesting that Susannah go back to the Asylum.

5. Billy Bereman, Emeline's brother in the 4th Iowa Cavalry, had been wounded May 29, 1863 near Mechanicsburg, Mississippi. The 4th Iowa Cavalry now served as Sherman's escort, and Ol, another of Emeline's brothers, became an orderly in Sherman's staff. (James R. Arnold, *Grant Wins the War*, page 321)

6. Benjamin Frank Taylor, who had enlisted as a drummer, died of disease April 1, 1863 in St. Louis.

[Mt. Pleasant, Iowa]
Thursday night
July the 2nd, 1863

Dear Husband,
    I wrote you day before yesterday and promised to write again

soon. In that letter I sent you two checks of $50 each which Stockton gave me to send to you to pay for Jim's coffin. He said for you to keep all that was over, sell the check to some sutler[1] or somebody that has money. But I suppose that you will get the letter all safe and then you will know all the particulars.

I received a letter from you today dated June 20th and was so glad you were alive and well. If you could only keep to, I should not mind the length of time so much. But the <u>uncertainty</u> is enough to drive me crazy. When will they take Vicksburg? And when will the war end? are questions that are heard continuously and are of vital importance to almost everyone. Oh, if we could only hear that Vicksburg was over <u>certain</u> the people would almost go wild with joy. But you all assure us that it will be before long. We have been looking for it every day for the last five or six weeks and maybe we will have to wait that much longer.

We are still all well. I am not very stout but think I will get along if I don't "work" too hard. Every little thing I do or walk up town I feel tired nearly to death. It is so hot and dry that I am really afraid it will be sickly. We haven't had but one little thunder shower this summer that I can remember. Indeed it hasn't rained enough to wet the ground more than an inch deep all summer, and not but a very few times that much. Everything nearly is done up. The corn has looked pretty well till within the last few days but today all curled up and looks as though it would die. A few more days will finish it. I am afraid we will have no potatoes at all. They don't grow scarcely any. They blossom when they were not much higher than your hand, of course they will not be worth much. I had a small mess of beans and potatoes the other day. The potatoes are an early kind. We have no cabbage at all. It has been so dry and the cut worms so bad that I couldn't get them to stand. The chickens were very bad and them too. I have only 17 growing chickens. I have a proudly nice patch of melons and cucumbers. Hope you will get here before the melons are all gone. I have them at the kitchen window so that I can watch the boys off. The lot all over is very clean, no weed to be seen, but the dust is a half foot deep all over it. I never saw such a time. There isn't a bit of grass for the cows. The ground is perfectly bare. We have begun to feed the cows corn. I don't like to do it but she will starve if we don't. We have only one little pig left, all died but it. It looks very nice. I have had the corn plowed twice. Guess I won't have it plowed any more if it don't rain. The most of it is as high as Nellie's head. I commenced killing the chickens off, but the garden isn't going to be any account, so I will keep the chickens . . .

The folks are making some preparations for the 4th. I hardly know what, haven't seen the bills. I guess the Sunday schools are all going to meet out at the campground and there is going to be speaking in Saunders Grove. Don't know what I will do. Tom Stockton is coming down for, is about to go up there to Jim's funeral which will be next Sunday. Ma and Sallie are going. Don't know whether I shall or not. My former boarders have all left and we are quite by ourselves. Ma had gone to keeping house. Went home the next day after she came. Zan has gone and Car, Lulie went home with Car. So you see, we are all alone. I guess Car will go and live with Ma next fall. I think Ma hated to come home from Missouri. She said she enjoyed herself so much there and had such a nice time. That Old Eye doctor of Lulie's that run off from London will be at the Brazelton house next Saturday. I have half a notion and go and demand that $15 that you paid him, for he didn't cure her eyes. We don't know anything about Billy yet, except that we heard he was at Memphis. Don't know whether he is bad or not. We are all so anxious to hear from him.

Poor Jont. I am afraid he will never get well. I wish you could send him home. I don't see why they don't let him come. He will never be able to do anything. The last we heard of Ike he was at Helena.

We got a letter not long since. Haven't heard from your folks since Zan went home. I must write to them soon. I saw Captain Smith the day that he sent me that letter. I talked to him about it. Oh! he [said he] did feel so bad about it, but he concluded it was your fault for you had packed it away with your business papers, that [he] didn't take time [to] look for a week after he come home. I guess he will go in to the school again, as Mr. Gunn made a failure and isn't going to teach any more.

I wish you will tell us something more about Freeman's death. You never said whether you buried him, nor how, nor whether you saw him fall or not, nor whether he ever said anything about being killed before he went into the battle. If there is anything you do not wish Car to know about it, tell me and I will not tell her. I heard by some means that he had crawled away and tried to pour water from his canteen on his wound. Poor Jim!! And poor soldiers, all of them.

This sheet is packed full of stuff. I guess you would have another like it. Please send me a lick of your hair in your next, will you? If you can spare it. You talk about being bald-headed and ugly. You

ought to see me. I am getting "grey." It is time. If you don't come
back pretty soon, you won't know me. I will be an old woman.

Your Own, Em

1. A sutler was a civilian traveling merchant assigned to the regi-
    ment, appointed by the governor of the state or by regimental or
    brigade officers. Prices were to be set by the board of officers,
    but many sutlers were accused of outrageous profiteering.

[Fragment]
[Mt. Pleasant, Iowa]
[July 1863]

[Dear Jacob,]

Lieutenant Gardner's body arrived yesterday morning while we
were at the depot to see Ma off. George Mason came with it. He
said he lived till he got to Memphis. I don't know whether he ever
spoke or not. Poor Josh, and poor Beck. I stopped to see her a few
minutes as we came home on Monday. She had just got the news
on Saturday of his wound, and the evening before I was there, she
heard he was dead. She seemed as though she couldn't stomach it.
Oh, it must be very hard to bear. I, through the mercy of God, have
been spared that pain so far, but perhaps it will be my time yet. But,
I pray that I may escape it.

There is one thing that I have never spoken to you about. If you
should fall, I want your precious remains sent home. I have always
thought that I couldn't stand it, but I believe I would be better satisfied. I have often thought that I would write to Lieutenant Steele
to that effect, to have you sent home if anything should happen to
you, but some how I have always felt that you would get home
alive, that you would be preserved through all the dangers and
return to us at last, but I have no right to think so. I know that you
are as much exposed to death as any of them and I thought however painful to think of, and or speak about, to be prepared for whatever comes. If you are still alive and well when this reaches you,
perhaps it will not be best to tell Lieutenant Steele, and I hope you
will not be in any more danger soon, if ever. But, there is no telling
when sickness or another battle may over take you. You may show
him, or some of the boys, this, or tell them what my wishes are, but
I hope and pray it may never be necessary for them to comply with
my request. But, it may be – Yet I don't feel so. May our Father in

heaven spare our lives to meet again in this world and spend many happy hours together. I have expected you right away after taking Vicksburg. But, if you can't come I will try and be satisfied. Indeed I could be satisfied till the end of the war if I were sure to have you home alive, then & well.

We are all well. I have got about as well as usual. You never told me that Baron was Lieutenant. Collie told me yesterday. I suppose you thought I knew it. Write often, and tell me all about your Company boys. I feel as though they were all my relations. Sometimes I think I can't wait a week for a letter especially when you are in such a place and you have been for the last 6 or 7 weeks – Goodbye, dear, and take good care of yourself.

Yours, Em

My pen is so bad.

Vicksburg Falls

Rear of Vicksburg
July 4, 1863

Dear Emeline,

Vicksburg has at last surrendered. We have taken the whole thing. A flag of truce was raised yesterday afternoon, and proposals made to surrender, but the thing was not concluded till this morning. We are very glad it is over. And yet we would just as lieve they had held out till this evening. We had got everything all ready to give them a grand 4th of July serenade today – one they would not forget for a while. We had a lot of heavy siege guns planted that have not been fired yet. And every gun on our whole line was to open this morning and fire just as fast as possible till ordered to stop. I guess the rebels had an idea of what was coming and concluded to quit in time. This will be another feather in the cap of Old 4th of July. I hope you are having a good time today celebrating the 4th. I wish we had a telegraph from here to there so you could get the good news.

We are taking it very quiet here today. There has not been a gun fired since yesterday evening. Both sides are on the breastworks looking at each other. The rebels seem very much down in the mouth. I suppose part of our force will march in and take possession before long, if they have not already done so.

As for the 25th, there seems to be no rest for us; we now have orders to be ready to march with ten days rations at a moment's notice. I suppose we go back to fight Johnston, if we can find him[1]. I thought I would drop you a few lines in haste, as I do not know what minute we will have to start.

We have been paid off again and I sent a package to the bank as usual. I sent $120.00. You can have it credited on the bank book. I have kept enough to take me home, but there is not much prospect that I will get there soon – can't tell anything about it. I have not heard from you since I last wrote. I look for a letter everyday.

I had two light chills and one real hard shake this week. But I think I have it broken now.

I have been very busy making muster and payrolls for a while. I am about through now for a while. You have no idea how hot and sultry the weather is here – one can hardly live in the sun in the middle of the day. I don't know what we will do if we have to march; I shall try it. A great many in the regiment are sick. Charley (now sergeant) Payne has been quite sick but is better; Samuel Garvin is quite sick, and Joshua Carpenter, Alvin Lock, Samuel Miller, Francis Waitman, James J. Jeffrey, William Fleagle[2], my clerk, and some others. Corporal David Coiner[3] shot himself yesterday through the wrist, and his hand was cut off at Division Hospital without any necessity whatever, as I think it was a sad accident.

I cannot give you any more particulars now about the surrender. I don't know how many prisoners there are or what amount of arms, &c, you will get all that in the papers. How I wish that all of Company B was here to enjoy the victory. I don't feel much like rejoicing. It takes off a great deal of the pleasure to me to think what it cost to win the victory. May their names to be remembered with honor and pride by a grateful people.

We have not heard anything from Captain Smith since he left. I am in hopes that something will turn up so that we will not have to go on the march, as we have been in front and in the rifle pits during the whole siege. It is perfectly astonishing to see the amount of work that has been done here by both sides. It would pay anyone to go a thousand miles just to see the works, the miles and miles of rifle pits, and breastwork, and the batteries and forts. But we have taken Vicksburg; and the 25th Iowa had a prominent share in the work – we are all proud of it now.

If we start today, I don't know when I will get to write again – if we don't, I will write in a few days. I hope this will find you all well. You must take good care of the children. Give my respects to Caroline and to Ma, if she is there. Tell them I often think of them both. I have not heard from Jont or Billy . . .

Your own, Jake

1. Confederate General Joseph E. Johnston was in the area and would soon occupy the previously captured Mississippi capital, Jackson.

2. Sergeant Samuel Garvin, Francis Waitman, John Jeffrey, and William Fleagle all survived the war. Joshua Carpenter, Alvin Lock, and Samuel Miller were all discharged for disability.

3. Corporal David Coiner, age 21, was discharged for wounds on July 29, 1863.

Vicksburg Falls – Mt. Pleasant

[Mt. Pleasant, Iowa]
Friday Morning
July the 10th, 1863

Dear Jacob,

I received a letter from you yesterday dated June 26th and was so glad to hear that you were alive and well. But you said you had had two chills, now I am afraid you are not so well as you pretend. Any person that has the chills don't feel very well. I know by experience. You must take medicine and not expose yourself more than you can help, for you will have them all summer. But to the all important subject, <u>Vicksburg has surrendered</u> at last. What glorious news!!! The people weep for joy and are wild with excitement. I suppose it is true this time for certain. We got the news here on Tuesday last between one and two o'clock, I guess. The girls had all gone to school and I was washing the dishes when I heard a church bell ringing. I didn't know what it meant, as there was no meeting. They rang it by jerks as though they were pounding it with a stick. In a few minutes every bell in town was ringing, the flags were flying, cannon roaring and men and boys shouting, horses and cowbells were making all the noise they could. I couldn't stand it. I thought I must go up and see what was the matter. Before I got halfway up, I heard that <u>Vicksburg had surrendered</u>. What joyous news! We had been <u>so</u> anxious and expecting it so long that it seemed almost too good to be true. I couldn't help but rejoice yet I felt so sad to think, how many brave boys we had lost there, and perhaps there are more that we haven't heard of yet, as your last letter was dated eight days before you got possession of the place. The report is that they surrendered the fourth of July at ten o'clock. I hope you had a glorious fourth in the city.

I understand that General Steele's division was the first to enter. I imagine I see the boys pouring in from every direction cheering and shouting and in the "highest" of spirits. You must write and tell me all about it. I do hope you will get to rest now awhile, but I am afraid you will be sent on to Port Hudson.

Some of the Old Copperheads got "cheered" that afternoon that we got the news. About 20 little boys got old cowbells and ran over to old Hill's and nearly deafened him with the noise. He got mad and shook his fist at them, would have thrashed them if he had tried to. From there they went to Goodman's and Lashes. The men made all three of these rebels put up the Stars and Stripes over their buildings. That night we had cannonading and the grandest fireworks I ever saw. The news from Penn.[1] is very good now, so that all Union people have great reason to be encouraged.

Ma and Sallie Nickle started after Billy and Jont yesterday morning. Billy is still in Memphis yet. Sallie Nickle will go on to see him and Ma will stop for Jont at St. Louis. They will bring them both home if they can get them. I am sorry you didn't get there in time to see Jont and get him discharged –

The Fourth passed off rather okay here, at least it did for me. They had a meeting in Saunders Grove. Several speeches made, &c, cannonading, &c and basket dinner afterward. I took the children and went down awhile. Saw the crowd (which was very great) heard some of the speaking though I was not close enough to hear much. We came away before it was over and got dinner at home, lunch. Jim Roberts and family went up all that day. Uncle Jim sent his best respects to you. Said he was going to write you a letter, was ashamed how he hadn't written sooner, &c. That afternoon Ma and I and Sallie went up to Jefferson.

Tom Stockton came after us to go up to James' funeral. It was preached by Mr. Wilson from Missouri. He brought us back on Monday. There was a great crowd there. Tom told me to give you his best wishes every time I write to you. He thinks he can never be kind enough to you for sending Jimmie home. He gives me about ten bushels of bran to feed my cow, hauled it down and wouldn't have any pay. They feel very bad about Bob being prisoner. He is no Copperhead about Tom. Some are a little suspicious of Robert (I mean Robert the senior). There has been no rain here since I last wrote to you. It has been very hot for awhile back. All my corn, garden is about to die. The ground is so loose and dry that it can't live much longer if it don't rain.

Em

1. Emeline is referring to the Union victory at Gettysburg, Pennsylvania over Robert E. Lee.

From Eleanor Bereman to Alvah Bereman (her son)

St. Louis, Missouri [where Eleanor was working as a nurse]
July 25, 1863

Dear Alvah,

I again seat myself to let you know how we are getting along. Billy's[1] arm is a little better. As far for his shoulder, it is no better. It swells up every few days then goes down his arm to his elbow. The hole in his back looks better today, but the one in front is swollen very much. They both run considerable. It seems to pain him most at night. Don't sleep much.

Jont[2] is not as well today as he has been. He feels little like talking. The chills, he had them on the boat when coming up the River. He told the Dr on the boat about it. He told him he had no opportunity to give him medicine till they got to St. Louis. He says if it hadn't been for Albeck Martin[3], he doesn't think he could have stood the trip. Albeck left the steamer in his __ and gave it to Jont and lay on a board himself so you see how a poor soldier is treated.

The poor soldier who gives up his life . . . does all the hard marching through cold and heat, does all the hard fighting loses his health, his limbs and dies and is no more thought of. He was nothing but a soldier and is soon forgotten. But, the ones that get the big pay are the ones that are honored and Remembered.

I sometimes think that if our Government had been worth so much it would have been better for us. There would not have been so many heartless scamps in office as what there are. But, men that would go for the good of their country are not the many and the ones that would have had instead of those, we have. I have seen so little regard paid to the soldier that I am disgusted with every big officer I see and that is quite often here lately. I am so tired tonight I can hardly get up to write this letter . . .

Write soon, E. H. Bereman

I got some milk this morning for the boys and must go and take it to them. I have milk mainly every day. They can't drink tea or coffee. Sallie[4] has been sick a couple of days, but is better this morning. I got over little yesterday coming home from the city. I don't feel very well.

1. Billy Bereman of the 4th Iowa Cavalry had been wounded on May 29, 1863, at Mechanicsburg, Mississippi. He later transferred to the Invalid Corps, but then returned to service and was mustered out December 4, 1864, at the expiration of his term of service. The Invalid Corps was for men recovering from wounds or illness, who were later expected to return to active service. The Invalid Corps also utilized the limited capabilities of men who could never return to full active duty, but who could do many behind-the-line jobs in their own units, hospitals, or prison camps.

2. Jont Bereman of Company B of the 25th Iowa Infantry had been ill for some time. He would soon return to Mt. Pleasant.

3. This is probably a reference to Alexander Martin of the 25th Iowa Infantry, who also was transferred to the Invalid Corps.

4. Sarah "Sallie" Bereman, Emeline's sister and Eleanor's daughter, had accompanied Eleanor to St. Louis to serve as a Union nurse

• After the successful siege and capture of Vicksburg, Sherman and the 15th Army Corps began a July 6 march back to Jackson, Mississippi, which they had previously captured in May. In Jackson, Confederate General Joseph E. Johnston had concentrated a force of 31,000 men. During this march, the Union soldiers continued to forage for food, and the troops no longer gave receipts for supplies taken as they had done previously.

Union forces shelled Jackson, and on the night of July 16, Johnston's army evacuated the city in the face of the advancing Union Army, burning factories and warehouses as they exited the city. The Union Army occupied the city, and further spread the fires.

Camp Near Black River Bridge, Mississippi
August 2, 1863

Dear Wife,

I take my pen to write you a few lines this evening to send home by Mr. Saunders[1], who starts tomorrow. If you got that book I sent you I guess you won't want much more from me soon— have you got it read through yet? I am scarce of paper yet, as you see. I have to use some that I had ruled for a muster-roll. I have not had a letter from you for so long I can't remember. I know that I got none either of the three last mails we got. But then I hope to see you before very long and then you will tell me all the news, won't you? That will be so much better than all the letters you could write in a month. I don't know yet for certain whether I will get to go or not, or when. But I think I will be at home by the middle of this month. I am working with all my might to get ready. And think a great deal of the pleasure I shall have in seeing you all once more, if it is only for a short time. I have been writing for the last three days all day and a good part of the night. It is now after ten o'clock.

We did not camp on Bear Creek as we expected when I wrote to you last, but we moved down here and came so slowly and there was so much delay that it has only been three days that I have had my tent and book-box so I could go to work. We have a very poor place to camp—on a sharp ridge with very little shade and ¾ of a mile to water. However our tent happened to come in a pretty good place, under a sassafras tree that makes a fine shade. We are right on the railroad, and about 1½ miles from Black River. The cars run regularly two or three times a day from here to Vicksburg, but I have not had a chance to go there yet.

Colonel Stone is there sick, and Lieutenant Colonel Palmer[2] is in command of the regiment. I have not had the ague any more but am not really well yet, though I am getting better. If I had a chance I would have my picture taken just as I look on a march, and see if it would be so <u>handsome</u> you would not know me!! I guess you would think I was a hard looking case. Did you know I am getting gray? But then I expect to show you the original some of these days.

I have your picture all right yet. I have carried it with me every place I have been yet. What have you done with mine? I have been working at my "muster-out-and-in" rolls so as to be mustered as captain before I go away—it takes a great deal of writing. But I think I will get that through tomorrow. Then I have my quarterly returns of clothing, &c and ordnance return, &c. to make out yet, besides final statements, sick leaves, furloughs, descriptive lists, &c to make, and clothing to draw for the men. But it all won't take me many days to get ready if I am not tied up with red tape. I shall be very much disappointed if I do not get to go. But officers, I hear, get only 29 days leave of absence out of the department—this will give me only 20 days from Memphis. So I am afraid I will not see much satisfaction with you and the children after all.

I must stop a day or so in St. Louis and see if I can do anything for Jont and Billy and some more of my men who are there, and then by the time I get home and attend to my business it will be time to start back. I think I can get furloughs for four men from the company—don't know who they will be yet. Billy Degroodt is quite sick and I am trying to get him home on "sick leave." Lieutenant Steele and all the men who were left at Vicksburg are out here now. Jolliff[3] and N. Hite[4] are quite sick; several others have the ague yet, but the health is improving rapidly. But I must stop. I have written this in great haste. If I should succeed in getting away as soon as I expect I will not write again—if I can't get off, I will let you know. Have the chickens fat and put on the big pot. I want to get fat while I am there. Tell the children I will bring them something—and maybe I will have something for you.

Your own, Jake

1. Mr. Saunders had been visiting the troops as part of the Iowa Sanitary Agency.

2. David Palmer, age 23, had been officially promoted from Captain to Lieutenant Colonel on June 9, 1863. The previous Lieutenant Colonel, Fabian Brydolf, age 44, had resigned on June 8.

3. Thomas J. Jolliff was able to return to Mt. Pleasant.

4. Nathan Hite, who had been captured and paroled near Arkansas Post with his brother Robert, was transferred to the Invalid Corps on October 1, 1863. No further information on Nathan could be found.

• In the late summer of 1863, Grant began to leave his army scattered in captured towns, doing garrison duty. Grant himself went to New Orleans for an inspection of Union forces that since early in the war had controlled the city. In his absence, Sherman was in charge of the Army of the Tennessee, but still was operating under Grant's orders. While in New Orleans, Grant was injured when he fell off his horse. Some say that Grant's horse was frightened by a streetcar, while others say that Grant tumbled off his steed because he was drunk. (Lloyd Lewis, *Sherman, Fighting Prophet*, pages 304-309)

[Mt. Pleasant, Iowa]
Aug the 7th, 1863

Dear Jacob,

I expect you have been looking for a letter from me for some time and I am sorry that I have not written sooner, but I will tell you why. I went up to Jefferson last Saturday to pick blackberries and didn't get home till yesterday and had no chance to write while there. We went to the timber two days for berries. I canned up 18 qts., not as many as I expected to get as it was such hard work and I couldn't find anybody that wanted to sell any, though there were hundreds of bushels sold at Marshall's . . .

But I must tell you the good news. We have had 2 or 3 heavy rains in the last few days, which is the only we have had since last spring of any consequence. Everything was about dried up. You couldn't tell that the prairie had ever been green and all, but the grass has started to grow again and I hope we will soon have feed for the cows.

Well, I must tell you some more. While I was gone, Ma by some means got a furlough for the boys and came home, every one of them. Jont is very low but is a little better than when he first came. He and his wife are at Alvah's. He is not able to be moved any place yet, looks dreadful poor and has such a bad cough. Billy is at Ma's. He is able to walk around but looks very poor, too. His wounds don't seem to be getting well very fast, though he is in no danger, I think. Now, Dear, if I had you here I think I would be satisfied. What has become of you anyhow? I have had only one <u>piece</u> of a letter from you for over three weeks. That <u>piece</u> was written on a half sheet of an old day book while at Jackson. (I was very glad to get that much I assure you.) You were then, ready to start on an expedition of 45 miles. Since then I haven't heard a word from you. I am so sorry that you went when you were not able. How I wish you could lay by awhile and rest. I am so anxious to hear again. It seems as though I will never get any more letters. Sometimes I think that maybe you are coming home but I try not to flatter myself with such hope, for I know it's hard for you to get off. I should not be surprised though to see you step in any day. The children all want to see you very much. They all are well except Nellie. She has a bad cough and has not been very well for sometime.

I believe I told you that Ike has come home and gone to Pella. We got a letter from Zan. They are still at Pella and Ike is very sick at Dr. Howard's. He has had the sinking chills but was getting some better expected to be down here in 8 or 10 days. The report at Pella is that Jim Ritner was killed at the Battle of Jackson, don't know whether it is true or not . . . Well, dear, I must quit. Do try and take good care of yourself and don't get clear down sick. Good bye.

Your own, Em

Jacob's Furlough

Colonel Stone granted Jacob granted his furlough in late August, and Jacob returned to Emeline in Mt. Pleasant for a brief, but longer-than-intended stay.

Chapter Four
Chattanooga, Tennessee

*Emeline's father, Samuel E. Bereman, was a member of the 37th
Iowa Infantry, nicknamed the Greybeard Regiment because it initially
only enlisted men too old for normal service. When Jacob returned to
Vicksburg after his furlough, his steamboat stopped for a few minutes
at Alton, Illinois, where the 37th Iowa was stationed to guard a Union
prison camp. When the boat docked, Jacob asked someone to notify
Samuel Bereman that he was to be in Alton for a few minutes. Samuel
came running to meet Jacob, but by the time he arrived at the pier,
Jacob's boat was pulling away. (Steve Meyer, Iowa Valor, page 484)*

[Mt. Pleasant, Iowa]
Sept. 19th, 1863

Dear Husband,

This is the "Sunday week" that I was to write to you and I
haven't heard a single word from you since you left except what
Father wrote. Ma got a letter from him the other day and he was
nearly mortified to death because he didn't get to see you. He had
been sick and lay abed that morning till somebody came and wakened him and told him that some person on a boat wanted to see
him. He jumped up as quick as possible and went down, but when
he got there the old boat had shoved off down the river so far that
he could not distinguish any person aboard. He felt so bad that he
cried like a child, thought they were the bitterest tears he ever shed,
and even while he was writing, the tears would flow in spite of him.
I felt real sorry for him, and want you write him a long letter and
explain why you didn't stop to see him. I suppose you didn't get to
write at St. Louis or I should have got it by this time. I am very anxious to hear how you got along . . .

Well, you ought to have stayed a week or two longer. The
Baptists had a grand festival last Tuesday night. There was a great
turnout and had a good time generally. Had oysters, ice cream,
peaches, lemonade, cake, &c. I was on the committee to deal out

peaches and ice cream so didn't get to see much fun. But, the committee of the whole concern had an oyster supper for their own especial benefit and didn't allow anybody else to come and on last Thursday evening. I was there, had many nice times. It was at Mrs. McClure's. Mr. & Mrs. Gunn were present. Colonel Swan and lady, Fryer, Ayers and several others. They adjourned to meet next Thursday evening at Colonel Swan's for the same purpose, that is, to have an oyster supper. Mrs. Swan says I must be sure to come, but it is too far unless you were here to go with me. They made $122 at the festival and cleared $68.00. It was held at the Union hall.

Lieutenant Crane & Lee have both quit shaking. I believe Lee intends starting next Wednesday. He wants to sell his house at any bid. Wonder if it is a good place for us to live. Don't know what his price is. He has a good house and lots of room around it and a considerable of fruit. If we could get it cheap, perhaps we could make it pay. I don't like the street much, but it is about as close to town as I would like. Yet Smith has sold out to a man by the name of Hunt. Mrs. Hunt is a Baptist, and a very fine woman—

I was at a wedding this morning. Mr. Gunn married a colored couple in church. It created quite a sensation. Monday morning. Just been out jawing to the old Dutch[1] woman for not bringing my wood . . . Can't get her to haul it at all, the old mean thing. Haven't engaged any for winter yet nor apples nor potatoes nor anything. Haven't sold the cows yet and don't expect I can sell Red at all. Corn is 50 ct. per bushel now. I am getting scared. Got your photograph. They are not good at all. The eyes are almost spoiled. I only took 9 of them. It was all that he had done at the time and I wouldn't take the rest. I believe I will send you one by Lee and let you see how it looks. You can send it back again. I want to get a letter so bad to hear from you how you got along. Mr. and Mrs. Gunn and Sarah Moore went for dinner Friday. I started the children to school this morning for school. Free School.

Em

---

1. As with many references to "Dutch" during that period, Emeline meant "Deutch" or German. Henry County had a large number of German-speaking people, whose parents had come from Germany. (Correspondence with Ann Crane Farrier)

This next letter is Jacob's first communication after returning from furlough. Unfortunately, Jacob stayed in Iowa longer than permission granted, and was reported "Absent Without Leave" for 24 days. But Jacob apparently was not alone in his late return—only 9 of 36 men on furlough had yet returned.

The Death of Jont Bereman, Emeline's Brother

Camp Sherman, Mississippi
September 20, 1863

Dear Wife,

This is Sunday . . . I got here yesterday evening after dark all safe and sound. They all say they never saw me look so well, or so fat and hearty. I do feel very well, and hope I will continue so. I had a very tedious time getting down river. I was eleven days on the way. But otherwise it was a very pleasant trip—the weather was fine and cool, and I had the good luck to get on a first-rate boat where we had the best of fare and accommodations every way. And if I had not been so anxious to get back, I would have enjoyed the trip first-rate. I did not have very much trouble with my boxes; everyone seemed ready to assist and accommodate me. I had more trouble to get them out here on the railroad from Vicksburg than all the rest of the way. They cost $21 to get them here. I found the men all anxiously looking for me and we had a great time last night opening the boxes and reading the letters. To see the pleasure and gratification it was to them more than repaid me for all the trouble I had to get things here, and I think it will be a real benefit to them. The health of the company has improved a great deal since I left.

The weather is quite cool and pleasant, and I think we will not have much more sickness. Lieutenant Steele and Sergeants Harlan & Yount are going to start home tomorrow—or next day and I will get one of them to call on you and tell you all the particulars about the men. Duran Nealey died here yesterday. Rich Kelly is very poorly just like Jont[1] was, before he went up the river. Degroodt is better but not able to do much yet. Only 9 out of the first 36 men that were furloughed from this regiment have yet returned, which is the reason we could send only two men now. If they had returned we could have sent five. I think they will get to go yet.

I find that I have been reported "absent without leave" for 24 days. But I think I can get it fixed up. I will have to report in writing to Brigade Head Quarters and give my reasons for staying so long. I think I can give a good excuse, don't you? It seems to me I was not at home any time hardly. I hardly got to see you and the children till the time to start away was so close at hand that I was all the time dreading to start and could get no satisfaction. I don't believe I will ever be so well satisfied in the army as I was before. I do wish the war was over so I could be at home with my dear, sweet wife. You don't know how hard it was to leave you all and go away that day, nor how lonesome I have felt ever since. I do hope the time will soon come when I can go back and get another good long—long sweet hug, like I did the day I got home that time. That paid up for a great deal of anxiety. But now I am away down here again in "Dixie" and all I can do is to remember you and love you, and live so as to be worthy of your love when I get back. It shall be my great care to do that.

I wouldn't give one of your sweet smiles and kisses for all the pleasures enjoyed in a life-time by those who spend their time drinking and gambling and carousing as a great many officers did on the way down[2]. I could not help wondering whether they had left a wife and children at home and whether they loved them. But I must tell you more about that some other time. I have got started now and would like to talk to you all day—don't you wish I could? But the men interrupt me so much coming to ask about their friends that I can't write. They have got two month's pay while I was away. But they would not pay any for me and they will not till I get my "absence" accounted for. This may take three or four months and perhaps only a few days. So I don't know when I get any money.

I have not seen Oliver yet. The 4th Cavalry is back here at their camp again. The boat only stopped a few minutes at Alton and I got a soldier to go and tell Father to come out, but before he got there we were so far from shore we could not speak. I saw him come running out and wave his hat. I was so sorry I didn't get to speak to him. I got a letter from him this morning written the same day. He says he felt like crying when he found the boat gone. I must write to him right away.

I found things changed around here a good deal. General Osterhaus[3] now commands our division. And our department has been put into an Iowa Brigade composed of the 4th, 9th, 25th, 26th, 30th, and 31st Iowa commanded by Colonel Williamson[3] of the 4th Iowa. We have division drill once, and brigade drill twice a week. I do not think we will be moved from here soon[4]. I do not think of anything now that I would like to have sent by Lieutenant Steele. I haven't had time to look around much yet. I will write again next

Sunday. I am so anxious to hear from you all. I hope Kitty has got well, and Nellie too. Kiss them all for me and tell them Pa loves them . . .

Your own, Jake

1. Jont Bereman made it back to Mt. Pleasant, but died of disease on August 22, 1863.

2. Some of the riverboats that transported the troops up and down the Mississippi River also transported prostitutes. (Thomas P. Lowry, M.D., *The Story the Soldiers Wouldn't Tell—Sex in the Civil War*)

3. Prussian-born General Peter Osterhaus replaced General Frederick Steele as commander of the 1st Division of the 15th Army Corps. Williamson was to lead Jacob's brigade for the Chattanooga and Atlanta campaigns. In 1895, Williamson received the Medal of Honor for his actions at Chickasaw Bayou.

4. On September 9, 1863, Union General Rosecrans, leading the Army of the Cumberland, occupied Chattanooga, Tennessee, which was recognized by many as the gateway to the South. With Vicksburg, this gave the Union forces the two most important strategic locations in the western Confederacy. General Burnside, with the Army of the Ohio, then captured Knoxville, Tennessee.

    Rosecrans continued his movements, but on September 19th and 20th, Confederate General Braxton Bragg caught Rosecrans and his troops in scattered positions, and thoroughly routed the Union forces at Chickamauga Creek, located south of Chattanooga. The Union Army lost 16,000 troops as killed, wounded, or captured out of 60,000 at the Battle of Chickamauga. Union General George H. Thomas's wing withstood the Confederate attacks, preventing a possible loss of the entire Union force, earning Thomas the nickname the "Rock of Chickamauga." Rosecrans then retreated with his army back to Chattanooga.

    Bragg allowed the Union forces to retreat north into Chattanooga, thinking they would soon retreat again, away from Chattanooga. Bragg's subordinates were extremely critical of Bragg for letting the Union retreat into Chattanooga, believing he missed an opportunity to complete the rout of the Union troops. Bragg's plan was to regroup his Confederates, then attack the Union Army during the anticipated second retreat, away from Chattanooga. When the second Union retreat did not occur, Bragg chose to not attack Chattanooga, but instead began a siege strategy, hoping to eventually starve the Union Army into submission.

Back in Chattanooga, the Union forces began to regroup. Lincoln was content to have Rosecrans secure Chattanooga, but Rosecrans himself, even after a series of successful battles, was unable to recover his self-confidence and presence of command after the loss at Chickamauga. Lincoln urged Rosecrans and Burnside to pursue the Confederates, but Rosecrans would not move. His responses to Lincoln contained little in military strategy but avowals of faith such as, "We must put our trust in God who never fails those who truly trust." Lincoln's famous complaint was, that since his defeat at Chickamauga, Rosecrans had been acting "confused and stunned like a duck hit on the head."

Lincoln then ordered Grant to bring his Army of the Tennessee from Vicksburg to Chattanooga to break the siege. Because Grant was still bed-ridden in New Orleans from the injuries received from his tumble from his horse, Grant placed Sherman in charge of organizing that movement.

On the Way to Chattanooga

Steamer *Sultana*[1]
September 26, 1863

Dear Emeline,

I wrote to you last Sunday and told you my trip down the river and how I found the men. This is Saturday evening and I will write a few lines again for fear I do not have a chance tomorrow. My health is still very good and so is that of most of the men. Harlan is not very well. Billy Degroodt is better. But I must tell you what has happened since I last wrote to you.

We were roused up Monday morning at 2 o'clock and ordered to march at 4, with one days rations[2]. I went with the company. We went 10 miles beyond Black River, and back to camp before night. It was pretty rough on me after resting so long, but I stood it about as well as the rest of them. It was a hard day on us all. We expected to gobble up some guerrillas but they weren't there.

Tuesday morning Lieutenant Steele started home, and at noon we got orders to be prepared to move the whole "shebang" "at a moment's notice."[3] This astonished us all greatly. We didn't expect anything of the kind. Not a man had heard anything of it, "at the Spring" or the depot, or the Sutler's, nor any other places where they generally get the news before the general does! Every man felt dead beat!! Company B was just getting into the merits of the good things I brought down and thought we ought to have been consulted, but we weren't! We got orders to be at the railroad at 4 o'clock on Wednesday morning, so we got up at 2 o'clock, took down our tents, packed up, and were at the railroad before daylight, lay there all day and till midnight before we got off. The whole division was moving and we were the last to get away.

We got to Vicksburg at 2 o'clock in the morning and lay in the street till morning, when we were ordered on board the *Sultana*. Up to this time none of us knew more than a fool whether we were going up or down river or sideways! But we had an idea we were wanted badly someplace or other, by the way they hurried us around.

We now found that Bragg had whipped Rosecrans in Tennessee, and we are going to reinforce him. I suppose there is going to be another big fight out there some place and it can't come off now till we get there. We have met a great many boats going down empty, and I suppose a great many more troops will be sent up.

Well, I suppose if Grant's army has to whip the whole Southern Confederacy, the sooner we get at it, the sooner we will be through[4]. For my part I think we have done our share, but if they can't get along without us I am ready to go in again—and may God defend the right, and continue his protecting care, for the sake of my dear family at home.

We are on the flag-boat, with General Osterhaus and staff. He says he selected us to go on the boat with him because we are the best disciplined and cleanest regiment in the division. So we have been trying to "look smart" and behave ourselves, so as to keep up our credit, and we succeed very well. We all like Osterhaus much better than we did Steele. He is quite "common." I had a long talk with him[5]. We are ahead of the rest of the fleet and will be the first regiment to reach Memphis. We will get there some time tonight, and I suppose will start immediately for Chattanooga. But don't know—we may go on to Louisville. If you watch the papers for Osterhaus' Division you will learn our whereabouts sooner than from my letters.

The "boys" got all their "good things" on the boat, and are having a fine time—they will get the good of them at last. The boat trembles so I can hardly write. I must stop for the present as it is bedtime. I will write to you every chance while we are on the move. You must be sure to keep on writing to me. You need not direct to any place but to the regiment and division. I am looking for a letter now. Haven't got any yet. Don't forget to think of and pray for

Your Jake

I did not get to see Oliver. I heard he was still at Sherman's Headquarters and well. All furloughs are stopped for the present and none of our company will get home! How do you like my pictures? I expect it will be several months before I can get any pay, because I stayed over my time.

1. Immediately after the war, on April 27, 1865, the *Sultana* exploded and sank near Memphis while transporting former Union prisoners of war back north. Over 1,500 men died in this largest marine disaster in United States history.

2. Union troops were looking for Confederate General Joseph E. Johnston.

3. The Army of the Tennessee was moving to Chattanooga to support Union troops commanded by General Rosecrans, now under siege in that city. (Lloyd Lewis, *Sherman, Fighting Prophet*, pages 308-311)

4. At this point in the war, the reference to Grant's Army is only a reference to the Army of the Tennessee.

5. Among other things, Jacob probably discussed with General Osterhaus the court-martial resulting from Jacob's extended leave in Iowa.

[Mt. Pleasant, Iowa]
Oct. the 4th, 1863

Dearest Husband,
. . . This is all cold, cloudy day and has been for 2 or 3 days. It rained some yesterday. I got a letter from you sent by Lieutenant Steele. It was the first I'd heard from you since you left and you may be sure I was glad to get it and glad to hear that you got down all right. Hope you will get your "absence without leave" accounted for

satisfactorily. I haven't seen Steele yet or any of your boys. I understand that Steele brought the news that you were up to Memphis. I wonder if it is true, and what are you there for? I do hope you want to go out to assist Rosecrans. I am so afraid you will have to go to fighting again. You must have started pretty soon after you got down and before the boys had time to eat up their good things. So it is too bad, but it is always the case with the 25th.

Baron Crane starts down tomorrow. I want to send this by him. If I can't get it up there, I believe I have no news to tell you, except that I have been about half crazy trying to prepare for the winter. I haven't done anything yet scarcely. Haven't got any apples, or potatoes, or wood, nor haven't sold the two old cows yet and don't know when I ever will. Corn is $.50 per bushel and it won't pay to feed the white cow, and I don't think she will do to kill unless she is fattened some. If I can sell her for $15.00 I will take it. It is going to be a great bother to me to get her butchered and sell the beef and hide and everything. I've been trying to sell Old Red for wood, but haven't succeeded yet. Haven't heard a word from your folks since you left. Have no idea they will come after him. I bought a barrel of molasses the other day at $.50 per gallon, which cost me $15.00. Isn't that extravagant. I tried to get the man to divide the barrel and let me have half, but he wouldn't do it. Molasses is scarce and I don't suppose I could get it any place for less than 50 cents and I was afraid I wouldn't get it at all. The man came along here, going to town to sell it. The old Dutch woman has brought the wood . . . and at last I sold your Iowa 1st coat to Brunnetts for about $4.00. Take it in wood cuttings. I want to go out to the Factory at Oakland Mills to see if I can't get a couple of blankets to keep us from freezing this winter. It cost me 10 or 12 dollars. By the time I get everything laid in that I need for this winter, I will be out of money not less than $75. Shall I use it or not? That is besides our clothing. It seems very extravagant that everything is so high that can't be helped. Oak wood is $3.00 per cord. Potatoes from $.80 to $1.00 bushel. Winter apples will be 50 ct at least. I so hate to use your money that you have come by such hard work and I at home not making anything at all. I will be as economical as possible though I must rather pay the enormous prices or do without things.

The children are all well. Lulie and Nellie go to the free school. I guess they are all doing pretty well. Lib has gone home to stay 2 or 3 weeks. We are staying by ourselves. How I wish you could be here. Annie expects to go on to Ohio the last of this week. She is at Alvah's now . . .

I must quit, or I shall expect a letter soon from you. I'm glad to hear you were well. Do take good care of yourself and don't get sick. It seems to me I wanted to tell you something else, but I can't think what it was. Good-bye, Dear. I am so lonely today.

Em

. . . I have got my new silk dress made, all together it cost nearly $28. I wore it to a festival last Tuesday night at the Union Hall (Congregational). Wasn't a bit proud. I owe Lib.

Historical Sketch—25th Iowa Infantry

*Upon arriving at Memphis, the troops disembarked and at once took up the line of march to Corinth, thence to Iuka and Cherokee Station. (*Roster and Record of Iowa Soldiers in the War of the Rebellion; *Published under the authority of the Iowa General Assembly)*

Lincoln took additional steps to reinforce Rosecrans in Chattanooga. He sent General Hooker and two corps of the Army of the Potomac, the 11th and 12th, to the Chattanooga area. Hooker and his troops arrived in Stevenson, Alabama, on the Tennessee River on October 3, 1863.

Camp Near Corinth, Mississippi
October 4, 1863

Dear Wife,

This is Sunday evening again and inspection is over and I have time to write you another letter. What a great privilege it is to be able to sit down and write to each other, isn't it? It is almost as good as to see each other and talk face to face, at least I feel so this morning. But at other times I feel like I would give almost anything to see you once more, and that it is very poor consolation to have to write. I suppose you have fixed up and gone to meeting. I wish I was there to go with you. I think I see you dressed up and one of the nicest and best looking ladies in town and think how proud I should be if I could walk beside you and sit with you at meeting. Well, I hope the time will soon come when we can live together again.

I have got two letters from you since I last wrote. Lee got here

Thursday evening and brought the first, but the other came the same night (the one you sent by mail). I was very glad to hear from you. You dear, good wife—you don't know how good it does me to get a letter from you. I love you better and think of you more than I ever did before. And I am more determined than ever to live as to be worthy of you. I don't know how it is with others. But I think there is no more excuse for a man in the army to drink and swear and play cards than for anyone else. I know I am not half as good as I ought to be, but I intend to live so as to preserve my own respect and that of my friends. There were a great many officers on the boat that I came down on; most of them had just parted from their wives and families, perhaps forever, but they carried on as if they had no restraint whatever. What disgusted me more than anything else was the slightly disrespectful way they talked about women. A lot of them tried hard to get me to join them in a spree one night. What do you think I did? I just took out my "picture" and showed it to them. They had sense enough to be ashamed of themselves and let me alone after that.

Lee has not said much to me about the "trade" yet. He says you and his wife are trying to trade. I do wish you had a good house. You deserve to have one, and shall have it as soon as we can find one to suit. But I think you had better be a little careful about trading with Lee's. The house is old and not well arranged for a family and then I don't think Lee can make a good title to anything. He can hold that as long as it is his homestead, but I think his creditors could take it from anyone else.

But you seem to think you would not like the house anyhow, so I will not trade, and you can do as you please about it. I am sorry you have such a time with the old Dutch woman. I would like to be hid someplace and hear you jaw her. I like to see you "spunky."

I hope you will get the wood yet. I suppose the weather is getting quite cold there by this time, and I hope you will be able to get a good supply of wood and corn soon—don't put it off too long. I wish I had had time to see more about getting you potatoes and apples, but it seemed like I had no time to do anything. I hope you will get them without much trouble. I think the Baptists might have had their festival while I was there. I am real spited that I was not there to go with you. I expect everybody wanted "Peaches & Ice Cream." I should have been very proud to see my sweet wife dealing them out. I'll be bound everybody wanted to buy of you? I shall be spited again if you did not go to the party at Colonel Swan's.

You are "fit" to go anyplace and I want you to go. No one whose good opinion is worth anything will think any less of you because we are not able to live in a fine house.

I have made out final statements for Jont and forwarded them. I am very sorry my pictures did not turn out to suit you. If I ever get paid I will try to have some taken here and send them home. I suppose you have seen Lieutenant Steele and got my letter. We did not know anything about having to move when he started, but we got to Memphis just five hours after he left there. We were moved on short notice.

You must tell me how the girls get along in school. I am anxious that they should learn fast. Tell them I want them to be good girls at school and they must learn at home too. I want them to learn to wash dishes and keep the house nice and clean and walk light and like ladies, over the floor—and not romp so much in the street and over to Morley's.

The last time I wrote to you we were on board the *Sultana* coming up the river. I must tell you what we have been about since. We got to Memphis[1] on Saturday night at 10 o'clock and went on shore Sunday morning and marched about two miles and camped just in the edge of the city. We expected to stay there some time from what they told us, and went to work and laid off a regular camp and put up our tents. But Monday evening we got orders to be at the depot the next morning at sun-up to take the cars to Corinth!

General Hurlbut[2] has command of the 16th Army Corps and has his headquarters at Memphis. His troops garrison that place and guard the road from there to Corinth. They are camped at different places along the road. They had all been in camp and doing nothing for the last 8 to 18 months. There are a good many regiments here that have never been in a fight yet. They all have good wooden barracks and live fine and are all fat and hearty!

Well, when Rosecrans was defeated General Hurlbut was ordered to take the field and the 15th Army Corps was to take his place. But he—Hurlbut—does not like Rosecrans and thinks he has a very good thing where he is. So he sent on to Washington and got the order changed so as to leave him where he is, and send us into the field again. So, because it is known that Osterhaus and his men can be depended on in a fight, we have to do all the hard work while others lie in camp.

We lay in the depot till Wednesday morning at 7 o'clock, when we got started for this place, which is about 100 miles east from

Memphis. It rained steadily all day, sometimes very hard. The men had to ride in open cars and all got wet through. It was 8 o'clock at night when we got here and it rained hard all night. We lay in the depot till morning. I paid 50 cents to get to sleep on a bare floor in a house.

Thursday morning, still raining, but we marched to this place, which is about three miles south of Corinth. I do not know how long we will stay here. We expect to move soon. But something may turn up so that we will get to stay. Our tents were all torn up and worn out so they were of no account and we left them at Memphis, mine with the rest. We were promised new ones when we got here, but we haven't got them yet and are just living out of doors.

I saw Will C. Ghost yesterday—he is a Lieutenant in the 39th Iowa. They have been in camp here since last January. He is quite well and hearty; the regiment is very healthy. His company has only lost three men by sickness while we have lost about 25. But I suppose all these things will come right some day.

There does not seem to be any great call for troops to reinforce Rosecrans just now, and we may be left here, or put on the railroad between here and Chattanooga to repair it. There is no way to get from here to Rosecrans except to go on foot, unless the railroad is repaired.

The health of my company is pretty good now. Billy Degroodt is a good deal better. Sergeant Harlan is not very well. Payne and Garvin are quite hearty. A few have a <u>shake</u> once in a while, and one man (Crow) has the bilious fever. He was my cook and a first-rate fellow. The Negro, Jack, I was telling you about was sick when I got back, and we had to leave him. No furloughs have been given to our company yet on account of the move. If we should go into camp here for any length of time, some of the men will get to go home yet.

My health never was better than at present. You would be surprised to see how fat I am. I think I am as heavy as I ever was. I have had a great deal to do, on account of Steele and Crane both being gone, but have a good appetite and make out to get something to satisfy it. I have opened the blackberries—they are <u>first-rate</u>. I am saving the cherries. Now I think you will be tired before you get through with this long letter. But I might as well write you all the news now, for if I put it off till I get home, I will either forget it, or have so much to tell you I won't know where to begin, like it was this time . . .

Your own, Jake

I have not heard anything from my court-martial yet. I wish they would hurry it up. I can't get any pay till it is disposed of, and I have had to spend a good deal lately and would like to get some more soon. But they may let it run 3 or 4 months if we keep moving.

1. Memphis had changed over the last year from a "half deserted town in which the spirit of rebellion was insolently rampant to a busy, prosperous mart where Northern capital and Northern men throve apace in trade . . . Memphis, the paradise of Jew sutler and Gentile siren." (*55th Illinois*, pages 272-273)

2. Major General Stephen Augustus Hurlbut, headquartered in Memphis, commanded the widely dispersed 16th Army Corps. After the war, he served as Grant's representative in Columbia and Garfield's in Peru. Throughout his military and post-military career, he was suspected and cited for mismanagement and corruption. (Stewart Sifakis, *Who Was Who In The Union*, page 208)

[Mt. Pleasant, Iowa]
Oct. the 11th 1863

Dear Jacob,

This is Sunday again and the time for me to write you another letter. But, I make a poor out writing, for I have two sore fingers. The very two that I hold the pen with so that I can hardly write it at all. I cut the fore finger and the other has the swelling right on the end around the nail. It swelled up and got sore all of a sudden and hurts me very much. I don't know what it will come to. I hope nothing bad.

I have just finished a letter to Ike. Got one from him yesterday. He had the blues because he couldn't get any letters and wanted me to write right away and tell him about you and everything else. He is still in the Hospital at Keokuk. Says he can be about all the time, but seems to get well "slower than seven year scratches." I guess he is almost discouraged by the way he writes. Well, Dear, where are you by this time? I got a letter from you dated Sept. 26th, a few days ago. You were then almost to Memphis. That is the last I've heard from you.

I understand that Mrs. Lee got a letter from the Lieut. dated 4 days after yours, & that he said you were all at Corinth. How true is it? I know not. I expect to go up and see her tomorrow morning

& learn the particulars. I do hope you will not have to go into any more battles. I am so afraid you will be hurt, be marching all over the country and [risking] your lives out after the mean Rebels.

When will the war be over? So that you can come home permanently rest? This is Sunday night. We are all out in the kitchen. Lulie is reading her Sunday school book. Nellie is trying to read the Bible. Tom is fussing around working to know what the figures are in a book. Kit has been to sleep and is just wakened up and crying. It is dark as pitch nearly & raining rather cold. Have to keep up fire all the time.

Lib has not got back from Danville yet. We are all alone. So you know our condition exactly. How I wish you were. Wouldn't we have a pleasant time? . . .

Haven't seen anything of Lieutenant Steele yet. Wonder if he intends to go back without calling. Haven't sold either the cows yet and there is no prospects of selling them. I hardly know what to do with them. I am certain it won't pay to winter them and yet I don't like to give them away. I have the poorest luck in the world doing business. This winter I can't make it go at all. I wish I had you here. My finger hurts. So I will have to quit for tonight.—

Monday. My finger is much worse. It has been raining ever since yesterday evening. This is an awful bad day. Can't get out any place. Guess I will have to send Lulie to the Post Office anyhow . . . Well, Dear, take good care of yourself and don't forget us at home. Hope you will get settled someplace soon.

Em

Iuka, Mississippi
October 12, 1863

Dear Wife,

This is Monday and I sit down to write you another letter. I should have written yesterday, but we were on a march and I could not . . . We are looking for Crane[1] back every day, but he has not come yet. I know he has a letter for me, and I wish he would hurry up. Though just between you and me, I don't care how soon he leaves again. I can get along with him very well myself. But he is very unpopular in the company. The men are all the time making fun of him and wishing he would never come back. He will be of no account here. I hope he will soon resign, for as long as he is an officer I will have to make the men treat him respectfully, which will be hard to do. You must not say anything about this. You will see from this date that we have moved from our camp near Corinth. Last Thursday night at midnight we got orders to march at 7½ in the morning. We didn't like it very well, but they did not consult us about it at all!! But just said "move" and we moved.

We had just got fixed so we could live tolerably comfortable. I had borrowed a tent from Colonel Palmer[2] and bought brick and built a chimney and was fixed as "snug as a bug in a rug." The men had built log cabins and slept in them that night for the first time. Some had built mud chimneys, but we had to leave the whole "shebang" (if you know what that is) and take our winding way over hills and hollows to this place. It is about 25 miles from Corinth here the way we came, and we got here Saturday evening.

It is a very rough, poor country, what they call "pine barrens." Saw some very nice tall pine timber and thousands of small pines like folks plant in their yards up North. Here they grow wild all through the woods. There is plenty of good springs, and clear running streams, so we have no lack of good water. This is a famous place for Springs. There are several fine hotels[3] here and the "quality" used to come here to spend the hot months and drink the pure cold water. It is on the railroad from Memphis to Chattanooga, and has been quite a flourishing place, mainly on account of the visitors to the springs. The country is very thinly settled; we only saw two or three houses on the whole road, and they were all sawmills!—built to saw for the railroad.

Well, as I said, we got here Saturday evening, and expected to rest yesterday and write letters. But our regiment was ordered out on a scout at six o'clock. We went 8 miles east on the railroad and back. Shot one rebel, and were very tired when we returned. Today I have been helping the men to jayhawk lumber and build shanties, as it looks like rain, but we will be all right by night. But I suppose we will not stay here long. I think I will not invest much in another chimney! I suppose we will go on to Chattanooga.

We heard that Sherman and Hurlbut were both contending for the field. We had nothing against Sherman but in that case we all hurrahed for Hurlbut. Not because we are afraid to fight Bragg "or any other man." But because we thought the glory of putting down the whole rebellion and whipping the whole South would be more than we could stand at once!! At any rate we are generous enough to be willing to share the honor with the 16th Army Corps. But I suppose from our being ordered forward that Sherman has succeeded, and we are in for another active campaign to be ended with a big fight.

There was quite a severe battle fought here about a year ago[4], and this place was then occupied by the Union troops, but they were all withdrawn some time ago, and the place has been held by the Rebels till we came. All the bridges have been burned on the railroad but we are repairing it, and the cars will run here by tomorrow. But we have just heard that the rebels attacked and captured a train near La Grange, Tennessee yesterday or last night, and that General Sherman and all his staff were on board and were taken prisoners[5]. This is very serious news to us. If the Rebels jayhawk the railroad between here and Memphis, how are we to get our letters or send any? And how are we to get our "hardtack and sowbelly"? I don't know what effect this will have. It may change the plan of the whole campaign.

In fact we are in a state of suspense, not knowing what minute something may "turn up." Captain Bell of Company E and Mr. Scott, who is the commissioner to take the vote of the regiment arrived here this morning, and we expect to hold an election[6] here tomorrow and give the copperheads a good drubbing, and then we will be ready to attend to the secesh.

My health continues first-rate. I am getting so fat I am afraid I will have to get another suit of clothes soon. I am pretty near as pudgy as Uncle Jesse! What do you think of that! The men that are with me are all well, and stood the march very well. But I had to leave Harlan and Degroodt and eight others at Corinth, they not being able to march. I have only 32 men now present. As there is no chance to mail this at present I will stop now and finish this tomorrow. I may have more news by that time.

* * * * *

Well, this is Tuesday evening, and I have not much more news to tell. It turns out to be all of a hoax about Sherman being taken prisoner. I believe a small force of guerrillas did attack and capture a train last Sunday, but General Sherman was not on it, and the train was soon re-captured and the rebels with it.

It rained last night was cold and damp today, so I got some more brick and am going to have another chimney. I bought two chickens today for fifty cents. I have had plenty to eat since I have been back, and never had a better appetite. We got a mail last night, but I got no letter. I wonder what is the reason. I am beginning to get the blues and I know you will think this letter real stupid. But I can't help it—if I only had one from you to answer, I could write you a long one so easily! We have not heard anything from Crane yet or Colonel Stone.

The railroad is now repaired to this place. The first train came in last night after dark. Our pioneers say they can build a railroad as fast as the rebels can burn it. I think we will be moved on East along the track in a few days. The 26th and 30th Iowa went this morning.

Our election passed off very quietly. I will try to get the results and send you with this. Some of the men would not vote for Captain Smith. But everyone voted for Stone (I mean in Company B). Now I believe I have told you all the news I can think of. I know you will think this is a very dry and uninteresting letter. But I will try and do better next time . . . Give my love to Ma and Car and don't forget

Yours truly, J.B. Ritner

N.B. Now ain't that curious! When did I ever write you a letter before, and had room enough left to sign my name in full? I always had just room to write "Jake."

1. Colonel George Stone and Second Lieutenant Baron Crane of Company B had not yet returned from their furloughs to Iowa.

2. Lieutenant Colonel David Palmer was in command of the regiment while Colonel George Stone was on furlough to Iowa.

3. The main hotel in Corinth was the Tishomingo Hotel, named for Tishomingo County. It was a long, two-story brick building located in the southeastern angle of the two railroad lines, facing the Memphis & Charleston tracks. It had a second story porch that had been rattled loose by the passing trains. (Peter Cozzens, *The Darkest Days of the War—The Battles of Iuka & Corinth*, page 22)

4. The Battle of Iuka was fought September 19, 1862, with Grant, Rosecrans and E.O.C. Ord opposing Confederate General Sterling Price. Grant and Ord missed the action when they did not hear Rosecrans' attack because of the direction of the wind.

5. On October 11, 1863, Confederate General James R. Chalmers' cavalry made an assault at Colliersville, Tennessee, on Sherman's train. Twice the Confederates reached the rear of

Sherman's train. They were unsuccessful in their attempts to set it on fire but they did capture Sherman's second-best uniform. (Lloyd Lewis, *Sherman, Fighting Prophet*, pages 310-311; John E. Marszalek, *Sherman, A Soldier's Passion For Order*, page 239)

6. Jacob is referring to state elections in Iowa. Captain J. Allison Smith ran unopposed for his previous position as Superintendent of Public Schools and received 2,033 votes. Emeline's brother Alvah Bereman successfully ran for State Representative. William Stone, Colonel of the 22nd Iowa, ran for governor.

•   In mid-October 1863, Major General Ulysses S. Grant met with Secretary of War Edwin M. Stanton in Louisville, Kentucky. Grant was promoted to command the newly created Military Division of the Mississippi, which gave him command of all western armies. This included the Army of the Tennessee, the Army of the Cumberland, headed by Rosecrans, the Army of the Ohio, headed by Burnside and also General Hooker and the two corps from the Army of the Potomac. Sherman was promoted to fill Grant's position as commander of the Army of the Tennessee, and Frank Blair was moved up to command the 15th Army Corps.

Headquarters Company B, 25th Iowa
Iuka, Mississippi
October 18, 1863

Dearest Wife,

This is Sunday again. Regimental inspection is over, and I am going to write you another letter and then go to the meeting house for preaching . . . Lieutenant Crane got here Thursday evening and brought a lot of letters, but <u>none for me</u>. Wasn't he a skeesicks? I had mind to give him a good scolding and send him back. But we got a large mail the same night after he came—and it didn't bring me any letter either! Then I wished the rebels would attack this post immediately; I wanted to fight! But I got along without doing myself or anyone else any damage till last night when we got another mail and I got a letter <u>from you</u>, dated October 4th and <u>mailed</u> the 7th!

I slept well last night and got up all right this morning! My health is still excellent. I weigh 193 lbs. Just think of that! 13 lbs. more than I ever weighed before. I just expect you would hug me now if I was to go home, I am so big—would you? We have made new arrangements about our cooking and eating in the last few days. We have formed two messes of the officers of the regiments. We are in a mess with the officers of Company's C, H, I, K, & B. We employ two good cooks and all eat together, and take two mess boxes instead of five. I think it will be a first-rate arrangement and cheaper than the old way. All I have to do is to go in and eat, and have no trouble about keeping a cook, and lugging a mess box and cooking utensils about wherever we go. I told you we had eaten the blackberries you put up; they were very nice. We ate the cherries this week; they were first-rate.

You say you heard that we were at Memphis; I suppose you know all about it by this time. We have marching orders now and expect to leave here today or tomorrow. I don't know how far we will go this time. But I think not very far. But we will keep moving forward and opening the railroad as fast as possible till we reach Rosecrans[1]. That is where we are going as fast as we can. But it will take some time, and be very hard and disagreeable work too, as we will stop just long enough to get fixed a little and then have to move on. This is the third camp we have fixed up since I came back. Then the guard duty is very heavy. My men have to go on every other day. Then the rebels are destroying the road in front of us all the time, and we have to drive them away as we advance. The 1st Brigade of our division had a skirmish yesterday six miles from here. We have very good news this morning from the elections in the North. We all rejoice over it, and feel that we have gained another victory over the rebels. I do think it will tend greatly to discourage them.

Our brigade gave Stone over 1,000 majority over Tuttle. Tuttle got only 5 votes.[2] The health of the company is pretty good at present. Sergeant Harlan has returned and is pretty well. I think this a healthy country.

I received an order from General Osterhaus yesterday evening stating that my case before the Court of Inquiry for being absent without leave had been dismissed[3]. So I got off very easily. Most of the other officers were called on to appear before the court, but they never called for me. The paymaster is here, and will pay us tomorrow or next day if we are not marching, and I will then get four months pay. I am glad the matter has been disposed of so easily.

I have not heard a word from our folks since I came back. I have written to them twice. I don't know what they are thinking about. I shall be spunky if they don't take that red cow off your hands. I am very sorry you have so much to do, and have so much trouble getting ready for winter. I ought to be there to provide for you, I know. It is real mean for me to go off and leave you so, isn't it? I do hope the time will come when we can live together again. And I just know I will never leave my sweet wife again. I hope you will succeed in getting clear of both the cows. I do not think you can attend to feeding and milking this winter. You would freeze off. I want you to get some potatoes and apples if they are high. You must have something for yourself and the children to eat, and the provision will be no cheaper. I think you did well to buy the molasses, you will use it all if it is good, and it will be better than to have to carry it home from town as you use it.

You must be sure to get plenty of wood and have it cut up. I can't bear to think of your being cold. If I can only earn enough to make my dear, sweet wife and children comfortable, I shall be very well satisfied. To be sure we should not be extravagant and should try to lay up something for the future. I may not always be able to earn money as fast as I do now. I may never get home, or get home crippled in some way. But I know I need not remind you of these things. I have full confidence in your management and good sense, and will be perfectly well satisfied with what you do. I think you need the blankets and should get them. I will try to be as economical as I can. I think I can send you $400 this time. And I will have two months pay more due the last of this month. So you have got your silk dress made! I am so glad of that. You were proud wearing it to the festival? No, I expect not! If I had been there to go with you, I would have been proud I know; I wish I had been there to see you outshine Lib, don't you?

Oh, you dear, good wife, how glad I am that you ever loved me. I want you to write me a long letter every week at least. Just sit down and write any nonsense or anything like I do. Everything you say and do is interesting to me. I hope you will not be sick when you write the next time. But it is nearly time to go to meeting and I must stop.

I am glad to hear that you think the children are doing well at school. I hope they will be good girls and learn fast. Tell me more about them next time. And don't forget to tell me about Josie and Kittie. What do they do and say? Do they ever talk about me? I cannot bear to think of their forgetting me. You won't let them, will you? I want you to think what that "something else" was you had to tell me, and tell me next time!! Give my love to Ma and Car, and tell me how they get along. I hope Father has got home before this time . . .

Yours forever, Jake

1. General Rosecrans and his troops were still under siege in Chattanooga, which is where the Army of the Tennessee was headed.

2. This is in reference to the 1863 election for Governor of Iowa between Republican William M. Stone, Colonel of the 22nd Iowa, and Democrat James Madison Tuttle, Colonel of the 2nd Iowa. Stone won the election and became Iowa's sixth governor. Before the war, Stone had been a judge and Tuttle the Treasurer and Recorder of Van Buren County. During the siege of Vicksburg, Tuttle commanded a division under Sherman. Although Tuttle was a loyal soldier, the local papers blasted him as a traitor for running as a Democrat. In March of 1864, Tuttle was made commander of the post at Natchez, Mississippi, where he proceeded to plunder army financial accounts entrusted to him, exact money from local citizens, take large bribes and arrested citizens suspected of being Confederate sympathizers. He resigned his post and returned to Iowa in June 1864, after Major General Henry Slocum issued an order for his removal. (*Historical Times Illustrated Encyclopedia of the Civil War*)

3. The charge against Jacob for being "Away Without Leave" was dismissed.

• On October 18, 1863, General Grant issued orders that Rosecrans was to be replaced as Commander of the Army of the Cumberland by General George Thomas.

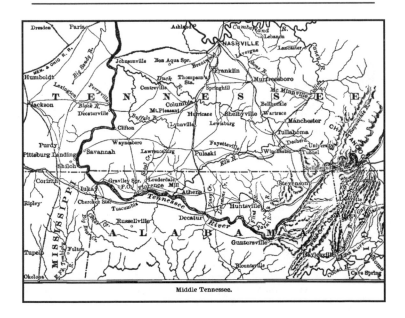

Middle Tennessee.

It Does Me So Much Good to Get Long Letters From You

[Mt. Pleasant, Iowa]
Oct. 19th, 1863

Dear Husband,

This is Monday. I should have written yesterday, but was so lazy I didn't get at it till it was time to get dinner and then by the time I got all the work done up, it was time to go to meeting. (I went after night, but didn't go again the forenoon. The wind blew a perfect streak all day yesterday.) We are all well. I have had a very sore finger ever since I wrote your last letter. I haven't been able to do a bit of sewing for a week. Guess it was a run around right on my thimble finger. It is quite sore yet. Don't expect to be able to sew any this week. Didn't wash any last week, didn't hardly milk or do anything else . . .

I got such a good long letter from you Saturday. It does me so much good to get long letters from you. Don't think I get tired, for I do not. I could read them 3 times as long without getting tired. The longer the better. Just you put in everything you can think of and it will all be read with interest I assure you. I got the letter that Steele brought, but didn't see him. I understood he has gone back. He didn't call here at all. I want you give him a good scolding for me.

I hear the other day that Tom Jolliff was here in town at the tavern very sick. Don't know what has become of him. Haven't heard anymore about him. I suppose he was too bad to be taken out home. Poor Jolliff. He went away from home such a lively mischievous boy and now it is more than likely he has come back to die. But, that is only one case out of a thousand of the same kind.

How I do wish something would turn up so that you would not have to go to Chattanooga. I am afraid there will have to be another big fight there. But, it seemed that the 25th is destined to have a hand in all the big battles. I hope that you may escape this one by some means.—My Dear, it gives me the greatest of pleasure to know that you stick to your good principles and don't give way to temptation, and mix in with the rowdy drinking, low men called officers. Persevere and so doing and never be tempted from the right by any set of <u>officers</u> or anybody else. No differences in that they <u>do</u> call you "Old fogie" or anything else. Their respect is not worth gaining while on the other hand, you will be <u>honored</u> and <u>respected</u> by all the noble and good. When they see that you have sense enough to persevere your own respect and that of your

Company and the friends you left at home. I hope you will always give them the cold shoulder when they want you to join in their sprees. I am sorry you can't get your pay. Hope you will get it soon.

The same committee are going to have another <u>oyster</u> supper at Tyner's so I will have a chance of going again if I feel like it, but I don't care about running around to suppers when you are away off to war. Mrs. Ghost said she was going to tell you & Morley and Mrs. & and I for going to the festival, but I knew you wouldn't care or I would not have gone.

Love, Em

Well, I didn't go to that Oyster Supper at Colonel Swans, but it wasn't because "I wasn't big enough" but because Annie and her father were here till almost night, and then I had no company at all to go with me. I <u>couldn't</u> go. I am very well acquainted with Mrs. Col. Swan, and am not a bit afraid of her. She invited <u>me particularly</u> to come to that oyster supper. If you had been here to go with me I should have gone.

Headquarters Company B, 25th Iowa
Camp Near "Dixie" Station, Alabama
October 24, 1863

Dear Wife,

This is Saturday. But as we are in camp now and may not be so soon again, I will write you a few lines. I am still quite well and hearty; so are all the men except Sergeant Payne, who is quite sick again. The weather has been quite wet and cold for several days. It is so cold today that I can hardly write—my fingers are so numb. But I will try to give you a short account of what had happened since I wrote you last Sunday. I told you I was going to meeting in the afternoon. Well, I went, and just as the preacher had taken his text and got started to preach, I was sent for. When I got to camp I found the wagons all loaded up and ready to move. It was sundown when we got started. We went 6 miles and "bivouacked" for the night. Monday morning we went about 4 miles farther to Bear Creek and camped. We were paid off that night. I got 4 month's pay, amounting to $456. I sent $700 home by express, $400 of my own and $300 I got from Lieutenant Lee. I sent it back to Memphis by the sutler and I hope it will get through all right. My watch did not run to do any good and I sold it for $8.00. I will buy another if I can get a good one.

Well, we got the bridge over Bear Creek built and started on Tuesday morning, and reached this place late in the evening. We marched in the rear of the train that day, but camped in the advance of the whole division. Our advance met the rebels a few miles beyond this place. We camped on the right of the road in thick brush and timber, and the 30th Iowa on the other side of the road in the field. We intended to move on the next day, Wednesday, but as it rained hard all day the order was countermanded. But about noon while it was raining and we were all huddled up in our tents shivering with the cold and damp, the rebels[1] came up and attacked us right in camp. They drove in our pickets and the bullets whistled over our camp before we had time to "fall in."

But we were soon in line of battle and marched out with the left of our regiment on the road, followed by the 1st Missouri Battery. We had gone about one-half mile when we found that we were close to the enemy. We could hear them talk and yell and the bullets came pretty thick. But we could see no one on account of the thick brush. Indeed I hardly ever saw such a thicket. We could not see our own skirmishers twenty steps in front. It was the worst place to fight in we have found yet. No one knew where the enemy was or how many there was of them. Then the rebels opened a heavy fire on the 30th and the left of our regiment, killing the Colonel (Torrence[2]) of the 30th and two captains and wounding several other officers and men at the first fire. The 30th broke and ran. The rebels gave a yell that made the woods ring and charged on them and routed them completely.

The rebels came up even with our line. We could hear the 30th retreating through the brush double quick, and at the same time a brisk firing was commenced on our right. I thought for a few minutes just at this time that the old 25th was going to <u>run</u>. The whole line began to waiver and gave back 3 or 4 rods before the officers got them stopped. I had to get behind Company B and talk pretty rough, but we rallied and fired one volley, and the rebels gave way. We then advanced ½ mile farther and came to an open field, and the rebels in sight about a mile off, retreating. There were about 1,500 of them. I got a bullet hole through my blouse[3]. It was the nastiest little fight we were ever in, just like fighting in the dark. There were 28 killed and wounded in the 30th, and 3 wounded in the 25th. There was one alarm last night at 2 o'clock and we had to get up and fall in. But it proved to be a hoax.

I don't know now when we will move from here; perhaps not until the railroad is repaired this far, which will take a week. I intended to write you a whole sheet but I have just been notified that a mail will leave headquarters at 4 o'clock and it is nearly that now. Colonel Stone and Lieutenants Steele and Simons got here last night, all right, but didn't bring me any letter? But we got a mail at bed-time and I got a letter from you dated October 11th! Lieutenant Steele started the day after the election. He was at your house that day and you were not at home. I am sorry you did not get to see him.

I am so sorry your finger is sore. I hope it will not get so bad you can't write to me. You must write with your left hand, but not a "left-handed letter"!! I wish I could be there to help you sit around the stove these cold, wet days. I am very sorry you have so much trouble about the cows, and to get provisions for the winter. I hope you will succeed yet. I wish I could be there to do it for you.

Yours ever, Jake

I would like to write a great deal more if I had time and tell you more about this country. We are all greatly pleased at the results of the election. I would like to write to Ike if I knew he was yet at the post. I haven't had a word from him yet. I think we will get to Tuscumbia in a few days and then I will write again. It is about 16 miles and the 1st Brigade is fighting in that direction today. We hear the cannon.

1. The Confederate Cavalry, led by General Stephen D. Lee, were wearing blue overcoats, which allowed them to get very close to the Union camp before being discovered.

2. Colonel William M. G. Torrence of the 30th Iowa Infantry was killed in action October 21, 1863, at Cherokee Station, Alabama. Before the war, Torrence was the Superintendent of Schools in Keokuk, Iowa. The previous colonel of the 30th Iowa, Charles H. Abbott, was killed in action May 22, 1863, at Vicksburg.

3. A blouse was a military coat of waist length worn for field services and field duty. In earlier times, as used in England and France, the word "blouse" meant a smock used by workmen. After the Civil War, the word took its modern meaning of a loose garment worn by women. (Daryl Lyman, *Civil War Wordbook*, pages 21-22)

The Death of Tom Jolliff, Such a Lively Mischievous Boy

[Mt. Pleasant, Iowa]
Oct. the 25th, 1863

Dear Jacob,

This is Sunday night. I wrote to you on last Wednesday. I believe I received a letter from you the same day and was sorry to hear that you had moved on towards Chattanooga. I was in hopes you would not have to go, but I see it as no use for me to flatter myself with such hopes. As you say, I expect you are in for another long siege to be ended with a big battle. Oh Lord, how I wish this cruel war was over and the poor soldiers all at home, away from the miseries of camp life and the horrors of the battlefield. When will it end?

Next Sunday will be just one year since the 25th Regt. left Mt. Pleasant. What an age!! But just to think that perhaps they will stay their time out. <u>Two long years</u> yet. Who can endure to the end? If Co. B has lost 25 men in one year, at the end of three years, at the same rate, then will be but a very small handful left. It is painful to think of. Yet I hope that Co. has passed through its severest trials, and that it may soon enjoy rest and health.

I told you about Tom Jolliff being sick. He died last Monday at the Brazleton house.—Was never able to get home. Poor Tom. I thought I would go and see him, but put it off till it was too late—

I am sorry you don't get my letters more regularly. You certainly have got them by this time. I thought I sent one by Lieutenant Crane, but his Father told me he went off and forgot it. So, he mailed it and sent it on. I suppose it will get there nearly as quick as he does. I don't think Baron will ever resign, so you must try and get along with him the best you can. Hope there will be no feud between him and the men. I think a considerable of the Crane family and will be glad if <u>you</u> could keep on good terms with Baron. I think if you would talk to the men and try to get them to like him, they would soon get over their prejudice . . .

Em

Historical Sketch—25th Iowa Infantry

At Cherokee Station, Alabama, the enemy was encountered. The following extract from the official report of Colonel Stone will show with what vigor the enemy's skirmishers were attacked, and how persistently the march was continued to Chattanooga to reinforce the troops which were so soon to become engaged in the tremendous conflicts around that place:

On Sunday evening, October 25th, 1863 at Cherokee, Alabama, our division received marching orders for 4 a.m. next day, and accordingly the division moved at the hour indicated, in the direction of Tuscumbia, Alabama, in light marching order and in fine fighting condition. The First Brigade, Brigadier General C. R. Woods commanding, had the advance, and ours, the Second Brigade, Colonel James A. Williamson commanding, the rear. General Osterhaus's orders were very imperative and strict concerning the tactical arrangement of battalions, as the enemy, but some three miles in front of us, was composed entirely of cavalry, and was fully our equal in numerical strength. About two miles from camp we met the enemy's skirmishers, and here formed our line of battle, the First Brigade on the right, and the Second on the left, with one of the other divisions of our Corps as reserve. My position was on the extreme left and, in accordance with orders, I formed a square to repel cavalry, first however, having covered my front properly with skirmishers. Our skirmishers pushed the enemy so vigorously, and our lines followed so promptly, that after a short resistance the enemy fell back to another position some four miles to the rear, and made another stand. The same disposition was again made by our division, the same sharp, short fighting with the same result, the hasty retreat of the enemy. We continued this skirmishing during the entire day, and renewed it on the 27th, literally fighting them from Cherokee to Tuscumbia. We entered the town at 3 p.m., on the 27th. Sergeant Nehemiah M. Redding, of Company D, was killed while skirmishing on the 26th. I have no other casualties to mention. Officers and men behaved handsomely. (Roster and Record of Iowa Soldiers in the War of the Rebellion; *Published under the authority of the Iowa General Assembly*)

In the Chattanooga area, Union General William F. Smith developed a plan to open a supply line to the Union forces besieged in Chattanooga. Smith's plan involved crossing the Tennessee River in three places – with a pontoon bridges north of Chattanooga, 1½ miles west of Chattanooga 1½ miles at Brown's Ferry, and then another 12 miles west at Kelly's Ferry. This would provide the most direct route to Chattanooga. The main obstacle was the Confederate Army based on Raccoon Mountain.

At 3 a.m. on October 27, a Union flotilla of 50 pontoon transports began its journey to Brown's Ferry. at 3 a.m. When they arrived at 5 a.m., *the Confederates had less than a brigade to protect Brown's Ferry and the Union troops easily drove them off in skirmishing that lasted less than 30 minutes. This capture of Brown's Ferry was the beginning of the end of the Confederates at Chattanooga.*

On October 28, Hooker occupied Wauhatchie in Lookout Valley and that night repulsed a Confederate attack. The Union supply line, referred to as the "cracker line," was now secure, and by October 30, Union troops were back to full rations. While this occurred, Sherman's troops were still making their way toward Chattanooga.

Chickasaw Landing, Alabama
November 1, 1863

Dear Wife,

Well, dear, it is late Sunday night and if you are not too tired and sleepy and will sit on my knee and listen, I will try to tell you what we have been about since I last wrote. I have a "bushel" of news to tell, but can't tell it all tonight, if I have to write it down. I wish I could sit down and talk to you till midnight, don't you! But I am very thankful that I have the privilege of writing to you—it is more than I expected sometimes through the week. Well, how are you all? . . . I am so anxious to hear from you, but it seems like we will never get any more letters.

I am still well and hearty, and can eat sweet potatoes and persimmons in unlimited quantities, which is about all this country produces. Company B is "all right"—the men were never in better health and spirits, and never were harder worked. But this good spring water and healthy climate is quite different from what we have been used to. This part of the country is very rough, almost mountainous, timber mostly pine, thinly settled, but full of the nicest springs I ever saw.

I told you in my last about the fight we had the day the rebels attacked our camp, and the Colonel of the 30th Iowa was killed. I see an account of the same fight in the papers, which is considerably stretched. It was not half the fight they make out and no troops were engaged except the 5th Ohio Cavalry and the 25th and 30th Iowa, and there would have been no fight at all that day if the enemy had not attacked our camp. But I have seen more rebels since then than I ever saw in my life.

Last Sunday night at midnight we began to strip ourselves for a fight. The tents and all surplus baggage was loaded up and sent to the rear; only one wagon was allowed to each regiment. Each man was furnished 3 days' rations and 50 rounds of ammunition. In short we made the most elaborate preparations for a hard battle and we all thought it was coming certain.

I have heard it said that "fighting is nothing when you get used to it." But I have been in a good many fights and never felt so gloomy and reluctant to go out as I did that morning. Indeed it is enough to make anyone feel sober to see an army prepare for battle. Every man is brought into the ranks and ordered to load his gun. The doctors get out their knives and saws and bandages, and you see a squad of men with a white rag tied on their arm in the rear of each regiment carrying stretchers, and waiting for someone to be shot, when they pick him up and carry him off.

Then we were opposed by the most daring and impudent set of rebels we have ever encountered; they attacked our pickets every night and we could hear them yelling through the woods. I believe I am about as brave as the most of men, but I thought a good deal, and anxiously that night about my dear sweet wife at home. And felt for the first time, that perhaps I might never kiss you again, and a good deal more the same sort.

Well, we started at 3 o'clock and by the time it was light we commenced skirmishing and driving in the enemy's pickets. The cannon opened at sun-up, and we had a lively time for 3 or 4 hours, but we out-flanked them and they retreated a few miles across a creek and made another stand. There we charged them and routed them again and drove them to within 6 miles of Tuscumbia, where they took a strong position on a high hill with a creek in front. We lay in the wood that night and the next morning after shelling them a while, they fled again, and we got to Tuscumbia late in the afternoon. Our advance drove them across the Tennessee River 5 miles from Tuscumbia. After the first shell went over our regiment about sun-up on Monday morning, I didn't care for all the rebels in the South—it seemed to <u>wake me up</u>, and after that I wanted them to <u>stand</u> and give us a fair fight.

Wednesday we marched back the whole distance (18 miles) to our old camp, and were all very tired and worn out, but we felt that we had driven them away so far that they would not annoy us soon again, and thought we could get one night's good sleep without being called up at midnight to drive them away. But don't you think the nasty devils attacked us the next morning before we had our breakfast? Yes, they did—they followed us right back.

They are nearly all mounted infantry. We did not go out that morning till after breakfast; most of the other regiments did. We found a strong force of them where we had the first fight on Monday. There were more of them than there were before and they advanced on us in two columns. We all thought we were in for a fight then certain. But when they came within reach of our cannon they halted, and then both sides maneuvered around all day in sight of each other, without coming to a fight except some firing by the skirmishers. They were all mounted and we had not much cavalry, and knew it was not worth while to try to catch them. We tried all day to get them into a trap, but they wouldn't "bite." The 9th and 25th Iowa were in the center on the road, and we fell back a mile or so, and wanted them to follow so we could surround them with the right and left wings. But they were too sharp. But you will see a full account of the whole thing in the papers, better than I can write it.

Friday morning we broke camp and marched back to "Dixie Station" or "Chickasaw Station"—I don't know which is the right name and from there North toward the Tennessee River, which we expected to reach that day. But it rained hard all day, the roads became very muddy and we could not get along. We only got 6 miles and lay out in the woods without tents or blankets. It was quite cold—it snowed a little in the night where we were, which was a "young mountain," as the boys called it. Yesterday was pleasant and we got here in time to put up our tents and be mustered for pay, as it was the last day of October. I have been hard at work all day today making payrolls and monthly returns. Now I believe I had told you all about it. And I believe I have written some very foolish things, indeed I know I have. You must not let anyone see this letter nor read it to them, now mind! If you do I shan't write you anymore.

I think we will remain here a few days, but not longer. This is a very small town, deserted and grown up in weeds, on the Tennessee River. Eastport just below here is another deserted town. The 15th Army Corps is all here, I think, at least three divisions of it, and we are going to cross over into Tennessee and march to Chattanooga, which is about two hundred miles from here. I think it was the intention originally to repair the railroad and go through that way. But we found so much opposition and the road destroyed so badly that it has been abandoned. And we are going to take the route on foot through Tennessee. I understand that Iuka is to be abandoned and our forces will fall back to Corinth again. We had the road repaired to our camp, but from there to Tuscumbia and beyond that it is almost totally destroyed. And it would take so many troops to guard it that it would not pay to hold it. I have heard that Degroodt is still at Memphis and doing well. William Harlan is here and getting well. Wils Payne had been sent back to Iuka but getting well as fast as could be expected.

I have not heard a word from Des Moines County since I came back. I wonder what they are all about. If we stay here a few days I will write to you again. I hope I will get a letter from you before we leave. The Tennessee [River] had raised so that boats come up here. There are two gunboats and two or three transports here.

But it is almost midnight and I must stop for this time. I expect you think I had better. I am ashamed of this foolish letter—if I had time I would tear it up and write another. I'll be real "spunky" if you let anybody see it. But I do love you and our children dearly, and I know that I am exposed to danger and am far away from home in an enemy's country. And I do sometimes think seriously of what would become of you if I should never get home to see all of you again. But I shall never do anything that I will be ashamed to have known, and if I fall it will be in a good cause and at my post doing my duty, and may God protect and comfort and provide for you and the children. Now, dear, I do not talk this way to make you feel sad or uneasy, or because I feel so myself, for I do not. You must keep on writing. You need not direct to anyplace, but to me, Company B 25th Iowa, Osterhaus's Division. Tell me all about how you have succeeded in making provision for the winter and all about the children. You don't say half enough about them. How do Ma and Car get along?

Yours ever, J.B. Ritner

Stevenson, Alabama
November 17, 1863

Dear Wife,

I know you have been looking for a letter from me for a long time, and wondering why you do not get one. I am afraid you almost have the "blues" over it, but it could not be helped, Dear. We have been on the march for the last fourteen days and had no chance to write or mail letters if we had them written. Come cheer up now dear and I will tell you all about it, if it takes all night. Don't look sober now or I can't write. I will just take another look at your picture and then go ahead. Well the last time I wrote to you was at Cherokee Landing in Alabama two weeks ago yesterday (Monday). I thought then I would get a chance to write you again before we left, but did not. We were ordered to start on Tuesday and were up all night crossing the river. And the next day at noon we started on the march. I had not got any letter from you for a long time, but just as were starting we got a mail and I got a letter from you dated October 26th and that evening I got the one dated October 19th! So you see I have been without letters too. I ought to have one later than either. I got one from Susan the day I got your first one. It was the first I had heard from any of them since I came back. She said Eliza had written me, but if she did I have not got it yet.

Well, we started on Wednesday, November 4th for the north side of the Tennessee River. The whole 15th Army Corps was then on the way to Chattanooga. But we saw nothing of any but our division (Osterhaus') on the way. The other three divisions were in advance[1].

I had just been out to eat my supper—had coffee, "hard tack" and ham, and that is what we have had to eat every day for two weeks. I am writing in a great hurry and I expect I will have this so mixed up you can't understand it. But I will try and do better.

I have not much to say about the march. We have traveled at least 200 miles in the last 14 days, and 300 miles since we left Corinth on the 10th of October and have had four fights in the meantime. If you have a late map you can trace our travels: from Corinth to Iuka, then to Tuscumbia, and back to Cherokee Landing, which is in the very Northwest corner of Alabama. From there to Florence, then to Pulaski—then to Fayette, then southwest till we struck the Memphis and Charleston railroad 12 miles east of Huntsville, then east to this place. It does not make much of a show on a map, but it is an awful long road when you come to travel it on foot. We did not see or hear anything of any rebels on the route. The country is very rough and hilly and rocky—indeed it is the roughest country I ever saw—beats Missouri or Vicksburg. For the last three or four days we have been among the Cumberland Mountains. I never saw such nice clear springs and running streams. We had an abundance of the best water and plenty of beechnuts and persimmons, which is about all this country produces.

We got some new tents just before we started, had plenty of rations, and got along very well, except that it was hard climbing the hills. The men all had good health and stood it first-rate. But we all wore out our shoes and the whole company is nearly barefooted now, and some have very sore feet[2]. We marched right along every day late and early, rain or shine, Sundays and weekdays. It rained hard all day the second day and I got wet through and the next day we had to wade a creek and I got my feet wet and then I had a "shake." I had three shakes before I got it broke up and took 40 grins of quinine. I was very sick one day, but had got entirely over it and feel very well now. But you wouldn't laugh at me now for being so "pussy." I have lost all my corporsity. I don't think I will have to buy a new suit till these wear out. In fact I can just about wipe my nose with the skin of my belly.

We generally start at 6 o'clock in the morning (get up at 4) and if we are in advance of the train, get to camp a little before sundown; if in rear of the train we don't get in till from 8 to 12 o'clock, according to the roads. It was 11 o'clock last night when we got in. Today we came 16 miles and I was very tired when we camped, but I thought I must write you a letter, so I went to work and put up the tent and fixed up the book box (which is the first time it has been unloaded since we started), and when I went to open it I found I had lost the key. But I broke the lock and got it open. I have felt very bad about not being able to write to you sooner. But I could not have sent it if I had written every day. We were in hopes, and it was reported all along the road, that when we got through to Stevenson we would get to rest a few days and get shoes and have a chance to write letters. But when we got there today we never halted at all, but marched right on toward Chattanooga. We are now four miles east of Stevenson, and go on at 6 o'clock in the morning.

We are yet 40 miles from Chattanooga, but we could hear the cannon from there this evening. They can be heard at Stevenson almost every day. I am in hopes yet that we will stop a few days at Bridgeport, which is eight miles farther on. If we don't get shoes I don't know what will become of us. I understand that we will have to leave all our tents and everything but what we carry, as the road is so mountainous that it is almost impossible to get wagons over it. I must go and warm my fingers. I hope your dear little sore finger has got well before this. Well, anything to put down the rebellion.

Our army never was in better spirits or more enthusiastic in the cause than at present. We all expect a hot fight before long, but we expect nothing but <u>victory</u>. And it does my heart good and I feel very proud of my company when I see with what fortitude and good will they bear hardship and fatigue. They don't talk now like they did in the "dark days" at Young's Point last winter. But they all say they don't want to go home till the rebellion is put down. But the regiments now are mere skeletons[3] to what they were a year ago, and I think the government does wrong not to <u>draft</u> men to fill them up.

There are 15 regiments in our division, which should number about 12,000 men, but in fact we have less than 4,000. The 25th is the largest regiment and has less than 300 present for duty. Company B is the largest company and has 40, all told present, 36 muskets only, leaving out cooks, &c. I have only 59 men now on the roll out of 97 that we started with. It is really sad to think how fast the war uses up men, and what a fearful destruction of human life, and what sorrow and misery follow in its track. But the end justifies the means; I feel that no sacrifice is too great to be made, and no loss can equal that of our country and government. It is reported that Lee[4] has command of the rebel forces at Chattanooga. If he has, he will find that he has not the "Army of the Potomac[5]" to contend with, and if he doesn't look sharp we will come Vicksburg over him.

But I must bring my scribbling to a close. Lieutenants Steele and Crane are both well and in bed asleep long ago—it is ten o'clock and I didn't sleep much last night and have to march tomorrow. I do not "like the Crane family[6]" much, especially Baron—he is too selfish and <u>snappish</u>—he sometimes forgets to treat me with the respect which is due from one officer to his <u>superior</u>. You know I am <u>Captain</u> of Company B and <u>must be</u> respected accordingly even by Lieutenants. But I will try to "be good" and not have any fuss, for your sake and because you asked me.

I don't think I ought to scold you for getting a new cloak, or for anything else. I have quit scolding you, don't you ever think I could be mean enough to scold such a dear sweet little wife as you are. I am so sorry you have so much trouble about the cows and wood and apples and everything. I hope you have everything ready for winter by this time.

I am glad to hear that the girls like their school and learn fast. I think if Lulie keeps on she can soon write me a letter. I am glad to hear that Tommy is so industrious; he must have that sled this winter if it snows, and the mittens and boots and then he will be a little man. Kitty must not eat so much bread next time. If she had to eat hard tack I don't think there would be any danger.

You must teach them all to love God and their country, and to <u>hate</u> a lie, the devil, and all traitors and copperheads; teach them to honor and respect the flag of our country, its rulers and institutions, and to love freedom and hate slavery, and everything and everyone that has caused this wicked war.

I don't think you had better trade with Lise, she won't suit you near so well as Lib.

Sergeant Harlan is getting better. I have not heard from Payne since we left him behind. If anyone inquires about the men, tell them they are all well. Now, dear I must quit and go to bed. It is quite cold, there will be a heavy frost. So good night, my pretty, sweet little wife, and may God watch over you and protect you, is the prayer of

Your Jake

I got a letter this evening from Dr. McClure[7] informing me of the death of Jolliff and asking me to send on his papers. Get Alvah to tell him that he must notify the surgeon in charge of the hospital from which he received his furlough and have him forward me his descriptive list. I can make out no papers till I get it and Dr. McClure has been in the army long enough to know it. If I knew where he got his furlough I could write myself.

1. In this final movement of Sherman's troops to Chattanooga, Osterhaus's Division was the last in line. This had later implications as to their positioning around Chattanooga, and in which specific battles they fought.

2. One of the contrasts between the Western Federal armies and the Eastern Federal armies was how well the Eastern armies were equipped with clothing and supplies. When they met, as part of this Chattanooga campaign, the Easterners scoffed at the appearance of the Westerners.

3. At this time, the Union Army was more inclined to create new regiments than fill existing units.

4. There were many rumor's concerning command of the Confederate Army of Tennessee at Chattanooga. Confederate General Braxton Bragg had been successful at the Battle of Chickamauga, but he failed to pursue and destroy the Union Army as it retreated back to Chattanooga. His unsuccessful siege of the Union forces in Chattanooga led to major dissent among his direct reporting generals. These generals included Longstreet, Forrest, Hardee, and Polk, who all wished to have Bragg relieved of his command. Some were calling for Bragg to be replaced by General Robert E. Lee, who remained in the east with his Army of Northern Virginia. Confederate President

Jefferson Davis came to visit his Confederate generals near Chattanooga and heard their complaints, but left giving Bragg his continued support.

5. This is a put-down of the Union armies of the east. The Army of the Potomac, despite its superior size, had generally been without success in most of its confrontations against Confederate General Robert E. Lee, although the Army of the Potomac had recently defeated Lee at Gettysburg.

6. The Crane Family, which included Second Lieutenant Baron Crane, was a large, prominent family in Mt. Pleasant. The family eventually became involved in many businesses in Mt. Pleasant, including hardware, jewelry, furniture, optometry, and undertaking. The Reverend Eber Crane was an active abolitionist and supporter of the temperance movement. Eber and Nancy had nine children, the oldest of which was Baron, born in 1838. (Henry County Bicentennial Commission including Ann Crane Farrier, *The History of Henry County, Iowa*, 1982, page 164)

7. Dr. Andrew McClure, M.D. of Mt. Pleasant was a local physician and surgeon. He had previously served in the 4th Iowa Cavalry, with Billy and Ol Bereman.

Headquarters Company B, 25th Iowa
Camp at Bridgeport, Alabama
November 20, 1863

My Dear Wife,

We have just gone into camp tonight and it is only half-past 5 o'clock and I have just received notice that there will be a chance to mail letters till 6 o'clock. So I thought I would write you a few lines for fear I would not have a chance soon again. I wrote to you two or three days ago, when we were four miles this side of Stevenson. But I ought to write every day for a while to make up for lost time. I got your letter last night dated November 3rd; the one you didn't write on Sunday because you hadn't time. But I have not yet got the one you said you "write in a few days." I ought to have two more, as we got the *Home Journal* today, dated November 14th. I don't see why the letters didn't come. You don't know how anxiously I look for your letters and how much good it does me to get one. It would do you good to see how eagerly the men all crowd around me when I come from Quarters with the mail. No matter what they are doing, they drop everything and run. And how disappointed and sad are those who do not get any. I know you and the children are anxious to hear from me and I will write every chance.

The next day after I wrote you last we came on to the river at this place, only about eight miles, but the roads were so bad[1] it was dark when we got there. Yesterday we lay in camp and I was very busy all day drawing and issuing clothing to the men and making returns, and was as tired as if we had marched. Today we only crossed the river and came out about a mile. We are to go on in the morning— I don't know where to. But I suppose out to where the fight is to be. I don't think we will go to Chattanooga, but to the right. I think we will be on the extreme right of the line, as we were at Vicksburg.

We cannot hear much that is reliable from the front. The rebels still hold Lookout Mountain, or part of it. I hear that our line is to be 25 or 30 miles long, and that we will try to outflank them. But I suppose we will find out something about it in a few days, as I have no doubt that things will soon be brought to a crisis here, and the rebels will have to fight or back out. A great many think they will fall back. For my part I don't care, I had just as lieve fight them here as any place. As near as I can find out it is 28 miles from here to Chattanooga and about the same distance to where we are to take our position in the line.

The Tennessee seems to be quite a large river here. The railroad bridge has been destroyed, but is nearly rebuilt—it will be done in a week or so. We crossed on a pontoon bridge, or rather two bridges, as there is an island here about 60 rods wide, and the river has to be bridged on both sides of it. There is no town here at all, not even a house, yet it is a great place for business. There are more quartermasters and commissaries' stores and mules and wagons than I ever saw at one place. The whole army is supplied from here. Part is hauled out in wagons and part shipped on steamboats to within 14 miles of Chattanooga.

We halted a little while just on this side of the river, and some of the officers found a sutler who had whiskey to sell at three dollars a quart, and about two-thirds of the officers in this regiment are now drunk and raising Cain generally all over the Camp. Company B boys are congratulating themselves that their officers are all right and minding their own business. They wouldn't swap officers with any company in the regiment. Don't you think they are right to be proud of us? Especially the Captain? And we are all proud of belonging to the Army of the West.

We see a good many soldiers here from the East, and there is a good deal of blowing between them and our men. Each one thinks their army is best. For my part I don't see what the Army of the East has to be proud of. If I belonged to it, I should be ashamed to own it.[2]

I received a letter from Saunders stating that the money I sent last had got there all right. I am glad of it. I had hard work to earn it, and would hate to lose any. It is costing me more to live here than it ever has before. We can get nothing in the country and have to buy all our provisions and we buy nothing at all but soldiers' rations. Everything in the shape of luxuries are so dear that we don't use any, and it costs me about $2.50 per week for board. And then I have had to buy a good deal of clothing,—a blanket, overcoat, undershirt, socks, &c, which took lots of money. Then I lost some clothing in issuing to the men which I had to pay for. But so I can send home enough to keep you and the children comfortable I shall be satisfied.

I am glad you have got rid of the red cow, and that the other one is going to have a calf. I hope you will get a good supply of wood and provisions and get along comfortably this winter. I am glad Father[3] got to go home. I would like to have been there. I wonder if we will ever all be together again. I hope so. Then won't we have a great time "when this cruel war is over." I wish Father and Ma would write me a letter. You never say a word about Ma. Why don't you tell me how she and Car get along? Tell Ma if we ever get to stop long enough I will write to her. You didn't tell me a word about Billy. I don't know whether he is at St. Louis yet or not. He has never written to me.

Pete and Uncle Jake were going to take Benton up to our house and send him to school. I think that is a good plan. I know he will be useful to you, and you can do him good. The mail is about to close and I must stop.

Your affectionate Husband,
J.B. Ritner

1. General Sherman described this road as "a ditch full of big rocks." (Lloyd Lewis, *Sherman, Fighting Prophet*, page 318)

2. Three Union armies were thrown together for the Chattanooga operations: the Army of the Tennessee, led by General Sherman, the Army of the Cumberland, led by General Thomas, and two corps from the Army of the Potomac, commanded by General Hooker. One of Grant's major difficulties was that the men from these armies did not get along with each other.

There was stark contrast as the Army of the Tennessee came in contact with the Army of the Potomac. The easterners had paper collars, polished buttons, knapsacks with neatly rolled blankets, and many wore French fatigue caps. Many of the Army of the Tennessee were without shoes, had shaggy beards and slouch hats. (Lloyd Lewis, *Sherman, Fighting Prophet*, page 317)

3. Emeline's father, Samuel E. Bereman of the 37th Iowa Infantry, arrived home on leave.

The Union Plan of Attack

General Grant placed General Sherman and the Army of the Tennessee on the north of Missionary Ridge, by Tunnel Hill, directed against the Confederate right, which Grant considered the opposing flank. According to Grant's plan, Sherman would lead the main Union attack, which would move across South Chickamauga creek, and eventually threaten the railroad at Chickamauga Station and possibly cut off Bragg's line of retreat.

General Thomas and the Army of the Cumberland were in the center, and were to attack only at the proper time after Sherman had turned the enemy's flank. Thomas was then to move to his left and meet with Sherman to drive the Confederates off Missionary Ridge. The Union generals did not plan a center assault by Thomas.

General Hooker, on the extreme Union right, was to secure Lookout Valley and just threaten Lookout Mountain, where it met the Tennessee River.

As a diversionary move, Osterhaus's Division (which included Jacob) was to feint an attack on the Union far right at Lookout Mountain. After attracting Confederate attention, Osterhaus's Division was to move during the night to join the rest of Sherman's troops. (James Lee McDonough, Chattanooga, A Death Grip on the Confederacy*)*

The Battle of Lookout Mountain
(The Battle Above the Clouds)

Grant's plan for General Hooker changed on November 23. Water levels had risen on the Tennessee River and washed out the bridge at Brown's Ferry, isolating Osterhaus's Division, which included the 25th Iowa, from the rest of Sherman's army. Rather than delay his original plans and have the pioneers repair the bridge, Grant instead ordered Osterhaus to report to General Hooker in Lookout Valley. Grant then instructed Hooker, with his enlarged detachment of 10,000 men, to capture Lookout Mountain if he could, as a preparatory step for assaulting Missionary Ridge. Strangely, Hooker's command included one division of each from the Army of the Potomac, the Army of the Cumberland, and the Army of the Tennessee.

On November 24, a murky, dense fog covered the region, and as the Union forces advanced, it appeared as if they were disappearing into the clouds. Confederates later reported that they had a hard time distinguishing any object at over 100 yards. The three Union divisions formed a common line, with the objective of sweeping every Rebel from the mountain, as Union artillery supported their advance. The Confederates were clearly surprised by the attack.

Despite being outnumbered 4 or 5 to 1, the Confederates put up a staunch defense. Initially, they were able to oppose the Union advance with artillery fire, but as the Union forces drew closer, the Confederates could not appropriately adjust the angle of their artillery, and consistently overshot the Federals. Eventually, the Confederate gunners lit the fuses of their shells and threw them over the side of the mountain, but this had little effect on the attacking Yankees.

About 2 o'clock on the morning of November 25, the remaining Confederate troops withdrew to the Rebel post on Missionary Ridge, which was now in an untenable position with the loss of Lookout Mountain. For the attacking Union troops, it was a cold, wet, miserable night on the slopes of Lookout Mountain.

Historical Sketch—25th Iowa Infantry

The troops continued to press forward by forced marches, and at midnight, on November 23rd, had reached a point near the foot of Lookout Mountain. The division under General Osterhaus was temporarily attached to the forces under the command of General Hooker. The Twenty-Fifth Iowa was assigned to a position in support of a battery of New York artillery. Following is Colonel Stone's official reports of the part taken by his regiment in the battles which followed in rapid succession, are here given in full:

Bridgeport, Alabama
Dec. 19, 1863
General:

I have the honor to report as follows, of the battle of Lookout Mountain, on the 24th of November 1863. Our division camped on the 23rd of November opposite

Lookout Mountain, and near General Hooker' s headquarters. At 9 p.m. I received orders to be in fighting trim at daylight next morning and accordingly, at 5 a.m. of the 24th, I was in line of battle, and received orders to support the First Iowa Battery during the day. It was intended that our division should act as reserves, while some of Hooker's division should storm the mountain, but this was partially changed, probably on account of one column being ordered further to the right than was first intended, and our division soon took an active part. At 9:30 am I had orders to go to the front, just under a point of rocks on Lookout Mountain, to support the guns of Battery I, First New York Artillery, then in position, and two of which guns were protected by being hastily casemated. This position I retained during the day, and, on account of the admirable place for defense, and the inability of the enemy to sufficiently depress his guns, I found at dark I had not lost a man.

Nothing could exceed the grandeur of this battle, from the point at which we viewed it. Every gun from Raccoon Mountain batteries to those of Moccasin Point was in plain view, and our lines of infantry so close that acquaintances were easily recognized. At 12 M [noon] the grand attack began, and soon the battle smoke hung over and enveloped the mountain like a funeral pall, and the whole battle, like a panorama, passed around and before us.

At dark, in accordance with orders from General Osterhaus, I reported, with my regiment, for special duty, to Major General Butterfield, General Hooker's Chief of Staff, and was ordered by him to a position on the extreme right of the army, to prevent an anticipated attempt of the enemy to turn our flank at that point. I occupied the point indicated, and made a personal reconnaissance of the ground in front of me. The enemy threatened some during the night, but made no attack, and, at daylight next day, in obedience to orders, I reported back with my command, to the division.

Very respectfully, your obedient servant,
George A. Stone
Colonel Commanding Twenty-Fifth Iowa

(*Roster and Record of Iowa Soldiers in the War of the Rebellion*; Published under the authority of the Iowa General Assembly)

Editor's Notes:

The 25th Iowa was in the brigade that also included the 4th, 9th, 26th, 30th and 31st Iowa Infantries. First Lieutenant Andrew G. Henderson of Maquoketa, Iowa, 31st Iowa Infantry, provided the following account of the Battle of Lookout Mountain:

"I do not wish you to think that all the time the battle was progressing everyone had his teeth tightly clinched and a dark frown on his countenance. Far different were the facts. In the height of battle we had some as amusing scenes and sounds as you would see or hear in a county circus or city theatre. A member of Company B [31st Iowa] sang an amusing song disparaging the chances of the Jeff. Davis Confederacy, the chorus of which runs as follows:

> 'Big pig little pig
> Root hog or die.'

While he was singing the rebels slackened fire at his end of the regiment to listen to the extraordinary songster, but as soon as he had ceased they redoubled their efforts to kill him, fortunately without success. A member of Company K has the gift of imitating a wild goose, and many times during the fight we could hear the signal notes of the Lost Gander, which would raise a cheer and laugh among the brave boys who were so heroically battling for the old flag.

Another of the boys would call out to the rebels to come over and get some coffee and wheat bread, (articles unknown in their camps) and would receive for answer, 'go to h-ll,' accompanied by a shower of bullets. Another member of the 31st changed the programme and raised a laugh by crowing like a rooster; while I seen and heard one of our boys who was shooting from behind a tree give some of the loudest and most unearthly yells I ever heard every time he fired his gun, which put me in mind of some excited individual at a camp meeting shouting 'glory, glory, glory.'

The next day some of the rebels that were taken prisoners on Mission Ridge by a Pennsylvania regiment wanted to know where the troops were from that fought them the evening before on Look Out. They said they were the d-d-t fellows they ever met in battle, as they had wild geese and roosters along with them, and a fellow to sing songs while the rest were fighting." (Private collection of Jack Hatfield; Steve Meyer, Iowa Valor, pages 267-270)

Missionary Ridge

On November 25, Sherman met stiff resistance at the north end of

Missionary Ridge, partially because he directed his troops into the assault in somewhat disorganized sections rather than sending a coordinated attack up the hill. At one point, the outnumbered Confederates, led by General Patrick Cleburne, conducted a bayonet charge down Tunnel Hill, allowing them to capture a large number of Union soldiers and forcing others to retreat.

The unexpected location of the Union penetration was in the center of Missionary Ridge—unexpected by both Federals and Confederates. Confederates had poorly positioned their troops such that when those near the base of the mountain retreated up toward the top, Confederate defenders at the top were reluctant to fire down on the combined Union and Rebel troops racing up the hill.

Historical Sketch—25th Iowa Infantry

Bridgeport, Alabama
December 19, 1863
General:

I respectfully report as follows of the part taken by this regiment in the Battle of Mission Ridge on the 25th day of November, 1863. On the morning of the 25th we left Lookout Mountain at 10 o'clock; passed through Chattanooga Valley, and arrived at the front of Mission Ridge at 2p.m.. We had just formed in line of battle for an attack, when the enemy's artillery became so annoying that we commenced to gain distance to the right for a more vulnerable point of attack. A messenger having now arrived with the intelligence that two regiments of rebel cavalry had passed down the mountain for the purpose of turning our left flank, General Osterhaus ordered me to take a position up the valley in the direction of the rebel cavalry, with my own regiment and the Twenty-Sixth Iowa. The skirmishing soon became very brisk on the right, with intimations of a general attack on our left. A division of the Fourth Corps now relieved me, and I at once reported back to my division, but had no sooner arrived at my former position than General Osterhaus informed me that the enemy was endeavoring to gain the mountain pass between Chattanooga Valley and Rossville [south of Missionary Ridge], and that I must gain it first and hold it at all hazards. I proceeded as ordered and held

that pass till dark securing one six-pound gun, one loaded
ammunition wagon, and 27 prisoners, (including three
Lieutenants), and a quantity of corn meal and bacon. I am
happy to say I have no casualties to report.

Very respectfully, your obedient servant,
George A. Stone
Colonel Commanding Twenty-Fifth Iowa

(*Roster and Record of Iowa Soldiers in the War of the
Rebellion*; Published under the authority of the Iowa General
Assembly)

The Rooster Brigade and the Battle of Ringgold

*On November 26, General Hooker began pursuit of the fleeing
Confederate Army and the next day reached Ringgold, Georgia, locat-
ed about 20 miles south east of Chattanooga. Hooker's detachment of
roughly 9,000 still included Osterhaus's Division of the 15th Army
Corps, which had been cut off from Sherman before the Battle of
Lookout Mountain.*

*Bragg had instructed Confederate General Patrick Cleburne to
offer brief but strong resistance in order to allow the rest of Bragg's
Army of Tennessee to retreat safely, particularly the artillery and transportation. Cleburne set up his defense at Taylor's Ridge by the gorge
caused by a branch of East Chickamauga Creek, just outside Ringgold.*

*An eager Hooker began the engagement before his artillery
arrived, and ordered a brigade in Osterhaus's Division forward. The
Confederates allowed the 76th Ohio to obtain an advanced position,
but then pinned them down under heavy fire. Williamson's brigade,
including the 25th Iowa, came to the support of the 76th Ohio, but they
too were placed in a tentative position where further advancement
was impossible, pinned down by Confederate fire coming from three
positions.*

*During this period, General Hooker became frustrated with the
lack of Union progress and ordered General Geary to send a brigade
forward to strengthen the attack. Both Hooker and Geary were from
the Eastern Army of the Potomac, and Hooker made derogatory
remarks about the slowness of the Western troops when he sent Geary
forward. Geary sent a brigade of two Pennsylvania and two Ohio regiments forward to the left of the Iowa troops on the mountain, led by
Colonel William R. Creighton.*

Colonel Creighton formerly commanded the 7th Ohio, which was one of the regiments in his brigade. The 7th Ohio was known as the "rooster regiment," and before ordering his men forward, Creighton stood on a rock and began to crow and flap his arms like a rooster. Soon the Lt. Colonel commanding joined him, and shortly the whole regiment was crowing and flapping their arms in support.

As Creighton's Brigade advanced, the Confederates temporarily held their fire. As they came upon the 25th Iowa, they refused to go to the left of the 25th, but instead marched directly through the 25th's entrenched position. Colonel Stone and others tried to stop them, pointing out the Confederate positions, but the 28th Pennsylvania announced that they would "teach Western troops a lesson."

After Creighton's men advanced about 20 yards beyond the 25th Iowa, the Confederates opened fire. Creighton's men initially returned the fire, then turned in panic. The Iowa troops were not able to support the 7th Ohio, in that they were directly in front of the Iowans. Almost immediately the Pennsylvania, Ohio, and Iowa troops were intermixed in a scramble down the hill in retreat. All suffered horribly in the process. The Lt. Colonel of the 7th Ohio was killed near the top of the ridge. Colonel Creighton was wounded in the chest and died six hours later.

The 25th Iowa suffered 29 wounded, including seven officers. Jacob was one of those wounded, having a bullet pass through his left hand.

Cleburne soon joined the Confederate retreat. Grant arrived and told Hooker to discontinue the movement and return to Chattanooga. (Wiley Sword, Mountains Touched With Fire, *pages 326-346)*

Historical Sketch—25th Iowa Infantry

Bridgeport, Alabama
December 19, 1863
General:

I respectfully make the following report of the part taken by my regiment in the battle of Ringgold, or Taylors Ridge, Georgia, on the 27th of November last, with the list of casualties of that day. Our [Osterhaus's] division had the advance that morning, and we had not anticipated the stubborn resistance the enemy would make there, or at least were not wholly prepared for it; or perhaps better still, both. We approached the hill or mountain by a right flank, perpendicularly to the face of the mountain, and, in order to get into line of battle, had to front and change front forward on first Company. Regiments therefore got into line of battle alternately, an evolution that more or less endangered each regiment to loss, without leaving it any means for defense or protection. My position being on the extreme left, I came into line last, and, when formed, found myself in open ground, and in easy range of the enemy above us, protected by abatis and breastworks. The fire here was very annoying, but the men responded so promptly to my command "Forward, double quick," that we cleared the open field and gained the base of the hill, with the loss of but three men.

The duty assigned me was this: to gain the crest as best I could and turn the enemy's [right] flank. The hill up which I had to go was very steep, a valley to my right and left running perpendicularly to the base of the mountain, and above a long range of rocks, barricades, etc. I was there exposed to three fires, namely, direct right, left and oblique. I discovered, by their battle flags, that two regiments confronted me, and, considering the odds about proper for an Iowa regiment, ordered an advance. The enemy had his skirmishers admirably posted and in strong force. The hillside was stubbornly contested, but we pressed steadily forward, and, in an hour from the time we started, had advanced to within seventy-five yards of the crest of the hill and driven the enemy completely off of it to his fortification.

I now occupied a splendid position, and, preparatory for a final charge, had ordered a halt for the men to obtain a few moments rest.

Three regiments of the Twelfth Corps now came up over the ground I had won by fighting, one passing on my right, one through the Thirtieth Iowa, still further to my right, and the remaining one through my line. I attempted to stop this silly maneuver of advancing, where men could barely climb, by a flank, and ordered and entreated the officers to go to my left and advance in line of battle, properly, with their skirmishers well forward. I pointed to them the fire they must meet, from three points, so soon as they passed my line, and reminded them that their men would be shot down like sheep, as marching thus, by a flank they could not possibly return the fire. All to no purpose, however. An officer of a Pennsylvania regiment [28th

Pennsylvania] said they would show western troops how to storm a hill, and that they were acting under orders, etc. They passed above me, and at once the fire of the enemy ceased, and at a glance I discovered the reason: He saw this column coming up by a flank, and commenced at once to mass a fresh column on its flank. Again I went to the officer, pointed out his situation, showed him where the rebels were massing; but he would listen to nothing, and went forward.

A moment of agonizing suspense to me, and the fire opened on them from the three places designated. I never heard a more terrific and incessant fire of musketry. The men stood manfully for a minute—till the next volley was being poured into them—and then, like a flock of frightened sheep, and with exclamations: We are flanked—they are coming—they are coming, came rushing down upon us, carrying everything before them, like an avalanche, and as far as we could see they were still running shamefully to the rear. I am credibly informed they organized again more than a mile from the scene of this disaster. My men were thrown into temporary confusion, but I at once re-formed in range of the enemy's fire, and, taking the hill at a new point, threatening to flank him in return, again commenced to climb the hill. Our entire brigade was now ordered forward, and this time we gained the hill, and, as regiment after regiment of the Iowa Brigade gained the plateau above us, the rebels, now threatened at every point, fled in confusion, and the Battle of Ringgold was over.

I lost 29 wounded, none killed, none missing . . . of 21 officers in the fight, one-third of them were struck. The day following the battle orders were issued reorganizing our division. We are now in the Third Brigade First Division, Fifteenth Army Corps, Lieutenant Colonel Palmer commanding the regiment, and I commanding the brigade[1].

Very respectfully, General, your obedient servant,
George A. Stone
Colonel Twenty-Fifth Iowa Volunteers.

(*Roster and Record of Iowa Soldiers in the War of the Rebellion*; Published under the authority of the Iowa General Assembly)

1. General Osterhaus promoted Colonel George A. Stone of the 25th Iowa to command of a brigade that included the 25th Iowa, and the 3rd, 12th, 17th and 32nd Missouri Infantry.

•   On November 28, 1863, General Bragg stepped down from command of the Confederate Army of Tennessee, issuing the statement, "I deem it due to the cause and to myself to ask relief from command and an investigation into the causes of defeat." Bragg continued to blame others for the defeat. In a report dated November 30, he wrote, "no satisfactory excuse can possibly be given for the shameful conduct of our troops on the left in allowing their line to be penetrated. The position was one which ought to have been held by a line of skirmishers against any assaulting column." Bragg, despite the defeat, did retain a position in the Confederacy, and effectively and unofficially became the Confederate Army's Chief of Staff, much to the dismay of many soldiers and Southern citizens.

[Mt. Pleasant, Iowa]
Sunday Night, Nov. the 29th, 1863

Dear Husband,
    I did not write to you all this week, kept thinking I would get letter from you. It had been so long since I had received one. I got two yesterday which made it just 18 days from the time I got the last one. I know you were on a long march and didn't expect to get one until you got through. We were uneasy about while you were on the march, but still more so, when you got through for we knew there must be a battle. Thursday we got a telegram of the fight. It stated Sherman's division was hotly engaged and suffered severely so we all were anxious to know the particulars. They took it Colonel Stone has telegraphed that he is all safe, but did not say anything about anybody else. We hope there is none injured from here, by his not making any mention of names. Oh, when will such great suspenses end? They seem to come thick one after another. May this horrible war soon come to a close, so that all the poor soldiers can come home. What a glorious time it would be and yet a very painful one to those who have lost friends there.
    Last Thursday was Thanksgiving Day. They had two Union services in the Methodist Church. It was crowded to its utmost. Rev Pickett of the Congregational Church delivered an elegant and appropriate discourse before the sermon. Rev Jocelyn read the good news of your victory over the rebels at Chattanooga when

the whole audience arose and sang the old doxology "Praise God from whom all blessings flow." After the sermon, a collection was taken up amounted to $117.00 for the "Freedmen's Relief Association." It is for the purpose of clothing the Negroes that are freed by the war. Those that are away down where they can't get work to do.

We are all quite well at present. Nellie staid out of school last week on account of mumps, but she is well now. All the connections are well as far as I know. You say I don't say anything about Ma. It seemed to me I mentioned her in every letter. She is still the same old Ma. They were all up here Thanksgiving night, their boarders Nickle & Wade came along and put our molasses vessel in the pantry (It has been sitting out in the porch ever since we got it. Never could get anybody to bring it in for us.) We made some taffy for them. Ate some pie and cakes (fried cakes) and apples. They all got to playing "cross questioned", "dumb quotes," "charades," "guessing the word," &c, &c, &c, and never went home till one o'clock. Tommy and Kitty and Freddie were wide awake at one o'clock.

It made one think of times gone by when you were home and Tom and all the rest of the boys, but alas!! Where are you all gone and when will we all meet again? God only knows. Perhaps never. Oh dearest, I have thought many times what if you should never get back, what would become of us? How could we stand it. I still flatter myself what you will be one that shall come through all safe. But why should I? I know that you are exposed to great danger and just as liable to fall as any. But I will not dishonor you by my forebodings, but let us hope for the best and trust to the Lord and pray that he may fit us both for whatever he sees best to implicit upon us. Good-bye for tonight, Dear. It is after ten o'clock. The babies are all abed asleep, long ago. They talk about you every day. Tommy has new boots & mittens, coat, pants, cap & comfort, but no sled yet. He is fixed pretty comfortably for winter. I have the children all a pair of mittens apiece. We have had a few days of real hard winter. Got both the hogs killed Monday morning.

Tommy got up this morning with the mumps on one side, but it don't hurt him a bit. He thinks it is very funny to have his jaw swelled up. They take it one at a time, and have a good deal of fun laughing at each other the other's big jaws.

Em

Post Hospital
Chattanooga, Tennessee
November 29, 1863

Dear Wife,

I sit down this morning to write you a few lines to let you know how I am. I suppose you will hear by the papers before you get this that I have been wounded, and will be anxious to know how badly.

I was struck by a musket ball, near the last joint of the thumb of the left hand. The ball passed through and came out in the heel of the hand. The bones are slightly fractured but I think not so as to disable my hand. It has been very painful and is swelled very much. But this morning it does not pain me much.

The fight was at Ringgold in Georgia, 18 miles from here. We were pursuing the retreating rebel army, our division in advance. We had marched nearly all night the night before, and day before yesterday (the 27th) we found them on a high ridge (600 ft. high) and very steep and rocky. The attack was made very precipitately and without any attempt to flank their position. We came upon the double quick for two miles, and as fast as the regiments arrived they were ordered to charge up the hill without waiting even to form the brigades[1]. Our whole division suffered severely, and after reaching almost to the top of the ridge, the whole division was driven back in considerable confusion. But formed again at the foot of the ridge. By this time a battery of parrot guns had been brought forward, when they again advanced and went over the hill in gallant style, routing the rebels completely[2]. They had in the meantime burned three miles of their train to prevent it from falling into our hands.

I was wounded about 10 o'clock and remained on the field half an hour afterward, but it bled so much I had to go back and have it dressed. We camped there for the night; it rained all night, and we had nothing but the heavens for a covering. We left all our wagons behind a week ago and have slept out of doors ever since. Yesterday was very wet and cold. But I was very fortunate. In the first place I had the good luck to get into an ambulance that was coming back empty for rations for General Hooker and staff, and so got out of the rain. And when I arrived here almost the first man I saw was Dr. L. C. Cook of Trenton, Iowa, who dressed my wound, gave me supper and breakfast, and a good bed in his room, and insisted that I shall stay with him till the regiments returns, which I think will be in a day or two. I am under great obligations to the Dr. for his kindness to me. Last night was very cold; the ground is frozen this morning, and I was very fortunate to get into shelter.

Lieutenant Crane is slightly wounded in the thigh, just enough to make a sore place for a few days. Miller Spry lost the fore finger of his left hand; he had a finger shot off the right hand at Vicksburg. Two or three others got scratched, but none serious. The 25th lost some 40 or 50[3] in wounded, I think none killed.

We helped to take Lookout Mountain on the 24th, having marched all night the night before to get there in time for the fight. And were in the fight on Missionary Ridge on the 25th. I will write again in a few days and give you all the particulars. I am so tired and dirty and bloody that I must get my valise and some clean clothes before I do anything else; my pants are nearly torn off, and I am bloody all over. You wouldn't own me if you were to see me now. Of all the fights where we have been with Hooker no one man here knew what has been done, except the general result which is that the rebels have been out-generaled by Grant, and defeated, routed, demoralized, and the whole army gone to the devil where it belongs. I saw 15,000 prisoners in town yesterday evening.

But I must stop for the present. I expect to be able for duty in a few weeks. Give my love to Ma, and kiss the children for me. I would like to write a great deal more, but can't now . . . There are a great many wounded in the hospital, but all are well taken care of. So don't be uneasy about me.

Your affectionate Husband,
J.B. Ritner

P.S. My stamps are all in the book box and I will have to frank this letter.

1. Hooker's directives to charge up the hill at Ringgold before forming the brigades, and before the Union artillery had arrived, has been considered bad generalship. Hooker's military behavior led to unexpected Union losses, and may have been one of the reasons that Sherman later stated that he did not even consider Hooker as a possible replacement to McPherson as a commander of the Army of the Tennessee. (Wiley Sword, *Mountains Touched With Fire*, page 334)

2. At this time, Cleburne withdrew his forces on orders from Bragg and Hardee. Ringgold was not a Union rout of the

Confederates as Jacob says, but a Union loss. However, the
Chattanooga campaign as a whole was a major Union victory.

3.   The official report lists 29 wounded from the 25th Iowa.

Chattanooga, Tennessee
December 1, 1863

Dear Wife,

I wrote to you a day or two ago, and have been thinking about
you ever since. I know how uneasy you are, and how anxious to
hear how I am getting along. Well, now, dear, just come and sit
down by me and I will try to tell you all about it. You must be careful, though, how you go to hugging me, if you touch my sore hand
I will squeal. Now I wish I had you here to growl and complain to.
There is nobody to pity me at all, and I feel quite lonesome away
from the company. You are the dearest, sweetest wife in the world,
and I know it. And if there was any way for you to get here and you
could leave home, I would have you come. It would be so nice. But
there is no use thinking of that. I have not seen but two white
women in this town. And they were both hugging and kissing an
old secesh who was just starting North with the rest of the prisoners. I didn't pity them a bit.

I haven't got a letter from you for so long I can't remember the
time. I do wish I could hear from you. What do the children say
about the secesh shooting their Pa. I think he was almost as mean
as a copperhead. Yet I am very thankful he did not hit me in the
other hand, for then I could not write to you, and what would
become of us then. Indeed when I see hundreds of our brave men
every day with wounds so much worse than mine, many with arms
and legs cut off, and many that will never get well, I think I have
no right to complain at all. And when I think of the dangers I have
passed through in the last week, I thank God that I have escaped
with my life. And that I still have a prospect of returning to my dear
wife and children and that I may yet see the end of this cruel war
and rejoice with all good and patriotic men over the downfall of
treason.

But I will try to tell you how comfortably I am fixed here. I am
in a large, three-story brick hotel, called the Crutchfield House[1]
and which is now used for a hospital. My room is in the second
story, southeast corner, is about 12 by 18 feet, has two windows on

the south and one in the east which opens onto a porch. It is nicely papered and has a fireplace. The occupants are Dr. Cook of Trenton, Iowa, Dr. McGraw of Michigan, and Captain Ritner of Iowa. The furniture is one bedstead with a good bed on it where the doctors sleep, one good spring sofa where I sleep, two tables covered with books, papers, surgical instruments, &c, where I am writing, three split bottom chairs, one rocking chair with a cushion in it, two wash stands, two looking glasses, one "contraband[2]" to sweep the room, make beds, and carry up wood and water!

There now, don't you think you see me sitting before the fire with my feet on the mantel piece making mouths, through the windows at the secesh prisoners penned up in the depot across the street? The doctors are out all day in their wards dressing wounds and attending to the sick, and I am here alone. My hand is quite sore—can't bear to have it touched, but feels easy when I keep it quiet; my arm is swelled considerable. The doctors say I will not be able to use it for two months, but I hope it will not be that long.

I am in a mess with the surgeons of the hospital. It costs us about $2.50 per week for grub, and we can get nothing but army rations. The building is quite large, twice as large as the Brazelton House[3], and contains between three and four hundred wounded men; many of them are rebels. We have 6 or 8 rebel surgeons here. I can't go along a passage or down stairs without meeting some lousy butternut. It makes me so mad I want to kick the rascals into the street. They are treated just the same as our men for all I can see. The rebel surgeons eat at our table—but not till we are all done.

Yes, I know what you are thinking about. I can see it in your eyes. You want to know if I ain't going to come home?

Well, dear, I don't know yet what I will do. I don't know whether I could get a leave of absence if I wanted it. I am waiting for the regiment to return from the pursuit of Bragg, which will be in a day or two. I will go home if possible rather than stay in hospital here or at any other place. But if the regiment goes into winter quarters here, and gets comfortably settled, I think I had better stay with them. But I will not attempt to follow them on march. It would cost me $100 to go home and back, and I could only stay a short time, and there are a great many things I can do if the regiment is in camp. And then my wound seems hardly serious enough to justify me in leaving the men and going home while they are in camp. Perhaps I can get a leave to go home and recruit for the regiment. I should like that first-rate. But

I do not think you need look for me very strongly. You know I would like to go home and stay with you a while this winter, and I know you want me to come. But you will not want me to do anything that would be considered discreditable, or would give cowards at home a chance to talk about me.

I wish I could only get a letter from you and hear how you are getting along. I am afraid it is very cold there and that you will nearly freeze. The weather has been very cold here for the past few days, colder than I thought it would get down here. The ground has been frozen for two or three days so it would bear a wagon. One or two days it froze all day in the shade. I pity the poor soldiers; almost the whole army is out among the mountains in pursuit of Bragg, with no tents, and no blankets except what they carry. They must suffer intensely. Then many of the wounded that have been brought back here had to be laid in open frame buildings or in tents, without any fire. I hear that some have actually frozen to death. It is horrible to think of. I have not heard a word from Oliver since I came back, don't know whether he is still with Sherman or not. I have not heard from Billy—if I knew where he was I would write to him. I heard today that the 4th Cavalry was on its way here. It is rumored that our division will go to Knoxville and go into winter quarters there.

* * * * *

December 3rd—I did not get this finished the day I commenced, and yesterday I heard that the regiment had come back from the front, and started out to hunt them. I found them in camp three miles south of town, but they had marching orders, and started this morning to Bridgeport. They expect to remain there a few days—perhaps all winter. I stayed out there with them last night.

We got a mail and I got a letter from you dated _____ in which you told about going to Ma's to cook the turkey. I hope you had a good time and ate some for me. But I was sorry to hear that they are so bad off. It must not be. You must pay them the interest on the $138 right away, and if Alvah does nothing for them, I want you to go and pay their tax. And let them have money to get anything they need. They shall never need for anything while I can help it. See Alvah about our tax and do as he recommends. I shall stay here a few days till the regiment gets into camp at Bridgeport, and then go there and perhaps stay with them if they go into winter quarters. If they move again I don't know what I will do. I am glad you got the money all right. We will be paid again in a few days and I will send some more. My hand does not get any better yet. I did sleep a bit last night. It comes very awkward to have to do everything with one hand.

Our division has been re-brigaded. We have now three brigades instead of two, and the third is composed of the 25th Iowa and 3rd, 12th, 17th, and 32nd Missouri, commanded by Acting Brigadier General George A. Stone!! I have no later news to tell you about the fight here. We are all anxious to get the Northern papers to hear the news from Chattanooga! The pursuit was continued 20 miles beyond Ringgold, but no enemy could be found. You will see all about it in the papers before you get this. Direct your letters to me at the regiment as you have been doing.

I wanted to write a great deal more and tell you all about our march, and the part we took in the fight at Lookout Mountain and Missionary Ridge. But I will have to put it off for the present. Tell the children I said they must all be good, and love each other and obey their Mother and must not forget their Pa . . .

Your affectionate Husband,
J.B. Ritner

I thought I had traveled some, and had seen some rough country. But I give it up that I didn't know anything about it. Missouri is a fine country! It is <u>level</u> about Vicksburg!! But if you want to see rocks and mountains come to Chattanooga—"among the jutting peaks and rugged cliffs of rock-ribbed, rude old Cumberland." The day we took Lookout Mountain was dark and cloudy and we could not see the top of the mountain for clouds. It did not rain in the valley till evening but the top of the mountain was among the clouds all day. It is 2,400 feet above the level of the water in the river. I was clear on the tip top of it the next day. It made my head dizzy to look down. Chattanooga is not half as large as Mt. Pleasant.

1. Before the war, the Crutchfield House was a famous hotel in Chattanooga where Stephen Douglas had given speeches in 1860 during his presidential bid, and where Jefferson Davis had made speeches after resigning from the U.S. Senate, on his way to Mississippi.

2. When Jacob used the term "contraband" he meant an ex-slave.

During the early period of the Civil War the Federal government demanded that the Fugitive Slave Law be enforced in states that remained loyal to the Union. This required military leaders to return slaves to their owners. General Benjamin F. Butler, not at all satisfied with this directive, declared that runaway slaves who came into his lines would be declared "contraband of war" and would not returned to their masters. At first, lawmakers tried to uphold the intent of the Fugitive Slave Law, but later passed the Confiscation Act that allowed the Union forces to seize and use ships, slaves, cotton and other Confederate property as they saw fit. After Butler's comment, the term "contraband" was used by Northerners as slang for ex-slaves. (Webb Garrison, *Civil War Curiosities*, pages 257-264)

3. The Brazelton Hotel of Mt. Pleasant was a large, four-story structure built circa 1859, located on the town square. (*The History of Henry County, Iowa*, page 27)

[Mt. Pleasant, Iowa]
December 8th, 1863

Dearest,

I received a letter from you yesterday, stating that you had your poor hand shot. I am so sorry & yet how thankful we ought to be that it was no worse—How do you get along without me there to dress it for you? And you passed through another series of battles and are still alive! Oh, it is nothing but the goodness of our Dear Father in heaven that has kept you safe through all those dangers that you have fought through. Let us thank him sincerely for it. We did not think, from what we could learn from the papers, that your division was in much of the fight, and were consoling ourselves that you were all safe. We know that you were out with Hooker and was not with Sherman in those dreadful charges and the paper stated that Osterhous' division was behind time in getting to some of the battles, so we had concluded that you were not in much danger. We hadn't got any of the particulars from you at all. Your letter was the first thing that gave us any definite news about the 25th. Colonel Stone had telegraphed that he was safe, but said nothing about the rest. I took your letter out of the office, and Julius Crane wanted me to open it to see if there was any news. I did so, and told him that you and Baron were slightly wounded. It soon spread around and I hadn't been home long till Mr. Crane came to know for himself how bad it was & the little later Alvah came out. I was glad to tell them that there was no danger, but I know your poor hand is very sore. I wish I could be with you a while and cure it up. Oh, I <u>do</u> hope you will not have to be in any more battles. I think the western Army has done its share of fighting. The Potomac boys ought to do their share now, and then the rebels would be ready for peace on any terms.

We all are well. The children have all had mumps, but are about well again . . . The cow will not have a calf for two months yet I guess. Perhaps I ought to have sold her. It will cost so much to keep her, but I could not get much for her & I expect cows will be very high in the spring. I know she is a good one and I thought I had better keep her.

Tell me in your next whether you can read my mixed up letters. Ma's folks are all well. Car has gone to Jefferson to stay awhile. Mr. Gunn has gone to Fairfield to hold a meeting.

I will just own up how <u>wicked</u> I have been. I almost wished your wound had been on the other hand and a little worse, so they would have discharged you (but, I don't though.) I am <u>mad</u> at the mean rebel that would take a drop of your precious blood. Forgive me for even thinking of such a thing.

Em

Historical Sketch—, 25th Iowa Infantry

*After the battle of Ringgold, the regiment, with its brigade and division, returned to Chattanooga, and, a few days later, marched to Bridgeport, Alabama, where it remained until December 23rd, [1863] on which date the division was ordered to proceed to Woodville, on the Memphis and Charleston Railroad, at which place it went into winter quarters. Colonel Stone's Brigade was engaged in two expeditions during the winter. The first of these expeditions ended at the town of Lebanon, Alabama, where there were a considerable number of citizens who had remained true to the cause of the Union. Many of them came to Colonel Stone's camp, where the men were organized into companies and furnished with arms and ammunition. They subsequently became part of a Union regiment and rendered good service to their country. Upon his return to Woodville, Colonel Stone was ordered to proceed to Cleveland, East Tennessee, at which place his command constituted a garrison for the post until early in March, 1864. At that point, the brigade rejoined the division at Woodville, where it remained until the beginning of the great Atlanta campaign, in which it was to take a most conspicuous part. (*Roster and Record of Iowa Soldiers in the War of the Rebellion; *Published under the authority of the Iowa General Assembly)*

Editor's Notes:

In December, the Union troops went into winter quarters with Jacob's division housed at Woodville, Alabama. Jacob returned to Iowa on medical leave because of his wound, suffered outside Chattanooga at Ringgold. During this period, many of the other veterans also took furloughs. While in Iowa, Jacob officially rented a room to act as a Recruiting Officer:

The diary of Dr. Henry Farr, Surgeon of the 25th Iowa who was also back in Iowa on furlough, includes the entry of February 6, 1864: "Went to the City—visited with Dr. Marsh. Called on Capt. Ritner, whom I found quite sick." By mid march, Dr. Farr had returned to the field in Georgia and his entries of March 18th and 19th, 1864, included: "Rev. Baird came from Burlington for the remains of M. Hinson; Superintended the exhuming of Hinson a dead private Co. G, who died in January [17th] of Pneumonia. Found body considerably decomposed. Placed it in an air-tight-coffin & shipped home to Burlington." (Diary of Dr. Henry Farr, Unpublished, Iowa State Historical Society, Iowa City, Iowa)

Chapter Five
The Atlanta Campaign

With the resignation of Bragg from command of the Army of Tennessee, Jefferson Davis awarded that post to Joseph E. Johnston, after giving consideration to William Hardee, Pierre Gustave Beauregard, and even Robert E. Lee. Bragg became, in effect, Chief of Staff of the Confederate Army.

On the Union side, Lincoln promoted U. S. Grant to Commander in Chief of all Union armies and Grant went east to personally guide the Army of the Potomac. Sherman took Grant's former position of command of the Department of the West. McPherson now commanded the Army of the Tennessee, which included the 15th Army Corps, commanded by John Logan, the 16th Corps, under Grenville Dodge, and the 17th Corps, commanded by Francis Blair. The 25th Iowa remained in Williamson's Brigade, Osterhaus's Division, reporting to Logan in the 15th Corps.

Also reporting to Sherman were George Thomas, commander of the Army of the Cumberland, and John Schofield, commanding the smaller Army of the Ohio. Hooker's 11th and 12th Corps were combined into the 20th Corps, and he reported to Thomas. Oliver Otis Howard led the 4th Army Corps, also reporting to Thomas.

Historical Sketch—25th Iowa Infantry

*The regiment had—prior to the commencement of the campaign— been again placed in a brigade composed exclusively of Iowa troops, as follows: The Fourth, Ninth, Twenty-Fifth and Thirty-First regiments of Iowa Infantry. These four regiments remained together until the close of the war and became known throughout the army as the "Iowa Brigade of the Fifteenth Corps." Colonel J. A. Williamson of the Fourth Iowa, by virtue of his seniority in rank, became the commander of the brigade, and Colonel Stone resumed command of the Twenty-Fifth Iowa. (*Roster and Record of Iowa Soldiers in the War of the Rebellion; *Published under the authority of the Iowa General Assembly)*

From Chattanooga to Atlanta.

I Have "Been Bad" Too. I Went to the Theater at Indianapolis!

No. 16, City Hotel
Nashville, Tennessee
April 22, 1864

My Dear Wife,

I sit down to write to write you a few lines this evening to let you know how I am getting along on the "Road to Dixie." Well, I have got "this far and no further."

I suppose you have got a <u>long letter</u> I wrote to you from

Davenport last Sunday. Well, I had the ague and no sense or I would have written more. I left there Monday morning, in charge of a detachment of 55 recruits, 10 stragglers, and one deserter, belonging to 12 different regiments.

I suppose the worst misfortune that could possibly befall an <u>officer</u> is to be placed in charge of a lot of raw recruits on the way south. They have no sense and can't learn any—and think the officer can do anything. I have been "bored" nearly to death. I have had two shakes since we left Davenport, but they didn't amount to much. It don't use me up like it did last winter. I rode all night last night in the cars and have been busy all day getting quarters and transportation for my "stock."

We arrived at Chicago at 5 o'clock p.m. and left at 9 p.m. and got to Indianapolis at 9 the next morning and had to wait there till 9 the next morning. I wished you had been there with me—it was the most lonesome place I ever saw. I didn't see anyone I knew till we were just starting away, when I found Lieutenant Steele, who had just arrived. He was on the same train to Louisville. I asked him for that picture you sent by him—he said he didn't have it. There now, what did I tell you? He said he forgot to leave his and you must go up there and get it!! I want you to send mine by Bowman or someone the first chance. I must have it, and haven't got time to come after it. Send my hair brush along too. I forgot it. I kept a sharp lookout all through Indiana to see if there were any more Hoosier girls as good-looking as the one I boarded with last winter[1], but I couldn't see her.

I have "been <u>bad</u>" too. I went to the theater at Indianapolis!

Well, we got to Louisville at 4 o'clock in the evening and Lieutenant Steele left on the train the next morning, but I could not get my detachment on that train and had to wait till 3 p.m. We got here at daylight this morning.

We leave at 6 o'clock tomorrow morning and will get as far as Huntsville [Alabama], and to the regiment Sunday. Steele would get there today. I am anxious to get there . . . It seems to me it has been more than a year since I saw you, and I have been thinking about you all the time, and wondering if you are well, and how you get along.

The weather here is very warm and pleasant. The trees begin to look green—some are out in their new dresses now, but the season is very backward here as in Iowa.

I hope you got the $100 I sent you from Davenport. I want it to pay my board bill for last winter[1]. It has cost me a great deal more than I expected to get down here, on account of being detained so much. They charge $3.00 per day at this place, and not half as good living as I got at your house. But I must quit and go to bed. I must be up at 4 in the morning, and didn't sleep a wink last night. So good night, dear—pleasant dreams to you.

Your own Jake

1. Jacob is joking about paying board to live in his own house with Emeline, who had once lived in Indiana, so was a Hoosier girl herself.

The Battle of Resaca

As the Atlanta Campaign began, the Confederates had their head-quarters at Dalton, Georgia, located southeast of Chattanooga on the way to Atlanta. Instead of attacking Dalton directly, Sherman relied on a flanking maneuver. Thomas and the Army of the Cumberland occupied the center of the direct route to Dalton, but McPherson and the Army of the Tennessee and Schofield and the Army of the Ohio went west and south of Dalton to Resaca to sever the Confederate rail lines to Atlanta. This complicated maneuvering took several days and included the Battle of Dug Gap on May 8 and the Battle of Rocky Face Ridge (May 7 to 12) by the Army of the Cumberland and the Army of the Ohio. The Confederates eventually realized the target of the Union assault, and on the night of May 12, they withdrew their forces from Dalton and moved to Resaca.

Sherman and Thomas mistakenly thought that Johnston would continue his retreat across the Ostanaula River, but Johnston decided that he must make at least a temporary defense of Resaca or risk being attacked in the rear while crossing the Ostanaula River. Fierce fighting that included all the Union armies took place in several locations around Resaca from May 13 through May 16, 1864. In the early evening of May 16, Johnston met with his generals and several division commanders and informed them that the Confederates would retreat to the south bank of the Ostanaula River during the night. This was the end of the first phase of the Atlanta campaign.

Historical Sketch—25th Iowa Infantry

On the 1st of May, 1864, the brigade and division marched from Woodville to join the army at the front. It first met the enemy in fierce conflict at Resaca, Georgia. The operations of the brigade in that battle are fully described in the official report of Colonel Williamson,

About 10 o'clock on the 13th instant the brigade was ordered into line of battle immediately on the left of the First Brigade, where it remained for two or three hours, when I received orders to move my brigade forward . . . taking the direction and keeping the alignment of the First Brigade until I arrived near the fortified hill from which the enemy kept up a heavy fire of artillery and musketry. At this point I halted, keeping my right aligned with the First Brigade, and advancing my left wing so as to bring them under cover, where I remained until the enemy fell back when I advanced, with the First Brigade on my right, and took possession of the hill immediately in front of the enemy's fortifications, where I remained, skirmishing until a late hour at night. On the morning of the 14th, commenced skirmishing at daylight, and kept it up all day, suffering considerable loss.

Late in the afternoon of the 14th, I was ordered by General Osterhaus to send one regiment to support a battery which was engaging the enemy's fortifications. In obedience to this order I sent the Twenty-Fifth Iowa, Colonel Stone. A little later in the evening I was ordered to send a regiment to support the First Brigade, which was assaulting the enemy's line on my right, and, in obedience thereto, sent the Twenty-Fifth Iowa, and moved the Fourth Iowa into position to support the battery. I remained in line of battle during the night of the 14th, skirmishing until a late hour, and again resumed the skirmishing at daylight on the 15th, and continued it through the day and until late at night. At daylight on the 16th, I received an order from General Osterhaus to advance into the town of Resaca, the enemy having evacuated it during the night. I have only to say in conclusion, that there was neither straggling nor cowardice in my command. All were anxious to do their duty.

Colonel Williamson reports the casualties in his brigade at Resaca as follows: Killed, 6; wounded, 37; total, 43. Colonel Stone reports the casualties in the Twenty-Fifth Iowa: Killed, 3; wounded, 15; total, 18. It will thus be seen that the regiment sustained a loss of one-half the number killed, and nearly one-half the number wounded, in the four regiments of its brigade at the battle or Resaca. (Roster and Record of Iowa Soldiers in the War of the Rebellion; *Published under the authority of the Iowa General Assembly)*

Monday, May 16, 1864

Dear Wife,

It is with great pleasure that I again seat myself to write you a few lines. I know, Dear, you will be very uneasy before you get this. I am very sorry it is so, but it couldn't be helped. Only think, I have not written to you since about the 27th of April! And I promised to write so often. Well, dear, when you know all about it, I think you will not blame me.

When I wrote to you last I said I thought we would soon move, but would not get to the front. Yet we started on Sunday the 1st day of May and came here as straight and fast as we could! and have been here a week and fighting for the last four days. We have not gained much on the rebels for the last two days and I don't know how much longer it will last[1]. But it will be till the rebels are completely whipped, which they are sure to be. John Laux[2] of my company was killed on the 13th. Corporal McPheron and James Scarff are wounded, but not severely. Three Sergeants in Company H, Barker, Boyles, and Parent[3], are wounded severely. Well dear, I will now go back and bring up the rear of my story.

On the very next day after I wrote I had a very hard shake and was very sick. The doctor was willing to leave me behind, but I started with the rest and got better for a while. When we got up as far as Stevenson [Alabama] I found my valise there at the express office. Everything was all right in it, so I had that much good luck. We thought we were not going to the "front" because we were ordered to take all our camp and garrison equipage with us. But as soon as we got across Lookout Mountain we were ordered to leave all camp and garrison equipage—turn over all the tents but three.

As we had so little transportation we were allowed only one valise for three officers. All the rest with the book-boxes, tents, &c, were sent to Chattanooga. Lieutenants Steele and Crane and myself put a change of clothing into one valise. I put in some paper and envelopes so I could write to you, and your picture to look at once in a while. Well, the second day the wagon broke down and the things were put into a wagon belonging to the 4th Division and several valises were stolen, ours among the rest! So we were out there in the wilderness without a thing except what we have on. I have not even your picture to look at. I hope Bowman will soon get here with another one. But that is not all the bad luck. I lost my blankets at the same time and lay out three nights without any covering at all, and caught a very bad cold— have been so hoarse I could not speak above a whisper. I have been with the regiment part of the time and part of the time at the rear in the hospital. It rained very hard a few nights ago and blew tremendously and I went to an ambulance to sleep and that night someone stole my haversack that I gave $5.00 for. Now don't you think I have got into a streak of bad luck. I never felt so much like complaining in my life. I know I ought not to write to you this way, for you have troubles enough of your own. But I can't think of anything else. I am now at the division hospital which is two miles in the rear of our advance works. The news have just now come in that the rebels evacuated last night and that our forces are pursuing. I suppose this is the fact, as there has been no firing this morning.

I came here from the regiments night before last. I have got my cold loosened up and the ague broke for the present, and will try to get to the regiment tomorrow. I must say that I have never been in so unpleasant a situation and so perfectly miserable as I have been for a week. Not because I was dangerously sick, but I could not speak so as to be heard by the company, and had a dull, stupid headache all the time, so I could do nothing, and yet I did not like to go to the rear at a time like this. Now I am growling again. I declare I have a mind to tear this letter up and not send it all.

This place is 12 or 15 miles southeast of Dalton near the railroad. The rebels have a strong force but not so many as we have, I think. They were driven back from Dalton several days ago and made a stand here, where they had strong and extensive fortifications, but we outflanked them and they have again fallen back—I don't know whether they will make another stand or not. We are sure to whip them if they do. And I think that will <u>end the war</u>. We have good news from Grant. We all expect to get home next fall. I got a letter from you the day we crossed Lookout Mountain and another one yesterday, dated May 2. You may be sure I was very glad to get them and they did me a great deal of good. I have thought a great deal about how uneasy you will be before you hear from me again. I do hope it won't be long till I can go home and stay with you always. Oh dear, won't that be nice.

I am sorry that Palmer is going away without fixing your fence. I don't know what you will do about it. I suppose all those 100 day men think they are doing great things and will take a great deal of credit to themselves for being willing to go for 100 days with the understanding that they will not be placed where there is any danger of their seeing a rebel![4] We are all glad the cowardly rascals are willing to do even that much to help us end the war. At the same time we despise the whole crew of them for not being willing to go to war in earnest, if they go at all.

I am glad to hear that the children are doing so well at school, and that Josey is so smart. I will write to Lulie and Nellie when we get back to camp and I get the book-box.

You may sell the house for what you think it is worth; I shall be satisfied with what you do. If you buy another house, have the deed made out to <u>yourself</u>. Although I have tried to keep my accounts correct with the government, and have been careful and honest in all my dealings, yet the regulations are such that I shall be afraid to own anything for years after this war is over[5]. But I must stop, dear, for this time. I will write again the first chance. Be assured, dear wife, of my true <u>love</u> for you.

Yours ever, Jake

You must excuse this grumbling letter, dear. I am ashamed of it. If I had time I would tear it up and write another.

1. At this point in Jacob's letter-writing, he is probably unaware that the Confederates had retreated from Resaca during the night of May 15–16.

2. John Laux, age 21, of Danville, was born in Germany. His name was on a list of soldiers that Jacob had recruited for the 25th Iowa Infantry during his winter furlough.

3. Corporal John W. McPheron, Jr. and John H. Scarff both survived the war. Sergeants Charles Barker and William Boyles survived the war, but John Parent, born in Virginia, died of his wounds on May 17, 1864 in Resaca. He was buried in the National Cemetery in Chattanooga.

4. Iowa mustered four regiments of 100 day men, whose purpose was to provide temporary garrison duties, to allowing veterans to be present for combat duties. The 45th Iowa was mustered May 25th at Keokuk with Alvah Bereman, Emeline's brother, as its colonel. All four mustered out in September. Jacob is complaining that the "100 day men" will consider themselves to be true soldiers, which he does not consider them to be. Harris Palmer, age 41, enlisted in the 45th Iowa as Third Sergeant instead of fixing Emeline's fence.

5. Jacob was referring to officers being in charge of equipment issued to companies. If this equipment of Company B of the 25th Iowa were lost or stolen, Jacob was afraid that he would be held financially responsible for it.

Historical Sketch—25th Iowa Infantry

*A summary of the report shows that, on May 16th, the Twenty-Fifth Iowa was on duty as provost guard[1] in the village of Resaca. Between the dates May 17th and 20th, 1864, the regiment marched with its brigade from Resaca to Kingston, Georgia (*Roster and Record of Iowa Soldiers in the War of the Rebellion; *Published under the authority of the Iowa General Assembly)*

1. The honor of provost guard would typically be awarded to the regiment or brigade that first entered the captured town.

Kingston, Georgia
May 21, 1864

Dear Wife,

Well, Dear, I wrote you a few lines yesterday in a hurry. And as we are yet at the same place with no prospect of doing anything today, I don't think I can spend the time more agreeably than writing to you again. You know I promised to write to you every chance. Oh, my dear wife, you do not know what a satisfaction it is to me to have you to think of and love and write to. I often lay awake for hours after marching all day, thinking about my sweet wife and children and wondering how long it will be before I see you all again.

I very unexpectedly got a letter from you yesterday after I had written. We got a mail in the morning but there was no letter for me. And I got the blues and felt meaner than a 100-day man. But about noon I got the letter you sent by Bowman with your photograph in it. I thought then I was the biggest man in the regiment. And had to go round and show the picture to all the other officers. I know they all thought they would like to have such a good-looking wife. I thank you a thousand times, dear for sending it. I think it is a very good picture. Your mouth is all right this time. I have nearly spoiled it already, kissing it. I am going to keep it. Bowman stopped at Chattanooga and had not got here himself. He sent the letter on by Milthone, who had been left there sick. He did not send the Ambrotype[1] or brush. I think he will be here with them in a few days.

We are camped about 2 miles back of Kingston, Georgia, in a large wheat field which was cut in heads when we came but is now out of sight. We are on the river Etowah or Hightower. And it is reported the rebels are fortified about 2 miles on the other side. I think we will go over and see in a day or two. I am sitting flat on the ground writing on my knee. The weather is very hot, and we have no shade except what we make by hanging up blankets. I have no clothes this side of Chattanooga except what I have on, and my shirt and drawers are the same I put on the morning I left home. But I had them washed the other day and am clean as the rest.

We came in here day before yesterday and may remain another day or two. But we are liable to move at any moment. It is reported that the rebels are reinforced. And I suppose we are waiting for our reinforcements to come up. But I can't tell you much about what is going on and nothing about our future operations. Everything is kept very close and every man and officer has to stay at his place. You can learn a great deal more from the papers than I can tell you. We are about 80 miles from Chattanooga and 60 miles from Atlanta. We have been driving the rebels before us all the way from Dalton. And the <u>moral</u> effect must be very greatly in our favor. We have pressed them so closely all the way they did not have time to destroy the railroad except the bridge at Resaca, and that was already framed and put up in 24 hours. There is a fine covered bridge across the river here, on which they had piled shavings and cotton but did not have time to set it on fire and we can cross whenever we get ready.

I am very glad to hear that your house looks so nice since you have got it fixed up. How I would like to be there and see it. I am so glad <u>you</u> think it is nice, for I was sorry after I came away that I did not buy you a new house when I was at home. If ever a woman deserved a nice house it is you. How I would like to see your new hat!—How proud I would be to go up town with you. Why didn't you have it on when you sat for your picture? I suppose Kittie goes to Sunday school with her hat and slippers. What does she do all day when the rest are all gone to school? I am glad to hear they do so well at school. I expect they will all be smart scholars when I get home. I hope they will be good as well as smart. I want Lulie and Nellie to learn to act like young ladies and not go with bad children or where they are told not to go. And they are getting old enough to think about something else besides playing and romping. Kiss them for me. Payne and Black are both well. Garvin and Crane both had a chill yesterday. I wrote a few lines to Mother this morning. Why don't you tell me something about Billy and Ol? I don't know whether Billy got his commission or not. Alvah ought to have been

<u>smart like we are</u> and then he could go to war—for 100 days!
My love to Ma and Car.

Your affection Husband,
J.B. Ritner

1. Collodian was a tricky transparent solution that held light-sensitive chemicals on glass. This was the key ingredient for all Civil War photography. An ambrotype was a variation on the collodian process, which produced a photographic negative on glass, that, when backed with black material, turned into a positive image. (Ross J. Kelbough, *Introduction to Civil War Photography*, page 48)

The Women's Dress Movement

[Mt. Pleasant, Iowa]
May the 24th 1864

Dear Husband,

This is Tuesday night. I have had no letter from you since last Saturday two weeks. When shall I ever hear again if we have had no information of your whereabouts since you left Woodville? But guess you were with Sherman. We had our intimation since that the Iowa boys had gone out with McPherson to take some position and afterwards, heard that McPherson's army was all cut to pieces. We were very uneasy for awhile, but not hearing it concluded it was all false. Today's *Hawkeye* gives an account of the battle at Resaca and states that Osterhous' division and 15th A.C. were engaged, but didn't say anything about the particular regiments. But, we almost know that you were all there.

Oh, how is it with you tonight? And when shall we ever get the particulars? I will still hope that you are all safe and that I shall soon get a long letter from you my dearest husband. What great hardships and dangers the poor soldiers have to endure—how I do pity them. This afternoon I was at Formal prayer meeting and such prayers as went up for the soldiers. If they were put up in faith (which I have no reason to doubt) the Lord <u>will</u> surely take care of the soldiers and soon give us victory and peace—

I was at a meeting this afternoon at the City Hall—A woman's meeting, for the purpose of pledging our selves not to buy any articles of dress for "three years or during the war." They have near a hundred names down. Some talk of laying by all their silks and finery and becoming calico dresses, and shakers. What do you think of it?

Thursday—worked the garden all day yesterday & didn't finish the letter. I was in hopes I would get some word from you, but didn't. Lib and I have concluded to go to Danville. Got a letter from Susan. She said we could have three pigs. It is most time to start and I must send you this piece of a letter hoping that before I write again I shall get a long letter from you. Sallie is going to stay with the children.

Your own Em.

All well.

The Battle of Dallas

Historical Sketch—25th Iowa Infantry

Remaining in camp at Kingston for three days, the 25th Iowa continued the march to Dallas, and arrived in front of that place on the 26th of May, 1864. In the skirmishes and heavier fighting, which ensued and lasted until the 31st of May, the Twenty-Fifth Iowa bore a conspicuous part, and again demonstrated fully the bravery and efficiency of its officers and men. During the night of May 28th, Williamson's brigade had built a complete line of defensive works. On the 29th, it occupied and continued to strengthen the works, all the time under the fire of the enemy. Soon after dark on the 29th, the brigade was ordered to leave the works and take a position on the main road, to cover the rear of the corps, which was then moving out. As soon as the movement began, the enemy made a vigorous attack, when the Ninth and Twenty-Fifth Iowa were ordered back to the original position, where they remained until daylight, holding the enemy in check. They were then joined by the other two regiments of the brigade, which remained in the works during the 30th and 31st of May, successfully defending them, delaying the advance of the enemy. At daylight, on June 1st, the brigade was ordered out of the works to another line one mile in the rear, which had been constructed to cover the withdrawal of the corps. When the corps had passed the works, the brigade moved out and acted as rear guard on the march to New Hope Church. The enemy following closely, as far back as Dallas. (Roster and Record of Iowa Soldiers in the War of the Rebellion; *Published under the authority of the Iowa General Assembly*)

- The battles in this area were the Battle of New Hope Church on May 25 (Hooker vs. Hood), the Battle of Picket's Mill on May

27 (Howard vs. Cleburne), and the Battle of Dallas on May 28 (Logan, including Jacob and Dodge, vs. Bate)

After the initial charge by the Confederates, Bate came to realize that the Union had more than a skirmish line around Dallas, as he had once thought, and he called off the Confederate attack. But the three Confederate brigades of Bate's Division did not get the order, and instead launched an uncoordinated attack aimed at Osterhaus's Division, which included Jacob. Confederate losses numbered 1,000 to 1,500 compared to Logan's reported loss of only 379.

During the night of May 28, Logan's and Dodge's troops stayed in their trenches, sleeping little and anticipating a night attack by the Confederates, which did not come. During the day of the 29th there were no large-scale attacks or flanking movements, but a great deal of fighting. However, at 10 p.m., as Logan and Dodge prepared to withdraw from their positions, the Confederates launched another series of attacks. The Confederate attacks did not cease until daybreak, and when they disappeared, many of the Union soldiers, a great percentage of whom had not slept for 72 hours, immediately fell asleep. On May 30, the Union troops were too tired to withdraw and the withdrawal, division by division, did not begin until the night of May 31, continuing through June 1.

The Battle of Dallas
Field of Battle, Georgia
June 2, 1864

Dear Wife,
   This is Thursday and I have not written to you since a week ago last Friday. I suppose you will be looking anxiously for this long before you get it. But it could not be helped. We have had no chance to write letters or send them back. My health is very good at present, but I don't know how soon I may have the ague again. I had a shake the same day I wrote to you last and one the next day. We were then lying about two miles back of Kingston, where we stopped to rest a few days. We started from there on Monday, May 23rd. We marched 18 miles the first day. I couldn't keep up and couldn't get to ride, and did not get to camp at all that night. But since then I have been right along, and feel able for anything now.
   Our army moved in three columns from Kingston, the 15th and 16th Army Corps on the right. On the evening of the 26th we

found the rebels in a strong position near Dallas. We came very near running into an ambuscade and getting cut up. This is the awfulest wooden country I ever saw—it is just like fighting in the dark. Our brigade was taken to the front and placed in line about dark. But the brush was so thick or the officers so drunk[1]—I don't know which—that the line was formed with the left flank of the brigade toward the enemy, instead of fronting them, and we were so close that the rebel bullets came right along our brigade all night. They kept up a regular fire, and we did not sleep a wink. The next morning they marched a regiment in on our left flank carrying our flag. The 9th and 31st Iowa were on the left, and thought they were reinforcements coming to help us and did not know any better till they received a volley from the rebels that caused the whole brigade to fall back, most of the regiments in considerable confusion. The 25th changed front to the rear in fine style and checked the rebels till the other two brigades came to our relief. Some of the other regiments lost a good many. We were on the right and did not lose any.

June 3rd

It rained so I had to stop here. It rained all afternoon and is wet and cloudy this morning.

On the evening of the 28th the rebels made an assault on our whole line, and came very near turning our right flank, and our brigade was again called out and taken on a fast run for a mile to reinforce the 4th Division of our Corps, which was about to give way. The rebels had already captured three guns of the 1st Iowa Battery and driven back the 6th Iowa Infantry. But we got there in time to retake the Battery and drive the rebels back—they got badly "salivated" all along the line, being repulsed at every point.

But I can't explain all our maneuvers to you in a letter, and I don't suppose it would be interesting.

On the evening of the 31st the rebels got a battery planted so as almost to take the breastworks of our brigade, which was then on the extreme right of our infantry line and next to Wilder's Cavalry[2], and they gave us the warmest bombardment we had ever had. The grape, canister, and shell[3] flew over and around us furiously. But we laid low and let them rip away till dark, when we were surprised to find that not a man in the brigade was hurt. It was very remarkable that we escaped so well.

The next morning just before daylight we "changed our base of operations." The whole right wing of our army fell back a short distance and then moved to the left. Our corps is now some 6 or 8 miles further to the left than we were, and have relieved the 20th Army Corps, who have gone still farther to the left. It was a very dangerous move to make in the face of an enemy, but it was well planned and executed without loss or accident. We think the object was to avoid a very strong position of the enemy in front of our right; they were strongly fortified in a range of rocky hills and had one high peak from which they could see all our movements, and we thought it easier to go around them than to drive them out.

We all have a great deal of confidence in Logan and McPherson[4]. The 2nd and 4th Divisions of our Army Corps are about one mile in front of us, pounding away at the rebels day and night. Their works are within 75 to 300 yards of the rebel lines. Our division is lying here in the woods as a reserve, but are ready at any minute to go to the front.

[This poem was printed on the stationary that Jacob used to write this letter.]

"To A Wife"
"Dearest, like the breeze of heaven?
Comes the solace you impart,
Dropping like the balm of heaven
On the weary home and heart.
Home with all its joys is present,
when those letters come from thee,
Household face bright and pleasant
Look with sunny smiles on me.
"When the cannon thunders near me
"Mid the clash of sounding arms,
Come the thoughts of home to cheer me
With its dear, familiar forms.
Then I see with eyes enchanted
All the loves that cluster there,
And I face with heart undaunted
All the fearful scenes of war."

(24 Sheets of Song Paper, free by mail for 25 cents, by J.R. Howells & Co., Jefferson, Ohio)

Well, my sweet dear, I did not write the poetry at the top of this page, but I want you to consider them my sentiments exactly. I could not express my feelings better if I was to try . . . Now I am writing this little sheet just for you, dear, and will try to tell you something about how we get along down here.

It is now 34 days since we started on this campaign from Woodville. Since that time all the officers in the regiment have been messing together. We have a pack mule and four cooks. We have nothing to eat but coffee, "hard-tack and sow-belly," and sometimes beef. Sometimes when we are "under fire" the cooks do not come up and we have to fast. We never have any table or anything of the kind, but everyone takes his grub, sits down on the ground, and goes to eating. So you see we have a nice "picnic" every day, and enjoy it very much. We are not troubled by tents or anything of that kind; each officer carries a woolen and a gum blanket and when night comes we lie down and go to sleep wherever we may happen to be—that is, if the rebels will let us. The pickets fire at each other here all night, and we always have to sleep with all our clothes, arms and accoutrements on, and sometimes stay awake all night. It is now about 24 days since we attacked the rebels at Resaca, and there has scarcely been a day since then that there has not been fighting someplace in hearing.

It was clear yesterday morning and I borrowed a pair of pants and sent my pants, drawers, shirt, socks, and blouse away to be washed. It rained very hard all afternoon and they are not dry yet. They are the same I put on the morning I left home, and are all I have this side of Chattanooga. So you see I have "nothing to wear" but shoes, pants and vest. Who wouldn't be a soldier! The way we kept dry in the rain was to roll up the woolen blanket and lay it on a stone, and then hang the gum blanket over our shoulders, and sit down on the woolen; in this way we kept perfectly dry. There is no house near here where we can get rails or boards. So last night I skinned a big chestnut tree and got a wide piece of bark, lay down on it and spread my gum over me and slept first-rate. I dreamed about you and the children and didn't get up till I was called to breakfast. I do think I love you better and think of you more since I was home last than I ever did before. Oh, how I do wish this was over so I could go home to stay. We have heard nothing of Grant's army[5] since the 19th of May. I hope he will succeed and I am certain that we will and that will surely crush the rebellion. Our lines are so long here and there are so many reports that we don't believe anything we hear and I can't tell you much about our operations.

Steele and Crane are both well. Sergeant Payne had the ague a few days ago, and Will Black had the sick headache a day or two—both are well now. Hall makes a first-rate soldier. The men are generally well. But all are worn down by hard work and loss of sleep. But I must stop and inspect the guns of my company. I will write again in a day or two if we do not move. I shan't write to anyone but you till this fight is over. You may write to the rest and tell them I am all right. My respects to Ma, Car, Alvah, Bro. Gunn, and all the friends.

Yours ever, J.B. Ritner

I had to write this on my knee and in a hurry. I am afraid you cannot read it. Excuse all mistakes—I haven't time to look over it.

1. Officers drinking continued to be a problem for the Union. On the morning of May 30, as the fighting lulled and many had food, water, and sleep for the first time in 72 hours, Lt. Colonel Benjamin Myers of the 83rd Indiana got so drunk, that in a "crazy fit," he made a solo charge on the Confederates and was killed. (Albert Castel, *Decision in the West*, page 250)

2. Wilder's Cavalry was named for its commander, John Thomas Wilder, who commanded the 3rd Brigade, 2nd Division, Army of the Cumberland. Wilder had converted one Union infantry brigade into mounted infantry and armed it with Spencer repeating rifles.

3. Shot, shell and cannister refer to ammunition for artillery. Cannister was similar to a large shot gun shell. (Jack Coggins, *Arms and Equipment of the Civil War*, page 67)

4. John Logan was the Commander of the 15th Army Corps, reporting to James Birdseye McPherson, Commander of the Army of the Tennessee. Jacob's opinion of major generals had changed from his boat ride near Vicksburg when Jacob complained about the aloofness of the "big bugs" that included Generals Blair and Steele.

5. Grant's Army had made little progress, suffering a defeat in the Battle of the Wilderness on May 5-7, 1864, and being halted at Spotsylvania Court House on May 8-20. The main Union plan going into the early campaign of 1864 was that Sherman would occupy Johnston in Georgia and Grant would defeat Lee in Virginia. So far, Sherman was having some success, but Grant was not.

• It rained most of the day of June 2, sometimes becoming quite heavy. This allowed a brief relief from the heat and humidity of the prior week.

- On June 4, Johnston withdrew again, despite a sarcastic telegram from Bragg: "General Lee, like yourself, has had no general battle lately, but in a series of partial engagements he has greatly damaged the enemy." The Confederates headed to Lost Mountain, six miles to the southeast. When Sherman learned that Johnston had retreated, he directed McPherson and the Army of the Tennessee, which included Jacob, to move from the New Hope Church area and march to Acworth, where McPherson arrived on June 6. McPherson then moved his troops along Procter's Creek, south of Acworth.

[Mt. Pleasant, Iowa]
June 3rd, 1864

Dear Husband,

I wrote you a week ago yesterday in a hurry as we were just starting to Danville. As we went past the post office I got a letter from you. The first I had had for near three weeks. You can imagine how glad I was to hear from you and more, but was sorry to hear that you was sick. Since things on Sunday last, I think I got two the same day. Wasn't I rich? Was so glad you had got well again, but I am afraid you are not going to be stout very soon again. When I got your first letter, I was tempted to sit right down and write for you to resign and come home. I don't believe you will ever get healthy in the army again. I suppose it would be hard to resign now, but I will say that if you still have the ague, and feel so bad as you have been feeling, you must try to come home to stay. I don't know that I am doing right in advising you so. But I feel that there is no use staying there and being sick all the time.

Did you ever get your blankets or haversack? What bad luck you do have and what are you to do without them? The loss of the blankets is worse than the rest for you will be so exposed to the cold without them and I am afraid you will have the shakes all summer. Hoping that you will have a reasonable portion of good health, or resign and come home . . .

The children had a letter from Ike saying that he had received a serious flesh wound in his thigh. I suppose you have heard something about General Steele's expedition up the Red River and after Price. How all his men and trains were gobbled up and destroyed. Ike was with him on that expedition and there received his wound. He is in the hospital and won't be able to do anything for some time.

Jim Campbell was here the other day and wants his money and

I don't know what in the world to do about it. Alvah is gone with the 100 days men, and there is nobody that knows anything about the papers. Al went to Keokuk and expected to be back again but couldn't get time. So he telegraphed for Sarah to come down. I told her to ask him about the Campbell papers. She did so and he said he didn't know anything about them. Didn't want to talk about his business, but gave her the key and told her we could find the papers. But, what am I to do with them when I get them? I am sure I don't know. I only wish we had nothing to do with the Campbell business. I am afraid it will get us into trouble yet.

What do you mean by saying that you are afraid to own anything for years after the war is over? If you have kept your accounts straight, there is no danger is there? Tell me the whole trouble. If you have got your business mixed up so that you are accountable to the government, let me know it, so that I can live according to our means. I am sorry if it is so, but I am willing to deprive myself of all luxuries and even comforts for the sake of keeping your money for you that you have earned so hard. As for having the property in my name, I don't know that it would be right. If we owe it justly, we must pay it though we should come to poverty. Though I pray that our dear children shall never know what it is to want for the common comforts of life, as you have been your hard labor always provides that for them . . .

Em

From Emeline's Mother to Emeline's Father

[Mt. Pleasant, Iowa]
June 5th, 1864

Dear Husband,

. . . Sarah Fleming came down Friday. She is gone to Em's today. It is first time she has been home since Jont died so there is not much satisfaction with her, as here was the last time she saw him. It brings him fresh to her mind, so she is crying all the time pretty near. I know it is hard. I can hardly realize myself that he and Jim have died. Oh that I could say the will of the Lord be done more fully than I do and not mine . . . Yours in trust affection. Good-bye.

E.H.B. [Eleanor H. Bereman]

Lizards, Spiders, Bugs and Ants

Near Acworth, Georgia
June 7, 1864

My Dear Wife,

. . . You said it had been <u>nine</u> days since you had a letter from me. Yes, dear, I knew it would be so, and that it would be nine more, likely, before you got one. I knew you would be very uneasy, but I couldn't help it. You can have no idea of our situation down here without seeing it and how difficult it is to write or send off letters. We are frequently long enough in one place (and doing nothing) to write a letter; but then it is merely standing or lying in line of battle with arms and accouterments all on, and liable to move at any moment. We generally move our position more or less after dark and are not allowed to take any of our clothes or make any fires. The cooking is done by a detail—we build fires and cook in some ravine away in the rear. Any fire that can be seen by the enemy is sure to bring bullets and shells. When we are not in this situation we are generally on the <u>march</u> in pursuit of the rebels. Now who can write in such a fix? I assure you, dear, it is not for want of a will that I don't write often, and then I have to beg for pen, paper, ink, and envelopes from the boys when I do write. But I am glad to be able to state that our position at present is not so bad.

On the night of the fifth [fourth] instant the rebels skedaddled from our front, and no one knows where they have gone to, as far as I can learn. They abandoned their line of works which was very strong and where they had fought us for ten days and we have heard nothing of them since. But I have no doubt we will find them entrenched some place between here and Atlanta. But I will go back to where I left off when I wrote last Friday and bring up my story.

Well, I told you about getting my clothes washed, and my sleeping arrangements. Well, it rained all that night, but my bark kept me all right. And I had just got a letter from you, and lay there thinking about you and the children and didn't care whether it rained or not. But there are several things that make a night's sleep down here, not just so pleasant as it might be. For instance, we always have to put our pants inside of our stockings at night to keep the lizards, spiders, bugs and ants, &c from crawling up our legs! Wouldn't you like to sleep in such a place? No, dear, I am glad you do not have to. But then, we have our own consolations with our troubles.

I often lie awake at night looking at the moon and stars and

thinking that they are the <u>same moon and stars</u> that shine on you.
And then I think that maybe you are sitting in the door at the same
time and looking at the same objects, or perhaps the same stars I
am looking at are shining through the window into your nice room
where you are sleeping in your snug bed, and then I feel very near
to you and love you, Oh! so much! And then I think again that however this may be, there is one thing certain, we have the same kind
Providence to watch over and protect us both, and the same
Heavenly Father to call upon for help in time of need. I feel very
grateful that I have a dear wife and kind friends at home who
remember me in their prayers.

But I have forgotten my story. Saturday morning it was still
rainy, but I went to work and dried my clothes at the fire, and
thought I would answer your letter in the afternoon, but about the
time I got ready we had orders to march in five minutes. We went
into the rifle pits to relieve a brigade of the 4th Army Corps. We
went into our first line of works in the p.m., but could not go to the
front lines till after dark. There was sharp skirmishing all day. We
took our position after dark and put out our pickets, and found that
we were only 160 yards from the rebel works. It rained and was as
dark as pitch. I didn't have my bark and had to lie down in the mud
and got wet. Sunday morning we found that the rebels had cut stick
and left for parts unknown. We went over to their works and found
them very strong. They had four lines that were thick enough to
stop a cannon ball. We found a good many Union Soldiers who
were killed at the commencement of the fight. Their remains lay in
front of our skirmish lines and could not be got at. It was the most
horrible, sickening sight I ever saw. They were so decayed as to be
past recognition—the flesh had slipped from the bones and the
stench was sickening. I hope I may never see such a sight again.

Finding the rebels gone along our whole line, we started on the
march about 10 o'clock and went about 7 miles northeast and
camped for the night. The weather was very hot and the road
muddy. A great many men gave out. I had another "shake" in the
evening—that was for getting wet the night before. Yesterday
morning we started at 6 o'clock. I took two doses of quinine and
marched at the head of my company till we got to our present
camp. We struck the railroad at Acworth and are now about one
mile northeast of the place. The whole Army of the Tennessee is
here lying in line of battle. The prospect is that we will stay a day
or two, but there is nothing certain. We seem to be on the extreme

left of our line now. I don't know where the rest of our army is, or
what they are doing. I suppose General Sherman knows all about it
and that is enough. We are now about 105 miles from Chattanooga
and 30 from Atlanta.

We have driven the enemy from three different positions, and it
has been accomplished without any great loss on our side, though
I can make no estimate of what our loss is. I am confident from the
rebels' own story that they have lost three to our one. And it had
been accomplished more by good generalship than by hard fighting—in fact there has been no general engagement yet[1]. There had
not been a great deal of artillery used on account of the thick brush
and the musketry has been mostly by skirmishers and sharp shooters. The same brigades and divisions have been hotly engaged and
lost heavily.

You need not believe a word you see, taken from the rebel
papers. They are the greatest liars unhung—their accounts tell
about us making charge after charge on their works and always
being repulsed with great slaughter!! No such charges were ever
made. But they tell their men the most outrageous lies to keep up
their courage—for instance, some prisoners we took day before
yesterday said they had the news that Lee had whipped Grant, that
<u>fifty thousand</u> of our dead and wounded fell into their hands, and
the balance were retreating to Washington, closely followed by
Lee; and that Hooker had been killed and his body fell into their
hands!! And then when we were around on the right they gave the
men whiskey till they were nearly drunk, and then told them there
was nothing but 100 day men in front of them, and if they would
charge on us we would all run, and they could turn our right flank.
They charged and got badly "salivated." The prisoners opened their
eyes very wide when they found they had run into the 15th Army
Corps instead of 100 day men. And then, don't you think, the hyp-
ocritical rascals will fight us all day and then have prayer meetings
at night. We can sometimes hear them singing and praying from
our breastworks[2]. The rascals! I wonder what kind of a deity they
must fix up for themselves who will hear the prayers of liars and
drunkards and slave holders and <u>traitors</u>.

But I must stop. I have just received orders to draw clothing for
my company. If I had nothing else to do I would write all day, for
I don't know when I will have another chance. I got a letter from
Spencer[3] the same day I got yours. I was glad to hear they were all
well and getting along so well. I don't know when I can answer it.

Tell them to write again. Now I must tell you one thing more. We got a large mail last night and I didn't get any letter from you!! I was so much disappointed. Lieutenant Crane got several, some written as late as the 25th of May. I don't blame you at all, dear, for I know you have written, but why didn't it come?

I got a letter from Till—he said that Isaac[4] was wounded in the battle at Sabine River. He thought not dangerously, but he had not seen him. I would like to hear more particularly. Tell me all you know about it. I suppose the 1st Iowa Veterans[5] are at home. Tell Tom I would like very well to hear from him, but I can't promise to answer his letter now. I suppose Alvah is Colonel of the 45th Iowa Infantry. We have the *Home Journal* of May 28th. Crane says that his folks speak in one of his letters about you being very uneasy about me. I do hope it would not be too long till you would get my letter. You shall not be so long again without a letter if I can possibly help it.

If Alvah went away without settling with Jim Campbell you may do it if you can. Pay him what the books at the judge's office show to be coming to him at the last settlement, as the money has been in the bank ever since and not drawing enough interest to pay the tax. Have him take the note on Peter[3] for part of it. I am glad to hear that you are likely to get the fence built at last. I hope you will not have much more trouble with it. I was pleased to hear that your garden is doing so well and that you are going to have some fruit. I hope I will be there to help eat it. The men are "able for duty," but none feel first-rate. We have not had a bite of any vegetable or anything sour, not even vinegar, for more than a month. What has become of the Sanitary Fairs? I could tell you something about Sanitary goods, if I had time, that would make your heart sick. But I must stop. Tell the children Pa loves them and often thinks of them.

Your affectionate Husband,
J.B. Ritner

. . . There now, I have gone and done it again. I thought I had this sheet full, and went and finished off on that secesh paper, and when I came to fold it up I found this blank. Well, I hope you will be able to find all and put it together right. I expect I will forget how to write if this war last much longer. But I don't think it will. If this rebellion is not put down this summer it will not be because we are not doing our duty in this part of the field. We will certainly take Atlanta within the next thirty days. And then if Richmond falls the thing is played out. I do think I will get to board with you next winter yet.

Jerome Bowman has not got here yet. I don't know what keeps him back. I expect the girls think their letter is never going to come. Well, I can't help it now. Tell them I said they must be good and kind to each other and mind what Ma says.

It is raining again and I must close. My best respects to all inquiring friends and my deepest, truest love to my dear wife.

Your own, Jake

1. Confederate General Joseph E. Johnston continued to occupy Sherman's forces without engaging them in a major battle. This was by Johnston's design. The elections of 1864 were approaching and Northern support of the war effort was waning without recent Union victories. If Lincoln were defeated in the 1864 presidential election, the North might give up the war effort and negotiate a settlement with the South. By avoiding an engagement and possible Confederate defeat, Johnston was following a strategy based on wearing out the Northern desire to continue the war effort. However, if this was Joe Johnston's strategy, it was certainly not the strategy of Confederate President Jefferson Davis, who continually pleaded with Johnston to engage and defeat Sherman. Davis did not like the strategy of trading space for time, which is what Johnston was doing. Johnston's response to Davis was that his Army of Tennessee was much smaller than that of his Union opponent, and that he must wait for the right opportunity to strike.

2. One of the Confederate Generals was Leonidas Polk, who, after graduation from West Point, left the military and became an Episcopal Bishop, rising to the position of Bishop of Louisiana. During the Atlanta campaign, Polk baptized both John Bell Hood and Joseph E. Johnston.

3. Spencer, age 14, and Peter, age 19, were Jacob's younger brothers.

4. Isaac N. Ritner was a younger brother of Jacob's in the 33rd Iowa Infantry. He was severely wounded April 30, 1864, at Sabine River, Arkansas, at the Battle of Jenkins Ferry.

5. Jacob's reference to the 1st Iowa Veterans was to the portion of the 1st Iowa Cavalry who had re-enlisted, thus earning the designation of a Veteran regiment.

• On June 8, the Union Party, which was the temporarily renamed Republican Party, met in Baltimore and nominated

Abraham Lincoln for a second term as President. Lincoln's running mate was Andrew Johnson, who before the war was a Democratic Senator from Tennessee, and was now the Military Governor of that state. The Republican platform called for the emancipation of all American slaves. (Albert Castel, *Decision in the West*, page 268)

- Also on June 8, Lt. Colonel David Palmer of the 25th Iowa "accidentally shot his hand through the metacarpi-Phalangeal joint; but refused to be reported wounded." (*Diary of Dr. Henry Farr*, Unpublished, Iowa State Historical Society, Iowa City, Iowa)

- On June 10, the Union armies began their movement. The 15th Army Corps moved to a mile south of a town named Big Shanty (presently named Kennesaw), which was another railroad station. Sherman himself arrived in Big Shanty mid-morning on the 10th. During this period, ending June 13, the soldiers were subject to eleven straight days of rain. McPherson moved most of his army opposite Brush Mountain, but did not attack. When not in his headquarters, Sherman spent much of his time with the 15th Army Corps, which he considered his favorite. (Albert Castel, *Decision in the West*, pages 270-272)

- On June 14, Sherman went to personally observe Pine Mountain. Using field glasses, Sherman saw a group of Confederates openly standing near one of their batteries. Sherman exclaimed, "How saucy they are!" and instructed General Howard to fire three volleys at the Confederates. Howard responded that General Thomas had instructed his troops not to not waste ammunition, to which Sherman said was correct as a rule, but "we must keep up the morale of a bold offensive." This order was passed down the line to the nearest artillery officer, Captain Peter Simonson, whose battery fired several shots to establish range, and then fired the three volleys.

  The group of Confederates that attracted Sherman's attention included Generals Johnston, Hardee, and Polk, who had been standing close together, surveying the situation. Confederate Colonel Dilworth saw the puff of smoke from the Union battery and quickly pleaded for the generals to separate and take cover. At first none of them moved, but after the second volley arrived, they walked in different directions. But the third volley was a direct hit on General Leonidas Polk, the Bishop, killing him instantly. William Loring replaced Polk in command of his corps.

- By June 18, the Confederates had retreated to Kennesaw Mountain, which had three distinct points: Big Kennesaw, Little

Kennesaw, and Pigeon Hill. From Kennesaw Mountain they could see Atlanta, which was only 20 miles south. On the morning of the 19th, the Union Army began moving skirmishers forward to Kennesaw Mountain, thinking that the Confederates had retreated again, across the Chattahoochee River. But the Union met resistance. By mid-morning, the Union began battery assaults, and by noon the bombardment was severe.

Although Union artillery could strike Kennesaw Mountain, the Union troops had great difficulty in advancing. The Army of the Tennessee became bogged down in 6 to 8 inches of mud, and the Army of the Cumberland declared the mountain to be unassailable. On June 20, there was more rain and more mud. (Albert Castel, *Decision in the West*, pages 284-287)

Camp Near Acworth, Georgia
June 8, 1864

My Dear Wife,

I expect you will hardly care to get another letter from me so soon after reading that long bungling letter I wrote to you yesterday, but we have received orders to march tomorrow morning at 6 o'clock, so I must write you a few lines anyhow.

I feel very well today, and think I shall stand it very well till the next spell of ague comes around.

I suppose we are going in pursuit of Johnston. But I have not heard where he is. Some think he has fallen back beyond Atlanta, but I still think we will have another fight before we get that far. The people in the North say he has at least 100,000 men. I don't know how many we have, but we have the most. Part of the 17th A.C., 15,000 strong, just got here today. They are camped not far from us, and I must try to go over and see Rodgers and Cady and Campbell and the other boys.

I have found out that there has been more hard fighting down here than I supposed. We all thought there had not been much done except by the Army of the Tennessee, to which we belong. But we find that the Army of the Cumberland and of the Ohio have been even more hotly engaged than we have. And the Rebels have been "Salivated" as the boys say, wherever they have been met. Our boys are all in good spirits and are willing to go in for another 40 days in the wilderness as hard as the last 40 days have been, and by that time, if we succeed as well as we have been doing, I think this accursed rebellion will be crushed.

There is a great deal of talk here about the Iowa Soldiers Orphan Asylum[1]. It is generally considered by the officers and men to be a great humbug. I have no doubt but it is a scheme to put money in some folks' pockets, because they can make nothing out of the "Sanitary." I think Bro. Gunn might be in a better business than to be helping run such a machine. If they really want to encourage the soldiers and do something for their families, let them give money to the widows and wives to enable them to keep their children together, instead of separating them and sending them to an institution.

I don't think Alvah gave it to the skulks any too hard. But I think maybe he would not have been so fast to go himself, if it had been to come down here, where Rebel devils howl through the woods and bullets whistle overhead two-thirds of the time. At least that I have not doubt is the case with nine tenths of them. But what will Sarah do now that he is gone? I suppose she can't put it off, to talk about when the war is over, as you say we are going to do. Oh Dear, if God will only spare my life till this war is over, that I may go home once more & take you in my arms and kiss you, I shall ask nothing more.

I want you to take the *Hawkeye* while this campaign lasts. I can tell you but very little in my letters. Sherman and his officers are wrong, I think, to keep everything so close as they do, but it can't be helped. We have never had such strict orders against skulking and straggling as we have now, & that is all right. But I must close. Write me a great long letter, dear; tell me about the children . . . I have got all your letters with me, and read them all over today. Take good care of the children.

Your affectionate husband,
J.B. Ritner

1. Jacob is echoing sentiments regarding the Orphan Asylum, as expressed in the May 14 and May 21, 1864, editions of *The Mt. Pleasant Home Journal*. Mrs. Annie Wittenmeyer, among others, had created a movement to establish an orphan's home, but *Home Journal* editorials espoused the concern that children would be better cared for in the homes of relatives and friends than in asylums. There was truth to this fear; after the war, the Gettsyburg headquarters of General Howard was turned into a Soldiers' Orphan Asylum and the abuse of the children began shortly thereafter, which proved to be a national scandal.

I Don't Think This War Can Be Carried On Without Me

Kennesaw Mountain
Georgia, June 20, 1864

My Dear Wife,

I believe this is Monday, but don't know for certain . . . It has been a pretty hard week. In the first place, I have had the ague three days and have been hardly able to get about, and don't feel near well yet, but I don't think I will shake any more till the next wet day. Then it has rained nearly every day and night for the last week. I never saw so much rain fall in the same time. It just pours down for 24 hours at a time. We have not had sunshine enough for several days to dry a blanket till today. And then we all have to stand right to our places. The fight goes on regardless of the weather. I have no time to tell you all about our movements and operations. The result now seems to be that the fight here is about over, and if reports be true, Johnston is so badly defeated that we will have no further trouble with him. They fell back night before last from their first and second line of works, where they were very strongly fortified on high ridges. This enabled us to move forward about two miles. Our division now occupies their first line of works in front of where we were before. And the 2nd Division 15th Army Corps is about one mile in our front, at the next line of works. They had to fall back because their left flank was turned by our right. And their communication with the rear was about to be cut off. I think they intended to make a general retreat across the Chattahoochee River. But we were too fast for them, and a large body of them got cut off and hemmed in on the mountains in our front. They made a hard fight yesterday, and show some resistance today, but they are evidently surrounded and will be "gobbled." One of our batteries is shelling the top of the mountain now, from a hill just to the left of our regiment. We have killed, captured, and wounded a great many.

Wednesday, June 22

We had to fall in and move to the front again day before yesterday and I had to stop writing and pack up. Osterhaus has found a gap in the front line large enough to let in one brigade by crowding out part of the 16th Army Corps. Our position is on a hill immediately in front of the left-hand mountain. Yesterday it rained steadily all day and the whole regiment worked all day building a breastwork and fixing an abatis in front of it. I don't know as much about the rebel situation now as I thought I did when I was writing the other day. They are still in our front and fight like the savage[1]. There was a very severe fight on our right the evening we came in there, but our men drove the rebels back and held their works, but they fought over them nearly all night. I don't know whether any part of Johnston's army has crossed the river or not. We are driving them back all the time and have got them out of their strongest works. Indeed they have no works except as they make them for the immediate occasion, except what they have on the two mountains on our front. They are very high and steep and cannot be taken from this side. It looks like it might be a clear day today—if it is I expect there will be hard fighting before night.

I have never found the valise with my clothes yet and never will. I have my blankets. I sent $5.00 back to Chattanooga and got another haversack. We also sent back and got some of the clothing we left there. I got a pair of pants and a shirt. We have five mails since I wrote to you, but had one letter from you, of date June 3rd. I was glad to hear that you were all well and that you had got letters from me at last. I don't think it would do any good for you to write to me to resign. I don't think this war could be carried on at all without me. Then I think this campaign is nearly over, and will end with the fall of Atlanta before the 4th of July, and then we have a rest, perhaps no more fighting at all.

I see a good deal about the women's dress movement in the papers. I think it is a very sensible thing and ought to be adopted by all—of course, what <u>man</u> wouldn't! I think there is a great deal more sense in that movement then in the Soldiers' Orphan Asylum project. But what has become of the "Sanitary" all this time? I thought that hundreds and thousand of dollars were raised in the North last winter and spring.

We have now been out in this campaign over 7 weeks and we have not had a mouthful of <u>any vegetable</u> or anything <u>sour</u> all that time—not even a taste of vinegar. I never wanted anything so much in my life as I now do something of that kind. And the men are all suffering for vegetables, but not a bite can we get. Coffee, salt pork and hard bread, with a mess of beef once if a while, was all we get. I can hardly eat it for the last week or two. I sent back and paid $1.50 for a quart of strawberries; they were first-rate. Have you had any yet?

You want me to tell you why I will be afraid to own anything after the war is over. I don't know, dear, as I can make you understand it in a letter. But it is not because my accounts are "mixed up" but just because of "red tape." The commander of a company is responsible to the government for all camp and garrison equipage issued to the company, such as tents, knapsacks, haversacks, canteens, camp kettles, mess pans, cups, pans, knives, forks, spoons, axes, spades, shovels, drums, fifes, &c. And their money value is charged to him at Washington, and he has it to pay unless the articles are properly accounted for. Of course if he has them on hand and returns them to the government at the end of his term, he is all right. But such things will wear out and get broken and lost and destroyed, and we must all the time be getting more to keep up the supply. The "regulations" seem to point out two ways in which property could be dropped from the returns. One is by having the article examined and condemned by the Inspector General. And the other, on the certificate of an officer that they were worn out, broken, &c by fair wear and tear in the public service. For more than a year there was no Inspector General that we knew anything about. And we used the latter method to get the worn out property off the return. But last winter we were notified that no property would be allowed to be dropped unless regularly condemned!! Now if that means only after the date of the notice, we are all right yet. If it applies to the whole time we are—broke. I say we for the officers are all in the same fix.

. . . Dear, how I do want to go and board with you a while. May I come? I will write soon again.

Your Husband

You must excuse this dull letter, Dear. There is sharp skirmishing just in front. No one hurt in the 25th since I wrote last. 2 taken prisoners by rebels.

1. Jacob is describing the Battle of Kolb's farm, which took place on June 22, where Hooker engaged Hood at nearby Powder Springs road. Hood's assault was a Confederate failure, with losses of at least 1,500 compared to Union losses of only 250. Despite the Union victory, Hooker's and Sherman's relations continued to worsen as Sherman felt that Hooker had overstated enemy strength and was too quick to call for reinforcements.

Mrs. Morley Is a Copperhead

[Mt. Pleasant, Iowa]
June 26th, 1864

Dear Husband,
    . . . What hard times you do have fighting every day or two
marching in the mud & rain & the hot sunshine, sleeping on the
ground among the lizards and spiders, having no clean clothes and
nothing to eat but hard crackers, &c. I don't see how you ever live
through it all. I wonder you don't all get discouraged, sick and
utterly fed up. But, the true soldier has the noble Union & the glorious old flag in view, and mind, not the hardships of the day
(though they are enough to kill him outright). There is fighting for
the right and right will prevail.

> "For right is right since God is God,
>   And right the day must win;
> 'To doubt would be disloyalty
>   To falter would be sin."

    Brave honored soldiers who wouldn't honor the soldier?
Soldiers who are giving their lives, some of them inch by inch to
save this land from ruin. Who wouldn't sympathize with pity and
aid a Soldier? He is a traitor that would not, north or south. And I
can't have any patience with such. I feel more and more bitter
toward them every day. When I know a person is "copperhead" I
can't feel that they are my friends; I heard the other day that Mrs.
Morley said she didn't believe one of the soldiers would ever go to
heaven. If she was not my nearest neighbor and I knew it was so, I
would never have anything to do with her again. Though she is a
very good neighbor, and I would like her first rate, if she were only
sound on the Union question. How I do wish this war was over so
all the poor soldiers could come home and the mean rebels made
to knuckle to the Union. I am so afraid that Lincoln won't be elected and then the war may last another 3 years. What do you think of
Fremont? Could you have believed he was that kind of a man? I
believe you used to be a Fremont man, didn't you?
                                Em

From Eleanor Bereman to Samuel E. Bereman

[Mt. Pleasant, Iowa]
June 28th, '64

Dear Husband,

   . . . It makes me think of Car's dream. She told me to tell it to you, but I believe I haven't so I will tell you now. She dreamed that a big Copperhead snake bit you on the thigh, but did not hurt you much, but the snake bit so hard that it died. Well, I guess that has nothing to do with my letter . . .

   I tell you in another letter what the Ladies of Mt. Pleasant were trying to do to help the war along. The war to bind themselves by the covenant not to buy any foreign goods, but go plain and dress in what America could afford. But, they can't come it. I told you that I was glad of it for I never had seen the people dress so fine in my life as they had done since this war commenced and it is the truth that the stares everybody in the face that their government is not humbled yet, and I fear the consequence. It seems to me if we would view this present war just as it is now, even if we gained every battle, it would be enough to humble any people under the sun, and if this war lasts till the people repent and become humble, there will be nobody to repent . . .

   I think sometimes of Sodom and think this government is like him. There is not enough righteous to save it. Well, God knows what is best to do, and we know that he is a righteous God. If wishing would do any good, I could wish Fremont and all our last Congress were on the side of the Sea . . . I hope you will keep writing and let us know from all . . . I remain your loving wife.

               E.H.B. [Eleanor H. Bereman]

The Battle of Kennesaw Mountain

Union skirmishers first encountered the Confederates at Kennesaw Mountain on June 19, and a week later the Confederates were still unlodged. Sherman responded with a frontal assault on June 27, with the day ending in a horrible failure for the Union troops, who were unable to move the Confederates from Kennesaw Mountain, and while suffering 3,000 casualties, compared to only 700 for the Confederates. Almost half the Confederate losses were pickets overrun at the start of the attack, which meant that after the assault began, the defenders inflicted almost ten Union losses for every one of their own. (Albert Castel, Decision in the West, *pages 304-320)*

Historical Sketch—25th Iowa Infantry

On June 27th, a general assault upon the enemy's strong line of works along the face of the mountain was ordered, in which the Twenty-Fifth Iowa, with its brigade, participated and suffered considerable loss. The assault was unsuccessful, and the brigade returned to its line of works, from which it kept up an incessant fire upon the enemy's line until the night of July 2nd, when the enemy evacuated his line of defenses on Kennesaw Mountain, and began his retreat in the direction of Atlanta. The enemy fell back slowly, stubbornly resisting the advance of the Union Army, and there were frequent skirmishes, in which the Twenty-Fifth Iowa and the other regiments of its brigade participated. (Roster and Record of Iowa Soldiers in the War of the Rebellion; *Published under the authority of the Iowa General Assembly)*

- On the evening of June 28th, Logan's command arranged for a temporary truce so that Union and Confederate troops could retrieve their wounded and dead, many of whom had been nearly devoured by maggots. The two sides mingled in friendly fashion for two hours, even assisting each other on occasion. Thomas' command accepted a similar Confederate offer on the morning of June 29. On the Confederate side Generals Cheatham, Cleburne, and Hindman joined in the conversations. (Albert Castel, *Decision in the West*, page 323)

Sherman continued to send his troops south along the Union right toward the Chattahoochee River and Atlanta, their intention to turn the Confederate left flank. As this maneuvering continued, Johnston planned another retreat, feeling that Sherman's entrenching tactics made it almost impossible to attack with success, and that the size of Sherman's Army would allow the Federals to successfully flank Johnston's Army. Johnston again pleaded with Davis and Bragg at Richmond to direct Nathan Bedford Forrest's cavalry to attack Sherman's supply lines, but again this request was denied. (Albert Castel, *Decision in the West*, page 328)

On the night of July 2nd, the Confederates began their retreat from Kennesaw Mountain, leaving behind skirmishers to delay Union knowledge of the retreat.

As the 25th Iowa continued toward Atlanta, Jacob was sent to the rear along with the rest of the Union sick and wounded.

Rome, Georgia
July 2, 1864

My Dear Wife,
    Well, dear, I have got settled in a new position, and take the first opportunity to write you a few lines. In the first place, I must say my health is not much better than when I wrote to you last from the hospital at Big Shanty. I don't seem to improve as fast as I thought I would. I think that one thing that is the matter with me, in that I have had the ague a good deal and have taken a great deal of quinine, and then lay out in the rain and on the damp ground, and it got into my bones and joints, and they don't seem to limber up very fast. But I think that with a few days' rest with the right kind of food and I will be able to go to the front and buck against the rebel breastworks again. But I suppose, dear, you don't care how long I stay sick! so I don't get very bad—so bad I can't write! But I do, and I shall go to the front just as soon as I can, and so would you if you were in such a hole as this is. But I must tell you all about it. I am sitting on the floor, with my paper on the bunk, writing, and if you will just come in and sit on the bunk beside me I will tell you all about how they use "brave and patriotic" soldiers in this country. I did not want to come back here at all. But the next day after I wrote to you before they got orders to break up the hospital at Big Shanty immediately and send every man to his regiment, or to the rear. As I was not able to go the regiment, I had to come back.
    We were all loaded onto the cars at midnight Thursday night, and lay there till after sun up next morning before the train started. We had nothing but common freight cars, very dirty, and the sick and wounded were all crowded in together, till there was not room enough for all to lie down. We got back to Allatoona Pass Hospital about 9 a.m. This is 12 miles from Big Shanty. Here they left all the wounded of the 15th Army Corps. We got to Kingston about noon, which is 16 miles from Allatoona Pass, and lay there in the cars roasting in the heat for three hours. Finally they put several cars loaded with wounded into our train and we started for this place, which is 16 miles from Kingston. We got here about 4 o'clock, and expected to find everything prepared to receive us, but were badly disappointed. We were all ordered off the cars immediately, and there we lay on the ground, sick and wounded together for two hours before anyone came near us, or we could find any

place to go. There was about three hundred all together. There were five other sick officers of our division along, but none from our regiment except myself.

Rome is pretty considerable of a town, or has been—contains a good many fine buildings and nice residences. I should take it to be about as large as Mount Pleasant. The inhabitants are mostly here yet, and it is not destroyed like most of the towns through which our army has passed. Well, we finally got to what they call the Officer's Hospital where we are now. We got no supper and had had neither breakfast nor dinner. This morning they brought us a little hard bread and coffee, no meat or anything else. I couldn't eat anything. I had the good luck to meet Captain Hanks[1] here of the 15th Iowa. I got acquainted with him last winter at Davenport, and like him first-rate. He is sick, but able to walk around more than I can. So gave him $20 and he went and hired boarding for us at a private house, and we are going to go it on our own hook after this.

We are in the second story of a brick building; the room is about 30 by 50 and contains about 30 sick and wounded officers. There is another room in front with I don't know how many in it. There is no Sanitary Commission here—nothing but army rations and not much of that. But we have good cast iron cots to sleep on, and some have bed ticks and sheets. I have not got any yet, but have two nice white blankets besides my own, and a pillow, which makes a first-rate bed. But I must stop and lie down awhile. I will try to finish this after dinner.

* * * * *

Well, dear, it is now 7 o'clock and I have had a good rest and my dinner and will try to write some more. Captain Hanks, Lieutenant Lee of the 16th Iowa and myself went out to the place I spoke of for dinner. We had corn bread and buttermilk! Pork, beans, and new potatoes, fresh butter, and blackberry pie! Wasn't that splendid. I thought I never sat down to so good a meal, and eat lots. It won't take long with that kind of living to make me able for another fight. I am afraid though we will not be allowed to enjoy it—the other officers say the surgeon in charge does not allow the patients to board away from the hospital. They must stay here and pay him $1.05 per day and get nothing then. The other officers have had no dinner yet.

We intend to run our own machine as long as we can, anyhow. The weather here is very hot and sultry. It seems to me as hot as it was at Vicksburg last August. I think this is a hot hole anyhow. It is situated at the junction of the Etowah and Ostanaula Rivers. The country is extremely rough and broken around here, ranging from low hills to high mountains, rocky and steep, in many places almost inaccessible, especially if surmounted with rebel cannon. Blackberries and huckleberries are very abundant and are getting ripe. There will soon be roasting ears. I had a ripe apple today. I forgot to say that the folks where we sent to dinner seem to be very nice people. They have no Negroes. There are two white woman who do their own work. They live in a nice two-story brick house and keep a cow. The men are at home, and work at their trade, shoemaking. They have a looking-glass, and I got to see myself for the first time in two months. I don't believe you would know your Jake at all, if you were to see me now. I never looked so slim and hollow-eyed, I know. But I will come out all right some day yet. I have been thinking about those gooseberries you put up for me. I am very much obliged to you, and think it very kind of you to put them up just for me. I hope I will get there to help eat them.

I have not got any letter from you since I wrote to you last, and have been uneasy about Nellie and the other children ever since. My letters will all go to the regiment and I will not get them till I go back, and perhaps not then. I know there are letters there now for me. I do wish I could get them. Whenever you get this you must write me a great long letter right away—get a big sheet like this and write two full, and direct to the regiment as usual, for I will be back there by the time it gets there. Tell me all about everybody. How do Sarah, Alvah, and Mrs. Morley get along? Did you go to the big show[2], and what did you do on the 4th of July?

Well, Dear, what do you think of the war now anyhow? I declare I am getting tired of it. I do wish I could go home and live with you the rest of my days. Oh how I long for that time to come. And I still think it soon will. I think prospects never were so bright. Sherman will certainly take Atlanta, but it may be some time yet. Johnston has fought us for 20 days in his present position. But we will "flank" him yet. We have very encouraging news from Grant's army[3]. And if both are successful, and the people of the North come up to the support of "Old Abe[4]" as they ought to, we will all be home by New Years. I see plenty of officers here who are not as sick as I am who have sent in their resignations and expect to go home soon, but that is not my style. I am bound to see it through. I will make one more effort at it anyhow, before I give it up. I know it is a hard life, full of privations and danger and temptations. Profanity and vice of all kinds abound as well as rebel bullets and shells. But I know that pure lips have promised to pray for me, and I feel that I shall be shielded and guarded and kept uncontaminated—true to my "North Star" which shines so brightly in my dear home. True to my wife, my country, and my God. But I must close for this time. I have your photograph with me yet. I am glad you have the children's. Send me a copy of each—I will take care of them.

1. Captain Romulus L. Hanks, Company G, 15th Iowa Infantry, was 39 when he was mustered as First Lieutenant. Hanks was promoted to Captain on August 1, 1862, when Captain William Cunningham was promoted to Major, who replaced William W. Belknap, who was promoted to Lieutenant Colonel of the 15th Iowa.

2. Jacob was talking about the Monster Equescurriculum Circus that appeared in Mt. Pleasant on June 27, 1864.

3. Grant's objective was to capture Richmond. That failed, and he was now participating in operations similar to Vicksburg. He disengaged his Army of the Potomac from the Army of Northern Virginia at Cold Harbor, then took it south of Richmond and crossed the James River to attack Petersburg. During the Battle of Petersburg, Grant began a nine-month siege operation against Lee.

4. Jacob was talking about the upcoming Presidential election in November 1864. Running against Lincoln was Democrat General George McClellan, who at one time was Commander in Chief of all the Union armies. The Democratic party platform included a plank calling for a negotiated settlement with the Confederacy, which would have been equivalent to a Confederate victory of the war. (Albert Castel, *Decision in the West*, page 480)

•   The Confederates retreated six miles south of Marietta to the Smyrna Camp Ground. The Confederates rested briefly and then began building their defensive lines. Sherman himself was surprised at Johnston's position of defense that was so close to the Chattahoochee River that it would hinder Johnston's next withdrawal. July 4th was an extremely hot day; half the men in

Osterhaus' Division dropped by the roadside during the march
and some died. (Albert Castel, *Decision in the West*, page 331)

Officer's Hospital on Lookout Mountain [Tennessee]
July 7, 1864

My Dear Wife,

You will no doubt be surprised to see by the heading of my letter that I have again "changed my base of operations." Well, I have,
and here I am on the top of Lookout Mountain, where the air feels
as pure and cool and bracing as it does in Iowa. We can see "all
over creation" almost, sleep under two blankets at night, and feel
comfortable in the daytime, when persons in the valley below are
sweltering and almost suffocating in the heat and dust.

I do not feel much better or stronger than I did when I wrote last
from Rome, but I think I shall improve rapidly now. And I expect I
will be "able for duty" as soon as I shall like to leave here, if not
sooner. I am afraid that I have got into such a good place I shall be
tempted to "take it easy" longer than I ought, that is, if the doctor
will let me. Well, don't you think I deserve to take it easy for a little while? But do you think I could "play off" and lie around here
when it is my duty to be in front! I think you know me better. But
I must begin back and tell all about it.

. . . When I got to Rome I wrote to Lieutenant Steele to send
my letters there, and they will go to Rome. I tried to make arrangements to have them sent from there here, but I don't much expect
it will be done . . .

Well, our hospital at Rome was a miserable affair. The officers
got only two meals a day, and then nothing but hard tack and coffee, occasionally meat, not a bite of fruit of any kind except as they
bought it from some peddler of pies. At our boarding house which
I told you of in my last, we did not get much but cornbread and buttermilk, and we soon got tired of that, and were all well pleased
when General McPherson sent back an order that the officers should
all be sent to Lookout. We were loaded into freight cars on Monday
afternoon July 4th and it was the driest old Fourth I ever passed. We
nearly melted in the dirty cars. We went 10 miles to Kingston and
lay there in the cars all night and till 6 o'clock the next morning.

We then got some good news from the front. Two trains loaded
with "Johnnies" came up from Big Shanty, some 800 in all, and we
learned that our forces had taken Kennesaw Mountain and Marietta

and captured a great many prisoners[1]. We have not heard for certain, but I have no doubt that our army is now across the Chattahoochee River and in Atlanta, and that the fighting part of the campaign is over. I hope it may turn out so, though I did want to be "in at the death," and if Johnston's army is used up, I shall always regret that I was not able to be there.

Tuesday was a very hot day, and we were till 9 o'clock at night getting to Chattanooga. I never saw such tedious traveling. There were five trains coming this way one right after another, and so many going out that we could hardly get along at all. But they say there is no "bitter without some sweet." Although I was very tired and nearly worn out lying so long in a dirty car, there were one or two things that gave me a great deal of satisfaction. The train in front of ours, and the two behind, were loaded with rebel prisoners. And the inhabitants, who are mostly of the female persuasion, had heard that the rebels had again been driven back, and that prisoners would be along that day on the trains. And we found them gathered for miles on each side of the road, at all the stations, with bread and pies and blackberries and tobacco and c, to give their friends. Many of them recognized friends, relatives, husbands, and sons among the prisoners and some heard that their friends were killed or wounded. And the way they cried and slung their snot around, was a sight. I enjoyed it hugely; it made me feel good all over. I felt like taunting them and adding to their misery if I could. But of course I could not insult a lady, so I kept my mouth shut. Now I expect you think these were not very Christian like feelings. I don't know about that. But they came very natural to me. And when I thought how I had to leave my own dear wife and family and spend years of the best part of my life, undergoing dangers and hardships of all kinds on account of their accursed treason, I could not help it. And then when I thought how I have shortened my own days and seen my best friends and nearest relatives lose their lives in endeavoring to sustain the government which these rebels were trying to destroy, I felt that I could see the direst calamity befall them with the utmost complacency. Indeed if Christianity requires love such enemies I acknowledge myself woefully deficient. I can't and I won't. I had been reading the 23rd Psalm[2]—did you ever read it?

Well, we had to lie over two or three hours at Dalton, and while we were there a notorious guerrilla and railroad burner was publicly hung[3] on a tree in front of the courthouse and in the presence of a large number of both citizens and soldiers. I enjoyed that too. If a few more of the leaders were caught and served in the same way there would be less depredations committed on our "cracker line[4]." I suppose you don't see it in the papers, but the fact is that scarcely a day passes without a bridge being destroyed or train burned between here and the front.

As I said before, we got to Chattanooga at 9 o'clock Tuesday night. The doctor who had been sent up in charge of us was drunk and sent us to the Crutchfield House, a public hotel. It was already full and we could not all get even into the barroom and some lay in the street. The next morning we got a little breakfast for a dollar apiece, and at 9 o'clock were still lying around on the porch in the street, when we found that the doctor was still drunk and had not reported us properly to the surgeon in charge of the post. So we reported ourselves and were sent up here in ambulances. It is 6 miles from town by the road. I was very tired and could hardly walk when I got here yesterday, but feel a good deal better after a good night's rest. But I am tired now and can't tell any more about this hospital today. I will write again in a few days, when I get better rested. Direct to the regiment, as I expect to be there in ten days from now.

Well, dear, I intended to close this letter just here, but I have taken a nap and had my dinner, and now I feel like writing some more—not that I have anything particular to say. But I love to write to you. I often wonder if my long prosy letters are interesting to you? I always feel nearer to you when writing to you than at any other time except when I am reading your last letter.

I got my valise at Chattanooga and what clothes I have left, and feel quite fine with my clean pants and white shirt on. I also got my hair brush and your ambrotype that Bowman left there. I think the picture is ever so nice. The eyes look so sweet and bright, it does me good to look at them! There are lots of officers here from all over the North, and they all have pictures but I'm not ashamed to show mine with any of them.

Now I wish the time would soon come when I could see you again and go home to board with you. I believe you have never told me yet whether you could furnish me with board and lodging next winter, if I should get to go. I expect it is in one of the letters I have not got yet.

This is a most horrible war, is it not, dear, to take me away from you for so long a time and to make it necessary to endure such dangers and labors as we both have felt on account of it. But you must not think that I regret that I entered the army, or that I begrudge to my country for a moment all that I have done and suffered in trying to serve her. I have never felt so for a moment. No, my dear, if only through this baptism of blood, our nation, freed and purified from the blighting curse of slavery, shall lift her radiant forehead from the dust, and crowned with the wisdom of freedom go on her glorious way rejoicing. I shall count my past suffering and shattered health only as the small dust in the balance compared with the priceless blessings of peace, freedom, and national unity, which they may have contributed however slightly to purchase. Only to have contributed something, however little, for the peace, something for the glory, something for the permanence of those beautiful and bright institutions which are the pride of the past and the hope of the future—will be a joy through life and a consolation in death.

Now Dear, I must stop and take another nap before supper—don't you think I am lazy? Well, you write me a letter as long as this. You could not write one so dull.

Your own, Jake

1.   The Union took control of Kennesaw Mountain as the result of another retreat by Johnston and the Confederates. Many Confederates stayed behind and allowed themselves to be taken prisoner.

2.   Psalm 23—A Psalm of David
     The shepherd psalm
     THE LORD is my shepherd; I shall not want.
     He maketh me to lie down in green pastures: he leadeth me beside the still waters.
     He restoreth my soul: he leadeth me in the paths
     of righteousness for his name's sake.
     Yea, though I walk through the valley of the shadow of death, I will fear no evil: for thou art with me; thy rod and thy staff comfort me.
     Thou preparest a table before me in the presence of mine enemies: thou anointest my head with oil; my cup runneth over.
     Surely goodness and mercy shall follow me all the days of my life: and I will dwell in the house of the Lord for ever.

3.   A continual problem for the Union was the presence of guerrillas—locals who sabotaged Union trains and supplies. The man that Jacob saw hung was named Edwards, who had been captured as a spy. (Lee Kennett, *Marching through Georgia*, pages 98-100)

4.   The "cracker line" was a supply line.

I Never Tried to Write a Letter to Such a Little Girl Before

Officer's Hospital
Lookout Mountain, Tenn.
July 11, 1864

Dear Daughter Nellie,

I have just written a letter to Lulie and as I promised to write one to you I supposed I had better do it now or your black eyes will look back at me. The doctor made me take a dose of calomel last night and a dose of salt this morning. And, I don't feel very bright this morning, but I am afraid I may not have another chance to write.

The last letter I got from Ma was written a month ago (June 15) and she said you had the sore throat. I have been very anxious to hear from you ever since, but it seems like I will never get any more letters. I hope you did not get very bad and that you are well as ever and going to school again long before this. But, I would like to hear all about it and whether Lulie and Tommy and Kittie got it too. I am afraid they did.

I never tried to write a letter to such a little girl before and I am afraid you won't think it very interesting. I suppose you don't care anything about "War News." If you do, I have none to tell. We are up here on this Mountain six miles from Chattanooga. We are not allowed to go to town and we don't get any papers or see anybody, nor hear anything that is reliable. And, that makes us all want to get away and go to the <u>front</u> where there is something going on and some excitement.

This country is not a bit like Iowa. It's covered with hills and rocks and there are no nice towns and houses. The people live in little old log cabins. I have seen a great many little boys and girls like mine who were dirty and ragged and had nothing to eat and looked very miserable indeed. And then, there are no <u>schools</u> in all the country and the children all grow up without learning anything. I've seen girls and boys a great deal larger than you and Lulie who never were at school in their lives. And I am so thankful that my little girls have a nice home and good clothes and plenty to eat and a good school and Sunday school to go to. Don't you think you ought to be very thankful that you have all these things and such a good, kind mother to take care of you? And then these wicked people down here would like to make our country just as poor and miserable as theirs is. And, if it was not for your pa and the other soldiers, you would soon have no nice homes or schools either. But I expect you think this may be hard to understand. Ask Ma to tell you more about it.

Now, you must be a good little girl both at home and at school and learn to write so you can write me a letter. Captain Hanks who stays in the same room with me has two little girls in Knoxville, Iowa, just about as old as you and Lulie and they both write letters to him. And I shall look for a letter from you some of these days to tell me all about Tommy and Kittie and Mandy and Maud and Edith and all the little boys and girls who go to school, about your lessons and the garden, the pigs and corn, the new fence and everything. And I will write to you both a whole sheet full of the next time. How many verses have you learned at Sunday school?

Your affectionate father,
J.B. Ritner

The Death of Samuel E. Bereman, Emeline's Father

[Mt. Pleasant, Iowa]
July 13th, 1864

Dear Husband,

Day before yesterday I wrote you a long letter and sent it up to the post office and got in return a letter from you written at the Rome hospital. I was so sorry to hear that you were sick enough to go to the hospital and glad that you had gone for I think you certainly will get a little more rest there. You requested me in that letter to sit right down and write you a great long letter. I intend to after writing to Henry. But, just after finishing his, I received a telegram from Alvah & Billy that poor father was dead. This dreadful news has us all into such a state of grief that I haven't hardly been able to write till today. I am now at Ma's in the little bedroom writing. I have been with Ma since we got the news. She thinks she can't let me go home. The telegram stated that he was dead, and that they would send the body home embalmed and that was all.

We were in great suspense, but were relieved somewhat by a letter from Billy yesterday, which was written five days before the telegram was dated. He said father was sick with the flu, but would soon get better he thought as he had brought him over to his quarters and was doing all he could for him. He also got a little note that Alvah sent in one of his letters to Sarah yesterday, saying that Billy had just been over there for him, to come over and see father, that he didn't think he would live. Alvah thought he might not be so bad and told Sarah not to alarm us. But, it seems that it proved fatal. We are so anxious to hear the particulars. We expect the body tomorrow or next day. It will be a week tomorrow since the dispatch was dated. Oh, how cruel and hard this war is. We are expecting the corpse of a Dear Father home and not a single one of the boys or you home to sympathize with, or help us to bear the pain of meeting it. I never realized how lonely we were, or how utterly destitute of a near friend. None of the children here but Sallie & I.

Judge Edwards was the first to come and offer his services. He is very kind & I shall never forget him. Taylor's folks have offered us to assist us in any way & today Brother Lee was out (a new member of our church) so, I think after all we shall find enough friends that are willing to do all they can. Brother Gunn is away, to be gone two weeks.

Ma takes it very hard. I thought at first she certainly would be sick. She went up to Alvah's that day and stayed all day. Came back by our house and rested awhile, and hadn't been home more than half an hour when the boy came with the dispatch for me. I could hardly take it and read it thinking it was from you. When I said father is dead, Tommy started for Grandma's and ran all the way down here, unbeknown to me. And while I was waiting for Sallie to come from town, and thinking how I would tell Ma, she came running up with Tom, almost give out. She asked him, when he jumped up on the porch, what he came for, he said he come to tell her Grandpa was dead. She said she knew it was so in a minute the way he looked. We could hardly keep her from giving up entirely. She laid down in the middle of the floor at our house & wrung her hands and prayed that the Lord <u>would</u> temper the wind to the shorn lamb. Oh it is <u>hard, hard, hard</u> to bear, but we must submit to the Lord's will. I have often thought if you should come home that way, how <u>could</u> I ever stand it? Giving up a Father or Brother's hard, but I <u>know</u> it is nothing compared to that. But, I am no better than a thousand others. I am even worse. I sometimes think that I deserve it for being so hard-hearted & living so far from the Savior and such. Such a prayerless life. Oh, that that Lord would bring us both to live a more Christian life than we have done and spare us to meet each other again.

Em

[Mt. Pleasant, Iowa]
July the 19th, 1864

Dear Husband,

I wrote you five days ago and told of the death of our dear father. I directed that letter to the regiment. Thinking that perhaps you would not get it for some time, I have concluded to write your hospital at Lookout Mt., but I do not know how to direct it so that it will go straight, but will risk it. I told you in my last how we were shocked by the receipt of a telegram from Alvah & Billy stating that Father was dead, and that they would send his body home embalmed. We got the telegram on Monday evening and the body came on Saturday morning. You may know that we spent a long week of suspense & anxiety & trouble. It was so sudden and unexpected that we can hardly believe it yet. We can't realize it, though we have seen and felt his poor body, stiff and cold in death, and followed it to the grave and saw it consigned to the dust. Oh, how can it be so that Father is dead and now lives out here at the cemetery by the side of poor Jont. But, it is so. We kept the body from Saturday morning till Sunday afternoon 5 o'clock. It was in a very good state of preservation and looked natural I think except that he was dark.

The funeral took place at Ma's. There was a good many out, almost a yard full. Judge Edwards talked awhile and Mr. Crane prayed. They sang one or two hymns and then repaired to the cemetery. There we left him alone to sleep his last sleep. Oh, how hard it is to give him up and how lonely it is here now. It was enough so before, but now it is doubly so. Ma took it very hard at first, and does yet, but bears it with Christian fortitude. I feared it was too much for her poor nottering frame. She feels so very lonely now that she can hardly stand it. I have stayed with her most of the time, night and day since the first news came. You know there is nobody there but Ma, Sallie & Amanda. They come up here Sunday night and staid all night. I thought I would keep them till Ma would get to feeling better, but the next morning she took a notion she must go home and try and get used to it there. We went down & stayed with her last night.

I do wish one of the boys was home with her. We have had letters from Alvah & Billy. They say Father had the flu, was only sick about a week, said that his mind wandered a good deal before he died, and he felt bad because he made blunders in talking. He said he had been sick a good many times before, but never felt that his time had come to die till then. Somebody told him not to be discouraged. He said he wasn't. All he dreaded was his present pains, otherwise he was all right. Alvah wrote to me that he & Billy had to borrow money there to pay the expense of coffin and embalming, &c and that I must pay the expense charges which would be about $50.00 or so, and the boys would make it all up to me as soon as they could. Ma happened to have some of Ol's money and she said she would use that, but I gave her $20, as my share towards the expenses. I felt that I must give something. Ma has no money to support her except Ol's and that won't last long as everything is so high now. The burial expenses cost $9.50.

Now my Dear, I must tell you what conclusion we have all come to here, & that is that you must resign and come home. I don't think your health will ever get any better in the army, for I think you are a broken down. That will take years to be well again, and if you still expose yourself, you may never get over it. You know I have never persuaded you before to come home to stay, but I think it is my duty to do so now. As you have served your country now for almost 2 years and have lost your health so that you can't be of much service any longer in the army. You must remember that you owe a duty to your family as well as your country. Now you have served your country faithfully, to the last minute without actually giving up your life for it. And why do that, when you have done all else that you can? And when that much more will do no good. But won't you.

Em

On July 8 and 9, segments of the Union forces began to cross the Chattahoochee River in two places, Roswell and Isham's Ford near Soap Creek, located north and east of most of Johnston's forces. Johnston responded by ordering another retreat, this time across the Chattahoochee River, which was another moral blow to Georgians who felt that Johnston would make a stand at the Chattahoochee and never let the Yankees cross that river. The citizens of Atlanta immediately heard of Johnston's retreat, which set off a mass exodus from Atlanta. By July 12, only a few thousand citizens remained, including Mayor Calhoun.

Jefferson Davis, who never approved of Johnston's strategy of retreats, finally decided to replace Johnston. After consideration was given to others, on July 17, Davis gave command of the Army of Tennessee to General John Bell Hood, who had a reputation as an aggressive fighter.

On July 20, Stewart and Hardee engaged the Union Army of the Cumberland at the Battle of Peachtree Creek about five miles north of Atlanta. Union casualties at the Battle of Peachtree Creek were about 1,900 killed, wounded, or missing, compared to 2,500 for the Confederates in what is considered a Confederate defeat.

Both Union and Confederate soldiers were aware of the political impact of the impending battles. The North was tired of the death and destruction wrought by the war, with little in the way of recent major victories to show for their efforts. The South felt if they could continue to hold out until the presidential election of 1864, then Lincoln would be defeated and the new administration would negotiate peace with the South. The Atlanta (Macon) Daily Appeal forecast: "the greatest battle of the war will probably be fought in the immediate vicinity of Atlanta," and that the outcome would determine "that of the pending November Presidential election. If we are victorious the Peace party will triumph; Lincoln's administration is a failure, and peace and Southern Independence are the immediate results." (Albert Castel, Decision In The West, page 395)

On July 21, Hood moved his troops toward the east side of Atlanta to block McPherson and the Army of the Tennessee. Sherman and the other Union officers were aware of this Confederate movement, but at first thought that Hood was abandoning Atlanta.

On July 22, the Confederates, following Hood's directives of frontal assaults, attacked the Army of the Tennessee in fighting east of the city. In the midst of the battle, General McPherson traveled into a gap between the 16th and 17th Army Corps, where he was surprised by a small band of Confederates who gave him a chance to surrender. McPherson refused and started to gallop away, but was shot through the lungs near his heart and died.

Historical Sketch—25th Iowa Infantry

On July 20th, 1864, the brigade marched near to Atlanta and built a line of earthworks. On July 21st, it again advanced and built another line of works, but had only just completed and occupied the new line when it was ordered – on the morning of July 22nd – to move about three-fourths of a mile to the west and occupy a line of works which the rebels had abandoned on the night of the 21st. Then followed the hard-fought battle of July 22nd, 1864, in front of Atlanta, the rebels attacking the Union lines in heavy force. In that battle, the Twenty-Fifth Iowa shared the honors won by its brigade, and suffered its proportion of the loss of 5 killed, 2 missing and 29 wounded. (Roster and Record of Iowa Soldiers in the War of the Rebellion; Published under the authority of the Iowa General Assembly)

The Battle of Atlanta

Near Atlanta, Georgia
July 22, 1864

My Dear Wife,
 I wrote you a few lines at Chattanooga on the 16th inst. and I suppose you are anxious to get another letter. I have had no chance to write since, and we have orders to be ready to march at a moment's notice, so I don't know how much I'll get to write now. We are now lying about two miles northeast of the city. We moved in here yesterday afternoon, and were then close to the rebel lines, and we built breastworks. But last night the rebels fell back about a mile and our skirmishers are now that far in front of us, and in sight of the city. But the rebels have strong works in front of them and are firing with artillery. I think we will move up today to a strong line of works which they abandoned last night. I don't think there will be much fighting here anymore[1] and we will have the town in a day or two.
 My health is very good now. I feel a great deal better than when I left the hospital. I left Chattanooga on Saturday morning and got to Marietta that night about midnight. I found the regiment had moved to the left and had crossed the Chattahoochee River at Roswell, 15 miles from Marietta. I got to Roswell on Sunday and found our train there, and left my valise and haven't seen it since. The train has not yet come up. I went on foot from there and found the regiment about 11 o'clock at night, 12 miles this side of the river (we moved immediately.)

*****[2]

 July 23—2 o'clock p.m. I did not get to finish my letter yesterday. When I was interrupted, we moved up ¾ of a mile and in sight of Atlanta to where the rebels had abandoned a strong line of works. But instead of going into Atlanta, as many thought we would, we had the hardest fighting we have had in the whole campaign. In the forenoon, the rebels massed their forces and turned our left flank and drove the 17th Army Corps back in some confusion. But they [the 17th Army Corps] rallied and were reinforced, and recovered all the ground they had lost. Then, in the afternoon, they [the Confederates] charged on the line further to the right where we were and the brigade next to the left of us were driven out of their works and their battery captured. Then our division (or rather two brigades of it) charged on the rebels and drove them back and recaptured the battery before they got it away. They fired on us like all vengeance, but shot too high, and there were only 8 or 9 hurt in the regiment. No one hurt in Company B except Sergeant Payne, slightly in the right arm. He is still able for duty. Every man did his duty bravely.

I was the first one to reach the rebel works, and captured a captain and two men myself. I started to "go for" the rebel flag which was floating over the works further to the left, but when I stopped a minute to send the prisoners back, the boys got ahead of me. Our division captured 200 prisoners, and the ground in front of us was covered with their dead and wounded. The fight was very severe all along the line and the rebels lost not less than 10,000[3] men in killed, wounded, and prisoners, and our loss was very heavy, but less. They captured a good many prisoners from us.

The "Iowa Brigade" in the 17th Army Corps lost a great many. The 16th Iowa has only about 40 or 50 men left. The 15th lost 154 men. But Captain Rogers and Sergeant Cady are safe—I saw them today. Captain Barr[4] of the 11th was killed. Archey Campbell was shot through the right hand. Captain Rogers lost 20 men yesterday and the day before, but none, I think, from Danville. But our greatest loss yesterday was the death of Major General McPherson, who was killed in the forenoon. We feel his loss deeply. We all loved him and had confidence in his ability and courage. General Logan[5] takes his place.

We worked all night last night fortifying. And this morning were relieved by the 23rd Army Corps and moved two miles to the left, where we are now fortifying again. There is a truce today— our men are bringing in the rebel wounded and burying their dead, who all fell into our hands when they were repulsed. They came very near getting our whole train yesterday—it was only saved by hard driving, but we are prepared for them now and do not fear any attack they can make. But I must go back to where I left off when we had to move yesterday.

When I got to the company I found that one of my best men had been killed while I was gone, Lewis Edwards. He was shot by a sharpshooter across the Chattahoochee River. He was a good soldier and leaves a large family. I was very sorry to hear of his death.

The rest of the company were all as well as usual, and are yet, with the exception of Lieutenant Steele, who had the diarrhea pretty bad, and has been at the hospital the last two days. Lieutenant Crane is well. He is *aide-de-camp* to Colonel

Williamson, so I am alone with the company.

. . . I have felt bad ever since I read your letter of the 27th, because I am afraid from the way you write that I said something I had no business to, and that hurt your feelings. If I did, dear, I beg your pardon a thousand times. I never meant to complain that you did not write oftener, but that the letters did not get here, and if I said anything rude or mean I hope you will excuse me this time and I will never do so again. You must give me a good scolding for writing you a piece of a letter from Chattanooga, and then we will kiss and make, won't you dear?

I think your man acted very mean about the fence, and I will attend to his case when I get home, and show him that he can't impose on the wife of a soldier without being called to account for it. The lower board was to be new and he had no right to any of the scraps, and the gates were in the contract. If you have not paid him the balance yet, don't do it till I get home.

I hear that the 45th Iowa has been disgraced for stealing and sent away from Memphis. That is a pretty story indeed. What do the folks think now of "the most intelligent, most patriotic, and wealthiest" company that ever left Mt. Pleasant? I suppose Company A has come down a peg. But I must stop.

I have just learned that the rebel General Hardee was mortally wounded and captured yesterday. He died at our hospital, today[6]. I thank you very much for your words of sympathy and encouragement in your letters. I thought of them when I started for the rebel flag—if I had taken it I would have sent it to you. Good-bye for the present.

Your affectionate husband,
J.B. Ritner

I send you a skein of silk, captured at Marietta on the 4th of July.

1. This was optimistic thinking. Roughly one minute after writing this, the Confederates launched their attack against the Army of the Tennessee, which included Jacob.

2. At this point, the Confederates attacked and Jacob put aside his letter.

3. Logan's official report estimated the Confederate loss at 10,000. Sherman's estimate was closer to 8,000. But further review by historians, including Castel, has lowered the estimate to 5,500.

4. Captain George W. F. Barr was one of three Barrs in Company
G of the 11th Iowa Infantry from Mt. Pleasant, Iowa. George
was age 25 at enlistment, David age 24, and John age 35.
Contrary to Jacob's belief that George was killed, he survived
and had been taken prisoner. He was released from prison
October 1, 1864. George, David, and John all survived the war.

5. From the diary of Dr. Henry M. Farr, Surgeon of the 25th Iowa
Infantry, July 22, 1864:

> Early this morning it was found that the enemy had left
> their outer works & had retired within their inner line.
> Gen. Hood had superseded Gen. Johnston & adopted new
> tactics. The main part of the Rebel army was hurled
> against the 17th Corps on our left. One of our regiments
> & a battery were taken prisoners. General McPherson was
> killed & things looked squally: But General Logan takes
> Command of the Army of the Tennessee. Sherman sends
> up reserves [and] the rebels are driven back within their
> inner works with great slaughter.
>
> Our Brigade was in reserve near Sherman's Quarters. I
> saw Gen. McPherson's remains brought in. Soon I saw
> Gen. Logan coming towards Sherman at full speed & see-
> ing him approaching, Sherman calls out to Logan saying
> "Logan, put a Brigade in the gap made by the captured
> regiments. The 17th Corps are in reserve. You can have all
> the reinforcements there is room for. Logan answers,
> "Gen. I have already done what you order. I had no time
> to wait for orders." Sherman answers "all right. Well give
> em h-ll before night." (Dr. Henry Farr, *Diary of Dr. Farr
> (Unpublished)*, Iowa State Historical Society, Iowa City,
> Iowa; Steve Meyer, *Iowa Valor*, pages 317-318)

6. The rumor that Jacob heard about General Hardee being mortally wounded and captured was not true. General Hardee survived the war and died in 1873.

In Rear of Atlanta, Georgia
July 25, 1864

My Dear Wife,
I wrote to you day before yesterday and as there seems to be no
signs of a move or a fight this morning, I will try to write again. My
health is still quite good. I have been gaining in flesh since I came

back, although we have worked very hard. We never stay more than
one night in one place. We got our works fixed first-rate at the
place I wrote to you from last, and were in hopes we would get to
use them. But yesterday morning we were relieved by the 16th
Army Corps and our division went back to and beyond Decatur and
tore up railroad. We are now lying in the brush some four miles east
of Atlanta. I lost my pocketbook while at work yesterday. It had no
money in it, but had your photograph, which I wouldn't have lost
for anything, and memorandum of the clothing issued the last three
months. I am afraid it will give me a good deal of trouble.
Lieutenant Steele is yet sick at the hospital and no better; the rest
of the company are all right.

There was no fighting yesterday. Our prisoners and detail were
still busy burying the rebel dead. Some of our batteries shelled the
city all last night. And this morning the rebels advanced their skirmishers and there is some firing in our front, but we do not expect
an attack. Our cavalry have been out along the railroad 40 or 50
miles and burned all the bridges and several trains, and destroyed a
great deal of provision and government property belonging to the
rebels. They came back yesterday with a large lot of prisoners. All
the other roads are destroyed more or less, and I think we will soon
end the campaign in this quarter by taking the city and the greater
part of the army. And I think that will about end the war. Things
seem to move slow about Richmond but perhaps they think the
same about us. But if they are as hard at work as we are, no one
should find fault.

The battle here on the 22nd was one of the hardest and most
effective of the season. And it was fought entirely by the Army of
the Tennessee (the 15th, 16th, and 17th Army Corps). We lost as
many prisoners as we took, perhaps more, but their killed and
wounded exceeded ours by ten to one. Their loss was not less than
10,000. They got 18 pieces of artillery and all the entrenching tools
of the 16th and 17th Army Corps, but we got thousands of arms
thrown away by them on the field. I could fill a dozen sheets if I
had time, describing to you the desperate fighting at different
points and the slaughtered rebels lying thick in front of our lines,
which were some three miles long, but it would not be interesting
to you. Our greatest loss was General McPherson—he will be
deeply mourned for by the whole nation. A great many prominent
rebel officers were killed or captured. The 16th Iowa lost every
man and officer that went into the fight[1]. 70 of the men were away

on detail and escaped.

. . . I told you there was a letter back at the train for me that came while I was away. Well, I sent back after it. I thought it must be the one next after the one you wrote about Nellie being sick. But when it came it was only a letter from Ed Hebard. I just tore it up. Your letter between June 16th and 27th is yet minus. I hope we will soon be where we can get letters regularly again. Your last letters were so good. I don't see how I could live away down here at all, if I did not get a letter from you once in a while.

I don't think you need to be at all uneasy about the election of Lincoln. The army will get to vote. And I have the first soldier to find yet who will not vote for Old Abe. I was a Fremont[2] man once but I am not now. He has turned out to be nothing but a selfish demagogue. Every soldier feels that the only way to end the war and save the country is to elect Lincoln. I will write again the first chance—do the same. My love to Ma and Car. I have written this in a great hurry for fear we would have to move before I got done. I am afraid you will find it very dull if you can read it at all. But remember that it is from your own Jake who loves you dearly and thinks about you all the time when we shall meet again day and night. I always think of a great many things I want to tell you, but when I come to write in a hurry I can't think of them.

Your own, Jake

1. The 16th Iowa was in the division commanded by Giles Smith, part of the 17th Army Corps commanded by Blair. They were in the left line of the 17th Army Corps during the battle of Atlanta by the gap between the 17th and 16th Army Corps, near where McPherson was killed. The 16th Iowa had fought fiercely and was in the process of accepting the surrender of the 2nd and 8th Arkansas with two Texas companies. As this began, they had twice as many prisoners as were in their regiment. While they were sending prisoners to the rear, they suddenly found themselves surrounded by Confederate reinforcements and isolated from other Union support. Since they were almost without ammunition, the 16th Iowa was itself forced to surrender. At one point, an Iowa soldier asked an Arkansas soldier which side was surrendering, and the Confederate responded "I'll be damned if I know." (Lee Kennett, *Marching through Georgia*, page 193; Report by Colonel Addison H. Sanders of the 16th Iowa Infantry; Steve Meyer, *Iowa Valor*, pages 319-320)

2. General John C. Frémont was considering running against

Abraham Lincoln for the Republican party nomination for president. Frémont had been the Republican nominee in 1856 and Jacob's grandfather had attended that convention as a delegate.

• After the Battle of Atlanta, Sherman moved the Army of the Tennessee from the east of Atlanta over to the west, then south to strike Atlanta from that position.

Following General McPherson's death, Sherman temporarily appointed General Logan to commander of the Army of the Tennessee, which included the 15th, 16th, and 17th Army Corps. After discussions with General Thomas, Sherman decided to promote General O.O. Howard to permanent command of the Army of the Tennessee. Logan was upset that he did not get permanent command but accepted the decision.

Far more upset with Howard's promotion was General Joseph Hooker, head of the 20th Army Corps under Thomas in the Army of the Cumberland. Hooker once led the Army of the Potomac and felt that he was the rightful choice to head the Army of the Tennessee. Hooker responded to Howard's promotion by submitting his resignation to Thomas, who passed it on to Sherman, who was happy to accept it.

[Mt. Pleasant, Iowa]
Tuesday morning, July 26th, 1864

Dear Jacob,

I wrote you a few days ago, and directed to the hospital Lookout Mountain. The next day I wrote another and directed to the regiment. But, as you don't get many letters of late, I thought I would write again today and Lulie has written a half sheet and wanted to send it, in mine. I will try and write the other half sheet. Though I expect she has told you all the news, (I haven't read her letter yet.) In the first place, we are all well, expect that Nellie fell down last Thursday and broke her right arm. She was playing and run over a snag and fell on her arm. I sent immediately for Dr. Marsh. He was not at home, so I got McClure. He came and set it. Said there was only one bone broken. She is getting along fairly well, but complains of it a bit. Only she don't like to have it bound up so tight. The other doctor charged me $3.00.

We had a nice rain last night. The first for a long time. I feel rather sleepy this morning. Was up all night at Morleys. They have a young "miss" about six hours old—Sarah hasn't "come in" yet.

I don't suppose you will ever get the letter I wrote to the hospital for you had started from there by the time I wrote you. I must give you a big scolding for leaving there before you got well enough. I told you in my other letter that I want you to stay there as long as the Dr. would let you so that you would be able to stand it better. I am so afraid you will get down sick again. I also told you that you must resign and come home if you possibly could for I don't think your health will ever get any better in the army, and that we need one man to the half dozen families that are left alone. Ma feels very lonely. I don't know how she will get along, as it is very hard on her. I told you all the particulars about Father's death in my other letters.

We heard good news yesterday, that was that Sherman was in possession of Atlanta, but that the death of General McPherson is a great loss to the country. I still take the *Hawkeye*.

Got a letter from Eliza the other day. She sent me her and Charley's photograph. I will write you again in a few days. Excuse this short letter. How do you like Lulie's letter? She did it all herself. Nellie is going to try to write to you when her arm gets well.

Yours, Em

What became of Capt. Hanks? Did he go to the regiment or not? Missouri is full of guerillas[1] and people are getting scared, for fear they will come up in Iowa. There is an order from General Baker to call out the state militia. I don't feel the least bit alarmed. I believe I can face a rebel if he should come here to burn my house down and shoot him too if I had a gun.

1. Independent commands of Confederate guerrillas continued to operate in Missouri, located directly south of Iowa. The most notorious of these guerrillas included William Quantrill, who had fought against Jacob in the Battle of Wilson's Creek, and "Bloody Bill" Anderson. In August 1863, Quantrill launched a savage and murderous attack against the civilians of Lawrence, Kansas, killing no less than 150 men, several of whom were barely more than boys. (Shelby Foote, *The Civil War*, Vol. II, pages 704-705) When Emeline wrote this letter, Tom and Till Bereman and the 1st Iowa Cavalry were in Missouri guarding rail lines against bushwacker attacks, so in addition to concern of possible attacks in Iowa, Emeline would have been very aware of actual guerrilla activities in Missouri.

    In September 1864, just two months after Emeline wrote this letter, "Bloody Bill" Anderson captured a train in Centralia,

Missouri, killing the crew and 24 unarmed soldiers on furlough.
Anderson also slaughtered civilians on the train who had tried
to hide their valuables. Three companies of the 39th Missouri
Militia, a new regiment formed only one month before, armed
with outdated weapons and mounted on farm horses, set out in
pursuit of Anderson, but they were also ambushed by Anderson
and his men. Of the 147 men in this force chasing Anderson,
116 were killed, two were wounded and six reported missing.
(Duane Schultz, *Quantrill's War*, pages 284-289; Stewart
Sifakis, *Who Was Who In The Confederacy*, pages 6-7)

The Battle of Ezra Church

*On the morning of July 27, the Army of the Tennessee left its
entrenched position east of Atlanta to move toward Lick Skillet Road,
located west of Atlanta. Charles R. Wood replaced Osterhaus as
Division Commander within the 15th Army Corps, and his division
was placed in line near a small frame church called Ezra Church. To
Wood's right was the rest of the 15th Army Corps, and to his left the
16th and 17th Army Corps.*

*The Confederates detected the Union movements the day before
and moved a large force to the area for a planned assault against the
Federals. Confederate General Stephen Dill Lee and his corps initiat-
ed the action and, despite setbacks, General Lee continued to order
his corps to regroup and attack the 15th Army Corps. When General
Alexander P. Stewart and his corps arrived, Lee gave him the impression that Hood wanted him to attack the Union right flank. Stewart
began to push his troops toward Ezra Church and the suicidal
Confederate frontal assaults renewed in several places against the
Army of the Tennessee. Both Stewart and Division Commander Loring
received disabling wounds during this period.*

*For the day, Confederate casualties came close to 3,000, making
the casualty ratio almost 5 to 1 against the Confederates.*

Historical Sketch—25th Iowa Infantry

*From the 22nd to the 29th of July, the regiment was actively
engaged in the siege operations [of Atlanta] with its brigade. On July
28th, the rebels made another attack in heavy force, ending in their
repulse. The heaviest part of this day's fighting was to the right of the
position occupied by Williamson's brigade and, consequently, it took
only a minor part in the engagement.* (Roster and Record of Iowa
Soldiers in the War of the Rebellion; *Published under the authority of
the Iowa General Assembly*)

The Battle of Ezra Church

The Dead Rebels Lie There All Over
The Ground, A Horribly Sickening Sight

Near Atlanta, Georgia
July 29, 1864

My Dear Wife,

I wrote you a few lines on the 25th inst. The next day I got two letters from you, one of the 11th and one of the 13th which contained the sad intelligence that Father was dead. It made me feel bad to think about your lonesome and trying situation. It is a great affliction to the whole family. I feel that he was as dear to me, and I shall miss him as much as my own Father. He was always a kind and indulgent father, an affectionate husband, and an honest man and a true patriot. As you say it is hard that such men must be sacrificed to the demon of slavery and treason. Our dear family circle is being broken more and more. One after another of the links are broken, and God only knows how many of us will be left to meet each other after the war is over. I can easily believe that it was a very severe stroke to Ma, as you say. I sympathize with her in her great affliction, and hope that God in mercy will hear her prayers. And that she will have faith and strength to look for comfort to Him in whom she has always trusted. You must stay with her if she wants you to, or have her stay with you. You must see that she has everything she needs. She must never want for anything while we have the power to relieve her . . . I do think it was too bad that none of us men were at home to comfort and assist you in your great trial but that was out of the question. I am very grateful to the kind friends who volunteered to assist you. And then I am in hopes that some of the boys would get leave to go home with the body. It is a great consolation that he did not die among strangers, but had some of his children around him.

I am still quite well. We have had hot and hard work since I last wrote to you. We were then on the railroad east of Atlanta. The next day we had orders to march at 4 o'clock. The whole Army of the Tennessee has been changed from the left to the right of our line. We are now on the extreme right about four miles southwest of Atlanta. We did not get our position until about 11 o'clock yesterday and hardly had our line formed when the rebels made a furious attack on our corps. Our men had used their time well and had built a temporary breastwork of logs and rails. The whole force of the enemy was directed against the 2nd and 4th Divisions and the 3rd Brigade of our division. We were in the front line, but they did not charge on our part of the line, but came within 200 yards. The fighting lasted all afternoon. The rebels charged five times and were repulsed with great loss every time. There was a great slaughter along their whole line of attack. I was over the battlefield this morning. The dead rebels lie there all over the ground, a horribly sickening sight. Their loss must have been several thousand; ours was nothing in comparison, as every lull in the fight was used in strengthening the works. It was a very hot day and a good many men died of sunstroke. There is some skirmishing in our front today, and there are some indications that they will make another attack. But we are well fortified now, and want to fight them right here, if we have to do it at all. But I can't begin to tell you all the news that's going here or all we have done for the last three days. We haven't got Atlanta yet, but expect every day that we will take it.

We had a short visit day before yesterday from Reverend Pickett of Mt. Pleasant. We were glad to see him. He promised to call on you when he gets home. Governor Stone paid us a visit today and he walked along on our breastworks and made a very neat little speech. He promised to take letters back for us, and I am in a hurry to get this done before he leaves. General Howard commands our department now and Logan the 15th Army Corps as before. I think we will like Howard very well. He managed the engagement yesterday admirably. Our cavalry has gone on a raid to destroy the railroad to Macon[1] and if the rebels don't soon get out of here it will be too late. I expect to date my next letter at Atlanta. I have heard and seen it stated that Atlanta was situated in an "open, level, plain." I can't see it in that light. I have been nearly around it, and the country is very hilly and broken, but not rocky and mountainous like it is on the other side of the river. And except where it has been cleared, which is a very small portion, it is covered with very thick timber and brush; and you can't see a man 50 yards in many places.

I think I would like the house you speak of very well, and the situation too. But I think that in 6 months after the war is over I can buy such property for $1,200. But if you can sell the house we now have for $1,000 you may buy it. I have five months pay due me which will amount to over $600. But I must stop. Give my love and sympathy to Ma and Sallie and tell Tommy I think he was in a great

hurry to tell bad news. How I would like to see the little rogue.
Your affectionate Husband,
J.B. Ritner

1. Sherman had plans to force Hood to either evacuate Atlanta, or to come out and fight. As part of this, Sherman directed George Stoneman's and Edward McCook's cavalry units to cut Hood's railroad lines from the south along the Macon Road, which is the action that Jacob is describing.

   Stoneman once held command of the cavalry of the Army of the Potomac, but lost it because of his performance at the Union defeat at Chancellorsville. Hoping to restore his former glory, Stoneman had other intentions beyond Sherman's directives. His plan was to capture Macon, which contained an arsenal, warehouses, a cannon foundry, and a terminal for three railroads. Stoneman's initial assaults on Macon were not successful and he backed off, wandered south, then north, then back toward Macon. His movements were closely followed by Confederates, who engaged and defeated him, finally accepting his surrender.

   McCook spent his time ripping up railroads and telegraph lines near Lovejoy's Station, but eventually ran into Wheeler's cavalry, who trapped McCook and his cavalry. In response, McCook disbanded his unit and directed his men to escape any way they could. McCook himself made it back but his losses totaled about 600.

   With these actions, the Confederates destroyed about two-thirds of the Union cavalry in Sherman's army. (Albert Castel, *Decision in the West*, pages 436-440)

[Mt. Pleasant, Iowa]
July 31st, 1864, Monday at Ma's

Dear Husband,
. . . Old Mr. Laird died yesterday morning and is to be buried this morning so I concluded to stay and go to the funeral. Well, Dear, let me tell you, I have had no letter from you since last Friday week. You had just started from the hospital and said you would write as soon as you got to the regiment. I have been looking in vain for it, and have been very uneasy about you thinking you had just got there in time for the battle of the 22nd. Hope you were not engaged in it as your health was too poor in undergoing such hard-

ships. Mr. Crane told me yesterday the chaplain of the 25th was in town the day before, and said he saw the boys the day after the fight and they were all right. This relieves me a good deal. I hope to hear from you very soon.

I still take the *Hawkeye* and see by it that the 15th A.C. has suffered severely. I hope that Sherman will get full possession of Atlanta without further fighting. Everybody is confident that it is ours by this time. You have, doubtless, heard of the last call for more troops (where the men are to come from, I don't know.) The draft will certainly be enforced this time, and then the North will begin to see trouble, as some of the Copperhead persons declare that they "will stay at home, and defy Old Abe and his minions to drag them from their families." "They hope that the people will at once put their feet down, and insist that not a man should be forced out of the state (New Jersey) to engage in the Abolition of butchery and swear to die at their own doings rather than march one step to fulfill the dictate this mad, revolutionary pontificator" meaning our president and government—I do hope every drafted man will be a Copperhead. The Adjt. Gen. of this state has ordered out the militia. There was a meeting here Saturday afternoon to organize companies.—

There is a good deal of talk about the guerillas, making a raid through Iowa. A good many people are frightened, and they are going to make preparations to resist them. Missouri is full of them, doing all kinds of mischief and the last *Hawkeye* said they were in the southern part of Iowa. The edition of the *Home Journal* thinks we may expect a raid any time. So far, I have not been the least bit frightened. They may come, but if they do, I shall just trust myself in the hands of the Lord. He is able, and all powerful to save to the uttermost. If I or mine shall must meet with disaster at the hands of such foes, I shall not feel that he has forsaken me—I am longing for the faith of the Apostle, when he said "Though He slay me, yet will I trust in him."

We are all well. So are Ma's folks. Nellie's arm is swollen and sore yet. We took off the bandage yesterday as the doctor told us. I think I shall take her up and let him see it again. It is a little crooked too. I am afraid he didn't set it right. She can't use it any, but don't complain of it hurting, only when she knocks it against something. I expect to go to Jefferson next week in company with Sallie and Mrs. Pat Hannah to pick our corn and blackberries. There is some in market now. I want to put up a good lot for you to eat again next winter.

Dear, I must quit as it is time to go to the funeral. I have written

several letters to you lately. Hope you have got them. I wrote one to
Lookout Mountain. Hope I shall get one from you today. Good-bye.
E.R.B. Ritner

Mr. Gunn has a brother here visiting him. He is a preacher too
and is truly a man of God.

Near Atlanta, Georgia
July 31, 1864

My Dear Wife,
I wrote to you the day before yesterday, and sent the letter home
by Governor Stone . . .
We were relieved yesterday about noon by a post of the 17th
Army Corps and our division moved back a short distance and are
now lying in reserve. We haven't got a very good camp—we are in
an open field with no shade except what we make by carrying
brush, and the weather is extremely hot. And we have built an arbor
the whole length of the regiment and twenty feet wide. There are
plenty of good springs near by. But we are so close to the battlefield of the 28th inst.[1] that the smell is very disagreeable. I suppose
you folks that don't know anything about war will think it is a good
thing to get to laying reserve. But we think just the reverse, and
don't like it a bit. We may lay here three or four days, but are to be
called out at any minute and sent to support some part of the line
that is in danger of being broken, and then we have to go into a
strange place and fight, it is a great deal better and safer to have our
own share of the front line to hold, so we can get the "lay of
ground" beforehand.
Well, this is Sunday morning, about time to get ready to go to
meeting. I expect you are fixing to go. I have just been looking at
your picture, and I think I see you now, putting on your things. I
know how nice and pretty you are looking, and that you will think
of me when you get to meeting. Oh, how much comfort there is in
that thought. I often think about you, and wonder almost if it is
really so, that a beautiful and pure-minded woman loves me and
thinks of me—yes, I know it is so. How I wish I was there with
you. I would have a kiss first, and go with you to meeting?
Shouldn't I? But here I am, sitting on the ground under our shade,
writing on my valise, which I got last night for the first time since
I got back. The men are all busy around me, some writing letters,

some washing their clothes, and others cleaning their guns and c. Lieutenant Steele is still at the hospital. I have not heard from him for several days. The balance of the men are all well as usual.

Well, dear, you see I was back to the regiment before I got your letters. In fact, I was here when they were written. There is a great deal of truth in what you say, dear, and I have been thinking on the same subject. But I have not been able to come to the same conclusion exactly as you did. I know that you are very lonesome at home and that you need me there very much. I sympathize with you in your great affliction and would like to be there to comfort and assist you and Ma. I feel too that I have a duty to discharge to you both and to our children as well as to our country. But which has the greatest and most pressing claims? If I were to consult my own feelings and inclinations, without regard to duty or patriotism, I should certainly be at home with you just as soon as possible. But my health is not so poor now as you seem to think. I feel quite well and hearty since I had my short rest at the hospital. I have been gaining in flesh ever since, although it has been the hardest part of the campaign, and we still have nothing to eat but hard bread, coffee, and bacon. But I can eat it first-rate, and I could not get out of the service on the plea of physical disability unless my health fails again. So you at least have the satisfaction of knowing that your husband is not such a broken-down cripple as you feared, but has a prospect of a good many years yet. I think the medicine I took had a good effect. But I am a little afraid I will have the ague again in the fall. And then another thing—I am very much attached to my company; I enlisted them all and came out with them with the understanding that I would stand by them and stay with them till their time is out. We have marched and fought and suffered together so far, and seen our ranks gradually thinned out till I have come to feel towards them almost as if they were my brothers. And what excuse could I make to them for leaving them while I am able to stand in my place and at their head and lead them. I don't feel like I could do it. They must stay till their time is out or the war is over. And unless I should become unable for service I think I must stay with them. Am I right about it? What do you think of these things? I rely a great deal, my dear wife, on your judgment and your sense of right, and will try to take your advice. Then I think some of the other boys might as well be home as me. Alvah's time will be out before long, and he is better able to see that Ma is provided for than I am. And I suppose he will do it. I suppose the time of the non-veterans of the 1st [Iowa] Cavalry is out now, and I thought Tom was going home then. How is that? You have not said anything about it.

Well dear, it is afternoon and it is time for the children to get ready for Sunday School. But it is thundering and looks like it would rain. I expect they will have to stay at home. But then they would feel bad and lose their tickets. I have been thinking what you and I would do while they are gone, if I was there—have you got that big rocking chair mended yet? I am glad the girls were pleased with their letters. I will write Tommy one when I get time.

I am glad you helped Ma to bear the expense[2]; we must do our part, and if the others do not do theirs we will do theirs too. But they are more able, some of them, than we are, but that makes no difference. I suppose that Car will come back as soon as she hears the news and will be company for poor Ma. There is no paper on which to credit the money from Sara Jont. I think it was all right to lend the money to James Campbell—he will pay it. I got a letter from him some time ago and answered it while I was at the hospital.

The 15th Army Corps did itself great credit in the battle here on the 28th inst.[1] The rebels attacked us with great fury—almost frenzy—many of them were intoxicated. They had two corps, and brought forward new men time after time, but failed to break our line in the least. Their loss was not less than 6,000 and ours, from the best information I can get did not reach 500. It was a perfect carnival of slaughter. We have buried 1,300 of their dead in front of our line, which was not more than a mile long.

We have just received orders to be ready to march at a moment's notice and I must close. I will write to you again in a few days, if possible. I think we are only going out on picket duty. I can't tell anything about when Atlanta will be taken, but believe it will surely fall. Give my love to Ma and the children, all friends.

Your own, Jake

1. Jacob is referring to the Battle of Ezra Church as the battle of the "28th inst."

2. Jacob is referring to the expense of Emeline's father's funeral.

Historical Sketch—25th Iowa Infantry

On July 30th, the brigade moved to the extreme right of the army and occupied that position until August 6th, when it moved one mile to the front and built a new line of works. There it remained—expecting an assault from the enemy every day—until August 13th, when it participated in an attack, made by its brigade and division, on the enemy's skirmish line. This resulted in a complete success, including the capture of nearly the entire enemy force in the rifle pits. (Roster and Record of Iowa Soldiers in the War of the Rebellion; Published under the authority of the Iowa General Assembly)

We All Like the Rebel General Hood First-Rate

Near Atlanta, Georgia
August 4, 1864

My Dear Wife

Well, Dear, it seems like I will never get done dating my letters "near Atlanta." We have been almost around the city, but don't seem to get any closer. I see the Northern papers say that Sherman is in no hurry to take the place, but is going to take his own time for it. That is all bosh. The whole army is anxious to have the thing over with, and are getting impatient of the delay, which I have no doubt is unavoidable and not the result of choice, on the part of Sherman or anyone else. You speak of the great relief and joy you felt at the fall of Vicksburg. I know there was great rejoicing then and will be when Atlanta falls. There will be more rejoicing in the army when we enter Atlanta than when we captured Vicksburg. It has taken more time and labor and hard fighting and cost more lives. But we all feel that it is a doomed city, and we are expecting every day to be the last.

I wrote you last on last Sunday, July 31st. Just as I finished we had orders to march. But we didn't go. We lay at that place till Tuesday afternoon and then moved about one mile to the right, where we are yet, lying in reserve. We have a strong line of breastworks. And there is another line one-half mile in front of us, and our skirmishers are from 300 to 400 yards in front of them. There was brisk skirmishing and heavy artillery firing on the line in front of us and to the right yesterday, and lines were advanced and a good many "Johnnies" captured. In the afternoon there was very hard fighting on the extreme left, at or near the city. It lasted about two hours. I have not heard who made the attack or what the result was. This is the poorest place in the world to hear news that is reliable. We all have to stay at our places so as to be ready at any moment to reinforce any part of the line that is in danger of being broken.

We have had a good deal of rain lately, and we have got wet several times. Captain Simons and myself have jayhawked a good wagon cover which we stretched up for a fly and it keeps us quite dry and comfortable when it rains, and makes a good shade when the sun shines. I was very busy yesterday drawing and issuing clothing to the company. They had all got very dirty and ragged but are now well supplied. In the evening I had—well, what do you think I did have?—I had a shake. Don't you think it too bad! The weather here is very hot. I believe it would kill half the men in the regiment to have to stand out in the sun a day. But we always manage to have a shade of some kind; if we stop in open field we cut and carry brush for arbors, or stretch up blankets.

Lieutenant Steele is still at the hospital; he does not get much better. Payne and Black are both well and stand it first-rate. Sergeant White is not very well. Bill White is in the hospital at Marietta. The general health of the army is good. And the men are all in excellent spirits considering what they had to go through with.

We all like the rebel General Hood first-rate. It is reported that he was wounded or killed on the 28th[1]. I hope it is not so. He makes his men charge on our works, where they are sure to get repulsed, and if he keeps on a few days longer, he will have no army left. I may be mistaken, but I think you will hear that Atlanta is taken before you get this letter. And then I think the 15th Army Corps will be sent back, west of Chattanooga, perhaps clear to the Mississippi River[2]. Unless I should get sick again, I do not think you need look for me home this fall, unless the war should close. I would like dearly to see you and the children even for a short time, and when I get to thinking about you sometimes I think I must go if possible. But then when I think of the parting again I think I could not do it and that I would rather stay here till I go home to stay. What do you say? Must I go home on leave of absence for 20 or 30 days if I can get one? If you say I must come I will try to do so. And suppose I should go home to stay, what would I do then? You will have to contrive some way to make me useful as well as ornamental. I don't know of anything I could do to pay my board.

We have just now got orders to be ready to march at a moment's notice, and I must close and pack up. I believe I will send this as it is, as it is uncertain when I will have another chance. I got a letter from Zan yesterday—was glad to hear from them. Have had none from you since I wrote last.

Give my love to Ma and all the friends. Does "Lib" live with

you yet? You haven't said anything about her for a long time. Excuse my "piece of a letter" and accept the true love of your own
Jake

1. Jacob is referring to the Battle of Ezra Church. Several Confederate Generals were wounded there, including General Alexander Stewart and General Loring. General Hood was not in attendance and the rumor of Hood being wounded or killed on that date was not true. Hood survived the war.

2. The 15th Army Corps did not move west as Jacob speculated, but stayed with Sherman as he moved east.

•   Sherman was cognizant of Grant's staggering losses and absence of victory at Petersburg, Virginia. His brother, Senator John Sherman, as well as Northern and Southern newspapers, told of the importance of Sherman's military efforts to the upcoming presidential election. It was feared that the Northern populace, tiring of this war, would vote Lincoln out of office, in favor of McClellan and a settled peace with the South.

[Mt. Pleasant, Iowa]
August the 7th, 1864

Dearest Husband,
    What shall I do? I can't get any letters from you. During all these trying times of anxiety and suspense, I have had not a single line from you. What is the reason? It has been seventeen days since I received your last letter. It was written on starting from the hospital at Lookout Mountain. You said in that, that you would write as soon as you got to the regiment. I have looked so anxiously for some word from you, but in vain. Never even heard that you got to the regiment till Friday night. Mrs. Crane told me that Baron said you were back. If you have written, I have never got it. After the battle of the 22nd and the news of the death of General McPherson and the 15th [Army Corps] being so terribly cut up, I thought it would be awful, the suspense of waiting for the particulars. But, I have lived over that and also of another after the battle of the 28th and still no particular word from you. Several letters came the first of last week and several more Friday and Saturday. Some from your Company. Beck Hanne was down Saturday and said they had got a letter from Billy dated 29th. Updegraph said he spoke of you being there and that they gave you their letters to make for them. And the way I understood it, he said you were going back to the hospital. My

Dear, why don't I get a letter from you telling me directly all about yourself. Are you sick again? If I know that you are safe, I shall try and be patient till you can write, though it would be a great comfort to get a letter when I am so anxious to hear from you.

This is Sunday night and Mrs. Hannah, Sallie and I are expecting to go to Jefferson tomorrow evening or Tuesday morning, blackberrying, and if I don't get a letter tomorrow morning, I shall certainly get the blues worse than ever and won't feel like going at all.

Have heard of Wils Payne being wounded. Hope he is not bad. Didn't hear whether there was anymore or not. Oh, how I <u>do</u> want to get a letter. When Lulie came home yesterday from the post office yesterday without any, I felt as though I couldn't stand it much longer, but since I have heard your name mentioned by some of the boys (though not a word about your health) I feel as though I could have a little more particulars hoping soon to get a letter from yourself.—

There is a good deal of excitement here about the guerillas. It is reported that they are in the southern part of the state and some expect them here any time. So you need not be suspicious to hear of Mt. Pleasant being burned down anytime. I don't feel alarmed yet, though there may be a great reason to fear them, as Missouri is (the northern part) is completely overrun with them. They are getting up several Co.'s for the militia here. One Cavalry Company came out here on our promise to drill Saturday afternoon. I think they will soon be ready to give any guerilla party a warm reception. I understand that that Price's army has been disbanded and sent back and cast over Missouri to plunder and kill. The Copperheads don't say much, but I guess they are doing all they can secretly. There is a good deal of talk of the Knights of the Golden Circle having meetings over the State. I guess they are plotting some mischief.

We are all well at present. So are Ma's folks. Nellie's arm is swelled some yet, but is getting along pretty well. They are not going to school now. The free school commenced the first of Sept. Guess I will send some of them again. Lulie wrote you a letter and put it in one of mine. If you get it you must say something about it . . . Her eyes are as well as they ever been . . .

Old man Arthur is here putting up a "privey" out of the old lumber that was left of the fence. It will be a rough concern, but better than none . . . I must quit. I know you write Dear, but it provokes me to so that they don't send me yours.

Em

Oh yes, Sarah Alvah has another <u>girl</u>. Don't that beat you? They are no smarter than we, are they? She thinks Alvah will be so disappointed because it was not a boy. He promised her if she would have a boy, he wouldn't reenlist when his 100 days was out. Ma wrote you a letter this other day. Hope you will get it. They are very lonely.

Bugs, Lizards, Scorpions, Snakes, Spiders, and Forty-Seven Kinds of Reptiles

Near Atlanta, Georgia
Wednesday, August 10, 1864

My Dear Wife,

I wrote to you last Sunday. We are still at the same place. I told you then that we were going to have a fight on the right in the afternoon. Well, it came off according to order, but did not come nearer than 400 yards to our part of the line. Random shots and spent balls came among us pretty thick, and wounded a few men, but nothing serious. The fighting was done by the 14th Army Corps. They advanced their line some 300 or 400 yards and held their ground.

There has been no very severe battle since the 28th of July on our part of the line. You will not learn from the papers that we have been doing anything. And perhaps you will think that we have been lying idle and resting. The fact is that we have been hard at work ever since, day and night. The rebel lines are where they were. But we are constantly advancing ours; our skirmishers keep up a brisk fight day and night. They are now close to the rebel works. No one who has not seen it can have any idea of the work it takes to advance an army in the face of an enemy. I thought I did a great deal of digging last summer at Vicksburg, but that was just nothing at all to what we have done here in the last three weeks.

I tell you, dear, I am getting tired, awful tired of this campaign. It has lasted now over 100 days; and I have no idea how long it will last yet. I should not wonder if Atlanta were taken tomorrow or next day. And I shouldn't wonder if it held out a month yet. But we are closing up on them and some one will have to fight or run before long. There is heavy artillery fighting all around as I am writing. We have four batteries and the rebels three, all within ¾ of a mile from here.

I told you Captain Simons and I had a "fly" to keep off the sun and rain. Well, don't you think the rebels have shot holes in it already ! and nearly spoiled it!. I would like to make as many holes in their hides. We are having a wet spell here—it rains every day. We had a mess of green corn (very soft) for breakfast this morning for the first—have had no apples or peaches yet. I suppose you have plenty before this time.

This is the meanest country I ever saw. It doesn't produce anything but traitors, and bugs, lizards, scorpions, snakes, spiders, and forty-seven kinds of reptiles that are never seen in any civilized country.

I do wish I was out of it and could go home and have a good talk with you—wouldn't that be nice. Here I am writing to you about "batteries" and "lines" and "right and left" and all that kind of war stuff, which I can't explain to you so you can understand it, and you don't care anything about it if you could. But I love to write to you and do every chance. But what I want all the time, is just to take you in my arms and tell you "something"—I do love you dear, and if I am spared to see you again, am determined to treat you more kindly, and show you that I love and appreciate you better than I ever done before. I got a letter from you last night, date July 31st. I am sorry you had been so long without a letter from me. I have written two a week for a while past, and I think you have had plenty of letters before this. You wrote from Ma's. I don't care how much you stay there; if she is lonesome and needs you, you must get her to go and stay with you part of the time.

There is one part of your letter I can't understand at all. You say "Nellie's arm is still swelled," "and she can't use it," and you are going to "take her to the doctor again." Well—what in the world has the little toad been doing to her arm? There must be a letter that I have not got yet, which will tell me all about it. But for fear it doesn't come at all, you must tell it over again, for I want to know. And while you are about it, tell me all about Tom and Kit (if you haven't got any other name for her yet) and about Lulie. You don't know how much I like to hear something about them. Do they ever talk about their Pa? Or have they forgotten me entirely?

I hope you will not be troubled by guerrillas. But I think it is wise for the people to be prepared. If they should get there, do you stay at home, and let on you are not afraid of them. That is the safest way. But it wouldn't be very safe for them to offer any indignity to my wife. I should follow them to the end of the world. You need not be uneasy about the draft. It will be enforced and the men will be found. I wish it had been done sooner—we need the men here right now. If we only had 20,000 more men it would be a short job.

I hope you had a good time at Jefferson and got lots of blackberries. If I don't get home to help eat them I will have you send me some down. I forget whether I ever told you that General Osterhaus has gone home sick and General Woods commands our division.

Good-bye, dear, and when you pray remember your Jake.

To Emeline's Mother on the Death of Emeline's Father

Camp near Atlanta, Geo.
August 14, 1864

Dear Ma,

I received your very welcome letter yesterday and was glad to find that you had not forgotten me. Though I did not think you had because I know you have enough to do without writing many letters. I have written to Emeline since I got one from her and I will write to you today and let her wait.

This is Sunday morning and we have been at this same place for a week. This is the first time we have been in one place so long since we left Woodville. We are close to the Rebel Works and can see them and hear them talk. The balls and shells come among us pretty thick, but so far we have escaped without much loss. We have had one killed and six wounded in the regiment during the last week. Yesterday evening we advanced our skirmishers and captured the Rebels skirmishers (200 men in all). Since that they cannot hurt us with muskets, but still shell us. No one has been hurt in my company lately. Will Black and Millhaus both got a light tap on the arm. The men are generally well and in good spirits.

I had heard of your great affliction[1] by Emeline's letter. It was a great shock to me and I know it was a terrible blow to you. It was hard to think that he died away from you and from home and that when his remains were sent back, there was not one of the boys and me there to receive it or comfort you. I do think it was too bad, but I hope you have found kind friends who did all that could be done. I shall always be grateful to them for the interest they took. And then you had that great friend on whom you have leaned for so many years. I know he did not desert you in your time of need and all earthly friends and relatives are poor comforters compared to him who has promised to be an ever present help to those who put their trust in him. I sympathize with you deeply and I know you must feel very lonesome. But, I hope and pray that you may be able to say "thy will be done."

I was glad to hear that father's mind was at peace in his last moments and that he felt that it would be well with him in the future. I always thought that his heart and his life and conduct were better than his doctrine and I think so yet. Then we have the consolation to know that he died in a good cause, that he gave his life for a worthy object.

When I think what this war has cost our family in blood and suffering, I detest more than ever the wicked traitors and their more inhuman abettors in the North. I do not think your feelings on the subject are unchristian. I think they are very right and natural. We are not required to love and pray for Public enemies and traitors. David and all the old prophets expressed their hatred and detestation of such men and prayed for their speedy destruction. I feel just as you do and when I think of the suffering that has been brought on you and our family by their stupendous wickedness, I feel I can never lay down my arms till they are conquered. I have taken some of them prisoners, but when I think of these things, I feel that it would not be safe for any of them to come in my way.

I could not sleep last night after reading your letter. I got up at midnight and went out and sat on the breastwork in the moonlight and thought of the difference in our family since the war began. How we were all at home—safe—contented—prosperous—happy—Now we are scattered everywhere and no one knows how many of us will ever meet at the old homestead again. I think a great deal about how you and Emeline get along with no one there to help you see to anything. I hope Alvah will soon be home. I don't know whether I will get to go home this Fall or not, but whether I am there or not, you must always let me or Emeline know if you need anything.

We can never pay you for your love and kindness to us and I have written to Emeline that while we have anything, you must never want for it. I always was a very awkward hand to comfort anyone in affliction with words, but be assured that I sympathize with you deeply in my heart and I pray that this severe trial may be blessed to the spiritual good of us all.

I have no idea when Atlanta will be taken. Everyone here feels that it will be captured and we all feel certain that it would have been ours a week ago if General Palmer had not refused to obey orders[2]. A little petty jealousy has caused all the delay and may keep us here a month longer. I am getting very tired of this campaign. It is hard work . . . We have just now got orders to fall in to our works with arms as the Rebels are making their forces in front of us and General Logan thinks they may attack us. We hope they will, but there is no such good luck. All we want is for them to come out of their works and attack us, but I have no idea they will. The artillery on both sides is firing. Goodbye for the present. I shall be very glad to hear from you again.

Your affectionate son, J.B. Ritner

1. Jacob was referring to the death of Eleanor's husband, Samuel E. Bereman.

2. This is in reference to Major General John M. Palmer, Commander of the 14th Army Corps, who reported to Major General Thomas, Commander of the Army of the Cumberland. On August 4, 1864, General Schofield, Commander of the Army of the Ohio, presented orders from General Sherman for Palmer to assist Schofield in an attempt to break through the Confederate lines on the east of Atlanta. Palmer refused, feeling that although Schofield commanded an army and Palmer only a corps, that he still outranked Schofield because of seniority. Many historians agree with the conjecture that Palmer's actions may have delayed the capture of Atlanta by a month. Palmer then asked to be relieved of command of the 14th Army Corps and was replaced by General Jefferson C. Davis, who was promoted to Major General. (Albert Castel, *Decision in the West*, pages 454-458; Webb Garrison, *Atlanta and the War*, page 184)

[Mt. Pleasant, Iowa]
Wednesday Night, Aug. 17th, 1864

My Dear Husband,
   . . . The Association commences day after tomorrow at Danville. We are all going, but Ma, she is going to stay with the children. Everybody expects to have a good time. Wish you were here to go too.

I don't think I was wrong in persuading you to come home if your health continued bad. But, if you had health, and strength and think you can stand it well as the rest of the boys, I can't expect to have my own wishes gratified in regard to you resigning. I feel it is a duty I owe my country, to give up my dear friends to fight and even this in her defense. I shall try to bear my part willingly though

I feel that I am making a great sacrifice, but not half so great as yours. You sacrifice home, friends, and all its comforts and pleasures besides enduring all kinds of hardships, privations and even suffering death, if need be, for the sake of those you left behind and your country. Tom says "we cannot now appreciate the glories that will surround the name of such a family as ours," yet what is a little glory when it is purchased at the sacrifice of those we love. It is only the proud consciousness of having done our duty first to God and then to our country.

You spoke of coming home this fall, if you could get leave of absence, I shall leave that for you to decide. The pleasure of seeing you home would be great, but I feel that the parting again would over balance the pleasure. If you can come to stay all winter, it would be nice, but if you only to stay a few days, I don't know but it would be more sorrow than joy in such a visit. I will have to leave all to you, Dear. Since thinking it over, I feel that one <u>hour</u> of your company be at most a year of happiness. I can't say <u>don't come</u>, but if you think best come.

Billy says his time will be out this fall and then he is coming home to stay. He didn't reenlist. Alvah is to so disgusted with the higher officers that he will not go again unless he is drafted, I guess.

We are all well. Nellie's arm is about well. But, it's crooked a little. We expect Car home before long . . .

Em

Near Atlanta, Georgia
August 20, 1864

My Dear Wife,

This is Saturday and I have not written to you since a week ago last Wednesday—ain't I mean? Well, I am still quite well, and have escaped the bullets and shells so far. And we are still at the same place I wrote to you from last. One reason I have not written before is that the "Johnnys" cut our "communications" and there have been no trains from Chattanooga for about a week till yesterday, they commenced running again, so that we could not send away mail or get any . . . I would like to give you an idea of our situation here and of what we are doing, how we do it, but I don't expect I can make you understand it.

When we came here, August 6th we were on the front line and

close to the rebels skirmishers. Our lines have advanced several times since then and our brigade was crowded out and there has been another line of works in front of us for a week or more. But the rebels are so close yet that the bullets and shells come into our camp and we can hear them yelling. Hardly a day passes that someone is not wounded or killed in the regiment. I have had two men wounded slightly the last week. And the Adjutant[1] was severely wounded in the leg night before last.

Most of the time we walk about our camp just as if there were no rebels within a hundred miles and do not pay any attention to an occasional shell or bullet. But every once in a while, both day and night, we get into a muss with the rebels. The skirmishers on each side are very vigilant and close to each other; a few men on one side or the other will see or hear something and fire—the other side fires back, the first fire again, and in less than two minutes the whole line is banging away as fast as they can. The artillery opens from a half dozen posts. Bullets and shells fly thick and the air is full of smoke in less time than it takes to write it. Then every man grabs his gun and every officer his sword and get into the works so quick you can't see how it is done. A beautiful state of society, isn't it! Whenever the firing commences both sides begin to yell, and we have got to think it nothing but fun.

But we came pretty near having something serious last night. Just at dark our regiment was ordered to build a new line works about 300 yards in advance of the front line, so as to make another advance. I went out with half my company, taking arms, axes, spades, picks, shovels, &c. We had just found the place and got the ground staked off, which is on a ridge about 300 yards from where the rebels skirmish line is now. When all at once they commenced like fury and shot low, too. We lay down, but had no protection whatever, and the balls whistled all over and among us. We fell back a little piece over the hill till they stopped and then built our works. There was no one hurt; everyone says that it was nothing but our usual good luck that saved us, and if any other regiment had been there they would have had a large list of killed and wounded. But I think it was all owing to the Kind Providence and watchful care of the God of Battles; no one else could bring us safe through such dangers; and to Him be all the praise. And I pray that His protecting arm may still be extended towards us.

Well, as I was going on to say, when the firing slacked up a little, we went to work and dug for dear life till we got a hole big enough to hide in. It commenced to pour down rain about the time we got to work, and rained all night, but we worked away, and by morning had strong works. I sent back my men that went out first at midnight and had the rest come out and I stayed till morning. They are putting in a battery of 6 guns at the left of our regiment and we will not move out till tomorrow.

. . . I hope the rebels won't cut our road any more, but if you don't get letters you must blame it all on the "Johnnys."

I hope you went and got lots of blackberries. Oh, yes, we had soft bread for dinner and supper at the "Officers' Mess" today, the first we had had since May 1st. We had to stand out in the rain to eat dinner but didn't mind that. I hope you get to go the Association. Tell me all about it when you write. I got a letter from Henry today, too—they are well. I don't think Alvah's are half as smart as we are. We have a fine smart boy, we have, and don't have babies in wartime, do we. If I was in Al's place I think I would "veteran," but as it is, I think I won't. I must stop.

It is now 7 o'clock and dark as pitch and raining. And don't you think, I have just now been notified that the works we made last night are not in the right place and I must go out tonight and move them back 40 feet! That's what's the matter! Who wouldn't be a soldier!

Well, the war won't last always, I hope . . . My love to Ma and all the rest.

Your own, Jake

1. Adjutant Samuel W. Snow of Burlington had been promoted from First Lieutenant to Adjutant on March 1, 1863. The previous adjutant, S. Kirkwood Clark, nephew and adopted son of Governor Kirkwood, had been wounded at Arkansas Post on January 11, 1863, and had died about a month later.

From the diary of Dr. Henry M. Farr, Surgeon of the 25th Iowa Infantry, August 1864, referencing the two weeks after Snow was wounded:

Thursday 18th—Adjutant Snow 25th Ia severely wounded in femur much hemorrhage. (At field Hospital the operating Surgeon wanted to amputate his leg above knee. But I prevented it—He recovered all right.) . . . making two soldiers whose legs I have saved. I believe hundreds of limbs are sacrificed unnecessarily.

Friday 19th—Had a serious time last night with Adjutant

Snow. His prostration from loss of blood was extreme. Took him to Field Hospital & made out a certificate for leave of absence home while his wound should heal . . .

Monday 22—Went over to Field Hospital. Adjutant Snow doing well. The Surgeon who wanted to amputate his limb still claims amputation necessary. (Snow got well & saved his leg) (Dr. Henry Farr, *Diary of Dr. Farr*, Unpublished, Iowa State Historical Society, Iowa City, Iowa)

Headquarters Company B, 25th Iowa
Near Atlanta, August 24, 1864

My Dear Wife,

It is now Wednesday evening, 7 o'clock, and I think I will write you a few lines before I go to bed . . . I am still well and hearty and have not been hit by a bullet. Just as I finished my last letter we were notified that the works we had built were not in the right place, although we had built them just where we were ordered to. But we had to go out and work all night to get them done. And Sunday night, after dinner, the regiment moved out. We had to build "double-breasted" breastworks to protect the rear ranks—if a man lies on the ground fifteen feet from the works he is not safe from bullets, but we are well-fixed now, and don't care how much they shoot. Captain Simons and I have our fly stretched up on a side hill in the rear of the company. We dug into the hill till the bank on the upper side is about two feet high, and have one story underground, then we have a log barricade on two sides high enough to cover our heads, and the dirt thrown up against the logs on the outside. We have a hoop pole bunk to sleep on, and two writing desks, made of cracker boxes. Now can you understand that? Don't you think you can see me sitting here writing to you by candlelight? We think it is a very nice "shebang" and feel quite comfortable and safe, and almost like we had a home again. The bullets hit our barricade sometimes, but they can't hurt us. I don't expect you would like to live here very well. But here is a great deal, you know, in getting used to a thing.

We have had some of our papers brought up from Chattanooga and are very busy making out reports and returns, rolls, and c, which have got very much behind, and it will take a great deal of writing to get them all straightened up. But I can sit here and write with bullets whistling over, and cannon firing, and shells bursting all around without being annoyed more than you would be by a fuss among the young ones, but then I have got used to it. Just now, while I am writing, there has been great cheering and yelling all along our skirmish line and it is reported that the rebels have fallen back or evacuated for good. Bully for us if they have. I will get someone to hold my hat and coat while I do some big yelling.

I was "Brigade Officer of the Day" last night and today—that is, I had charge of all the skirmishers from our brigade and just came in off the skirmish line when I began this letter, and the Johnnys have not fired a shot since dark and did not fire one cannon today, although we shelled them like fury. What if they are gone—won't we be the happiest fellows in the world! But I don't believe they are. I am just writing this because I want it to be so and can't think of anything else. And there is some prospect that we will move from here in the morning anyhow, so I must finish this letter tonight. We have had four mails since I wrote to you last, but I didn't get a letter either time. I think I am sure of one the next time.

Charley Barker got here today direct from Mt. Pleasant. He did not bring anything for me, but it does us all good to see anyone who had just come from home.

I heard this evening that Ed Shreiner is at Marietta as agent for the Christian Commission, and that he is coming out to see us. It will be quite a treat to see him—maybe he will bring us some "Sanitary." Did Reverend Mr. Pickett ever call to see you? Lieutenant Steele has got well and came back to the company a few days ago. I have four men sick, none of them very bad—they are Randles, Bowman, T. A. Black, and Gregory.

* * * * *

Good morning, dear, did you have a good sleep? I did. I got sleepy and did not finish this last night. And the rebels have not evacuated. Just as I expected, they kept very quiet all night, but are firing about as usual this morning. But our whole army is about to make another grand move to the right and we have no doubt but we will take Atlanta. The action of the copperheads in the North gives us more uneasiness than the rebel army. If the people at home will only do their duty, we will attend to the army here, but we need more men and I am glad the draft is so close at hand. I hope the government will be able to enforce it strictly in every state—if it does, the war is about over. Did you get many blackberries and did you have a good time at the Association? . . . I can't help thinking about Al's having another girl. It is a good joke on them. I guess they will have to try again. We will have to show them how to have boys. When the war is over, we can do it, can't we?

Your affectionate husband,
J.B. Ritner

Near Atlanta, Georgia
August 29, 1864

My Dear Wife,

You see we are still "near Atlanta" but we are not so "near" now as we were the last time I wrote; we were then within three or four miles and now we are about sixteen miles from there, in a south-eastern direction[1]. My health is still good, and I yet have a whole skin. I had to let out my sword belt the other day, and if we keep "raiding" round among the green corn I will have to lengthen out again.

I wrote to you last Wednesday evening and finished the next morning. I told you there was some talk of the Johnnys evacuating, but they didn't do it. And so we concluded we would leave ourselves and let them stay there if they wanted to so bad. So on Friday night at eight o'clock almost our whole line fell back, very quietly, and started on one of the greatest military movements, or one of the greatest raids that has been made during the war. We marched all that night to the next day. The weather was very hot and it rained some; I don't think I was ever so tired in my life. A great many men gave out. And when we halted a little while about daylight I lay down right in the road and went to sleep—wasn't that a pretty fix to be in? But we camped at noon on Saturday, and had lots of roasting ears, without salt or butter, and the next morning we were all right again. I have got broke into the business now, so I think I can stand as much as anybody. Yesterday we came onto this railroad. We expected to have a fight before we got to it, but didn't. We got here at 2 o'clock yesterday, built a line of fortifications, and then went to tearing up the road, been at that all day today (Monday). We burn the ties, bend the rails, and then fill the cuts with brush and logs and fill up with dirt, and bury torpedoes[2] every few rods. Sherman says he has sent the cavalry round to destroy this road two or three times, but the rebels always fix it again in a few days[3]. I don't think they will fix it in a hurry this time.

I don't understand this movement. But I think it can't help but compel the rebels to evacuate Atlanta. I suppose we will go on from here towards the Macon Road. There has been no fighting for the last two days, except a little skirmishing with pickets, and I don't know where the rebels are, but I guess they are around some-place. We have fifteen days' rations along with us, and that with what we can get in the country will last us twenty, and I think before that time somebody will be whipped. The more I see of the country the worse it looks—it certainly is the woodiest country I ever saw. We only passed one house and three or four cabins in coming round here; nothing but brush—brush. Where we lay in the works from the 28th of July to the 26th of August, I did not see a single human habitation, though we were near Atlanta.

Day after tomorrow is Muster Day and I must have my rolls ready; no matter what is going on; so I rigged up a desk out of a cracker box this morning and have been hard at work all day. I got two done and have two more to make tomorrow—if we don't move. I am writing by the light of a piece of candle I carried in my haversack. We have got no mail since we started out on this march, and I don't think there is any chance to send letters back now. But I thought I would write you a few lines anyhow. I don't believe anyone could go back alone the way we came; we are out in the country and have no communication open to the rear, but it will not be so long. I did not get a letter in the next mail. We got two mails before we left the other camp, but yours did not come. But I think now I will get one the next time, sure.

I tell you what it is, my candle is getting very short—"small by degrees and beautifully less" and I am afraid it will be done before my letter is—won't you just bring out the lamp and light it?

Well—I understand the 45th Iowa have agreed to "veteran" if the citizens will raise the $200 bounty. Well, that is the famous patriotic regiment, is it? According to "our correspondent" in the *Home Journal*, they did not "go for money!" Oh no, not they— patriotism was their motive and they did not claim "any praise except what they won." But it looks to us as if they were trying to sell out at a pretty good price now. When is their time out? Is Alvah going to stay in the service? What do they call their new girl? What did they want another girl for, anyhow? Just now when boys are going to be scarce and girls and women so plenty on account of the war? I think Al had better veteran. Now if he was raising a boy to serve his country and take his place some day—like I am—he might stay at home. How is Nellie's arm by this time; and what was the matter with it in the first place? I haven't heard that yet—I expect it will be well before I know what to pity her for. I can't "say anything" about Lulie's letter till it comes.

My candle is about to wink out and I don't see the lamp coming, so I will have to dry up. I wish you a sweet, sound sleep and pleasant dreams, and won't you tell me what you dream about. Oh yes, we are here surrounded with rebels. But I assure you we have thought and talked more about the rebels that meet at Chicago today than about these, and we hate them worse and fear them more[4]. The sentiment of the army is universally for Lincoln.

My love to Ma, and Sarah, and all the rest.

Your own, Jake

1. During this period, Sherman was pulling back his armies to prepare for another attack. The Confederates were confused by this movement, some thinking that Sherman had decided to retreat back to Chattanooga. On August 28, the 15th and 17th Army Corps reached the West Point railroad at Fairburn and the 4th and 14th Army Corps arrived at Red Oak, both south of Atlanta.

2. Sherman had instructed the soldiers to begin to destroy the railroads, saying, "Let the destruction be so thorough that not a rail or a tie can be used again." The purpose of destroying the railroad leading into Atlanta was to cut off Hood's supplies. The process of creating "Sherman's Bow Ties" usually included two-thirds of the troops standing guard while one-third accomplished the damage. With two men to a tie, they would lift up a segment of rail and flip it over, then take sledge hammers and what ever was available and pry loose the spikes and then the rails. They would then pile up the ties and set them on fire, while laying the iron rails on top. When the irons were red hot, the soldiers would twist them around trees or telegraph poles. The Union also buried shells or torpedoes so that they would explode if the Confederates tried to remove them. (Albert Castel, *Decision in the West*, pages 489-491)

3. Several days earlier, Sherman had sent Kilpatrick and his cavalry on a raid on Jonesboro with the idea that they would destroy railroad lines feeding Atlanta. At first, Kilpatrick had success and was able to rip up rail lines, but the rain prevented the bonfires necessary to twist the iron rails. Eventually, Kilpatrick was surrounded by the Confederates and had to make a bold dash to escape. He returned to Sherman and reported his success, predicting that the rail line would be disabled for ten days, but the Confederates repaired the damage within two days.

4. On August 29, the Democrats convened in Chicago and nomi-

nated Major General George B. McClellan, the former commander of the Army of the Potomac, as their presidential candidate. One of the chief writers of the party's peace plank was Clement Vallandigham, whom Jacob had discussed with Confederate pickets near Vicksburg. (See Jacob's letter of May 30, 1863.) Vallandigham's peace plank stated:

> *Resolved*, that this convention does explicitly declare . . . that after four years of failure to restore the Union by the experiment of war . . . that immediate efforts be made for cessation of hostilities . . .

At this time, Lincoln's chances for re-election were considered slim, even by many prominent Republicans. Several Republicans wanted Lincoln to step aside for another candidate, such as Salmon Chase, the Secretary of the Treasury.

The Battle of Jonesboro

On August 30, the Army of the Tennessee set out for Jonesboro, along with Kilpatrick's cavalry. Initially, the Confederate resistance was light, but it soon increased. As word of the Federal movement made its way back, Hood ordered reinforcements to Jonesboro.

The Confederates were led by Hardee, with an estimated force of 20,000, which was nearly three-fourths of the Army of Tennessee's infantry. Union General O. O. Howard's force was approximately equal in number, but was better rested and better fortified.

As the battle began on August 31, the Confederate's pre-battle weariness was apparent against the more confident and stable Union forces. One Confederate division, contrary to plans, was led away from the battlefield while chasing the Union cavalry. General Howard commented that "Nothing, even if I had planned it, could have been better done to head an entire Confederate division away from the battle field."

On the first day of the Battle of Jonesboro, the Union casualties were only 172 compared to Confederate losses of 2,200. This was the third consecutive battle in which Union General Logan and the 15th Army Corps inflicted heavy losses on the Confederates and only suffered small losses itself.

The second day of the Battle of Jonesboro, September 1, 1864, was also a Union victory, conducted primarily by the 14th Army Corps. The Army of the Tennessee was entrenched close by, but did not participate.

Early in the morning of September 1, Hood learned of the Confederate set back on the first day of battle and began to orchestrate the Confederate withdrawal from Atlanta, selecting Lovejoy's Station as the assembly point for the retreating Confederate forces.

Unfortunately for the Confederates, Hood's instructions for a timely removal of ordnance from Atlanta did not take place. As a result, five locomotives with eighty-one boxcars packed with gunpowder, shells, 5,000 new rifles, and 3 million cartridges were destroyed to prevent them from falling into Union control. After clearing out civilians, the rebel soldiers set the boxcars on fire, which set off "flaming rockets" and "innumerable spangles." The explosion was a signal to the Yankees that Atlanta was being abandoned, although Sherman at first thought that Union General Slocum had attacked Atlanta and that the sounds were those of battle.

Sherman learned on the morning of September 3 that Slocum had entered Atlanta the previous day, and with that he wrote the famous note back to Halleck, "Atlanta is ours and fairly won." (Albert Castel, Decision in the West, *pages 494-535; Webb Garrison,* Atlanta and the War, *page 194)*

Lovejoy's Station, Georgia
September 4, 1864

Dear Wife,

I have just been informed that there is a chance to send letters back, and that the mail will close in a few minutes. We are 25 miles from Atlanta on the Macon Road. We (Company B) are all right—had hard fighting, but whipped the rebels badly. We have been notified that our task for the present is done, and well done, and we expect to go back toward Atlanta soon. But the rebels are still in our front. Three men have been killed or dangerously wounded in our regiment this morning, two in Company F by one bullet, close to where I was lying, but the fight is over for the present. Tell the folks that Company B, is all right.

Yours ever, J.B. Ritner

- The reaction across the North to Sherman's taking Atlanta was immediate. As Atlanta fell, the North realized that it could, and was, winning the war. With this, Abraham Lincoln's political future took a dramatic swing. Horace Greeley, who had been promoting the replacement of Lincoln on the Republican ticket, declared: "Henceforth, we fly the banner of Abraham Lincoln for our next president." Conversely, support for John C. Frémont soon dwindled. The Republicans who had thought they faced almost certain defeat were now almost assured of victory.

- The Democrats delayed their national convention in Chicago to better sense the military situation, as their platform had called the war "unwinnable," a military failure. One newspaper responded by saying, "Sherman's capture of Atlanta makes slivers fall from the Chicago platform." The New York Herald declared that McClellan's nomination on the platform an "absolutely worthless one now." McClellan quickly tried to distance himself from the Vallandigham plank, saying he would continue to prosecute the war if elected. The Republicans then promptly attacked this contradiction between the Democratic party platform and the Democratic presidential candidate. (Albert Castel, *Decision in the West*, pages 541-543)

From Spencer Ritner, Age 14

Danville, Des Moines Co., Iowa
September 4, 1864

Dear Brother Jacob,

I received a letter from you some time ago but did not have time to answer it until today. I will try and give you all the news this time. Well, we had an awful sight of work to do this harvest. More than ever we had to do before, but we got all of our grain and meadow cut and put up in a good time. We have got about as big a stacked yard as anybody around. We had the barn cram full of hay and one stack besides. Our meadow was the best in the county, our small grain was first rate and our corn is just as good as anybody's. We went all through it and cut out all the weeds before the seeds got ripe. We intend to sow our wheat and oats on it next spring. We are done fall plowing and have nothing to do except have out the manure which will not be a very big job this fall and to thrash and to pull the corn when it gets ripe. Eliza intends to come home and stay in two or three weeks. She is a going to teach the garden school this winter, the same school she taught last winter. Lulie and Nelly are coming down here next week to give us a visit.

We received a letter from Isaac yesterday. He was not very well and was anxious to hear from you since the fight at Atlanta. They had been paid and he sent home $25.00 and said he would send more the next mail; Mr. Lake's youngest child died today about 11 o'clock. He lives in Mr. Stice's house . . . We have two year-old colts from last spring which we rode the other day. They are both pretty wild.

The news came yesterday that Atlanta was taken and we are all anxious to hear from you. That child is to be buried today and I must write this letter done and send it along over to the office. The draft comes tomorrow, but I don't think they will draft here. The quota of this township is not full, but the quota of this congressional district is, so we do not know whether they will draft or not. I hope they will.

Hogs are from 6 ct. to 8 cents per pound. We have 25 to sell this fall. We are fattening them on new corn, feed stalk stock at all . . . We all send you our love. Uncle Jim and Jake and Aunt Eliza send you their best respects. Write soon and I will try and answer your letter a little sooner next time.

Spencer A. Ritner

Camp at East Point, Georgia
September 9, 1864

My Dear Wife,

I wrote you a few lines on the 4th inst. which I hope you have got long before you get this, and be relieved of your anxiety. I had only two minutes and a half to write, but I thought it would be better than nothing. I am still quite well and hearty, the campaign for the present is over, and I have escaped all the bullets. How thankful I am, and what great rejoicing there was here, over the result of our last great battle. We all feel like we would weigh about a ton apiece.

I have not time now to tell you all about our operations since we left our position before Atlanta. And I doubt if I could make you understand it. We had hard work, hard marching, and hard fighting, but we accomplished the great result—we out-maneuvered General Hood and defeated and scattered his army and have Atlanta, and don't mind now what we have done. But the Army of the Tennessee that really did the work and fighting that captured the place, have not seen the city yet, except at a very respectable distance, and are not likely to soon. The Army of the Cumberland, that gets all the favors here[1], and runs the machine to suit themselves, have got located in camp there, and we expect to stay here.

We attacked the rebels at Jonesborough on the Macon Road on the 30th of August. Our regiment did not get into position on the front line till 10 o'clock at night. We built five lines of fortifications in thirty-six hours, and [the Confederates] were driven beyond Lovejoy's Station. Some of my men who were on the skirmish line on the 1st of September wore out their guns shooting. None of my company were hurt, though we were under fire for a week, day and night.

When we left our works before Atlanta and started on the flank movement, General Hood and the rebel army thought we were falling back across the Chattahoochee!! And Hood telegraphed to all parts of the south that the Yanks were defeated and falling back and the citizens of Atlanta would have a grand picnic in our deserted fortifications, and a ball[2] at night on the 26th of August. A great many of the chivalry from other cities went up to take part in the sport. But, alas! For worldly glory—while they were carousing, cannonading was heard in the southwest and presently word was brought that the Yanks had cut the Montgomery Road, and that the whole army was going for the Macon Road.

This makes a great deal of sport for our army. It put me in mind of the poem on "Waterloo" that we used to speak at school and if I was a poet I would get up something like this:

There was a sound of deviltry by night
And Georgia's capital had gathered there
Her beauty and her chivalry
&c, &c—
But hark! What sound was that? Did ye not hear it?
No, 'twas but the wind or the cars on Chattahoochee bridge—
On with the dance, let joy be unconfined.
No sleep till morn when Hood and Hardee meet
To chase the fleeing Yanks with flying feet.

But you know I never was a poet—if you didn't you do now. But you must excuse me. I feel good all over—we have whipped the rebels, and now I like to make fun of them. We got the news of the capture of Atlanta on the 3rd inst.; it was read to each regiment and then the boys began yelling. I could hear them for miles through the woods, sending up cheer after cheer as the news reached them. It was a big thing. On the 5th we lay under fire, and had to lie low too, but we talked of nothing but the draft, which we suppose was enforced on that day. I have no doubt but that there are a great many cowards and copperheads in the north who wish they had been born a girl, or had died when they were young. But I say go on with the draft. If Old Abe doesn't enforce it this time I won't vote for him.

On the night of the 5th our regiment had the "softest thing" we ever had since we have been out. It rained hard all day and the night was dark as pitch, and we had to fall back from Lovejoy's to Jonesborough, 5 miles. The mud was from shoe-mouth to knee-deep. I fell down two or three times and was the dirtiest man you ever saw; my coat was all torn to rags. The boys got to tearing pieces of the tail to wipe their guns with, which all did very well to laugh at. But I thought it was rather a deplorable condition for a "brave defender of his country" to be in!!! We got the President's order expressing thanks and &c, on the 7th inst., and yelled again. But were sorry he neglected to order the Mt. Pleasant Battery to fire a salute! Hope they did so on their own responsibility!

We are now some six miles south of Atlanta. Our permanent camp has not been assigned to us yet, but we expect it will be in this vicinity. We just lay around loose yet. We have not been paid since I came down last spring. There is eight month's pay due the men and six month's due me. I have worn out and lost nearly all my clothes and will have to keep $150 if we ever get paid.

I got two letters from you last night, one of July 26th with Lulie's letter in it, and one of August 18th; we got the *Home Journal* of the 27th, and there must be letters still behind. I was very glad to get Lulie's letter. I think she did first-rate—she told me more news than you did, and it is spelled very well, and I could read it right along. I think it very smart and she must write to me again. Nellie must not run so fast and get upset and break her arm. The other officers all rear up when I talk of getting leave of absence—they think I was at home long enough last winter. I guess if they had pitched into the fight and got shot they would have gone home too. But there is no order yet allowing "leaves of absence" to anyone. And if there was, I guess there is no show for me. But one more year—and then.

Yours ever, J.B. Ritner

1. Contrary to Jacob's opinion, historians say that Sherman favored the Army of the Tennessee over the other two armies.

2. As Sherman's troops withdrew from Atlanta and moved south in preparation for the attacks on the Macon railroad and Jonesboro, General Hood incorrectly thought that Sherman was abandoning Atlanta and was retreating north to Chattanooga. Hood telegraphed Richmond that the Confederates had won a great victory, and the Confederates immediately began planning a victory ball. (Webb Garrison, *Atlanta and the War*, pages 187-188; Albert Castel, *Decision in the West*, pages 485-486)

Camp 25th Iowa Infantry,
East Point, Georgia
September 11, 1864

My Dear Wife,

This is Sunday evening . . . We have been trying for three or four days to get into camp, and after being moved about a dozen times and clearing off the whole county, we have at last got located and commenced fixing up. Our camp is about 300 yards east of the railroad at East Point. We built a line of fortifications today and began to police the camp, which is right in the brush, but we have good water close by and can make it a pretty good camp.

Your letter was of date August 24th. I was glad to hear that you had been to the Association and that you had a good time and enjoyed yourself so well. I wish I could have been there. Where is it to be next year? I think I will go. I think "Old Bets" is the biggest fool out, I don't care how many pictures you give Uncle Jake. If she don't like it, tell Lib to tell her to send me one of her pictures, and then you will be mad! That is the way to fix you! You know I lost your photograph with my pocketbook; well, it is lost yet. I want you to send me another and send the children's along too—I want to see them. Did you ever find that "pin"? I hope you have. We haven't heard anything of the paymaster yet. Some "lousy cuss" from the "Army of the Cumberland" stole my haversack, sword-belt, hair brush, towel, and nearly everything I had left, night before last. I expect it will take half my pay to buy clothes again.

I was detailed today as a member of a court-martial at Division Headquarters. We meet tomorrow, so that knocks my going home all endways; we may be engaged there all the time we are in camp. I think it is pretty rough. I have been flattering myself this long time that when the campaign was over I would get some rest and time to fix up my papers, &c. I worked hard all day on payrolls and forty other things that have to be done. But here I have to go and be shut up on a court-martial. But one year more and then!

We hear it rumored that the draft is postponed again. If that is so I tell you there is not one soldier in a hundred that will vote for Lincoln; I won't. Our railroad has been cut and we have had no papers from the North since the victory here. But I suppose there was great rejoicing, and all think we have done a big thing—we think so too. And no one who has not been here knows anything about what we have done or the dangers we have passed through. I realize it more myself, now that it is over, than I did at the time. The 25th Iowa started [the Atlanta campaign] with about 365 men and have lost in killed, wounded, and prisoners, 65. Our division lost 889. We have been under fire 87 days out of 130 since we left Woodville. You think it strange that we should be exposed so much and no more hurt. It seems just as unaccountable to us. As you say, it was "only the kind, protecting power of the ruler of all things" that saved us, and to Him be all our thanks. We all got so used to the danger that we did not think of it. I have lain down and slept many a night and passed many days, in almost perfect unconcern, when the balls were striking all around, and I was liable to be hit any moment. It makes me almost shudder to think of it now that it is all over. We have all graduated in the art of building fortifications. I can take Company B and beat the world "or any other man," building works; I always carry a spade myself, and we have two axes, three spades, 2 picks, and one shovel in the company. It takes just four lengths of a rail, or logs 40 feet long, to hold the company. And if there are any rebels close about, the way we can get up a breastwork in a hurry is a caution to lazy folks. But I will tell you all about these things when I get home. We have whipped the rebels anyhow and captured Atlanta. And that is glory enough for once, but it cost the company two good men, killed, and four wounded.

We have not had as good fare since the fighting was over as we had before, and there is a great deal of complaint. Our Officers' Mess have not had a bite of meat for three days, and can't get any for five days more—nothing but hard tack and coffee and sugar, and the men are in the same fix, except that we get plenty of hard bread and they don't. What has become of all the Sanitary? I know that the men at the front who do the fighting never got any. I am more than ever dissatisfied with the way the thing is managed. The whole army is suffering for vegetables—we have got none in the country except a few messes of green corn. There are a great many cases of scurvy[1].

Captain Hanks, who was with me at the hospital came back when I did, but got sick again and has gone home. I saw Rodgers and Cady a few days ago. They are well.

So Mrs. Morley has another girl, has she? Well, I did not expect anything else from a copperhead. But Al's might have known better.

I am no hand at match-making and can't get Lieutenant Steele to write to Lib. I think they would make a good match[2]. But if they do, they will have to take it the natural way. I am sorry she failed to get the school. But I don't know what you would do without her. I think Dr. McClure[3] ought to have his back broke for not setting Nellie's arm straight. I will write to Tommy as soon as I get time. I am glad he is a good, smart, boy. I think he is the best little boy in the town. But what about Kittie? You haven't said anything about her for a long time. I have not forgotten the little dear. I want you to send me her picture.

Billy Degroodt has the ague again and is quite poorly. Lieutenant Steele is well. Billy Black and Sergeant Payne are quite well. I have 11 men absent sick and 7 absent on detached service. But had not lost one this summer by disease. I will write you again in a few days and describe our camp and my headquarters.

Good night and pleasant dreams to you, my dear.

Your own Jake

1. Scurvy is disease caused by the lack of ascorbic acid. A soldier suffering from scurvy would bruise easily, his gums may bleed and teeth become loose, and he might have sore joints. (*World Book Encyclopedia*)

2. Jacob was unable to get his friend Lieutenant Samuel Steele matched with his cousin Lib Alter. About one year after the end of the war, Steele married Miss Sarah Margaret Everts and they had one child. Sarah died in 1868. Steele was married a second time in 1872 to Martha D. Oaks and they had five children. (*Portrait and Biographical Album of Henry County, Iowa— 1888*, pages 221-222)

3. Dr. Andrew W. McClure, MD, graduate of the Ohio Medical College at Cincinnati, served as surgeon for the 4th Iowa Cavalry that included Billy and Ol Bereman. He also operated a drug store in town. After the war, he became a trustee of the State Hospital for the Insane, a member of the American Medical Association, and was a prominent and successful citizen of Mt. Pleasant. (*Portrait and Biographical Album of Henry County, Iowa—1888*, page 286)

[Mt. Pleasant, Iowa]
Sept. 12th, 1864

Dear Husband,

It is just a week today since I wrote you and just two weeks last Friday since I had a letter from you. We are all very anxious to hear from you as we have had no news from any of you since Atlanta was taken. I don't know yet whether you were in the fight or not or whether there was much fighting, as I don't take any papers. I take the *Hawkeye*, but have nobody to go to the post office for me . . .

I hope that you got through all safe with all your boys. I have been very anxious of the taking of that place and am now, very glad that it is taken and that you will all get to rest awhile. But it has taken so long and I have got so discouraged about the war being over that I am afraid that it is no nearer being over now than before it was taken. But I will try and hope for the best . . .

Well dear, I do so wish you could come home and board this winter with us as it is going to be very tedious winter I know without you. . . I spent a good deal of money last winter, but is going to take a good deal more to keep us this winter. Clothing of every kind is very high. Calico is 50 cts per yard and everything else is up in proportion. Provision of every kind is very high and we have a pretty good size family to board, but you see I am through my sheet and a very well letter it is I believe. I am half sick. Excuse this and I will write again soon. Hope I shall get one from you first.

Yours, Em

East Point, Georgia
September 14, 1864

My Dear Wife,
. . . Oh, my dear, sweet wife, how I would like to take you in my arms again, and have a good hug and a kiss! I have been thinking a great deal about what you said about going home, and the more I thought the more I wanted to go, till I finally made application to the Colonel yesterday for a leave of absence. But nearly all the officers want to go home, and only seven can be gone at once, because the orders require one commissioned officer to be left with each company. So we had a meeting last night to determine who should go. They all seemed to think I ought not to go now, because I was home so long last winter. I couldn't see it in that light, but thought I wanted to go as bad as any one. But I finally agreed to stay and let the rest go. I run Company B and the court-martial[1], and Lieutenant Steele takes command of Company G, while Captain Utter goes home. There now, what do you think of that? Don't you think I was very accommodating to stay when I had a

Lieutenant to leave with my Company? I do. And the officers have nicknamed me "Old Magnanimity"! What do you think of that! But the truth of the matter is that it didn't make a bit of difference, for Colonel Stone would not have "approved" my application anyhow. Colonel Stone, Captain Simons, Lieutenant Crane, and Dr. Marsh are all going home—at least they have sent in their "applications" and I suppose they will be approved. If there is any chance to go after they come back, I am to have the first "put in," but I don't think there will "be any hereafter" in this case. We will be ready for another campaign by that time, and no leaves of absence given. So you see there is not much prospect of my seeing you soon. But just wait till about this time next year, and see.

This court-martial is the greatest bore I have come across in the army. I think it is rather hard to be put in such a place right away after coming off a long campaign. The other officers lay about loose in the shade, go in their shirt-sleeves, and keep cool and take things easy generally. While I have to black my boots, put on my best clothes, button up my coat, tie on my sash and sword, and go to General Osterhaus' headquarters and sit up on a high bench and look dignified all day—what do you think of that? There are ten captains and one Colonel in the court.

We had a visit today from Mrs. Horner, the lady who takes Mrs.Wittenmeyer's place. We all felt much flattered, but she didn't bring us any "Sanitary." We are putting up a regimental bakery, and expect to go to housekeeping and have soft bread some of these days! What do you think of that?

Sergeant Payne has been quite sick since I wrote to you last, but is now better. The general health and spirits of the army is good. We still have conflicting rumors and do not know whether the draft will be enforced or not—that is the great topic of interest here now. If it is not, Old Abe is gone up the spout with the soldiers; we won't vote for him if he backs down again.

There is a "truce" now for the purpose of removing the citizens from Atlanta[2]. They go out the road in sight of our camp. General Sherman is moving every citizen from Atlanta. They think it pretty hard. But I think it is just right. We have possession now and will run the machine to suit ourselves and not for the benefit of either speculators or traitors. The truce agreement is to last ten days. General Howard and General Logan have issued congratulatory orders to the Army of the Tennessee, and to the 15th Army Corps, which have been read to each regiment[3]. They are to the point and contain nothing but the truth. I tried to get copies to send you, but couldn't. I suppose they will be in the papers and you can see what our officers claim for us.

General Logan says the 15th Army Corps has placed hors du combat[4] more rebels than there are men in the corps. And I do not doubt but we have. I gobbled up three myself, that I know of, and if all the rest did as well, we must have made a large hole in their army.

We have not got a very nice camp. It will take a great deal of work to fix it up nice, and we haven't got room enough. We are jammed in between the 2nd Division on the left and the 9th Iowa on the right, and a battery in the rear. I suppose the State of Georgia is too small for a camp for Sherman's Army. But I must go to bed. Give my love to Ma and Car and Sallie and all friends.

Your own, J.B. Ritner

1. The court-martial would be composed of eight company commanders appointed by the division commander, hearing cases ranging from gambling to rape and murder, although reported rapes and rape attempts were very rare. A different officer would serve as the judge advocate, or prosecutor. The defendant had the right to have an officer or other soldier serve as counsel, but the defendant usually represented himself. (Joseph T. Glatthaar, *The March to the Sea and Beyond*, page 86)

2. Sherman arrived in Atlanta on September 7 and soon handed a letter to Mayor Calhoun directed to General Hood, telling Hood that Sherman would be expelling all citizens from Atlanta. Those citizens were given an opportunity to go either north or south. (Albert Castel, *Decision in the West*, pages 548-549)

3. Logan's congratulatory order of September 11, 1864, includes: "You have marched during the campaign, in your windings, the distance of 400 miles, have put 'hors-du-combat' more of the enemy than your corps numbers, have captured twelve stands of colors, 2,450 prisoners and 210 deserters . . . When the time shall come to go forward again, let us go with the determination to save our nation from threatened wreck and hopeless ruin, not forgetting the appeal from widows and orphans that is borne to us upon every breeze to avenge the loss of their loved ones who have fallen in defense of their country. Be patient, obedient and earnest, and the day is not far distant when you can return to your homes with the proud consolation that you have assisted in causing the old banner to wave from every mountain's top and over every town and hamlet of our once happy land . . . "

Howard's order of September 9, 1864, includes: "Our rejoicing is tempered, as it always must be, by the soldier's sorrow at the

loss of his companions-in-arms. On every hillside, in every valley throughout your long and circuitous route, from Dalton to
Jonesboro, you have buried them. Your trusted and beloved
commander; his name, the name of McPherson, carries with it
a peculiar feeling of sorrow. I trust the impress of his character
is upon you all to incite you to generous actions and noble
deeds." (Charles W. Wills, *Army Life of an Illinois Soldier*,
pages 299-303)

4. Hors du combat meant casualties of war, either killed, wound-
    ed, or captured. It is a French term, literally translated as "out of
    combat." The use of the term in the English language dates to
    the mid-1700's. (Darryl Lyman, *Civil War Wordbook*, page 86)

The Most Outrageous Rascality

Headquarters of Company B, 25th Iowa Infantry
Camp at East Point, Georgia,
September 16, 1864

My Dear Wife,
    I wrote to you night before last. But the court-martial does not
meet this afternoon. I don't think I can enjoy myself any better than
by writing to you again. If they won't let me go home to see you, I
have the consolation to know that they can't prevent me writing to
you, just as often as I please. That is one good thing, isn't it! We get
a mail now almost every day, but I have got no letter from you since
I wrote last. The last I got was dated August 24th, more than 20 days
ago. Lieutenant Crane has letters of the 3rd of September. I don't
know what has got the matter with mine that they don't come along.
You don't know how much good it does me to get a letter from you,
nor how anxiously I wait for the mail. I think about you a great deal
more, now, and miss your letters more, than I did when we were in
the field. My attention was then called more to other things, and we
had the excitement of a battle or skirmish all the time. But now all
that is over for the present, and the more I think about you the better I love you and the more I want to see you.
    We have Regimental Inspection this afternoon but I don't have to
go out. My health is still very good. I don't think I will have the ague
this fall. Sergeant Payne is a good deal better. The rest of the men
present are all well. We are having the most delightful weather I ever
saw—the nights are cool and pleasant, and in the daytime we have a
fine breeze and very pleasant in the shade—the sun still shines pretty

hot. It looks and feels almost like "Indian Summer" in the North.

The citizens are still moving South[1]. Trains loaded with them go by here every day. I don't think we will move from here very soon unless Hood should undertake to send part of his force to reinforce Lee at Richmond—if he does that, we will "go for" the balance of his army. No leaves of absence have come back "approved" yet.

I haven't got any news to tell you, dear. But I felt lonesome and thought how nice it would be if I could have an hour or two with you. I think like you that it would be worth a year, yes, ten of them—with anyone else. But I couldn't have that, so I thought I would try to keep the blues away by writing to you.

I tell you, dear, I am getting very tired of this war—not only tired, but utterly disgusted and out of all patience with the way some things are managed. I am like Alvah—if I was out of the service once, they might try if they couldn't run the thing without me. Everything goes by favors, and the more anyone does, the more is expected of him and the less credit he gets. Everyone who knows anything about it knows that the Army of the Tennessee has done the greater part of the hard marching and fighting on this campaign. We have been changed from one flank to the other two or three times, and so have traveled twice the distance the others did. But the Army of the Cumberland, at least till lately, have had the credit of doing all that was done. The papers have been full of letters which may do to read to the Indians, but not to soldiers who know anything. And now they are camped in and around Atlanta which we captured, and are paid off, and have an abundance of supplies of all kinds for both officers and men, while we can get nothing but a very scanty supply of hard bread and coffee. In fact we get nothing till the Army of the Cumberland is supplied and then if there is anything left, it is sent on to us. We don't get as good rations as we did while in the field. And then "our dear friends at home" can't see any difference between a soldier at the front and one who has never been in sight of a rebel. A man who has been in the army 100 days[2] and never fired a gun or smelt powder gets as much credit as one who has fought 90 days out of the 100 and been through 13 regular battles. No one who has not been to the front and seen men in line of battle and stripped for a fight has any right to say he has been to war. Any one might go within three miles of the front and yet know nothing whatever of the circumstances of men in immediate presence of the enemy. All this is very annoying to a soldier. I don't care anything about it myself. But I like to see justice done to men whom I have labored and fought and suffered with, all summer.

But the most stupendous humbug, the most damnable imposition, and the most outrageous rascality, is shown in the way the "Sanitary" is distributed and used. But I will tell you more about that sometime when I am in a better humor.

. . . I almost forgot to tell you that this is my birthday—did you know it? Why don't you come and whip me, or throw a bucket full of water on me? Maybe you would, if you had known it in time. Well, I am 36 years old today. I will soon be an "old man" if I live. I cannot help wishing that the balance of my life whether it be long or short, may be spent better than what has gone before, and that I may be allowed to pass the remainder of my days with my dear wife and children, free from all the alarms of war, and for that reason I want the rebels completely subdued now.

Your own, Jake

Don't let anybody see this letter.

1. Jacob is referring to Sherman's forced exodus of the 1,650 civilians from Atlanta. (Webb Garrison, *Atlanta and the War*, page 209)

2. See comments regarding Alvah Bereman, the 45th Iowa Infantry, and the 100 day men following Jacob's letter of May 16, 1864.

Headquarters Company B, 25th Iowa
Camp At East Point, Georgia
September 19, 1864

My Dear Wife,

Colonel Stone and Lieutenant Crane and Sergeant Garvin are going to start home tomorrow morning . . . I have to go the court-martial twice a day, and attend to all my company business besides, which keeps me very busy. Indeed I don't see any more rest now than I did while on the campaign, but I can have a better chance to write when I have a few spare moments, and I mean to improve them, too. No man deserves to have such a dear, pretty, sweet wife as I have if he won't write just because he hasn't got a letter since he wrote last. But I got two letters from you yesterday (Sunday). It rained all day and I could not answer them. You must know that I have a very poor protection from the "inclemency of the weather." It is a wagon cover stretched over a pole. It is an old rip of a thing, and has several holes torn in it, and some bullet holes, and is entirely open at both ends. It does very well in dry weather, but when it rains everything gets wet.

We have heard of the paymaster at last. He sent for our payrolls today. I think we will be paid in about a week. The men have not been paid for eight months and need it very much. It is a shame that they have not been paid long ago. There is six months' pay due me, up to August 31st. You had better engage someone to haul you 6 or 8 cords of wood as soon as you can. You need not look for me home this fall—I don't think I will be able to get away. General Sherman thinks he can't get along here without me this fall!! I would like to be there for a few days anyhow to get your potatoes and apples and &c, and help you to eat them, too. Garvin is here now waiting for this letter and I haven't got it half done. If we should remain in camp and I can get leave to go home, it will only be for a few days. What time of the moon[1] had I better come? The more I think about it the more I want to go, although I really have very little hopes that I will be able to do so.

One of the letters I got from you was dated September 12th, and mailed that day—it came very quick. I suppose you have got my letters before this time and know all about the "taking of Atlanta." The Army of the Tennessee did the marching and fighting that took the city, but we were 28 miles southeast of there on the Macon Road. There was no fighting at the city after we left. General Slocum[2] was left there with the 20th Army Corps but did not enter the city till Hood had evacuated it, and then was afraid to go in till the mayor of the city went out and invited him in. But he is the bully big man that took Atlanta!! Well, I suppose it is all right.

The rebels are still moving south. A train of cars with 950 prisoners went out today to be exchanged. Sherman is going to exchange 2,000 prisoners[3] (the last that have been taken). The cars run to Rough & Ready, a station about 4 miles from here. The rebel army is camped at Jonesborough, 28 miles from here.

We have fortified our camp very strongly, and commenced putting on style. General Osterhaus has ordered that all officers shall wear shoulder straps and go neatly dressed at all times. We have roll call at daylight on the color line, which must be attended by all officers, Colonel and all. We have company drill twice a day and battalion drill four times a week. In fact we are put through the hardest I ever knew. The men are tired of camp already—they would rather be in the field.

Payne is about well. I think Bill Degroodt will get either furlough or a discharge. He is quite under the weather, but able to be around. The rest of the men are all well. I think Sergeant Yount and perhaps a few more will get to go home on furlough. I am trying to get them through.

One of your letters had a letter from Lulie in it. I think she does first-rate; she can write a very good letter. I wish she would write often—she always tells some news that you forget. I hope she and Nellie will have a nice time down at Danville. I am sorry the bugs eat your potatoes and that the moles destroyed your melons. I have not had a taste of either this summer, except one mess of potatoes at the hospital.

I expect you had better trade Tom off for one of Snell's boys? How would he like that? But I would rather he would play with them than with Frank; they are not copperheads. But he must take care and not get into another bumble-bee's nest. He must have looked funny with his eyes bunged up; if I ever get time I will write him a letter. And tell Lulie I will write to her some of these days.

I don't know what effect the fall of Atlanta will have on the spirit of the rebels. I think it will be a very hard blow, and one that will discourage them a great deal. But I don't feel much like fighting any more here till I see what they are going to do in the North. If the north is going to be divided and McClellan elected, we have already done enough for nothing. All our labor and fighting and suffering will then be for nothing; all the blood that has been shed and the lives that have been lost will be in vain.

I see that the draft is to be enforced, and the army will support Lincoln. And I believe he will be elected. And I believe that if he is, the war will not last much longer. But I am like you—I have prophesied so often about the close of the war and been disappointed that I do not pretend to know anything about it. You must get Crane and Garvin to tell you the rest of the news.

Your own, Jake

I will send home by Garvin a package of old letters that I have no way to carry here. They are mostly from you and I don't want to lose them. My book-box and tent have not got here yet.

1. Jacob's reference to the "time of the moon" is probably a reference to the rhythm method of birth control.

2. Major General Henry Warren Slocum had previously served under Hooker at Chancellorsville, but was highly critical of Hooker for his cautiousness. He thereafter refused to serve under Hooker. After Hooker left the army because he was not given command of the Army of the Tennessee, Slocum gained command of the 20th Army Corps, which was comprised of the old 11th and 12th Army Corps of the Army of the Potomac. During Sherman's March to the Sea Slocum commanded the Left Wing, eventually known as the Army of Georgia.

3. Sherman had roughly 2,000 Confederate soldiers and another 1,000 Confederate workmen to exchange. Hood had proposed the prisoner exchange when communicating with Sherman about the expulsion of civilians from Atlanta. Hood had proposed following "the stipulations of the cartel" that Grant had stopped. Initially, Sherman agreed to this, but later added complications that precluded the exchange.

Andersonville prison, which held an estimated 32,000 Union prisoners, was located in southern Georgia. Sherman, feeling that the Union prisoners could not initially help him, while the Confederates that were to return were relatively healthy, stated that he would only accept men that had fought in his armies. He also would not accept men whose term of service was about to expire. (Garrison, *Atlanta and the War*, pages 209-211; Lee Kennett, *Marching through Georgia*, page 212)

The Dogs Were Not Taken Prisoners— Neither Will They Hunt Soldiers Hereafter

Camp 25th Iowa Infantry
East Point, Georgia
September 26, 1864

My Dear Wife,

This is Monday morning . . . It rained every day and night last week, and my "shebang" is so poor I can't write when it rains. I was very busy at the court-martial all week. But we got through Saturday evening, and I will not have so much to do now. The weather has cleared up, too, and is very clear, cool, and pleasant— rather too cool at night to sleep out of doors. This morning and yesterday morning it was almost cold enough to frost. I must get a wall tent and build a chimney to it as soon as possible.

I went to town yesterday, and saw the great city of Atlanta, that we read so much about in the papers. I had seen it several times before, but always from a respectable distance, and from the top of a tall pine tree. But never was in the city till yesterday. It has been a pretty large place, perhaps two or three times as large as Mt. Pleasant. It is not laid off regularly, like towns in the North; the streets cross each other at all kinds of angles. The most of it is built very scattering and it covers a great deal of land—if cities were measured by the acre Atlanta would be a great place.

Part of it is very much damaged by our artillery. I saw a great many houses that were struck by cannon balls on three sides, some of them a dozen times. I should think it was rather uncomfortable quarters there about that time. How would you like to have your house shot to pieces in that way?

But the greatest curiosity in the city is the bomb proofs—there is one in almost every yard. They are made by digging a hole in the ground about four feet deep and large enough to contain the family when packed in like stock in a railroad car—then lay boards over the top, and cover with dirt till it is four or five feet thick. They have a hole just large enough for a man—or a woman without hoops on—to crawl in it. When the fighting commenced the women and children and citizens retired to these underground houses and remained there till the danger was over. They frequently had to stay all night. Now would you like that way of keeping house?

Most of the citizens have gone. I saw a few families there yet. I presume they will all be gone in a few days, as General Sherman is determined to make it a purely military post.

I went to the hotel there yesterday (kept by a northern man) and got my dinner. I had a cup and saucer, a white plate, a cloth on the table, and sat down on a chair and ate like folks—didn't use any "tin fixings." We had a very good dinner, I thought. But it had been so long since I saw anything of the kind I hardly knew how to go about it. And it took me just an hour and a quarter by the watch to eat my dinner, and I ate as fast as I could, too! I paid a dollar for the dinner. There were three other captains down with me—they say I ate at least two dollars and a half worth of raw material, to say nothing about the cooking, and &c. And that it will never do for me to go north at the present prices of provisions there—what do you think of that?

My health is first rate. I have never felt so well since I have been in the army as I have the last two months. We are ordered to prepare immediately for an early and vigorous campaign. So I suppose there is no show for me to go home this fall.

You had better commence in good time and lay in a good supply of provisions for your command during the winter campaign. I have no idea if you will have to board me, but it is well to have the Commissary Department well supplied at all times, and then if your communications are cut or the road becomes impassable, you will be all right . . . I think some of my men will get to go home on furlough; if they do I will get them to call and see you . . .

I learned in town yesterday that the rebels captured and burned a train of cars night before last at Big Shanty[1]. We have had no mail for four days. I have no doubt but there was a mail on the train with a letter in it for me, and the Johnnys have got it—ain't that too bad? And I just expect that my book-box with all my papers and my wall tent were on the same train and are gone up too! They were on the way here from Chattanooga that time, and it would be just my luck to have them gobbled up.

The exchange of prisoners is still going on[2]. The most pitiful sight I have seen during the war is that of our soldiers coming back from the southern prisons. I have seen several lots of them as they came into our lines; hardly one of them had shoes or socks, many no shirts, all were dirty, ragged, and so wasted away with hunger that they looked like mere skeletons. It is really affecting to see the joy they express at being once more under the protection of a civilized and humane government. They tell the most heart-rending stories of their treatment while prisoners. Some of our prisoners were brought up to Rough and Ready yesterday to be exchanged, but for some reason the exchange did not take place and they started to take them back to Andersonville. Some of them (the prisoners) broke away from the guards and were pursued by bloodhounds. Some of them came through our picket line this morning, and soon after the dogs came following the trail. The dogs were not taken prisoners—neither will they hunt soldiers hereafter.

Almost everyone here is in favor of Lincoln and Johnson. They will get nearly the whole vote of the army from present appearances. We have just heard of the victory of Sheridan[3] over Early in Virginia, and are anxiously waiting for the particulars, and to hear that Grant has taken Richmond, and that the war is over. Give my love to Ma. I suppose Al is home now, and will see that she does not need anything. You must write and tell me all the news over again—maybe the rebels won't get it the next time.

Your own, J.B. Ritner

1. Hood had begun a northward march to destroy Sherman's supply lines from Chattanooga and Nashville. (Albert Castel, *Decision in the West*, page 552)

2. See comments regarding the prisoner exchange in previous letters. Approximately 150 former prisoners of Andersonville broke through ranks and escaped during this process. (Lee Kennett, *Marching through Georgia*, page 212)

3. On September 19, 1864, Cavalry Commander Philip Sheridan attacked and routed Confederate Jubal Early near Winchester in the Shenandoah Valley in Virginia. He launched a second successful attack at Fisher's Hill three days later. Sheridan caused devastation in the Shenandoah Valley similar to Sherman's destruction in Georgia.

- During this period, the Confederate Army underwent a reorganization, transferring Hardee, who had unhappily served under Hood, to command South Carolina, Georgia, and Florida. Hardee would again confront Sherman in the upcoming months. Cheatham took command of Hardee's former corps. (Albert Castel, *Decision in the West*, page 552)

[Mt. Pleasant, Iowa]
Wednesday night, Sept. 28, 1864

Dear Husband,

I started you a letter on Saturday last and I believe I told you I would write in a few days ago. Is now twenty minutes past nine and I can only write you a short letter, that in a hurry. There is no one in the house but Sallie and me, and she has gone to bed. So you see if I stay up longer the "bugger" will catch me.

Mrs. Blazer and I intended to go to Burlington in the morning at half past seven, to the fair and so I sent Tom and Kit down to Grandma's so that I could get off soon. But don't you think it commenced raining before dark. Has been pouring down ever since. I have no idea we will get to go on the morning train. We intended to go to town and stay all night at France McClures and spend two days at the fair. It commenced last Monday (The Sanitary). And the Agricultural commended Tuesday.

So you see they are having two at once. It will be worth going to see and I shall be sorry if I don't get to go. I think it ends Friday. The girls haven't come home yet. I am getting anxious to have them come. If they don't come in a day or two, I shall write for them. Lib wants to stay till after this fair, so she will certainly be home the last of this week.

The boys from old Co. B arrived Monday evening and Sargt. Garvin came out here on Tuesday afternoon and brought me a letter from you and told me all that I could think to ask him about. I was very much surprised to see him. He came to the front door and I met him and was going to call him Champ Miller, but he corrected me. I was not dreaming of Garvin being a way up here. I think you was very "magnanimous" to stay & let all the rest come, but I suppose it is all right, as you was home so long last winter . . .

Garvin thinks that you will come, and I think from the way you write, that you think you will come, so I will begin to make up my mind that you will be here in less than two months. I can't tell you now what time in the "moon" you had better come, as I have forgotten what time exactly that the moon changed last, but I will find out in time to write to you before you come. I suppose you will not start before these boys get back, and I will know something about it by that time. I haven't seen Lieut Crane yet. I think he must have taken them by surprise . . .

Marth Roads baby died before she left home. Had the encephalys (can't spell it). Well, it is after ten and I must quit and write you a big one when I come back from the fair if I go. Raining still. Goodbye.

Yours, Em. R.B.R.

They Attracted As Much Attention
As The Great General Himself

Camp 25th Iowa Infantry
East Point, Georgia
October 2, 1864

My Dear Wife,

This is Sunday and I must write you another letter. I sent you a letter by Sergeant Yount a few days ago. I expect you will see him and get all the news before this letter gets there. I got a letter from you a few days ago dated September 19th. I was very glad to hear from you again and learn that you were all well. I think it strange that you had not heard from us since the taking of Atlanta. I wrote so many letters I thought you would be certain to get some of them. I suppose you have received them all before this. And have seen some of the officers who have gone home who could tell you all about everything.

My chance for getting to go home this fall "grows small by degrees and beautifully less." We received an order from General Sherman day before yesterday that no furloughs or leaves of absence would be granted, and all those already granted are revoked[1]. Lieutenant Colonel Palmer received a leave of absence the day before that, but had not gone yet, and now he can't go at all. Then last night we got orders to "keep the men well in hand and be prepared for any emergency." I believe we are "prepared"; but would be very thankful if no "emergency" would come along for a while yet. A large part of the army is now moving; part is going back to different points on the railroad, and another expedition started yesterday towards West Point, on the Montgomery railroad. I think they are going to Sweet Briar, about 20 or 25 miles west of here, where the rebels are said to be crossing the Chattahoochee River to attack us in the rear and cut our railroad.

So you see there is no use in me talking about going home soon. It would be just our luck to have to move soon. We have scratched around and gathered up things till we are pretty well fixed.

Company B has the nicest quarters in the regiment and puts on more style than you ever saw. We have our street graded up nice and swept two or three times a day. The men all have bunks fixed up and take pride in keeping themselves and their quarters clean and neat. There is a detail made every morning from the regiment for picket guard, which is posted out about two miles or so from camp, and stands 24 hours. But twelve men who have their arms and accouterments and clothes in the best order, and who present the best military appearance, are selected for the detail to stay here for headquarters guard. I hardly ever have one of my men on picket—they are always picked out by the Adjutant for guard here. I suppose it is because they have such a good-looking Captain— don't you think so?

I got my wall tent all right and have a floor in it, a good bunk for Steele and me, have the book box fixed up, and another table, made of a cracker box, and a looking glass, two camp stools, and everything nice. We have three hickory trees in our street and a large black oak close beside my tent. (But I must stop and fix up for inspection.)

* * * * *

Inspection is over and we can hear cannonading in the direction of Sweet Briar, or Sandtown.

My health is still excellent. I never felt better. We are having short rations now, that troubles me more than anything else. We can get no flour or meat (except beef) nothing but hard tack and coffee, and not very plenty of that. We borrowed some money and sent to Atlanta yesterday to get some grub, but couldn't get a bite. There has been no train here from Nashville for a week, and we may be starved out here yet. But I think not. Part of the army has been sent back, and I have no doubt the road will be kept open now. We have not been paid yet—don't know when we will be. We have heard that the paymaster will be here this week.

The weather still continues very wet. We have a hard rain almost every day. I wrote you in my last about sending me the cape to my overcoat, but I have changed my mind about it. You need not send it. I don't think it would do me much good here. I haven't got any letters for a month except the one I got from you. And I have not written to anyone but you since we came here. I expect they think I am mean, but I can't help it. I haven't time to write. I haven't been idle an hour since we got into camp and have not got my business near all done yet. I like to hear from all my friends, but if I could only get a letter from you every week I would not fret about the rest. Some of them have not written to me for 6 months, and some not at all.

We have been having some grand reviews in the last few days. General Woods, who commands our division now, reviewed each brigade. We are the same old brigade with the addition of the 30th Iowa. But we have a new number; we are now the 3rd Brigade. And day before yesterday General O.O. Howard, who commands the Army of the Tennessee, and General Osterhaus, Commanding 15th Army Corps[2], reviewed our division (1st Division 15th Army Corps). Our division has a good name for marching as well as fighting, and all the generals came to see us in review—there were fifteen generals on the ground.

After we had been reviewed by General Howard, General W. T. Sherman came out upon the ground and we passed in review before him. He came out from Atlanta in a fine carriage with three ladies—real northern ladies—had hoops on, and were dressed up like folks! It had been so long since we had seen anything of the kind that it was quite a treat to see them. They attracted as much attention as the great general himself. General Sherman said if he had 25,000 men like the "Old 1st Division" he could go anyplace in the Southern Confederacy.

You did right to get the pump. I am glad you got it. If we have to leave there we can take it along. I think you had better see about getting your wood and cow feed right away. I know everything is high, but you must have those things, and I don't want you to get out in the winter, when the weather is bad. I don't want you to pay Brumits another cent. He is the meanest white man I ever knew. He said "he didn't believe you were honest" did he? Well, just wait till get home. I will attend to his case. I will cram that down his throat.

You must have a lonesome time there, with Lib and the girls gone away. Don't you wish I could be there to keep you company? I do. It would be so nice. I often feel lonesome here, where I have so much company, and so many things to call my attention to, and then I want to see you. There is a place in my heart for you, dear, and no one, or anything else, can fill it. I do wish the nasty rebels would behave themselves so we could go home, if it was only for a few days. I suppose Colonel Stone and Crane and Simons[3] are all having a good time at home now and the 100 day women all have their men at home. Well, I am going to keep a stiff upper lip, keep clear of the "blues" and vote for Old Abe and think I will come out all right yet. There is one thought that cheers and strengthens me more than anything else, and that is that I have a dear, sweet wife at home who loves me and is true to me. What more could a man want? I don't think there is a day that passes that I don't get your picture out and look at it, and kiss it.

Yours ever, Jake

1. General Hood and the Confederate Army of Tennessee had moved north with the intention of destroying Sherman's supply lines between Chattanooga and Nashville. Sherman was preparing the Union pursuit of Hood and revoked all furloughs for soldiers not yet departed. Sherman was also concerned about strikes against the supply lines by Confederate Nathan Bedford Forrest. Jacob is making reference to the two Union divisions previously sent to Chattanooga and the one Union division sent to Rome to guard supply lines against Hood and Forrest. (Albert Castel, *Decision in the West*, page 552)

2. General Osterhaus replaced General Logan as Commander of the 15th Army Corps on September 23. Logan returned north to help campaign for the upcoming fall elections. General Charles R. Woods, previously Brigadier General of the 1st Brigade, replaced Osterhaus as Division Commander. Williamson continued to lead Jacob's brigade.

3. Colonel George Stone, Second Lieutenant Baron Crane, and Captain William Simons had already gone back to Mt. Pleasant before the revocation of furloughs.

• On October 2, Sherman learned that Hood's entire army had crossed the Chattahoochee River and was moving toward Marietta. Sherman then sent his entire army in pursuit of Hood, except for the 20th Army Corps that remained in garrison duty in Atlanta. (Albert Castel, *Decision in the West*, page 552)

Historical Sketch—25th Iowa Infantry

*On the 8th of September, the regiment went into fortified camp at East Point, where it remained until the 4th of October, when it joined in the rapid pursuit of the rebel General Hood's army. (*Roster and Record of Iowa Soldiers in the War of the Rebellion; *Published under the authority of the Iowa General Assembly)*

• Sherman tried for two weeks to trap and attack Hood, who was striking at the Western and Atlantic Railroad, destroying track from Big Shanty to Acworth and between Dalton and Tunnel Hill. Hood's army recaptured Dalton where the Confederate Army of Tennessee had spent the previous winter. Eventually, Hood had to retreat toward Alabama to seek supplies for his troops. (Albert Castel, *Decision in the West*, pages 552-553)

Bivouac in the Field Near Rome, Georgia
October 13, 1864

My Dear Wife,

I have not written to you for about ten days, first because we have been on the march after the rebels, and I couldn't write, and second because the rascals tore up our railroad so we could neither send letters home nor get any from there. I guess we have made them wish they hadn't done it! I wrote you last from East Point about the first of this month. I think I told you then that we had orders to store our company and garrison equipment in Atlanta and prepare to go on a campaign in "light marching order," which means that you must carry everything you have on your own back, march day and night, and be ready to fight at a moment's notice. We are now about seventy-five miles from East Point, and have traveled not less than ninety miles to get here.

The Johnnys crossed the Chattahoochee River below Sandtown,

and struck our railroad near Kennesaw Mountain and tore up the track and destroyed the road completely from there to Acworth, a distance of eight miles, and did some damage between Acworth and Allatoona Pass, which is six miles this way. But there they were met by General Corse[1] with the 4th Division of the 16th Army Corps, which had been sent back along the road several days before. They had a hard fight there, but "our side whipped," as usual, and drove them off the road, captured their artillery, and a large number of prisoners. I have heard so many reports about the numbers that I don't know anything about it.

But the fight was very obstinate, and our loss was considerable. The 39th and 7th Iowa lost heavily. I have heard that 7 officers of the 39th were killed. I have had no opportunity to learn anything about Lieutenant Ghost, who belongs to that regiment. It was the first fight of any consequence they were ever in. But they had to come up to the scratch at last as well as the "old 25th."

We marched over the battle ground a few days ago, saw many graves of both our men and rebels, but could not stop to get any particulars. We left East Point at daylight the morning of the 3rd inst. and marched till midnight. The next day we reached a point about six miles south of Marietta, where we rested a few days. We moved in the night to the west side of Kenesaw Mountain (I mean we marched ten miles and camped near Kenesaw.) We lay there one day and I went to the top of the mountain. The view from the top is the most sublime and extensive I ever saw. I can't describe it so you would get any idea of it. I wish you could see such a sight once. I am going to bring you down here "when this cruel war is over"!! and show you the Southern Confederacy from the top of Lookout and Kenesaw. Won't that be grand. I know you would enjoy it, and you must see it.

We left there at 6 o'clock in the evening of the 10th inst. and marched 12 miles by 4 p.m., making 32 miles in 22 hours! The reason of our hurry was that the rebels had attacked Rome, and it was reported that our force there was surrounded and about to be gobbled up. But they have been driven away from there and we are now resting for today in an old field about 4 miles from Rome. We have a fly stretched up to keep the sun off and I am sitting flat on the ground writing on my valise. We got here about sundown, and after dark we got a large mail!! The first we have had for two or three weeks. I got two letters from you, one mailed September 24th, and the other September 29th. I was very glad to hear from you again. General Sherman did not pay the least attention to your wishes about letting me have a good rest.

We have done the hardest marching and had the least to eat and the most to carry, while on this march, that we have ever had. It had rained several times and been quite cold part of the time. One morning there was white frost and we all nearly froze. But we are all in good spirits. Sherman is in fine spirits. He says he has the Johnnys just where he wants them. They are going to try to get to Nashville, and that is just where we want them to go. They had about 30,000 men, and we have 60,000 besides the force that General Thomas is organizing at Nashville[2]. The 4th, 14th, 15th, 17th, and 23rd Army Corps are here; the 20th Army Corps is yet at Atlanta. We are all right; if they do cut our railroad some places it doesn't take us long to repair it again. But I think we will soon teach them better manners.

I think Lulie and Nellie make a long stay. I think you must be very lonesome without them. I wish I could be there to stay with you a while. But I don't think you need be so certain about my going home this fall. I don't think there is any show for it myself. In fact, I wouldn't go now if I could.

We are on the rampage after the rebels and there is a prospect of a fight, and it is fun to sky-hoot over these hills and mountains after them, and sleep out in the woods. It gives a man such a good appetite for his hard tack and coffee. You need not "take on" so about "Old Abe." I am going to vote for him, since you say he is enforcing the draft! And so will Company B, every man of them. They are all right, just the bravest, best, and noblest set of men in this army. They will do their whole duty all the time, and I am proud to be the leader of such a company, and would not leave them for anything. And General Sherman thinks he can't get along without me anyway, so you need not look for me. And then you didn't tell me what time in the moon to come, so I won't think anything more about it.

I think Sarah Jont[3] has gone and done it sure enough. I think she was bad off—she ought to be ashamed of herself. I don't know anything about Zink, do you? Is he a soldier or a copperhead?

I am glad that Car has gone home. I hope she had a very pleasant visit. But I think Ma will be better contented now, and she will be company for both of you. So the great hundred day men have got home at last. I suppose they had quite a splurge. I reckon a three years' soldier would stand no chance at all there now. The fair sex couldn't see us at all. We haven't made any "indelible footprints" like the 45th.

I suppose you have seen Captain Simons before this time, and Sergeant Yount. I sent a letter to you by him. He has no doubt told you all the news. You said you were going to send me the girls' pictures, and didn't do it. I would like to have them, and Tom's and Kittie's too. I have your ambrotype yet, which will do. I think it is just the prettiest picture in this army.

I hope you got to go to Burlington to the fair. I would be very sorry if the rain spoiled your trip. I did expect to get another letter telling me all about what you saw. But I have just heard that the rebels have cut our road again at Resaca (between here and Chattanooga), and there is no chance to send or get letters! We will have to give them a good thrashing yet before they will behave. I don't know when you will get this, but I will start it anyhow, as I don't know when I will have a chance to write again. I am writing this in a great hurry as we have inspection this p.m..

I read your letters last night by the light of a fire and then thought about you and dreamed about you all night. I thought of lots of things then to tell you, but I am in a hurry now and can't think of anything. There is a man going to Rome in a few minutes to take letters. One of my men (Gregory) was discharged a few days ago and has gone home. I think he will call to see you. He lives in Mt. Pleasant. I left Wm. Degroodt at Marietta in the hospital. He was quite poorly, and ought to be discharged.

I do not know what to think about the war ending this winter. We have heard that Richmond is taken[4]. If that is so, I don't see how it can last much longer. I am certain that we can use up all the rebels in this part of the country, and if Grant attends to Lee's army as he ought, I don't see how they can hold out. I believe Lincoln will be re-elected, as he ought to be, and that will have a good effect, and tend greatly to shorten the war, and hasten an honorable peace. But I don't count much on getting home to stay till my time is out. The rebels are going to strain every nerve to do something before the election to help McClellan and encourage the northern rebels. But we intend to see that they don't make anything off us. You must excuse this long scribble. Write soon and write long letters.

Your own, Jake

It is now 4 o'clock and we expect to march tonight. We will

follow the rebels, I think. "The boys" are out in the woods gathering chestnuts[5] and persimmons—they are very plenty here.

1. Allatoona Pass served as a Federal supply base along the railroad, which had become the target of General Hood. Sherman sent General John Corse with 1,900 soldiers to reinforce the 900 men already there.

   Confederate forces, led by Major General Samuel French, surrounded the Union supply base. French demanded unconditional surrender by Corse, but Corse refused and the two sides engaged in an intense battle. Union casualties were 706, with Confederate casualties roughly 800. The 39th Iowa suffered casualties of 40 killed, 52 wounded, and 78 missing or captured. Jacob's friend, Lieutenant William Ghost of the 39th Iowa, was not among the casualties at Allatoona Pass, and he survived the war.

2. Hood eventually lay partial siege of Nashville, which housed General Thomas and his troops. During this period, Grant suggested to Sherman that he pursue and destroy Hood, but Sherman felt that no army could really pursue and destroy the fleeing Hood. Sherman was instead planning his march through Georgia.

3. Sarah Jont was the widow of Emeline's brother Jont Bereman. Jont died on August 22, 1863, just a little more than a year before his widow ran off with Zink.

4. The rumor about Richmond being taken by the Union Army was not true.

5. Chestnut trees once ranged from central Maine along the Appalachian Mountains to Arkansas, but a disease that entered in the 1890's, probably from Japan, killed most of the chestnut trees in the United States. (*World Book Encyclopedia*)

[Mt. Pleasant, Iowa]
Oct. 14th, 1864

Dearest Husband,

I intended to have written two days ago, but have been so busy. Yesterday Mrs. Blazer and I were gone all day hunting apples and only got two bushels apiece. We were around through the country southeast five or six miles. Mrs. Blazer has a two-year-old colt and a "buckboard," and that was our conveyance. We could not get the promise of any winter apples at all and I guess we will have to do without. They are worth a dollar a bushel in town, and we can't afford to eat many at that price . . .

How I wish you could be here to buy things for us. Wouldn't it be nice? It will be a week tomorrow since I had a letter from you. You said in your last that you didn't expect to get to come home. That is too bad, isn't it? I should think you might get a furlough after you go into winter quarters, but I shall not think too much about it, nor insist on it, but leave it to you to your judgment whether it will be best or not. It would be very nice for you to be at home awhile. You keep looking ahead to the times when you will be discharged, but I can't see that far. One year longer is a long time and there is no telling what may happen to us both by that time, but we will hope for the best and pray that the time may speedily come when you shall be permitted to come home to stay.

There was a soldier here the other day while I was away. The children didn't know him, but I expect he was one of your boys. I will send the cape of your overcoat if I can find anybody that will take it. I saw Garvin the other day. He said he had all that he could carry and could not possibly take it. I will see if Lieut. Crane will take it. If he can't, I don't know how you will get it, for I don't know as I will get to see any of the other boys. I will try and write a letter to send by then and send the girls photographs. I told you I would send them in the "next letter," but thought I had better send by someone as it would be apt to go safer. The girls all come home next Monday morning, well pleased with their visit . . .

Billy can't come home and has sent for his Sally to come to Memphis to stay this winter and she is going to start Monday next. Billy thinks he will be apt to stay there this winter. Haven't heard from Tom for a long time. Alvah & Sarah and children came out here last Sunday. Mrs. "<u>Sarah Zink</u>" hasn't showed herself down here since she was married. Alvah says he is going to have himself appointed guardian for the children so that Manda will get her share of the property. When you write again, tell me what you think of buying government bonds with our money. I spoke of it in my last letter. Good bye and take care of yourself.

Yours truly, Em

Sargt. Garvin expects to start to his regt. the first of next week I believe. Don't know whether Crane is going down or not. Haven't hardly got to speak to him yet.

Historical Sketch—25th Iowa Infantry

*The pursuit [of General Hood] was continued by forced marches until October 16th, when the regiment went into camp on the bank of Little River, Alabama in sight of Lookout Mountain. October 20th, the regiment participated in a skirmish with the rebel General Joseph Wheeler's cavalry. (*Roster and Record of Iowa Soldiers in the War of the Rebellion*; Published under the authority of the Iowa General Assembly)*

Camp In the Field, Atlanta [Little River, Alabama]
October 23, 1864

Dear Wife,

. . . We are camped about 30 miles west of Rome and South of Stevenson. Don't know how long we will stay here, or where we will go when we start. The rebels were in our front day before yesterday when we stopped here, and our cavalry had a hard fight with them, and drove them ten miles that day. The rebels have now gone off south. They are not going to cross the Tennessee River this time. I guess it would not be healthy for them up there. I suppose we will go after them when we get ready.

There is a rumor that we are to be paid off before we leave here—we need it very much. I haven't got any money and my clothes are all worn out, or lost. I washed my shirt and drawers and socks yesterday, and then tried to mend and darn them up, but made a poor [show] out of it. We are all in good health and spirits, and get plenty of meat and vegetables in the valleys among the mountains. But we live in a very primitive style. We have no tents at all, and no blankets except what we carry on our backs when we march. There is not a plate or knife or fork in our Officers' Mess—each one has a tin cup for coffee, and we eat meat and "taties" with our fingers. We have had a white frost the last two nights, and we have to sit up round the fire and parch corn and roast potatoes to keep warm. But anything to put down the rebellion. I have got used to it, and enjoy it very well. If it was not for being away from home, I would not mind being a soldier. But my dear, wife, you don't know how much I want to see you once more. I do wish I could go home, but I see no prospect of it soon.

We are all going to vote for Lincoln and I hope that after the election we will have peace and all go home. You may be certain that I will go home "on leave of absence" just as soon as we get settled some place, if I don't get on another court-martial or something to prevent me. I would not go and leave my company on a campaign if I had a chance. They wouldn't know what to do if I was gone. They say they are all going to come and live with me when the war is over. They are the best company in this army, and there isn't a copperhead among them. Will Black has not been very well for a few days, but is better—nothing serious. Wils Payne went out foraging this morning and came back a little bit ago carrying two hogs, four geese, two chickens, and a sack of sweet potatoes!

We have had very hard marching—often all night. My feet got clear worn out.

None of the officers or men who went home on furlough have got back yet. We look for some of them every day. Our railroad is all right again. We got a mail a few days ago, and I got a letter from you. I want you to get Alvah to buy Government Stock with our money and the Campbell money too. I intended to tell you long ago, but always forgot it. Keep enough to last you a while. I don't know when I will be able to send you any. Buy your provision and wood for the winter.

I wrote to Eliza this morning and told her to send those girls home! I am "Brigade Officer of the Day" today and have to visit the pickets this evening and tonight. Now I have written this just as fast as I could scratch it down, and if you can make any sense of it you can do more than I can . . . But my time is out and I must stop.

Your affectionate Husband,
J.B. Ritner

[Mt. Pleasant, Iowa]
Friday Nov. 4th, 1864

Dearest Husband,

I wrote you last Wednesday (a week) by Sargt. Yount and expect to have written again long before this, but have been prevented. Wednesday morning I had to go to Mrs. Sypherd's to help take care of her baby. It has been at the point of death for several days. I stayed all day and sat up all night. Didn't sleep a wink until Thursday near noon. That afternoon, there was to be a bee at Mrs. Lee's to sew carpet rags to make Mrs. Gunn a carpet. We spent the afternoon and evening till ten o'clock. Got enough sewed for the compact, and had a real nice time. Only I ought to have been at home writing you a letter . . .

I spoke for a barrel of molasses from Uncle Jake. Don't know what he will charge me. They are selling from .45 to 1.00 per gallon. He is coming up before long to bring them and some buckwheat flour and corn meal. Meal is worth 1.20 per bushel.

Ma's folks are all well and think they have a pretty hard time of it.—Allie McClure and Frankie Roads are here and they all keep so much noise that I can't think of anything to write besides have the headache so I will give you a goodbye (kiss) and quit. The children are all well. I should expect to see you home before a great while and then I can think of something to say. Maybe you will find some of the particulars in the letter I sent by Sargt. Yount. I told you in that what time to come home.

Em

Camp 25th Iowa Infantry
Near Vinings Station, Georgia
November 7, 1864

Dear Wife,

. . . I wrote to you last when we were on "Little River," Alabama, (I don't know whether that was what I called it then or not)—I think it was the 23rd of October the next day the 15th Army Corps went on a reconnaissance southwest. We went 20 miles and back in two days and a half. Had two or three skirmishes with the rebel cavalry. But they would not stand and fight. But at Fergus Plantation they had two pieces of artillery and shelled us for an hour or more, but we soon routed them out. We got back to camp on the 26th, very tired and hungry. We had marched 40 miles in 2½ days, took no rations with us, and found very little in the country.

One night we had coffee and beef broiled on the coals for supper, and coffee and "parched corn" for breakfast. When we got to camp the boys all went to work and boiled corn ears and then grated them for meal, and Lieutenant Steele took ten bushels of corn to a mill 4 miles from camp and ground it. But our scarcity only lasted a few days, and then only because our train could not move as fast as we did. We had an abundance of rations at Rome and in the wagons, but could not wait for them.

We lay in that camp two days after we came back, and then moved back to Cave Springs, which is about 20 miles southwest of Rome. We stopped there over one day, October 31st, to be mustered for pay.

Colonel Stone, Crane, and Garvin got back there. But none of them brought me a letter! But we got a mail the morning of the 1st November, and I got a letter from you. We marched that day ten miles to Cedar Springs, and then Yount and the other men from my company, got back, and brought me another letter and the girls' pictures. I was glad to get them. I think they are good likenesses—they look very natural. I wish I had Tommy's and Kittie's too. I would look at them every day. I am afraid I will never get time to write to Lulie and Nellie again—they must not think I have forgotten them. I think of them every day and would write them a letter if I had time, and would like to have them write me. I hope they had a good school, and that they will be good children and learn fast . . .

[Letter continued in the next chapter]

Chapter Six
Sherman's March to the Sea, the Occupation of Savannah and the Carolinas Campaign

Planning and Preparation for the March to the Sea

As the Federal armies of the West occupied Atlanta, both Sherman and Grant contemplated Sherman's next move. During October, Sherman proposed a movement toward the ocean through Georgia that would "make Georgia howl!" but Lincoln, Grant, and Chief of Staff Major General Henry Halleck were reluctant to approve it. They feared the uncertainty of that move, and felt that Sherman should continue to contend with Hood, who had taken his army north toward Tennessee and Kentucky. On October 11, Sherman telegraphed Grant: "Instead of being on the defensive, I would like to be on the offensive, instead of guessing at what he means to do, he would have to guess at my plans. The difference in war is a full 25 per cent." He also began to present that his real objective was Savannah, writing, "The possession of the Savannah River is more than fatal to the possibility of Southern independence."

Finally, on October 12, Grant reversed his position of reluctance and wired Sherman that "on reflection, I think better of your proposition." Shortly thereafter, Lincoln, Stanton, and Halleck gave their approval and blessings – "Whatever results, you have the confidence and support of the Government" from Stanton and "the authorities are willing" from Halleck.

On November 1, Grant telegraphed, "Do you not think it advisable, now that Hood has gone so far north, to entirely ruin him before starting on your proposed campaign?" Sherman's response was, "No single army can catch Hood, and I am convinced that the best results will defeat Jeff. Davis's cherished plan of making me leave Georgia by maneuvering." Grant agreed with Sherman's arguments, and on November 2nd gave Sherman permission to start his march when he was ready.

In Atlanta, all the sick and wounded, along with excess supplies, were shipped north as Sherman narrowed his army down to the fittest and most capable. Sherman notified Grant that during the march, he would not be sending couriers back to the North with progress reports, *but that he would "trust the Richmond papers to keep you well advised." On November 11, Sherman told his engineer, Captain Poe, to start knocking down the remaining factories in Atlanta. On November 15, Poe and his engineers set fire to the downtown area. Over a third of the city was in ashes by the time that Sherman left Atlanta on the morning of November 16.*

Historical Sketch—25th Iowa Infantry

On October 26th, the countermarch began and, on the 12th of November, the regiment was again in camp near Atlanta. With only a brief rest, after its long and toilsome march, it joined the army of General Sherman in his famous march to the sea. During this memorable march, the Twenty-Fifth Iowa performed its full share of duty . . . (Roster and Record of Iowa Soldiers in the War of the Rebellion; *Published under the authority of the Iowa General Assembly)*

We Elected Old Abe With A Perfect Rush

Camp 25th Iowa Infantry
Near Vinings Station, Georgia
November 7, 1864

[Continued from the last letter in the previous chapter]
     . . . But to go on with my story. We reached this place on Saturday evening, November 5th. I suppose we are about 100 miles east of where we started on Little River. The 15th and 17th Army Corps came through on three or four roads, several miles apart, and cleaned out a large strip of the Southern Confederacy. It won't pay to make any more raids through that country. We found plenty of forage, but left nothing behind, and that is the way we propose to do with all the rest of their country—eat and drive off all we can and burn the balance.
     We are now on the railroad 6 miles east of Marietta and about 12 from Atlanta. Immediately on arriving here, we were ordered to prepare immediately for a "vigorous campaign," and have been very busy fitting out with arms, ammunition, and clothing, and expect to start in a day or two for Savannah or Charleston, or some other seaport, and kill, burn and destroy everything we can't eat. The [14th,] 15th, 17th, and 20th Army Corps[1] and Kilpatrick's Cavalry are going on the expedition, about 50,000[2] men in all. And we expect to cut a road through the south that will teach them what it is to fight "Uncle Samuel."

We are going to have an election tomorrow before we start—elect Old Abe, and then go to smashing things generally[3]. And if we don't happen to get busted ourselves you will hear us about New Years on the other side of the continent, but you need not expect to hear much from us between now and then, for we are going to operate without a base. Everything is being rapidly moved back from Atlanta, Rome and all places between here and Chattanooga. Atlanta will be abandoned and burned, and the railroad to Chattanooga torn up and destroyed. All our tents, book-boxes, mess boxes and &c, have been either burned or sent back. We are allowed only one wagon to each regiment, which is to carry the baggage for all the field and line officers, and blessed is the man that has no more clothes than he can carry on his back—and that is my fix. I wore out and threw away one suit of clothes on the last march. I have no shirt of my own—but have borrowed one—have no money, and don't want any. In fact, I feel perfectly independent and don't care whether we have any "transportation" or not. But the officers who have just come back from the north are in a great deal of trouble about their fine clothes.

It is said that Hood has crossed the Tennessee with his army, and is at or near Pulaski, Tennessee. But General Thomas has plenty of men there to attend to his case while we turn the thing wrong side out, without much opposition down here. He can do no harm in Tennessee, while we can ruin their country here. I think Hood and Beauregard have been completely out-generaled again[4].

The only thing that can prevent us from dealing the rebellion a mortal blow is the weather. We have had a great deal of rain lately and the roads are very bad and it is very uncomfortable for soldiers in the field without any shelter. We have had several very frosty nights, and the leaves are falling from the trees. And if the rains should continue, it will be almost impossible for us to move. But we hope for better things.

But what about my "leave of absence"? I am afraid I won't get to go home soon! I may as well tell you now that I have had a "leave of absence" ever since about a week before we left East Point—more than a month ago, but before I could get started an "order" came from General Sherman stopping all officers and men from going home for the present, and that order is still in force. I have been trying to trade my "leave of absence" for a shirt, and can't do it! When we get through to Charleston I will get a new one and go home through Washington City and see "Abe."

The paymasters are here and at work on our rolls and we expect to be paid before we leave here. But we don't know whether to take our pay or not. The railroad will be torn up by that time, and no way to send it home. I have a mind to take only two months' pay now, and keep it. But if we find that there will be a good way to send it home we will take all we can get. I will try to tell you before I close this what we are going to do about it. I will stop for the present and finish after the election.

* * * * *

(Monday night) [November 7] Well, Dear, I have got a piece of candle, and will write some more tonight for fear I don't have time hereafter. We have just heard that Dr. Charley Marsh has been promoted to surgeon of the 25th since Dr. Farr resigned[5]. The appointment gives very general dissatisfaction in the regiment. There is not a line officer that would have signed a recommendation for him for that position. But I suppose the "Old Dr." pulled the wool over Colonel Stone's eyes when he was at home. He is entirely too young[6] and inexperienced, and has the big-head too bad to be entrusted with the lives of 400 men.

I was sorry to hear that you had the sore throat. I hope you have got entirely well, and that you have laid in all your supplies for the winter. I don't think you "wicked" at all—I just know you are not. You are the best and sweetest woman in the world, and worth all the "Green Backs" Uncle Sam has. And I think I am the one that ought to be thankful that I have such a dear, good woman for my wife and the Mother of my children. And I am so, and I would be willing to work harder and suffer a great deal more if necessary to provide you everything you need. I want you to use all the money that is necessary to make yourself and the children comfortable. I know you are too sensible and too patriotic to spend money for useless luxuries at a time like the present, if you had ever so much of it. I hope you will get a good supply of apples, if they are high. Tom & Kit must have one every day. Get a good load of corn and a big load of hay, lots of wood and potatoes. I would like to be at home and act as quartermaster and commissary for you a while, but I suppose I am needed worse here—at least General Howard thinks so.

* * * * *

(Wednesday Morning) [November 9] Well, we had an election

yesterday, and elected Old Abe with a perfect rush. I acted as one of the judges of selection. Our regiment poled 338 votes, 323 for Lincoln and 15 for McClellan. I think it was doing first rate. McClellan got only one vote from Henry Co. in the 25th, and none in Company B. Our brigade the 4th, 9th, 25th, 30th and 31st Iowa—gave Lincoln about 1,325, McClellan 101. We are all highly pleased with the result and hope the folks at home have done their duty as well.

The paymaster is still fooling around and has not paid us yet. He is slower than the 7-year itch and as mean. We hear brisk cannonading this morning in the direction of Atlanta, and I expect marching orders every minute. If we get paid I will send my money and that of the men in one package to Saunders Kibben & Co. We got a mail this morning and I got a letter from Susan. I won't have time to write to them before we leave here.

You must not be uneasy if you do not hear from me again for some time. My health is good, and we have managed to fix so as to make ourselves comfortable on the campaign. It is not expected that we will meet much opposition from the enemy. The weather is still wet. Atlanta has been entirely stripped. And I should not wonder if the artillery we hear this morning was being used merely to destroy the city. Give my best respects to Alvah and tell him I got acquainted with Mr. Streeter (Old Black Hawk), who is here as Commissioner. Give my love to Ma and Car, I hope they will get along comfortably this winter. Write as before for the present, but I hear that our mail is sent via New York. Good bye for the present.

Your affectionate Husband,
J.B. Ritner

I send you a couple of sescech ballads that we captured under the floor of a house when out on a foraging on Little River in Alabama.

1. The 14th and 20th Corps composed the Left Wing of Sherman's Army. The units became the Army of Georgia, General Slocum commanding. The 15th and 17th Corps under General Howard formed the Right Wing and retained the name "the Army of the Tennessee." Regiments from the 16th Army Corps were folded into the 15th and 17th Corps.

    The 15th Corps was commanded by General Peter Osterhaus, and the 17th Corps by General Francis Blair. The men of the 15th and 17th Corps were primarily from the northwest and had fought along side each other since the formation of these corps during the Vicksburg campaign. Generally, during the March to the Sea and during the Carolinas Campaign, these men got along with each other very well.

The 14th Corps was led by General Jefferson C. Davis, and the 20th Corps by General Alpheus Starkey Williams. The 14th Corps was also primarily from the Northwest, but the 20th Corps had come mostly from the East, first arriving at Chattanooga as the 11th and 12th Army Corps under the command of General Joseph Hooker. These men did not always get along so well with the Western troops.

2. The actual number in Sherman's armies was closer to 62,000.

3. Sherman wanted to wait until the last balloting for the Presidential election on November 8 before commencing his march. Due to delays, the march did not begin until November 16.

4. Historians agree with Jacob's comments that Sherman out-generaled Hood and Pierre G. T. Beauregard. Hood, rather than forcing the Union Army to chase after and attack him, instead attacked the Union Army supply lines. Beauregard was convinced that Sherman only had 36,000 men and that Sherman could be manipulated to return to Tennessee. To provoke Sherman to move north, Beauregard sent Hood and his army toward General Thomas. (Joseph Glatthaar, *The March to the Sea and Beyond*, page 4; Lloyd Lewis, *Sherman, Fighting Prophet*, page 441)

5. Dr. Henry Farr included in his diary entry of September 15, 1864, "Learning that . . those Surgeons who had served with a Regiment & had been honorably discharged would be employed under the title 'Acting Staff Surgeons,' with same pay and emoluments as pertain to Regimental Surgeons; and being willing to open a way for the promotion of Assistant Surgeon of 25th Ia. To be full Regimental Surgeon, we formed the plan that I should resign & that Dr. Chas. F. Marsh should be promoted to be Surgeon of the Regiment & I agreed to take my chances of getting the appointment of 'Acting Staff Surgeon.' Dr. French was a friend of Dr. Marsh & agreed to help along the scheme." (Dr. Henry Farr, Diary of Dr. Farr, Unpublished, Iowa State Historical Society, Iowa City, Iowa)

6. Dr. Charles F. Marsh of Mt. Pleasant was now only 22 years old. When he enlisted in 1862, he was appointed Hospital Steward and rose to Assistant Surgeon five months later, and then Surgeon after another year and a half.

[Mt. Pleasant, Iowa]
Nov. 10th, 1864

Dear Husband,
Once more I seat myself to write you a letter. I have had no word from you since I last wrote you.—Last letter was written near Rome. You were there after Hood's army. I am very anxious to hear from you again. Hope you have got through with that campaign and are now ready to go into camp and as soon as that is accomplished, I expect to see you at home. I dreamed last night that you were here. Hope I shall soon get a letter from you again. The folks here haven't heard from the boys that went back—they got to the regt. if they even got there. The last they heard they were at Chattanooga. I wrote you a long letter by Sargt. Yount. Hope you have it by this time.

Well Dear, this is Saturday. The young all talked so much the other night that I couldn't write, so I put it away till the next evening. Well, before I got my clothes all on the next morning, Mrs. Sypherd sent for me. Her baby was dead and she wanted me to come up. So I was there all day yesterday and didn't get to write any. The consequence is that you will have to be without this letter two days longer, for which I am real sorry.—. . .

Good bye, dear till I see you. If you are coming home at all it will be pretty soon.

Yours, Em

[Mt. Pleasant, Iowa]
Nov. 20th, 1864

Dear Husband,
I received a letter from you yesterday dated November 7th. You said you were preparing for another campaign and expected to go to Charleston. I was not surprised for I had heard that a week ago, and that Sherman had burned Atlanta. I had hoped that it was not true, but it seems to be for I also heard several days ago about you having a "leave of absence." . . .

I suppose General Sherman knows what he is about, but I don't see the advantage in burning Atlanta and moving on to Charleston. Could the Rebs go and fortify Atlanta again and make it a good position on the railroad for themselves as they had it once? I should think to leave so much country in the hands of the enemy in your rear would be rather dangerous business, as you might possibly be cut off from your supplies and be starved or taken prisoners. But just to think of you going away to Charleston to the <u>Atlantic Ocean</u>. If there was no war I should like to accompany you and see all the sights of the Southern Confederacy. If the reelection of Lincoln is to insure peace, we may expect it soon, as he is certain to be president again for every place that we have heard from has given him an overwhelming majority. I don't know what they have heard from all the states or not. This election will certainly give a deathblow to the rebellion, but it will be apt to die out by inches . . .

I must tell you what a big taking down I got today at church. I had my hat done over in the winter style and wore it to church today for the first time, and old Mrs. Burnett just <u>raked me</u> right before the people after meeting was over because I wore an "old ugly hat." She was so mean. She looked as though she could have stomped me with her feet. She said when people talked of soldier's wives <u>dressing</u>, she always held me up as an exception, but now I was as bad as any of them. Everybody that gets a new hat has to take a thrashing from her and so my time came today. I haven't got over it yet, but I don't intend to lay it by for her.

. . . perhaps I will get some of your letters. If you can't send them back, you can have a big pile ready when you do get a chance. Goodbye, dear, with my best wishes for your health and safe trip through <u>to the sea</u>.

Yours ever, Em

The March to the Sea

As it transpired, Sherman's "March to the Sea" held the attention of the North, the South, and even Europe. As Lincoln expressed it, "I know the hole he went in at, but I can't tell you what hole he will come out of." The London Herald said that Sherman's campaign would result in "the most tremendous disaster that ever befell an armed host . . . [or] the very consummation of the success of sublime audacity." If Sherman failed, "he will become the scoff of mankind and the humiliation of the United States," but if he succeeded, his name would "be written upon the tablet of fame side by side with that of Napoleon and Hannibal. He will either be Xerxes or Xenophon." The British Army and Navy Gazette stated "he has done either one of the most brilliant or one of the most foolish things ever performed by a military leader . . . the plan on which he acts must really place him among the great Generals or the very little ones." (Lloyd Lewis,

Sherman, Fighting Prophet, *pages 457-458)*

Sherman's intention was to demonstrate that the Federal army could march at will, and relatively unobstructed, through the South and cause open destruction in its path, in order to press the civilian element of the South to call a halt to the war.

Each day during the march, brigades would send out details of men to forage. These details were given instructions as to where the main army planned to camp for the night. The forage parties had flexible orders to set their own paths, meeting up with their brigades later in the day or early in the evening, bringing foraged supplies.

Officially, only Sherman and the four corps commanders had authority to order the torching of buildings, but many homes, barns, and other buildings fell to the flame anyway. Guerrilla warfare, also referred to as bushwhacking, prompted harsher treatment of the Georgians by the Union Army. In some situations, if Southerners had burned a bridge to slow the Northern advance, Sherman would order nearby houses to be burned in retribution, and to set examples for others in Georgia communities.

As the army made its way through the farms and villages of Georgia, the Union soldiers took as many civilian valuables as they could find, often threatening inhabitants with violence unless they revealed where they had concealed them. Through practice, the soldiers became adept at finding these items, digging up fresh graves and checking wells in most locations.

Livestock, horses, grains, and other supplies that could not be used or carried were destroyed, leaving a stench of rotting flesh at many sites. Sherman's original plan called for the men to travel about 15 miles per day, but once underway, this slowed to about 10 miles a day, to better achieve the intended destruction.

During the march, Sherman's Army was joined by fleeing slaves who had hoped to accompany and assist the army in its journey. But Sherman did not have the supplies nor an organization to help these blacks, and told them to return to the farms and later achieve their freedom. Sherman successfully enlisted the aid of Negro preachers to help spread this message. The biggest disaster for the Negroes occurred at Ebenezer Creek where Union General Jefferson C. Davis removed a pontoon bridge after his Union troops had crossed the Creek, preventing the trailing Negroes from crossing. Many of those Negroes drowned as they attempted to swim the creek rather than deal with the Confederate soldiers that followed. Others were then killed by the pursuing Confederates.

During the march, the men remained relatively healthy. The Army of the Tennessee reported less than 2 percent unfit for duty, including the wounded. Sherman had long been cognizant of the problems of a sitting army, and had usually endeavored to keep his command on the move.

On December 10, as Sherman neared Savannah, he encountered Confederate defenses about 8 miles before the city. Although he wanted to capture Savannah, his stated goal had been to achieve communications with any Union fleet on the seacoast. But even more importantly, Sherman needed to open a supply line. Without a supply base, it was essential that Sherman and his army keep moving; otherwise, the available forage would quickly diminish. The only way to establish a supply base was through the waterways to the ocean, and the Ogeechee River, which was the closest deep-water river. The main obstruction blocking this connection was the Confederate Fort McAllister, which lay at the mouth of the Ogeechee River. Beyond the fort was Ossabaw Sound and salt water from the Atlantic Ocean.

On December 13, Sherman sent Hazen's division of the 15th Army Corps to capture Fort McAllister, while Sherman and several other officers, some distance away, watched from the top of a rice mill on the other side of the Ogeechee River. Shortly Sherman was able to send a message to Slocum, "Dear General; Take a good big drink, a long breath and then yell like the devil. The fort was carried at 4:30 p.m., the assault lasting but fifteen minutes." (Lloyd Lewis, Sherman, Fighting Prophet, *page 463)*

Dr. Henry Farr, outgoing surgeon of the 25th Iowa, included the following entry in his diary for December 14: "Horse Race between Surgeon Marsh's mare and Q.M. Brown's. This was an exciting race, enlivened by the bursting of shells overhead, sent from the fortifications of Savannah."

By December 15, General Halleck had received a message written by General Howard sent through Port Royal, South Carolina. "We have met with perfect success thus far, troops in fine spirit and General Sherman near by." And with that, jubilation broke out across the North. Lincoln's message to Sherman was "God Bless you and the army under your command. Since cutting loose from Atlanta, my prayers and those of the nation have been for your success."

While the news was a widely celebrated glorious result for the North, the actual march itself had been an enduring disaster for the Southern people in its path.

At this point, Sherman wrote to Grant and others, that "I regard Savannah as good as gained . . . we have utterly destroyed over 200 miles of railroad." "I estimate one hundred million dollars, at least twenty million of which has inured to our advantage, and the remainder is simple waste and destruction. This may seem a hard species of warfare, but it brings the sad realities of war home to those who have

been directly or indirectly instrumental in involving us in its attendant
calamities." Although Sherman provoked greater Southern hatred
than Grant, Sherman's policy was primarily to destroy property and
morale rather than population.

The Swamp In Our Front Is Full Of
Alligators, Which Bellow Like Bulls At Night

Camp 25th Iowa Infantry
Near Savannah, Georgia
December 16, 1864

My Dear Wife,

I once more seat myself to write you a few lines. I know you are
very anxious to hear from me, and will often wonder why you
don't get a letter before this gets there. It is over a month since I
last wrote to you and during all that time I have not heard a word
from the North or had a chance to write or send a letter. But we
have at last got through safe and sound. My health is excellent and
has been all the time, and I enjoyed the march very well. We had a
good time most of the way through. And I got here with every man
I started with, all in good health and spirits. I think the 25th lost
only one man on the way and he was captured while foraging[1]. We
got here three or four days ago, but have not taken Savannah yet,
nor got our communication fully opened with the fleet, though that
will be accomplished as soon as we can remove piles and torpedoes[2] from the Ogeechee River. Fort McAllister, which was the
main obstruction, was captured by assault by the 2nd Division of
our corps on the 13th inst. We have not got any letters or papers yet
and don't know a thing about what has been going on in the world
for the last month. We expect to get both rations and mail[3] this
evening or tomorrow. Our present camp is about 8 miles south of
the city[4] on the Darien Road. But our line extends from the
Savannah to the Ogeechee River.

The whole country here is one great rice swamp, a great deal of
it under water—the hardest place to fight in I ever saw. There is a
swamp between our lines and the rebels—the whole length of the
line which cannot be forded or crossed except where there is a
levee or high bank thrown up for a road, and at every such place the
rebels have a fort on their side. We have planted batteries on all the

roads in short range of their forts, and our skirmishers wade out as far as they can, and keep up a continual firing day and night. There is heavy cannonading every day from a dozen different points, and altogether we are having a lively time. But I don't know anything about the prospect of taking the city. The swamp in our front is full of alligators, which bellow like bulls at night. And the tide from the ocean causes it to rise and fall about six feet. But we all expect that "Uncle Billy," as the boys call General Sherman, will find some hole to get in at before many days.

The weather is very warm and pleasant. We had a little frost one morning since we came here, but the trees, bushes, and weeds are all as green as though it was July instead of December. We are camped in a forest of tall spruce pine with undergrowth of brush, briars, and vines so thick one can hardly walk through them.

I wrote to you last on the 9th of November at Vining Station. We had not then been paid. We were paid on the 18th. But there was no chance then to send anything back as the railroad was destroyed to Chattanooga. The paymaster did not get through in time to go back—there are two companies not paid yet. And the paymaster came through with us; and I put my money and a package for the company in his safe which will be sent home the first chance. I got $745.30. I got six $100 7-30 bonds with coupons attached[5], which I made payable to you and put them in a package directed to you. You can detach the "coupons" as they come due and get the money at the National Bank. The men's package is directed to the bank.

We left Vining Station on the 13th and went to Atlanta and started from there on the 15th, one month ago yesterday. With the exception of a few days while we were near Macon, we had very fine weather and got along first-rate. We made a few hard days' marches, but generally took our time and lived on the fat of the land. We found plenty of forage and provisions. We lived on yams and fresh pork, chickens, honey, molasses, peanuts, &c. We had only one baggage wagon to the regiment. But we brought all the officers' valises, and a wedge tent for each four officers, and we have only slept out of doors two or three times during the march. We had more accommodations then we ever had before on a march. We marched on several roads. The army was spread over a strip of country from 40 to 60 miles wide, which was completely cleaned out and ruined. We ate all the hogs, and kept and drove off the cattle. We got hundreds of good horses and mules and Negroes, and did an immense amount of mischief generally. We destroyed the railroad and all its branches from Macon to this point. We did not capture Macon, but the 2nd Brigade of our division had a fight with the rebels a few miles east of the city and whipped them badly[6]. We lost 78 in killed and wounded, and the rebels 1,500. After that they made no opposition till we got near this place. The citizens mostly left their homes and hid themselves and their stock and household goods in swamps, but our foragers ransacked the country far and wide and found everything.

On the 6th inst. our brigade was started out at 4 o'clock in the morning to reconnoitre for a crossing of the Ogeechee; after marching ten miles we struck the river at Wright's Bridge, five miles from Station No. 2 on the railroad, found the bridge burned. We tore down some houses and fixed the bridge so we could cross on foot and five companies of the 25th went over and fortified. Then I was sent out with a detachment of two companies (B & H) to go to the railroad if possible. We had not got more than a mile and a half till we were fired on by a regiment of mounted infantry. The woods were full of them, and they shot like fury. We were within less than a hundred yards before we saw them. We fought them ten or fifteen minutes, when they began to swing round our flanks, and we fell back just in time to save ourselves. They followed us back to the edge of the swamp next to the river, where we made a stand and drove them off. I did not have a man hurt, but we found 4 dead rebels in the woods afterward. It only lasted two or three hours, and that is all the fighting the 25th has done since we left Atlanta, except what our skirmishers have done here.

Now what have you been doing all this time, Dear? I should like to get a letter and hear from you once more. I suppose you are freezing and shivering round the fire up there, wondering what has become of Sherman and his army. While I am writing out of doors in my shirtsleeves, and too warm at that. I hope you have plenty of wood and lots of provision, and that you and the children are well and comfortable. And you must see that Ma has plenty of everything she needs. I am afraid that she will be neglected and have to work go round so much seeing to things herself through the cold weather that she will get sick. You must do all you can to make her comfortable.

Now I expect you are waiting to know what I am going to say about that "leave of absence." Well, I hardly know what to say about it. I am going home the first chance, you may be sure of that. But I don't know when that will be. I have my "leave" yet—don't know whether it is worn out or not. I don't suppose there will be any chance to get away till Savannah is taken, and there is no knowing how long that will take. And then Sherman may start on an expedition against Charleston immediately, and allow no one to leave. But I have rigged up a desk and am fixing up my business as fast as I can. But it is uncertain and you must not look for me too strong. I will go home sometime during the winter if I can. If I don't you may be sure it will not be because I do not love you and wish to see you. Take good care of the children and kiss them for me. Give my love to Ma and Car and all the folks, and write me all the news.

Your affectionate husband,
J.B. Ritner

1. Sergeant James Barlow, who had previously been taken prisoner August 15, 1864, near Atlanta, was captured again in November at Cave Springs, Georgia. No later record was found.

2. Both the North and the South were using torpedoes that would float beneath the water surface and explode upon contact. Toward the end of the war, both sides had also developed torpedoes that could explode electrically and others also torpedoes that were detonated according to a clock mechanism. The torpedoes at Ft. McAllister were "Spar" torpedoes that were mounted on pilings. During the war, almost every waterway capable of floating a warship had been planted with torpedoes. (Webb Garrison, *More Civil War Curiosities*, pages 66-67)

3. One of those soon meeting Sherman after the connection between army and fleet was established was Colonel A. H. Markland, Sherman's mailman, with sacks of letters for the Army of the Tennessee. Sherman had sent him north from Atlanta with instructions to collect the mail and bring it to the coast in anticipation of Sherman's arrival. (Lloyd Lewis, *Sherman, Fighting Prophet*, page 465)

4. This camp was probably on the Lebanon Plantation, the neighboring Cottonvale Plantation, or Judge Lloyd's place. (Roger Durham, former Historian at Fort McAllister, currently U.S. Army Historian at Fort Stewart near Savannah)

5. The cost of supporting the Union war effort was a tremendous strain on the U.S. Treasury. Bureaucrats in the War Department designed a method to give some relief by paying the soldiers with interest bearing notes or bonds rather than cash. These were not legal tender and could not be deposited for weeks or months. (Webb Garrison, *More Civil War Curiosities*, page 192)

6. On November 19, three divisions of the 15th Army Corps had

moved out, but the last division, commanded by General John Corse, had difficulty crossing the Ocmulgee River because of rain and boggy roads. Six miles separated this division from the rest of the 15th Army Corps as it tried to catch up to the rest of the troops. Confederate General P. J. Phillips, leading Georgia Militia, discovered that they outnumbered their Union foe and ordered an attack on November 22 at Griswoldville by the untrained militia. In the fighting that followed, the Confederates lost 51 killed and 472 wounded, compared to Union losses of only 13 dead and 79 wounded, despite the Confederate's superiority in size. Most of the Georgia Militia were young boys and old men who had been reluctantly forced by Wheeler's cavalry to join the Southern fight. The Union soldiers quickly realized they were fighting untrained troops because of the suicidal charges conducted by the Confederates. (Jim Miles, *To The Sea, A History And Tour Guide Of Sherman's March*, pages 145-149)

- Sherman thought he had Savannah and Hardee's 10,000 troops surrounded, and in certain ways he did; Sherman was on the west of Savannah; 35,000 U.S. troops were occupying Hilton Head; and the Federal Navy blocked the east. Sherman sent a demand to Hardee that he surrender Savannah, but Hardee rejected Sherman's ultimatum, and on the night of December 20, Hardee surprised and outwitted Sherman by successfully evacuating his Confederate troops from Savannah. (Lloyd Lewis, *Sherman, Fighting Prophet*, page 469; Roger Durham, Savannah–Mr. Lincoln's Christmas Present, *Blue and Gray Magazine*, February 1991, page 48; Roger Durham letters)

Historical Sketch—25th Iowa Infantry

. . . on December 21, 1864, [the 25th Iowa Infantry] closed the triumphal march at Savannah, where it went into camp and enjoyed a brief period of rest. Colonel Williamson was at this time promoted to the command of a division, and Colonel Stone again succeeded to the command of the brigade, which he continued to command until the close of the next campaign, and the end of the war. Lieutenant Colonel Palmer again succeeded to the command of the regiment, which he also retained until the close of the war. (Roster and Record of Iowa Soldiers in the War of the Rebellion; *Published under the authority of the Iowa General Assembly*)

Savannah Is the Finest City I Ever Saw

Camp 25th Iowa Infantry
Savannah, Georgia
December 25, 1864

Dear Wife,

Christmas Gift to You!!![1] Christmas gift all of you—there now, didn't I catch you all that time? A merry time to all of you. I hope you will have a good time today, and that the children all found something in their stockings this morning! I am still well and hearty—have my "stomach and heels" and that is about all a soldier wants.

I wrote to you last on the 16th inst. and have got three letters from you since, the last dated November 20th—more than a month ago. Now I must tell you why I have not written sooner. You know one cannot always write when they wish to, even when they are at home. In the first place, we have been very busy; we have taken Savannah and had a great deal to do and to see. Then it has been so cold and windy for the last few days that I could not write without a fire and that we can't have except just out of doors, and we have all been shivering and smoking our eyes out, trying to keep warm. But the main reason I did not write was that I expected to go home myself, and get there about New Years. After we had taken this city, I supposed I could go home and get back before there would be much more done and I was determined to do it. So the day before yesterday I washed my hands and face, blacked my boots, put on a clean collar, &c, and took my old "leave of absence" to department headquarters to have it re-dated and to get permission to go with it now. But General Howard couldn't see it. He said he could not spare me just now. He is very much of a gentleman, seemed willing to accommodate me if he could. I told him it would be a great disappointment to me not to get to go now. He said that in a short time, or as soon as there was transportation directly from here north he would let me go. But I don't go much on that promise. The general opinion is that we will leave here within a week and then there will be no chance to go for some time. If it is so I can, I may apply again about the last of January. But it is uncertain where we will be by that time; the general opinion is that we will go from here to Charleston. And if our army goes into South Carolina I want to be along. Yesterday the 15th Army Corps was reviewed in the city by General Sherman. Company B led the 3rd Brigade and done it up in fine style. General Sherman said it was all done just right, couldn't be beat. And our Brigade Adjutant said the 25th Iowa beat everything in the corps marching.

Today is cloudy and looks like it might rain, but is warm enough to be comfortable without a fire, and I am going to write a while and then "our mess"—nine line officers and the chaplain—are going down to town to Mr. Haywood's[2], a wealthy citizen who we have engaged to get us a "Christmas Dinner." We thought we might as well try to have a little social enjoyment as it is Christmas, and not let you folks at home have all the nice things to yourselves. I will tell you about the dinner when we get back.

I am very well satisfied with the disposition you made of the money, only I am afraid you did not keep enough for your own use. I think the money is safe with Shaw, if Alvah says so. If you get any money from the farm, you had better keep it for the present. I have found no way to send mine home yet, and when I do it will all be in "bonds." There will be four months' pay due me in a few days from now, but I don't know when I will get it.

I don't allow you and Lib to saw wood, you must get someone to cut it all up, so you will have nothing to do but burn it. I wish I was there to keep you warm in these cold nights—wouldn't that be nice. Well, dear, I will be out of the army before another winter and then see if ever I leave you again! I don't allow Mrs. Burnett or anyone else to scold you, and you can tell her I said so. You have more sense than all of them and I say you may wear your hat whenever you please. You must wear it when I come home—won't you?

We were in hopes that our division would be left here to garrison the place, and then I was going to have you come down here and stay a while. But the 1st Division 20th Army Corps has got that position and we have to take the field again—just our luck.

Well, I suppose you would like to hear some war news. I don't suppose that I can tell you anything that will be new by the time you get this. We got very short of rations after I wrote to you last. There were so many obstructions in the Ogeechee that even after Fort McAllister was taken it was some time before boats could come up. The men got rice and pounded the hulls off in wooden mortars and in holes cut in stumps. There was the greatest pounding for a few days you ever saw; every soldier was going his best, and they got some hand corn mills, such as the Negroes use to grind with, and ground corn, and parched corn, and so made out till we got a partial supply.

Then we commenced pushing up on the rebels, and were just about ready to cross the swamp in spite of them, when they evacuated. We had land bridges and other contrivances[3] all ready to go for them the next night. Some of our men had been over and examined their position. They left on the night of the 20th and we marched in force and took possession of the city early on the 21st. Our army having marched over 300 miles and captured the city of Savannah in thirty-five days and that with a loss of less than 500 men!! The rebels crossed the river in front of the city on a bridge made of flat boats[4], and went towards Charleston. We thought they were surrounded on that side so they could not get away, but it seems not. They left all the guns in the forts and a great deal of ammunition. I don't know the number, but I think that including Fort Jackson, which has also surrendered, we have captured as much artillery as we did at Vicksburg. But the principal thing of importance is the cotton. There is an immense quantity of that here. I hear that it is estimated at fifty million dollars' worth[5].

Savannah is the finest city I ever saw. The population, white and black, was about 30,000. A great many of the citizens are here yet and are almost in a starving condition. They look like they were well pleased that we have come here, but I don't go much on the Union sentiment here. There are a great many fine residences here, and the streets are lined with live oak and other shade trees. The monument to Pulaski[6] is the finest thing I ever saw. They have a park with a fountain in the center that is a splendid affair[7]. And they have some church edifices that are said to be the finest in the United States. I wish you were here to see it. I will bring you down when the war is over. We found here about thirty engines and a great deal of rolling stock. And I can't begin to tell you what all. I have not seen the ocean yet, but the water in the river is salty at high tide. But I must stop and go to dinner.

* * * * *

Well, Dear, I have been to dinner. But I got something else just as I was starting that was a great deal better and more welcome than any dinner could be—and that was a letter from you. I was very glad to hear from you. Your letter was dated December 4th. I knew you would be very uneasy. And then it would be two or three weeks more before you could hear from us. I hope you and Tommy have both got well by this time. You must get those sore lips of yours cured up before I get home. I won't allow you to "pout" a bit while I am home.

But I am afraid you will have time for a good long pout before I get there!! What in the world will you do without Lib? I don't care for the expense. I wish she had stayed there. You will be lonesome and have too much to do. But I think it will be better for her.

You need not be uneasy about General Sherman going on a "wild goose chase" and getting his men into trouble. He is all right, and knows what he is about! He was a little uneasy himself for a while! When he saw our flag go up on Fort McAllister he knew he was all right. He clapped his hands and exclaimed, "Thirty days without a base! Thirty days without a base! Such a thing was never heard of since the days of Alexander!"

You need not believe anything you see from southern papers about the opposition we met on the way here. We didn't meet it. We just ran around loose and did pretty much as we pleased. We did not take Macon, did not try, and never intended to. We could have done so, but it was strongly fortified and would have cost us a hard fight, and we would have got a great many wounded men on our hands and no way to take care of them or send them back. We destroyed the railroad all around it so it is useless to the rebels. Our prisoners had all been removed from Andersonville[8], so it was useless to go there. But we captured and destroyed Milledgeville, Gordon, Mellen, and several other places, and all the railroads in our route. And got through in better health and spirits and with our transportation in much better condition than when we started. I think it the boldest and most successful move of the war.

It is currently reported here now that Hardee's retreat has been cut off, between here and Charleston by General Foster[9] and that he surrendered yesterday with 10,000 prisoners. I don't vouch for the truth of it.[10]

I wrote to you again before we left Atlanta, but did not get to send it. I put the letter with the money in the package and it is here yet. The railroad from the north was destroyed several days before we left. I made out to get some clothes there. I got one shirt from the "Sanitary," one from the government, and bought one from Dr. Tibbetts. I also got 2 pairs of socks, an overcoat, pants, and drawers from the government. But I am nearly out of clothes again that are fit to wear. I had to borrow boots and pants to wear to the dinner. If ever I get to "God's Country" again I am going to have some good clothes!

There are a great many torpedoes in the Savannah River, and our fleet has not come up yet. We are pretty short of rations again, but expect to get plenty by tomorrow.

But I must tell you about the dinner. We had a very nice civil time. Mr. Haywood was an ice merchant, was worth $100,000 before the war. He lives in a three-story brick, one of the finest residences in the city. The furniture is the nicest I ever saw. He is an intelligent and sociable man, but a full-blooded rebel. But we talked politics all day without getting "excited." For dinner we had roast beef (that we furnished ourselves), chicken, rice, cake, cookies, coffee, and pies—don't know what they were made of. They charged us thirty dollars, which we thought very cheap.

Now Dear, I think I have told you all the news. You will be sorry to hear that I could not go home, but you can't be more disappointed than I am. But keep in good heart, my own sweet dear. I will come yet, this winter if possible, and if not I will at least love you and remember you night and day. Direct your letters to me at Savannah. Give my love to Ma and all the folks.

Yours ever—Your own,
J.B. Ritner

1. The most notable mention of Savannah as Christmas tidings was Sherman's offering to Abraham Lincoln:

    To his Excellency President Lincoln,
    Washington, D. C.
        I beg to present you, as a Christmas gift, the city of Savannah, with 150 heavy guns and plenty of ammunition; also about 25,000 bales of cotton.
        W. T. Sherman
        Major General

    (Lloyd Lewis, *Sherman, Fighting Prophet*, page 470)

2. Mr. Alfred Haywood, the ice merchant, lived on York Street between Montgomery Street and Jefferson Street in Savannah. Haywood, who was born in Oxford, England, was also a grocer, city councilman, and had temporarily served as Mayor of Savannah. (Georgia Historical Society)

3. Jacob is referring to scaling ladders, fascines and gabions built to give the soldiers a means to cross flooded rice fields, streams, and other similar obstructions that protected many of the Confederate defenses. (Roger Durham letters)

4. The Confederates were short of the pontoon bridges so they laid

them end to end as opposed to side by side. They constructed three bridges – the first to Hutchinson Island, another across the back channel to Pennyworth Island, and the third crossing to a rice dike on the South Carolina side. (Roger Durham letters)

5. There were many parties that claimed this cotton. See comments following Jacob's letter of January 12, 1865 concerning Secretary of War Stanton's visit to Savannah regarding ownership and distribution of this cotton.

6. An 1857 drawing of Monterey Square and the Pulaski Monument, which Jacob described as "the finest thing I ever saw." (Margaret Wayt DeBolt, *Savannah Spectres And Other Strange Tales*, page 197)

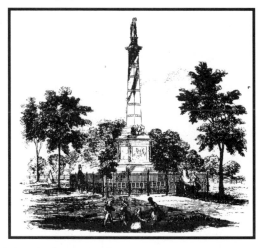

7. Jacob is referring to the fountain in Forsyth Park.

8. Jacob had described the failed prisoner exchange in his letters of September 19, 1864 and September 26, 1864. The Confederates soon abandoned Andersonville. Some prisoners escaped, but most captives moved to other prisons before the Union Army had a chance to rescue them. (William Marvel, *Andersonville, The Last Depot*, pages 202-203)

9. General John Gray Foster had been given charge of operations against Charleston in May 1864. Foster and his troops were Eastern troops who had not participated in the March to the Sea, but met Sherman near Savannah. (Stewart Sifakis, *Who Was Who In The Union*, page 141; Roger Durham letters)

10. The rumor of Hardee's surrender was not true.

Savannah, Georgia
January 4, 1865

My Dear Wife,
   I again sit down to write you a few lines. I intended to write last night, but I heard that we would get a mail, and I waited till bed-time, thinking I would be sure to get a letter from you. It came at last, and there was just one letter for Company B and that was for me! But when I opened it, it was from Ol! I was mad enough to bite it. I was very glad to hear from him, but I do want to get a letter from you again. I can't wait. I know you are looking for me home now any day, and are wondering why I do not come or write. Well, I was very much disappointed that I did not get to go. But it can't be helped now. We are still in camp at the same place as when I wrote last, but we expect to leave before very long. The 17th Army Corps has gone already—don't know where[1]. I am still in good health; so are all the men. We don't get full rations yet, and have drawn no clothing[2], so are ragged and hungry and not so fat as when we first got here, but in other respects we are all right.
   We had a rather dull New Years—at least I did. We did not go to town for dinner as we talked about doing. Some of the officers went down to the coast on Saturday and got about ten bushels of oysters in the shell and had a great time eating them. They ate all day. First they ate all they could raw, right out of the shell (ugh! the nasty things!) then they roasted them in the fire in the shell, then they had fried oysters, then oyster soup—then they ate some more raw, then had some with pepper and vinegar, &c, &c, all day. It made me sick at the stomach just to see them swallow the nasty things and I didn't taste one (hah!) So I had nothing for dinner but hard tack and coffee, neither sugar nor meat. I wish I had you to cook me dinner—they might go to thunder with their oysters if I had a chance at those sausages and ribs you wrote about!
   I see by the papers and letters that you are having very cold weather up north, with plenty of snow and good sleighing. I hope you have plenty of good wood and keep warm. We have had a good deal of cold, disagreeable weather here, some very frosty nights, but not what we would call cold at the north, but enough to make it uncomfortable to sleep in a tent without fire, and eat out of doors as we do. Then when it rains our shebang that we write in leaks. There has nothing new or strange happened here since I wrote last. Everything seems to be settling down and becoming regulated as

fast as possible. We have a Union paper published here and are promised a daily mail soon. Most of the stores and shops have been opened, but there is very little in them, and they ask an outrageous price for everything. There is a great scarcity of provision among both citizens and soldiers. Apples sell at 6 to 8 for a dollar, butter $2.00 per pound, cheese the same, &c; no clothing (except rebel) to be had at any price.

Our brigade was reviewed today by General Woods, and the 15th Army Corps is to be reviewed again next Saturday by General Howard. I wish you could see a review once; and we will make a fine display next Saturday. We can beat anything in the army marching. But I don't think half so much of Sherman and Howard as I used to. First because they won't let me go home! And then they seem to have certain pets and favorites who get all the favors and soft places. The 20th Army Corps and the 4th Division of our Corps will be left to garrison Savannah, while our division that has always been in the field, that has never been whipped, and has done more marching and fighting than any division in the army, has to go again. It seems that those who are deemed the most unreliable in the face of the enemy are the very ones who get the most favors in the army, and the most credit at home. It makes me so mad sometimes that I think if I could get out of the service I would, and let the whole thing go to the devil.

Myself and three other captains have made arrangements to take a trip down to the coast through Ossabaw Sound, next Saturday if the weather is fair. I want to see the Atlantic Ocean. The tide runs up here, but the ocean cannot be seen. If we go I will have a long story to tell you about it in my next.

We have heard the good news from our Army in Tennessee[3] and also that Butler has attacked Wilmington[4]. Everything looks favorable for a speedy termination of the war. I do hope it will soon come. My time is getting short, only nine months more, at the farthest, but I hope I will not have to stay that long.

Ol's letter was written at Memphis December 10th; he is well then. Neither Tom nor Alvah have written a word to me since I was at home last spring. I don't suppose they care to hear from me. Do you think I ought to write to them? As long as you write to me and love me, I don't care. You will always remember and pray for your soldier husband, will you not? I know you will. And may the good God that has protected our lives so long, soon return me safe and sound to your arms, and the society of our dear children. I have no fears but that you will train them up correctly, but long to be there to assist and help bear the responsibility. Kiss them for me, and teach them to pray for their unworthy father.

Your own, Jake

I have not been able to get any stamps yet and will have to "frank" this letter. Good night, my sweet dear, and may you have sweet dreams.

1. Elements of the 17th Army Corps were sent to Liberty County to destroy the railroad and to forage. (Roger Durham letters)

2. Jacob makes this comment three weeks after the fall of Fort McAllister. This helps underscore the need that Sherman had to establish a supply base after marching through Georgia, now that his army remained stationary in Savannah.

3. Jacob is referring to the Battle of Franklin, where Hood launched another unsuccessful frontal assault, and the Battle of Nashville, where Hood had established a partial siege against a much larger army commanded by Thomas. After much urging by Grant, Thomas attacked and routed Hood on December 15. Because of Thomas's delays in attacking Hood, Grant almost replaced him with Logan. Logan had actually arrived in Nashville with the orders of replacing Thomas, but had been instructed not to present them if Thomas had acted against Hood by the time he arrived.

4. The last major port open to the blockade runners of the South was Wilmington, North Carolina, protected by Fort Fisher. The Union plan was to attack Fort Fisher by fleet under Porter, and then by infantry under General Benjamin Butler. Porter did his work, silencing the Confederate batteries, but then Butler would not move, announcing that he would not waste the lives of his men. Grant then removed Butler and replaced him with Alfred Howe Terry, who commanded a successful attack against Fort Fisher on January 15. After the war, Terry joined the regular army and was General George A. Custer's superior officer when Custer was killed at the Battle of the Little Big Horn. (Lloyd Lewis, *Sherman, Fighting Prophet*, pages 477-478; Stewart Sifakis, *Who Was Who In The Union*, page 408)

Camp 25th Iowa Infantry
Savannah, Georgia
January 8, 1865

My Dear Wife,
    This is Sunday evening and I sit down to write you a few lines, as I may not have another opportunity for several days. We have just received orders to march tomorrow morning at 7 o'clock on the "Thunderbolt Road!" This did not surprise us any. It is the first order we have had on the subject, but you can't fool an old soldier! We can always tell when a move is on hand before the order comes! I have felt it in my bones for a week. "Thunderbolt" is down the river on or near the coast. We go there and embark on transports, and go by water to—someplace—don't know where, probably Beaufort, South Carolina. Since we have to go, we had just as lieve go now as any time.
    General Logan has got back and takes command of the corps again. We are all glad of that. "Old hell-smell" as we call General Osterhaus goes to St. Louis[1]. It is reported now that General Sherman has played off on the 20th Army Corps. That General Foster of the 18th Army Corps takes command here, and the city is to be garrisoned by Negro troops! If that is so, it is all right, but if the 20th Army Corps or any division of our corps is left here, and we have to go again, I shall always think it is a piece of the most gross injustice. We have got about half the clothing we need, and may get the rest before we leave. And there comes in another grand imposition. They are forcing us to take a lot of old and indifferent clothing that the pet Eastern Army would not have, just because we can't help ourselves. I suppose they think anything is good enough for us. I have been fighting mad about it for two or three days. But grumbling will never put down the rebellion!
    We had another grand review yesterday; the whole 15th Army Corps was reviewed in the city by General Sherman. It was a very windy, cold day, but we did the best marching that was ever seen in this city. The citizens mostly turned out to see us, and the streets were lined with soldiers from the other corps.
    We got a mail yesterday evening, and I got a letter from you, the one you wrote December 22nd . . . You still talk about the "ugly cold." I am really afraid it will get to be something worse. You must take good care of yourself, dear. You must take something for your cold. I wish I was there to make fires, and milk for you. But never

mind, dear! I will be there next winter, and then see if you shall go out in the cold and freeze your dear, sweet self. I am glad to hear that Annie is going to stay with you. You will not be lonesome now.

We did not go down to the coast yesterday, as I told you in my last that we discussed. We knew we would move, and then there has been a high wind off the shore for the last two days and we were afraid we might blow away and not get back. But tomorrow we embark on the briny ocean—"the deep blue sea." I am anxious to see it and take a ride on it. I will have something to tell you about it in my next letter.

Pem Howe[2] got here today as a recruit to Company H (glad he didn't come to my company). I have not had time to talk with him yet.

This is Sunday but I have been hard at work all day. I am Brigade Officer of the Day and went out with the pickets this morning, then made out my ordnance return and I have to go to the picket line tonight at 12 o'clock. Then I shall be thinking about you— perhaps you will be asleep in your warm bed, dreaming about me. Only think how far we are apart! I hope you will see me at home, but I hope there will not be "anything the matter" with me. I won't make any more promises about going home. I don't know but Sherman intends to keep us hard at work till our time is out or the war is over. And I won't promise to wait for the "first of the month" if I get leave to go. I would go that far, if I could, just for one of your sweet kisses. Now you must not fret yourself and be uneasy about our going into another fight—we may not have any. If we could move from Atlanta here without fighting, I think we can go any place else.

I see that almost all the generals and other officers of the Potomac Army have gone home to spend the holidays. Well, poor fellows, I suppose they deserved it[3]. They couldn't have any fine dinners or other nice things sent to them! Then they have had such a hard time, and done so much! If we could only do some big thing we might get to go home too. And perhaps have a dinner sent to us! I don't mind these things myself. I know it is unavoidable, but there is a great deal of complaint and hard feelings among the men. But I am grumbling again. I don't often take such a spell. But I have felt awful crabbed all day. I hope I will get up in a better humor tomorrow. My men are all well, and so am I. And we will give a good account of ourselves the first time we meet the rebels. Good night dear.

Your own, Jake

I haven't got any stamps yet. I don't like to "frank" my own letters, but will have to do so again.

1. General Logan had not participated in the March to the Sea, but had returned to the North to participate in the election campaigns for the Republicans. During his absence, General Peter Osterhaus led the 15th Army Corps. Osterhaus, not wanting to replace one of the division commanders within the 15th Army Corps, asked to be reassigned. He then became Edward R. S. Canby's Chief of Staff of the Military Division of West Mississippi, based in St. Louis.

2. Warren Pembroke Howe was a son of Samuel Howe, the founder of Professor Howe's Academy in Mt. Pleasant, Iowa. This was the same Professor Howe who had taught William Sherman and his brother John at a school in Ohio. Another son, Seward, took over the Academy in Mt. Pleasant in later years. As described in *The Palimpsest*, edited by John Ely Briggs in 1931, "Warren Pembroke Howe, Pem as he was called, remained in Mt. Pleasant and became a thorn in the flesh to his father and Seward. Brilliant and well-educated, he possessed many exceptional qualities as a teacher, but he was at the same time impulsive, unstable, and unwilling to work under authority. During his later years, his convivial habits diminished and finally destroyed his usefulness to the school and to the community. His mind, if it had been susceptible to discipline, would have placed him high on the honor roll of a distinguished family."

 Jacob was very familiar with Pem Howe, as he and Jacob both were from Mt. Pleasant and both had served as privates in Company F of the 1st Iowa Infantry in the Missouri campaign culminating with the Battle of Wilson's Creek.

3. Jacob is being sarcastic in reference to the 20th Army Corps that came from the Army of the Potomac.

Historical Sketch—25th Iowa Infantry

The operations of his [Colonel Stone's] brigade, in that last great march through the Carolinas and onto Washington, are fully described in the official report of Colonel Stone and, for the purpose of showing the part taken by the Twenty-Fifth Iowa, in that closing campaign, the following extracts are taken from the report:

 In accordance with orders, I respectfully report a summary of the part taken by this command in the campaign just ended. The campaign commenced on the 10th day of January and ended, with my command, on the 26th day of March, 1865, making the duration two months and sixteen days. On the 10th of January last, I had orders to march from our camp near Savannah, Georgia, to Fort Thunderbolt. On the 12th of January, I took shipping at Fort Thunderbolt for Beaufort, South Carolina with all the regiments of my command, save one, (the Twenty-Fifth Iowa), which was left behind to assist in fetching up the transportation of the division. This regiment [the 25th Iowa] reported to me at camp near Beaufort, South Carolina, on the 14th day of January, 1865. (*Roster and Record of Iowa Soldiers in the War of the Rebellion*; Published under the authority of the Iowa General Assembly)

Camp 25th Iowa Infantry
Thunderbolt Landing, Georgia
January 12, 1865

My Dear Wife,

As we are lying here today doing nothing I think I will write you a few lines again, though I . . . have no news of any kind to tell you. I do love to sit down and write to you. I can always find something to say. I hardly ever write to anyone else now. We got a small mail today and I got nothing but a notice from a quartermaster at Louisville, Kentucky. I am very anxious to get your next letter. I think you would get my first letter from Savannah before you wrote it, and I would like to hear that you had got it and had been relieved from your anxiety.

I wrote to you last Sunday night. We then had orders to march the next morning at 7 o'clock. Well, that order was countermanded at midnight, and we did not move till Tuesday morning at 9, when our division came down here, which is four miles from Savannah, expecting to go on board of transports and go to Beaufort immediately. But the 17th Army Corps had not got away yet, and are not all gone now, and we have to wait till they get out of the way. We think we will get off tomorrow.

There are several ships, brigs, schooners, propellers, and side-wheel steamers engaged in carrying troops to Beaufort. They make one trip each day. It is very slow work loading; the wagons and artillery, &c have to be taken apart and hoisted in one piece at a time with block and tackle. The boats are not at all like those that run on the river.

The rebels had a strong fort here. There are 10 or 12 heavy siege guns here yet, all dismantled. One is a 200-pound "rifled parrot." Thunderbolt is on a narrow passage of water that runs between the mainland and one of the Tybee Islands. The country all around here is level as a prairie; a good deal of it overflows when the tide is in.

I saw the first Palmetto trees yesterday I ever saw, and they are the greatest curiosity I ever saw. I can't describe them so that you would know what they look like. They had no branches at all, and no leaves except a few right on top, but they have stems three or four feet long, and the leaf is as large as—well, as large as a news-paper, and green. They are what they make palmetto hats of! It looks very odd to see the trees and bushes all green in January.

I went yesterday to see Bonaventure[1], which is an old cemetery used by the aristocracy of Savannah. It is one of the most pictur-esque, as well as the most gloomy places I was ever in! I wish I could describe it to you. It is planted with live oak and cedar, so thick that they make a dense shade. The trees are large and tall, and have very long branching boughs, which are hung thick with "moss." I never saw it grow so long, or the trees so loaded with it before. This gives a gloomy, spectral appearance to the place that seems very appropriate to the last resting place of fallen greatness. The vaults and monuments are of marble and very costly.

We heard last night that Honorable E. M. Stanton[2] and Q. M. General Meigs[3] had arrived at Savannah. I don't know whether it is so or not—and don't care. We don't want to see either one of them. If they will stay at Washington and mind their own business, General Sherman can run this concern without any of their help.

My health is good, and I hope you have got over that cough of yours. You must tell me about it when you write—if you don't I shall think you are worse. Company B is well. We have got nearly all the clothing we need at present. But we do not get full rations yet. We have all, officers and men, lived pretty hard since we came here. I do not think we will "take the field" for two or three weeks yet. We are first of our corps to cross, and at the rate they are going, it will take that long to get the corps across.

If they had let me start home on Christmas, as I wanted, I could have been back long before they will want me here (They don't give but 20 days' leave)—don't you think they are mean for not let-ting me go? I think the war will end yet before my time is out. But we don't know much about what is going on at other places. We get no northern papers here at all. I don't see why they do not have them here for sale. Tell the children not to forget their Pa—and that

I said they must all be good children. I think about them every day. I have Lulie's and Nellie's pictures yet, and am looking in every letter for Tom's and Kitty's. Give my respects to Ma, Car, Annie, and all the rest. And accept my love for yourself.

Yours ever, Jake

1. Bonaventure Cemetery, from an 1865 print by T. A. Richards in Harper's Weekly. (Margaret Wayt DeBolt, *Savannah Spectres And Other Strange Tales*, page 193)

One of the early owners of the land that was to become Bonaventure Cemetery was John Mullryne. Mullryne and his son-in-law were both prominent citizens in colonial Georgia but sided with the English during the Revolutionary War and had to flee Georgia. After the Revolutionary War Tatnall's son, Josiah Tatnall, Jr. returned to Georgia and purchased Bonaventure. Tatnall, Jr. was a successful planter who introduced cotton to Georgia. He also served in the state senate and was elected Governor in 1801.

Governor Tatnall's son, also named Josiah, served in the Confederate Navy and while in command of naval defenses of Georgia and South Carolina Commodore Tatnall led his fleet in an attack against the Union ships at Port Royal in November 1861. (Terry Shaw and Margaret Wayt DeBolt, brochure prepared by Friends of Bonaventure; correspondence with Terry Shaw and Margaret Wayt DeBolt; Stewart Sifakis, *Who Was Who In The Confederacy*, pages 275-276)

2. History well records the animosity between Sherman and Secretary of War Edwin McMasters Stanton, but apparently it was also known by the active troops in the field. Stanton had come to Savannah to take possession of the large amount of cotton, whose ownership was claimed by the British and several other parties. Sherman was particularly incensed by the British claims on the cotton since they had been paying for the cotton smuggled out of the South with cannons, shells, and other ammunition used against the Federals. (Lloyd Lewis, *Sherman, Fighting Prophet*, pages 479-480)

Stanton's unofficial purpose for visiting Sherman was to check on Sherman's treatment of the Negroes. The story of Union General Jefferson C. Davis and the tragedy at Ebenezer Creek had created a substantial concern in the administration in Washington over Sherman's conduct toward the blacks. Stanton and Sherman held a joint meeting with area Negro preachers. At one point, Stanton dismissed a fuming Sherman from the meeting and questioned the blacks in private:

> "State what is the feeling of the colored people in regard to General Sherman, and how far do they regard his sentiments and actions as friendly to their rights and interests, or otherwise.
>
> *Answer*: We looked upon General Sherman, prior to his arrival, as a man, in the providence of God, specially set apart to accomplish this work, and we unanimously felt inexpressible gratitude to him, looking upon him as a man that should be honored for the faithful performance of his duty. Some of us called upon him immediately upon his arrival, and it is probable he did not meet the Secretary with more courtesy than he met us. His conduct and deportment toward us characterized him as a friend and a gentleman. We have confidence in General Sherman, and think that what concerns us could not be under better hands. This is our opinion now from the short acquaintance and intercourse we have had." (*Official Record* Series 1-Volume XLVII/2 as published by the Guild Press of Indiana on CD-ROM)

Sherman's and Stanton's animosity toward each other boiled over near the close of the war.

3. Early in the war, Sherman's friends had sought the position of Quartermaster General for Sherman, but instead, this position was awarded to Colonel Montgomery C. Meigs, a Georgian.

Sherman was then appointed Colonel of the 13th Regular Infantry. Meigs held his position throughout the war. (Lloyd Lewis, *Sherman, Fighting Prophet*, pages 161-162)

The Death of Isaac Ritner, Jacob's Brother

[Mt. Pleasant, Iowa]
Jan. 31st, 1865

Dear Husband,

You see I have run two or three days over my time again. Please excuse, won't you? I keep thinking every day I will certainly write, but you know, dear, how hard it is for me to get at writing a letter when there is so much to do. It is now 12 o'clock and past. I have been to church tonight and then I had some work that must be done before commencing the letter. I should promise to finish it for my eyes hurt me now. I will say in the first place that last night after dark when we were just finishing supper, two gentlemen came in and introduced themselves as David Alter and Henry Alter, your uncles. They were looking out for a situation to move to . . .

They brought up the sad intelligence of the death of Isaac. I suppose they have written to you from home by this time telling you all about it. I've heard nothing but what your uncles said—that he died in a hospital of some fever. Oh, what a hard stroke to the already bereaved family—one after is another is taken till that larger family is nearly broken up. Who shall be next? Oh, let us all be prepared that when our time comes we may be ready . . .

I have no "city" news to tell you except that Mrs. Harvey's house burned down last Thursday afternoon. She was up to Taylor's sewing. The children had all gone to school, but Anna— she ironed and then filled the stove full of wood (for it was very cold) and then started to school about 3 o'clock. When they got back, the house was all on fire and so far gone it couldn't be saved. Mr. Harvey is at Pittsburgh. He has sent for them to come there. The goods were all saved except the kitchen furniture.—

I have given up looking for you till I see you. I suppose there is no chance while you are on the march. You must not "fret" about it and scold your superiors. I expect they know what is best. I will try & be contented and look forward to the time that you can come home to stay which will not be very long anymore.—I got your money at last, the 600. Goodbye.

Your Em

- Jacob's brother Isaac was severely wounded April 30, 1864, at the Battle of Jenkins Ferry on the Sabine River, Arkansas, and died of disease January 16, 1865, in a regimental hospital. He is buried in the National Cemetery, in Little Rock, Arkansas.

I Wish There Was Not An Oyster In A Thousand Miles of Here!

Camp, 25th Iowa Infantry
Beaufort, South Carolina
January 22, 1865

My Dear Wife,

This is Sunday and I will try to write you another letter . . . if I don't write today my letter will not go by the steamer that leaves Hilton Head tomorrow . . . I wrote to you last from Thunderbolt Landing. I wrote a letter to the children a few days ago. I hope it will please them and keep them from forgetting me. I will write to them again if I don't get where I can't write at all. I have also mailed to Tommy a Confederate spelling book that I confiscated on the march. You will find it a great curiosity; don't let them destroy it. I want to preserve it as an evidence of Southern civilization and intelligence! And I think I will send to each of them in this letter a little book that I got from the Christian Commission. I think that will please them and help them to remember their Pa.

We have heard that a steamer on the way here from New York was wrecked off Cape Hatteras and two hundred and sixty lives lost[1]. I have no doubt but our mail was on board of her, and lost, too. And I am very much afraid that some of my men were on board. Sergeant Keller was left at Chattanooga when we started through here. Will Black was left there in charge of the book boxes and extra baggage of the regiment, and Henry C. Carper had been at home on sick furlough. Some or all of them may have been on the unfortunate vessel.

The men here are all well. Ed Hall is detailed as clerk at Brigade Quarters. I don't know what this army would do for clerks if it was not for Company B. Garvin, Payne, Bill White and all the boys you know are quite hearty. And the old Captain himself is well and hearty, and anxious to start on the next raid.

Since we left Savannah January 10th, we have been camped "in the field," without any regular quarters. And it has rained constantly for the last three days and nights, so you may know we are in no very comfortable fix. Many of my men have no tents except what they make with gum blankets. The tents they have are nothing but shelter tents, or "dog tents" as they call them, which is two pieces of cotton drilling about as large as a sheet; these are buttoned together at one side and stretched over a pole, making a kind of a shelter that two men can crawl into, but it is open at both ends. Lieutenant Steele and I, and Captain Young and Lieutenant Anderson of Company A, have a wedge tent, just large enough for us four to lie down in it. It leaks when it rains. Then the whole regiment officers and men, and the whole army as far as I know—have nothing to make bunks of; all sleep on the ground. Just think of lying out on the ground without fire in a rainstorm for two or three days! But we have got used to such things and don't mind it much.

When we are in the "enemy's country" we always tear down houses, barns, churches, or anything we come to for boards to lie on. But we had not been on shore here five minutes when General Howard came down on us with a "general order" stating that all the property on this island (Port Royal) belongs either to the U.S. or to Union citizens, and that any interference with it would be severely punished. So we have to keep our hands off the lumber and rails and burn green fire! We are all keen to get out where the citizens are not all Union! It doesn't suit us to soldier in a friendly country. The land here belongs to the government and is cultivated by "freed men"—there are a great many refugees from slavery here. They all seem to be contented, industrious, and doing well. They are generally clean and decently clothed. There is a great contrast between those here, and the poor, ragged, starved wretches we see on the plantations as we march through the country.

Beaufort is quite a business place; a great many stores and sutlers where almost everything can be bought that you could find in a northern city, and at reasonable prices. It looks more like civilization than anything I have seen since I left God's country. The streets and every store and grocery are crowded with black men and women, buying, selling, and trading, just like white folks. There are schools for both old and young, and they seem to improve rapidly. I saw the other day a northern school-marm, "young and pretty," ride through town in a buggy with a buck negro. What do you think of that?

We have got plenty of rations since we have been here, the first time we had had enough since we got through to Savannah. The men have been furnished several rations of soft bread from the government bakery here, the first they have had since we left Woodville, the 1st of May—it was a great treat to them. Then we got quite a lot of "Sanitary" from the Christian Commission. My company got one dozen cans of tomatoes, some canned meat, pickles, butter, crackers, &c. It was a great treat to them. This is the greatest place for oysters you ever read of. "Our mess" gets them for 25 cents per quart, hulled. They eat 6 gallons a day, so you see it is pretty expensive—at least for me, when I have to foot my share of the bill, and don't eat any oysters! I wish there was not an oyster in a thousand miles of here! The government price of rations is a great deal higher than it used to be. It costs me twice as much to live as it did the first year.

The 17th Army Corps came over here before we did and moved out to Ft. Pocotaligo on the Savannah and Charleston railroad, which they captured several days ago, and cut the railroad at that point. They did this without much of a fight, and with very little loss. But General Foster with 18,000 men had been trying to take it for two months and couldn't. If he had done it, Hardee could not have got away from Savannah. But one brigade of our army captured the place at the first trial! That is the difference in the two armies.

Our division [the 1st] and the 2nd Division of our corps all came here by water and are nearly all here yet. The 3rd and 4th Divisions are coming across by land. General Sherman has played off on the 20th Army Corps, sure enough; the 18th Army Corps garrison Savannah, and the 14th and 20th Army Corps and Kilpatrick's Cavalry are moving across the Savannah River into South Carolina. The 17th Army Corps made another advance yesterday and drove the rebels ten miles, and there is heavy cannonading today in the direction of Charleston. I suppose they are still pressing on. It is only about 45 miles to Charleston on a straight line. We expect to start for there tomorrow, but we don't know certain where we are going[2]. But I have no doubt that is the point. The 1st Brigade of our division and the pioneers[3] are out now about 18 miles. I do not think we will have much fighting. It is an unfavorable season for a campaign[4], but everything else is favorable and I am anxious to give the rebellion another lick, before they have time to get their breath. We have no order to march yet, but we have soldiered long enough to know what is coming before we see it. We have heard the news of the capture of Ft. Fisher and

Wilmington. The navy at Hilton Head and the forts here have been firing salutes over the news for the last two days. It does seem to me that the war is about played out. I don't see how the rebels can hold out much longer, unless they should happen to get the advantage in some way of Grant's Army. Have no fears at all for our army, it can't be whipped, and whatever point we start for will be reached and taken—if it is Richmond itself[5]. One report in camp is that our train is to be loaded with 60 days' rations and that we are to start on a march of 400 miles. All right, if General Sherman thinks we can take Richmond, we can, and will.[6]

I don't know whether we will have a way to send letters back or not. If there is any opportunity I will write to you frequently—if not, you must have patience and not be too uneasy. I have no doubt but that I will get through all right. If I had got to go home when we first got to Savannah, I might have had a good visit, and been back by this time. But a good soldier ought not to grumble, and I have concluded to let come what will, if I can only see this rebellion put down before my time is out I shall be satisfied. I do not now expect that we will be mustered out before the end of our term. But I still hope I will get to go home on "leave of absence" before that . . . This is a very dull place. We don't get any papers from the north at all, and no news but what comes in circulars from headquarters. I would like to know what you have been doing, and how you have got along for the last month. But I hope you two Mrs. Captains (I mean you and Annie) have had good health and kept each other company, and that with the help of Billy you will get through the winter comfortably. Next winter I intend to make it my special business to wait on you myself. Now I have written you a very long, dull letter. But you must remember that it is cold and rainy and I am sitting flat on the ground writing on my knees, and have to stop once in a while and go out to the fire and warm my fingers. How I wish I could sit down beside you and put my feet on the stove. How about that rocking chair? Have you got it fixed yet? Better have it ready.

Your own Husband, J.B. Ritner

P.S. I have just heard that Major General Howard is to preach[7] in town this p.m.. If I had known it in time I should certainly have gone to hear him. We all think a great deal of Howard. There is not a man in the army that does not love him.

Your own Jake

I have concluded not to send the tracts to the children, but will give them to my men, for whom they are more suitable. If I can find some nice present to send them, I will do so.

1. Cape Hatteras is located on the coast of North Carolina, as is *Cape Fear*. No vessels meeting Jacob's description went down off Cape Hatteras during January 1865. Two Confederate blockade runners, the *Cape Fear* and the *North Health*, were lost in January 1865, near the Cape Fear River in North Carolina. (Helen Mills Wilson, Administrative Coordinator, Graveyard of the Atlantic Museum, Hatteras, North Carolina; William Trotter, Ironclads and Columbiads)

2. Sherman did not attack Charleston, but instead moved to Columbia, the capital of South Carolina. The feint toward Charleston was intended to confuse the Confederates. Some have speculated that Sherman spared Charleston because of fond memories of Charleston in his days before the Civil War.

3. The word "pioneer" referred to those soldiers detailed to build roads, bridges, barricades, earthworks, and the like.

4. Between January 27 and March 10, during the march through South Carolina, it rained over 50 percent of the days, frequently in downpours. (Joseph T. Glatthar, *The March to the Sea and Beyond*, page 108)

5. Grant and Sherman both had ideas for Sherman's army to assist in the capture of Richmond. Grant's plan was to have Sherman's army travel north by ship, but Sherman was determined to go by land, a continuation of his march through Georgia. Grant acquiesced to Sherman's plan and the march continued.

6. These are statements of determination by Jacob, consistent with the internal perception of Sherman's army. Others would later agree. Joseph Johnston wrote after the war, "But when I learned that Sherman's army was marching through the Salk swamps, making its own corduroy roads at the rate of a dozen miles a day and more, and bringing its artillery and wagons with it, I made up my mind that there had been no such army in existence since the days of Julius Caesar." (Lloyd Lewis, *Sherman, Fighting Prophet*, pages 490-491)

7. General Oliver Otis Howard was a deeply religious man. He had been a Sunday School teacher while at West Point, and one of his students was Willie Hardee, the son of Confederate General Hardee. (Lloyd Lewis, *Sherman, Fighting Prophet*, pages 516; Official Records)

A Set of Horned Barbarians from the Backwoods

Headquarters of Company B, 25th Iowa Infantry
McPhersonville, South Carolina,
January 31, 1865

My Dear Wife,

I am very glad that we don't have to march today so I have a chance to write you a long letter. In the first place, I am quite well, with the exception of a bad cold that I caught last night. I am so hoarse that I can hardly speak today. When we came here yesterday, our mess took possession of an old Negro cabin with two rooms and a fireplace. I might have known it would make me sick; if I had lain out on the ground I wouldn't have had a cold. I shall be more careful how I sleep in houses hereafter. In the next place we got mail on Sunday (day before yesterday) and I got a letter from you, dear, the first I had for three weeks. It was dated January 12th. The last one I got before was dated December 22nd and if you wrote any between these dates they have not come yet. We got several mails and lots of letter for everybody but me. I was very much disappointed every time that I had to go without a letter from you, my dear good wife. But when it did come and you scolded me for not writing oftener, I felt worse than ever! Now there, my sweet dear, if I could get you in my arms, I would kiss you till you couldn't pout a bit! Won't you take the will for the deed and give me one of your sweet smiles? Why, I have written three letters to you and one to the children without getting any answer. I would have written again several days ago, but I had a boil on my right hand and could not write for a week. I was very anxious that you should hear from me.

So last Sunday morning I went over to brigade headquarters and told Crane to tell his folks to tell you that I was well, but had a sore hand, so I could not write, and that you must not be uneasy because you didn't get a letter! And that puts me in mind of what you said about them always getting the most letters and the latest news. Wasn't that provoking? They will have the latest news again! I had a mind, after I got your letter, to go over and tell him to say nothing about me! And then, my dear, ain't it strange that I should have often thought just the same as you do. When I don't get a letter Crane is sure to, and if I get one, he gets one a week later! For instance, a few days after I got yours of the 22nd of December, he got one of January 10th, and then kept on getting letters almost every mail, sometimes two or three at a time, and when I got yours of the 12th he got one of the 16th, and we got another small mail last night and he got one of the 17th! But I know that he has half a dozen brothers and sisters besides other "sisters" to write to him, and I have no one but just you. And I don't expect to get as many letters as he does. And then one of your letters is worth a bushel of his. I wouldn't give one of them for all he ever got. He has a great deal more time to write than I have; in fact I can't see that he has anything to do; if he has, he doesn't do it. He has a tent hauled along for his use, and a horse to ride, and an "orderly" to ride after him wherever he goes and to hold his horse when he gets off, to bring him when he wants to ride, and to wait on and take care of him generally. As he never does anything, I think they must keep him at brigade headquarters for an ornament. Indeed he is generally known by the appellation of the "the ornamental part of the brigade staff"! I said he did not do anything. But when we arc in camp he reads novels and plays cards day and night—this is the sober truth, but I hope you won't tell anyone I said so. But being at brigade headquarters and having plenty of time to ride around, he frequently finds a chance to send a letter home by an officer or man that is mustered out, or by some messenger or dispatch that I know nothing about. I can only put my letters in the mailbag at regiment headquarters and so on to the mail steamer. If I had a horse and could get a pass and take them to department headquarters myself, I have no doubt they might get north a week earlier sometimes.

There has been a great deal of irregularity about the mail since we came here, more than we ever had in the west, but we don't blame the folks at home. They don't even send papers for sale.

If the Chicago papers had the opportunity that the New Yorkers have, they would have this army flooded with papers. But the eastern folks think we are a set of horned barbarians from the backwoods that can't read and have no use for papers or letters! But never mind, we expect to do something yet on this campaign to show them that we know how to put down a rebellion.

I knew you would be looking for me home. I am very sorry you were disappointed, my own dear. I do hope I will get to go yet. I am so anxious to see you again, I don't see how I can wait till my time is out. But perhaps I will have to. But I do hope that you won't think that I have forgotten you, or that I love you less, or that I neglect to write to you whenever I can. My own dear darling! I would not do or say anything for the world, that could give you a moments pain or uneasiness. I think of you more and love you more dearly than ever. And I do hope it will not be long till I again return to your arms and spend the rest of my days with you and our children.

I was glad to hear that you had been taking medicine for that cold. You must keep on till it is entirely well. I am glad to hear that you are not forgotten by our old neighbors. I hope you will have a good time eating fine dinners. Give them all my best respects and tell them that next winter I will be there to go with you. Do they ever "say anything about me?" I suppose that Mrs. Rhodes and the Mrs. Coles and all the rest of them think they are having quite a fine time with their husbands at home with them all the time! But don't you think they would be just as proud after all, if they had a husband who was a captain in Sherman's Army? It will all come right some day.

It must have been a mistake in the *Hawkeye* about 200 officers going home on "furlough" from the army. I don't think any went but those whose time was out, and they were mustered out. General Osterhaus and his staff went, and perhaps a few others who made out that they had very urgent business, but that is all. Now I know you are getting impatient to hear something about what we are doing, and where we are.

Well, when I last wrote to you, on January 22nd, we were at Beaufort, expecting to start on a campaign. But it rained incessantly for four days and nights, most of the time with a high wind. We had to lie on the ground, our blankets all wet, the wood would smoke but wouldn't burn. I never saw such a storm, and this regiment never had a more disagreeable time. The bottom fell out of the road, and nearly the whole country was under water. The 20th and 14th Army Corps and the 3rd and 4th Divisions of our corps, which had started across by land from Savannah, got swamped, and most of them had to go back and either come round by water or wait for the weather. But it cleared up at last, and has been very cold and wintry, windy since till today, it is quite pleasant. We left our camp 3 miles from Beaufort on the 27th and marched out to Garden's Corner, 10 miles. We crossed Coosaw River on a pontoon bridge. The roads were through ponds and rice swamps till yesterday, and then marched out to Ft. Pocotaligo, 6 miles, then across the railroad two miles from the fort, and then to McPhersonville, 4 miles northwest of the railroad, where we now are.

This is a one-horse town about the size of Trenton, built right in a pine forest—no farms or fields in sight, just the natural forest as far as you can see, yet there are a few fine houses, two nice churches, &c. The inhabitants are all gone but one poor old Negro who was of no account, so they left him to shift for himself. But we are in the enemy's country once more and are glad of it. We are allowed to "appropriate" what we find to our own use.

So as I said before, our mess took possession of a deserted Negro cabin, and proceeded to make ourselves comfortable. I wanted to put on a little "style" while I could, and sat down by a window in a draft and read a while, and caught a bad cold. I see Company B from where I am sitting now. They are putting on style too—they have a load of fine cane-bottom chairs and a mahogany table, &c and are reading books and papers and rebel letters which they found here. We don't want anything better for a trough to feed our pack mule in than the drawer of a rosewood bureau! Well, we didn't come all the way here for nothing! We will leave our mark.

While we were at Beaufort the 30th Ohio had to pay $800 for a meeting house they tore down for wood, and the 6th Iowa was charged $150 for a shanty they took for boards to sleep on, and everybody had to pay for all the mischief he did, which made it very annoying to old soldiers. This army doesn't know how to soldier in such a place. We all breathe easier and feel better now that we have got started on another raid! I can't tell you where we are going now, nor how long it will take us to get there, for I don't know anything about it. From what I can see, my own opinion is that we are not going to Charleston, at least not now. The 17th Army Corps is just in front of us. I don't know where the rest of the army is. We are not going to have as nice a time as we had on the other march. The weather is too cold. We have a heavy white frost every night for a week and the ground, frozen solid, does not thaw out during the day. I had no idea it got so cold down here. Just think of sleeping out on the frozen ground all winter! We got an order before we started that no tents would be allowed on the march, so we had to throw away our tent poles and rip the tents open behind so as to make flies of them—a very poor thing for winter, but better than nothing. The men are all in good health and spirits.

William Mason was left in hospital at Beaufort. He was not very unwell, but not able for a hard march. I don't know much about the enemy in our front. I have heard a few cannon shots since I have been writing—I don't think they have much force. I am afraid I will not have a chance to send this letter back now. I shall be very sorry if I can't . . . Give my love to the children and Ma, Car, Annie, Sally, Billy, and all my friends.

Your own, Jake (kiss)

Whenever you get this letter I want you to go up to Leisenring's[1] and see if they had the negative yet of the photograph they took for me last winter; if they have, get 2 dozen more taken and send them to me by mail. I want to exchange with the other officers and get theirs to put in an album. Let me know right away if they have got it yet. And God bless and protect you, my dear sweet wife.

We are all anxious to know if our money got home safe. You did not say anything about it, so I suppose it had not got there. But Company A sent theirs at the same time, and it got to Washington, Iowa, on the 10th . . . I hope you will have a good meeting. You must remember me there. Give my best respects to Brother Gunn, Burnett, and all the rest, and tell them to remember me.

1. Leisenring Brothers located their photography studio in Mt. Pleasant on the third floor of the State Bank Building, opposite the Brazelton House.

Camp 25th Iowa Infantry
In the Field, South Carolina
February 5, 1865

My Dear Wife,

This is Sunday afternoon. We have got into camp and have our breastwork built. We have our fly stretched up and an armful of corn blades to sleep on . . . After we got our work done I lay down here and thought about you, and wondered what you were doing. Perhaps you are gone to meeting or down to Ma's or someplace else. Maybe you are at home writing to me. Wherever you are may God bless you and take care of you. You are my dear, sweet wife, that I love dearly and think of you constantly. And I can't help thinking every day how far apart we are and how long it has been since I saw you. Sometimes I think it is not right and that I have no business to leave you go off so far and so long. But when I think of the good and great cause I am serving, I feel that it is worth even this sacrifice. But I can't help feeling the bitterest hatred towards the wretches who brought on this war. What comfort and happiness I might have enjoyed at home with you and the children during these three long years, instead of traveling all over creation to force them to respect a government that is intended for a blessing to them. I hardly ever say anything about these things. I can't express my opinion without using hard words.

Well, as I don't know what you are doing this p.m., I will tell you what we are doing, as well as I can. I wrote you a letter at McPhersonville on the 31st of January. We marched from there the next morning and have traveled about northwest. I suppose we will strike the Charleston and Augusta railroad about 20 miles west of Branchville. We have come slowly. We are about 60 miles from Beaufort, and 10 miles from the railroad. The country is very flat and swampy—nothing but swamps. I never saw such a place. We had to corduroy the road nearly all the way, which is the main reason we have made no better speed. But we have found the enemy in front of us all the way. We have more or less been skirmishing every day, and every day they fire at our foragers and flankers, and cut trees across the road. We have had no regular battle, but have lost some men every day—I mean our division. The 25th has lost only one so far, and he was captured, of Company D[1]. They annoy us a great deal more than they did in Georgia. But our cavalry is not here yet. They are with the other wing to the left, but will join us at the railroad. The 17th Army Corps is 8 or 10 miles to our right.

Yesterday our division had to advance and we reached the Salkehatchie River at noon. General Sherman expected a hard fight there, and that it would take at least four days to force a passage, at what is called Beaufort Bridge. There is a swamp a mile wide on the south side of the river and the rebels had a fort and a long line of works on this side. It would have been a very ugly place to take. They could rake the wood through the swamp with their cannon, and the river is not like any civilized river, but just a great flood of water running around loose through the woods, without any banks. But the enemy was good enough to evacuate without firing a gun, but destroyed the bridge. So we went to work to get over. We tore down barns, houses, and churches for lumber and got across by building 22 bridges and making a plank or corduroy road between them across the swamp. The 25th worked from 3 o'clock till after dark. This morning at daylight we moved out here, five miles, where I suppose we will wait till the whole army closes up and gets over. Our advance drove the rebels back this morning, but it is supposed to be only Wheeler's Cavalry[2].

I am in good health and spirits; so are all the men. They are all quite well and hearty. The commissary only issues half rations, but we get plenty to eat. We find lots of meat and chickens and yams, honey, &c. Our mess got a keg of kraut today. We have men detailed purposely to forage; they go to the houses, demand the keys to the smokehouse, and go in, take everything there is. We find bushels of peanuts every day. I don't know when I will have a chance to send this letter, but I will have it ready if there should be one. We have no communication now, and may not have for some time. I am afraid it will get rubbed up so you can't read it.

Tell the children I send my love to them all. Give my love to Ma and all the rest.

Your own Jake

The weather was quite cold and the ground frozen the first part of last week, but the last two or three days have been very warm and pleasant, like summer. I hope our winter is over.

1. Oscar Stout, Eighth Corporal of Company D, a resident of Burlington, was taken prisoner February 3, 1865, at Hickory Hill, South Carolina. Previously Stout had been wounded near Atlanta and had a finger amputated. He survived the war.

2. Joseph Wheeler had commanded the cavalry of the Army of Tennessee since October 13, 1862, and was at the time of this letter the ranking general of the Confederate cavalry at age 28. Cavalryman Wade Hampton was promoted to Lieutenant General on February 16, 1865, and on that date Wheeler and his cavalry reported to Hampton.

• Sherman was successful in confusing the Confederate generals as to his intended target. They had suspected that Sherman would attack either Charleston or Augusta, and had planned and positioned their troops accordingly. Sherman's real target was Columbia, the capital of South Carolina.

Little Congaree Creek Near Columbia, South Carolina
Historical Sketch—25th Iowa Infantry

[Report from Colonel Stone] On the 27th day of January, we broke up camp and resumed the march. During the campaign this brigade has had four engagements with the enemy; first at Little Congaree Creek, near Columbia, South Carolina, on the 15th day of February, 1865. The Second Brigade had the advance that day, and commenced

skirmishing with the enemy within two miles of the camp we [3rd Brigade, 1st Division] had left that morning. They drove the enemy without further assistance until, near Little Congaree Creek, when, from the nature of the ground, the enemy was enabled to make a stubborn resistance. Here my brigade was ordered up, and went into position on the left of the Second Brigade . . . The whole division now crossed and formed a line of battle on a plateau about a mile from the creek. I again went into position on the left. Some rebel cavalry skirmishers threatening my front, I moved on them with four companies of the Twenty-Fifth Iowa, and we soon drove them back to their main line. (Roster and Record of Iowa Soldiers in the War of the Rebellion; *Published under the authority of the Iowa General Assembly*)

On the night of February 15, Wood's Division of the 15th Army Corps, which included Jacob, carelessly camped within range of Confederate artillery, based on the east side of the Congaree River. Their evening campfires gave away their location, and during the night the Confederates bombarded the Union camp, resulting in one death and several wounded. This enraged Sherman, who contemplated the destruction of Columbia in retaliation, but officially let stand Special Field Order No. 26 that said to spare the libraries, asylums and private dwellings of Columbia. (*Marion Lucas,* Sherman and the Burning of Columbia, *pages 47-50*)

Columbia, South Carolina

Sherman and Logan ordered Colonel Stone and his brigade of Iowa regiments forward to accept the surrender of Columbia. This occurred, but not without problems.

Historical Sketch—25th Iowa Infantry

[Report from Colonel Stone] My next engagement with the enemy was at the city of Columbia, captured by my command on the 17th day of February, [1865] an official account of which, with the casualties, and the number of prisoners, was made to you, under date of the 19th of February . . .

Everything being now in readiness, the signal was given, and the assault made by all the regiments at the same time. The result proved no mistake either in planning or the execution. Before the enemy was hardly aware of it, we were right into the skirmish pits and scattering them in every direction. The Thirtieth Iowa here captured 23 prisoners. I accompanied this regiment in the charge, and can by personal observation testify to the gallant manner in which they made it. In front of the Island are a number of small bayous running parallel to the river about 20 feet wide and waist deep; few stopped to find logs on which to cross, but plunged in, holding guns and cartridge boxes above the water. The enemy seeing his skirmish line destroyed, and the eagerness with which our success was being followed up, became confused and soon broke, leaving our way open to the city . . .

When within a mile of the city, a carriage was discovered approaching, flying a flag of truce. It proved to contain Mr. Goodwyn, Mayor of Columbia, and the city aldermen, who came to offer terms of capitulation. I refused anything but an unconditional surrender. After some words had passed, they unconditionally surrendered to me the city of Columbia . . . When near the suburbs of the city I noticed some of the advanced skirmishers, say fifteen in number, being driven back by apparently a battalion of rebel cavalry. I at once called a corporal and three men, who happened to be near me, and put the mayor and aldermen in the corporal's charge, and with Major Anderson took about forty of my flankers and advanced on the cavalry. The corporal was instructed that in case one man was killed or wounded he should at once shoot the mayor and his party. Joining the retreating skirmishers with the forty flankers we speedily dispersed the rebel cavalry, having no more trouble in gaining the city.

Proceeding to the State House with Captain Pratt, I planted the first United States flag on that building. To Iowa alone is credit to be given for capturing the capital of the State that has been disloyal since the days of John C. Calhoun, and the contemplated Capital of the Confederacy, as none but Iowa troops were engaged.

I was absent from the brigade about an hour in placing the flag on the state-house, and when I rejoined my command found a great number of the men drunk[1]. It was discovered that this was caused by hundreds of Negroes who swarmed the streets on the approach of the troops and gave them all kinds of liquors from buckets, bottles, demijohns, etc. The men had slept none the night before, and but little the night before that, and many of them had no supper the night before, and none of them breakfast that morning, hence the speedy effect of the liquor. I forthwith ordered all the liquor destroyed, and saw fifteen barrels destroyed within five minutes after that order had been given. (Roster and Record of Iowa Soldiers in the War of the Rebellion; *Published under the authority of the Iowa General Assembly)*

1. As described by Colonel Stone, most of the men of his brigade soon became drunk. Jacob did not drink alcohol, so he would have been one of the few sober Union soldiers of this first brigade that entered Columbia. A short while later, Stone's brigade was escorted out of the city and other troops were put in control of the city. This was a necessary and unfortunate break in tradition of the Union Army that held that the first troops to enter a city were given the honor of being in charge of it.

- As the Confederates evacuated Columbia, they brought large quantities of cotton that had been stored in warehouses out to the streets, with the intention of taking it out of the city and destroying it; but because the Union Army appeared sooner than expected, they only removed the cotton to the streets before fleeing. Some claimed that the Confederates set fire to the cotton as they retreated from Columbia to prevent it from falling into Federal hands, as had happened on many other occasions. Other reports stated that Union troops set the cotton on fire, with only minimal efforts made by Union officers to stop that devastation. Nature added to the destruction and pushed it passed the point of control. High winds blew the cotton across the city to such an extent that many of the Union men commented that it appeared as if they were in the midst of a snowstorm. Unfortunately, it was burning cotton that filled the skies, spreading fire to trees, houses, and other buildings. The proper blame of who started the fires remains unresolved today, and Jacob's letters do not solve, nor add to, this historical dispute.

[Fragment of Jacob's Letter—Evidently soon after the capture and burning of Columbia, South Carolina, on February 17, 1865]

I have no sympathy for rebels any place, especially in South Carolina. But no man, even if he had a heart of stone, could stand by and see women and children in such distress and not help them. I thought what if you and our children were in such a situation, how thankful I should be to anyone who would help you. It is supposed that the city was fired by escaped prisoners, as they were heard to threaten all sorts of vengeance against the city. I hope that whoever did it will be arrested and hung.

One of the beauties of the "peculiar institution" was brought prominently to my notice that night, and that was that the white folks were more afraid of their own Negroes than they were of our soldiers. They did not dare to go into the street without a guard. "Why" they said, "the niggers will kill us" and were dreading what the negroes would do after we left. But there are a thousand things I will have to tell you about when I get home—it would take too long to write them. A great many citizens and negroes, men, women, and children, are trying to follow us through, and are having a miserable time in the mud and rain. General Woods had our train searched today and found over 3,000 lbs. of tobacco and other kinds of plunder brought from Columbia.

We left there on the 20th and on the 24th we crossed the

Wateree River at Peas Ferry, about 40 miles north of Columbia. The next day I was sent out with a forage party of 17 men. It rained all day and was so cloudy and dark that I got lost. I went to a place called Flat Rock Post Office, and there captured a company of 60 states militia[1]. They were just on the way to Camden to be armed and equipped. I found I could not get to camp that night[2]. So I took possession of a Baptist Church and camped on my own hook. It was very risky business, as we were five miles from the nearest regular camp, but we were not interrupted. I found the brigade the next day about noon, and turned my prisoners over to Colonel Stone. They are mostly old, gray-headed soldiers.

I have just been notified that John Pratt, one of my men, who was acting as orderly at division headquarters, was taken prisoner day before yesterday. He is the first man I ever had captured. They took three others of the regiment at the same time[3].

But I must stop for today . . . I have dreamed about you several times lately. I dreamed the other night that I had you in my arms and was kissing you. I thought you were just as pretty and sweet as ever, but that you looked pale and thin, like you had been sick for a long time. I hope you have taken medicine and got over that bad cough. Give my love to the children and Ma, and all the folks.

Your own, Jake

1. To help with the defenses of South Carolina, Governor A. G. Magrath called for all men, including boys and old men to report for military service. Magrath also threatened to arrest any member of the 23rd South Carolina Militia that failed to report for duty on February 26. This produced an anonymous letter to the colonel of the state militia stating "No tyrant has ever dared to issue such an infernal order as that of Lawyer A. G. Magrath. It will be a perpetual disgrace to Carolina that 'she' forced old men for the hardships of wars . . and children 16 years of age to be butchered in opposing strong and well-disciplined Veteran troops under command of such an experienced General Sherman, and for what? To save the life of a few aristocrats, who deserve to be hung? We did not expect such a man as you in whom we have had perfect confidence, that you would be a shameful tool to tyrannical rulers. All we have to say is that if you execute that order, know that a bullet is prepared for you and your house will be razed to the ground." (John B. Barrett, *Sherman's March Through The Carolinas*, page 65; Taylor Papers, South Carolina Library, University of South Carolina)

2. Many of the Union fatalities on foraging parties occurred when

the foragers strayed too far beyond the body of their army, just as Jacob did.

3. John Pratt of Mount Pleasant was taken prisoner February 24, 1865, near Camden, South Carolina. He was returned to Company B on April 9, 1865. Others captured included Sergeant Hiram Dunn, who survived the war.

• The religious General O.O. Howard, tiring of life with men in the field, issued the following order:

GENERAL FIELD ORDERS No. 12.
HEADQUARTERS DEPARTMENT
AND ARMY OF THE TENNESSEE,
Cheraw, S. C., March 5, 1865.

The attention of officers and soldiers of this army is called to the gross and criminal practice of profane swearing which prevails and is increasing amongst us, so much so that every sense of good principle and good taste is outraged. Have we forgotten that God is our kin Father and that He is helping us? Every insult to Him is a scourge to ourselves and invites disaster to our noble cause.

• The Confederates soon began to construct an army to block Sherman. The most dramatic addition to their forces was the re-entrance of General Joseph E. Johnston, who President Davis had removed from command of the Army of Tennessee during the Atlanta campaign.

• On January 23, 1865, Jefferson Davis appointed Robert E. Lee Commander-in-Chief of all Confederate armies. In this role, Lee sent a telegram on February 22 to Johnston instructing him that he was to command the Army of Tennessee and all troops in the Department of South Carolina, Georgia, and Florida. At first Johnston hesitated, thinking that the role given to him was only for him to orchestrate the surrender of the Confederate troops, but acquiesced after discussions with General Beauregard, who became his second in command. Others in Johnston's command included Generals Braxton Bragg, Hardee, Hampton, and Wheeler. Sherman learned of Johnston's appointment on March 1. (Mark Bradley, *Last Stand in the Carolinas: The Battle of Bentonville*, pages 25-31, 39; Stewart Sifakis, *Who Was Who In The Confederacy*, page 168; Jacob Cox, *Sherman's March to the Sea*, pages 181-182)

• The 15th Army Corps crossed the Pee Dee River on March 6

and then the Lumber River on March 9 in the middle of a blind-
ing rainstorm. (Mark Bradley, *The Battle of Bentonville*, pages
67, 78-80)

Fayetteville, North Carolina
March 14, 1865

My Dear Wife,
    I wrote you a few lines yesterday. We were notified that "mail
would be received for half an hour," and we all went to scribbling
in good earnest—I suppose there never were so many letters written
in the same time before! It is now 8 o'clock p.m. and we have just
been notified that mail will be received till half past ten! So here
goes to write another letter[1]. We have got no mail yet, but a boat
came up this evening and brought some northern papers—some as
late as March 6th. I have not had time to read them much yet. But
it seems like getting into a civilized country again, to be where we
can see a New York paper. You have no idea how lonesome and lost
one feels to be a month or six weeks in these woods and swamps,
without hearing anything from America! We expect to get a mail
yet, before we leave here. I do hope we will. We are not going to
stop here—nor any place else till this rebellion is put down.
    We are to draw ten days' rations here, and then "strike for tall
timber," but where that is we don't know—probably either
Goldsborough or Raleigh. I don't wonder at the rebels being
bewildered by Sherman's movements—for we never know ourselves where we are going till we get there—and then we start
right away for some place else. Cape Fear River here, and the 20th
and 17th Army Corps are over, and our corps is crossing today. We
left camp at noon today, and are now lying in the town waiting for
the 3rd Division to get over. We will probably cross about midnight.
    I am quite well and hearty—so are all the men. The health and
spirits of the army never was better. It is wonderful what men can
stand when they get used to it. I believe that we can go any place
or do anything we please. We wade swamps and creeks waist deep,
march through mud and rain, day and night, sleep out on the wet
ground with clothes and blankets wet through and through, eat
nothing but "slap-jacks" and meat—yet no one gets sick or discouraged[2].
    If I had time I would like to tell you about the time we had on

Lumber River. It rained three days and nights and the road became awful. The first day we were in rear of the train and worked till midnight and couldn't get it to camp. General Woods would not let us come in without the train, so we lay out along the road. The next day we had charge of 31 wagons loaded with ammunition and got it to camp at 2 o'clock at night, and started at 4 the same morning and got to camp at 10 o'clock, &c. Our route all the way from Savannah has been right across the streams; we have from one to six of them to cross every day.

But the great satisfaction is that we are cleaning out the Southern Confederacy. I don't think it can last much longer. But I have given up all hopes of getting a "leave of absence" till the war is over or my time is out. I would go home yet if I had a chance. But I don't think we will stop long enough till the thing is over.

But Oh! the horrors of war! You can have no idea of the desolation and suffering caused by the invasion of a hostile army; words cannot describe it—it must be seen to be realized. We have had about three mounted foragers from each company. They go sometimes 25 miles and destroy a great many things that are of no use to them. They go into the houses and search every nook and corner, up stairs and down, for meal and meat. Hundreds of families are left without a mouthful of anything to eat—not even a chicken or pig, cow, or anything. I suppose we have not less than 15,000 head of cattle now that have been gathered up in the country, and none of them are fit to eat. As fast as they give out or stick fast they are shot and left lying. Every few days the

There the bugle sounds the assembly and I must go—

March 15

– I did not get to finish this last night. We crossed over sooner than was expected. We are now on the north side of the river[3], two miles from the bridge. I don't think we will move today and I will get to send this away yet.

I was about to say, when I had to stop, that every few days the army has to be cleaned up of extra mules and horses; if this was not done the whole thing would soon be mounted. Then we have to cross a pontoon, guards are placed at the end to prevent more than the proper number of animals from going over. We are allowed 13 pack animals to the regiment; the rest are turned into a corral; those that are of any account are put in the train and the rest shot. They are shooting hundreds of them here that might be of some use to the people, if they were left.

We burned a large cotton factory[4] at Saluda River near Columbia, and another at Little Rock Fish near this place. Also a large paper mill and several smaller factories. They had a large arsenal here which has been burned. Indeed we have done an immense amount of damage, and caused a great deal of suffering and misery. But they began the war and should not complain at the natural and inevitable consequences.

But God forbid that our country should ever be invaded by a hostile army. I candidly believe that if Lee has as good an army as Sherman has, and knows as well how to use it and manage it, that he could march from Pennsylvania to Iowa unless he could be confronted with a large part of the army now in the field. Citizens and militia can do nothing against such an army. We laugh at them and their futile attempts to stop us. And after what I have seen here I believe it would be the same to a great extent in the north. The peace and security of our homes depends on the army in the field.

Our foragers came in last night. They have been out 8 miles towards Goldsborough and 15 towards Wilmington. They had a fight with the rebels but drove them back and came in loaded with forage. Our mess got 3 gallons of honey and lots of meat and meal. The rebels capture a good many of our foragers and sometimes shoot them after they surrender, but they are perfectly reckless and ride over the country as if they were at home. They get a great deal of meal by taking possession of mills and grinding corn for themselves.

We have just been notified that five days' rations are to be issued today, and that the supply train will then start to Wilmington to reload and join us at Goldsborough, which is on the Neuce River[5] 60 miles from here.

All our contrabands (about 10,000) are to go to Wilmington with the train. I never felt as much pity for any one as I have for those poor Negroes. They are nearly all bare footed and almost naked. A great many small children. They suffered terribly before they got here, but bore it all without a murmur. I am afraid many of them will be sadly disappointed when they come to realize the liberty they have been so anxious to obtain. I do hope the people of the north will endeavor to supply their wants. There are also a great many white refugees from Columbia and other places, and a great many escaped prisoners that we have picked up along the way, who are going to Wilmington and from there north.

And this reminds me that Dr. Charley Marsh has two female refugees along with our regiment ever since we left Columbia— has hauled them in the regimental ambulance and the sick men had to walk. One of them was the "kept mistress" of a fancy man at Columbia who got her in the family way and then turned her off. She had a baby in the ambulance about two weeks ago, and is there with it yet. She calls it "Iowa." The other is said to be a public prostitute. It is the most disgraceful thing I ever knew of. I never spoke to either of them, and would not if they were here a year. I would not be as big a fool as Marsh for a thousand dollars a day, and have told him so. But I won't say anything more about him now. There are some folks at home who ought to know how he carries on. But I don't want them to hear it first from me.

But I must stop for this time . . . Give my love to the children and tell them I love them all and have not forgotten them. Give my love to Ma, Car, Billy, Annie, and all the rest, and tell me all about them when you write.

Your own Jake

I don't know whether you can read this scribbling or not. It has been so long since I wrote any that I have almost forgotten how. Then I have to sit flat on the ground and write on my knee.

Jake

1. During this part of the march, the men in Sherman's army were not able to send nor receive letters, but for this exception at Fayetteville, North Carolina, when every soldier had the opportunity to send one letter. (Joseph T. Glatthaar, *The March to the Sea and Beyond*, page 87)

2. On an average day during the March to the Sea, less than 2 percent of Sherman's men were unfit for duty because of sickness. During the Carolinas campaign, the number averaged slightly higher than 2 percent. This was 46% fewer illnesses per 1,000 men compared to other Union campaigns. (Joseph T. Glatthaar, *The March to the Sea and Beyond*, pages 19-20)

3. Jacob is referring to the Cape Fear River, which is just north and east of Fayetteville.

4. When Union troops arrived at this cotton factory on the Saluda River near Columbia, there were still women in the factory tearing cotton cloth from the looms to take to their homes. As the Union engineers rebuilt the bridge crossing the Saluda, Union sharpshooters placed themselves in the factory to oust the remaining Confederate skirmishers in the brush who were firing

at the Union engineers. When the Union forces crossed the bridge, the Confederates quickly fell back. (Lucas, *Sherman and the Burning of Columbia*, page 73)

5. As Sherman was in Savannah gathering his last supplies before his march through the Carolinas, he and Grant had planned for General Schofield and his army to gather at the Neuse River in North Carolina with supplies at New Berne, a town on that river. Schofield was then to march to Goldsborough with those supplies and meet Sherman. (Lloyd Lewis, *Sherman, Fighting Prophet*, page 173)

• The Brevet rank of Brigadier General United States Volunteers was conferred upon Colonel George A. Stone, Twenty-Fifth Iowa Infantry, on March 13, 1865. (Report of Adjutant General of Iowa, 1867, Vol. 1, page 159)

The Battle of Bentonville

As the Federals pressed northward, Sherman spread his four corps so that they could obtain enough forage to sustain themselves before their final rendezvous with Schofield and the 23rd Army Corps, who were to meet them with supplies. Slocum's two corps, the 14th and the 20th, were about a day's march apart from each other, and about the same distance from Howard's wing. This allowed the Confederates to strike against a smaller, divided portion of Sherman's army. Johnston ordered all his troops to be concentrated at Bentonville on March 18.

On the 19th of March, the Confederates began their attack against portions of the 14th Army Corps, with the battle continuing all day.

Early in the morning of March 20, Sherman directed one division of Logan's 15th Army Corps to provide assistance to Slocum. The other divisions of Logan's Corps, including Jacob, were near Falling Creek Church, about three miles from Cox's Bridge. (Jacob Cox, Sherman's March to the Sea, *page 186-194)*

Historical Sketch—25th Iowa Infantry

[Brevet Brigadier General Stone's report] I did not meet the enemy again in any force till the 20th instant, [March 20, 1865] on our march that day from our camp near Cox's Bridge on the Neuse River toward Bentonville. The Second Brigade, Colonel Catterson, had the advance that day, and skirmished freely with the enemy, driving him easily until we had arrived within about three miles of Bentonville.

The enemy here became stubborn, and threatened an attack on the

Second Brigade. I was ordered up and went into position on Colonel Catterson's left. We now advanced our line of battle of two brigades about half a mile, and put up works about 3 o'clock p.m.

Major General Logan, commanding the corps and Brevet Major General [Charles] Woods, commanding the division, directed me to take three regiments, and, if possible, clear the road in our front, and open communication with the Fourteenth Corps, now fighting apparently about a mile from us on our left front.

I placed the Twenty-Fifth Iowa Lieutenant Colonel Palmer commanding, (which regiment I had ordered out about an hour before as skirmishers) to take the advance, and directed the Thirtieth Iowa, Lieutenant Colonel Roberts commanding, and the Thirty-first Iowa, Lieutenant Colonel Jenkins commanding, to follow as a reserve. The Twenty-Fifth Iowa was deployed as skirmishers, with their colors in the road I was going to clear, and my first movement with the regiment was to change direction to the right. This movement was made steadily until about three-fourths of the regiment had crossed the road, when our proximity to the rebels on my left and in the road caused very severe skirmishing.

Two regiments of the Second Division now came up on my left rear, (I think the Sixth Missouri and Thirtieth Ohio) one of them, the Sixth Missouri, deployed as skirmishers. I made arrangements with the officer commanding the last mentioned regiment to join the two regiments with mine, and, at a given signal, the Twenty-Fifth Iowa and Sixth Missouri should make a charge. The charge proved entirely successful, although at a severe loss in the Twenty-Fifth Iowa. We drove the enemy's skirmishers, composed of Hoke's Division from the Virginia army, back to their works across the swamp clearing the road, and opening communication with the Fourteenth Corps.

The officers and men of the Twenty-Fifth Iowa behaved handsomely and fought desperately. Lieutenant Colonel Palmer, commanding the regiment, and Captain Allen, acting Major, (who lost his right leg in the engagement) deserve notice for exposing themselves freely, and for the gallant manner in which they cheered their men forward. At night I retired to a new line, and my place was occupied by other troops . . .

On the 21st instant [March 21, 1865] I had orders to erect a new line of works on the skirmish line, and at 10 o'clock p.m. I moved three regiments to the front line, the Fourth Iowa on the right, connecting on the left of the First Brigade, Brevet Brigadier General [William] Woods—commanding—the Thirtieth Iowa in the center—and the Ninth Iowa on the left. The Twenty-Fifth Iowa and Thirty-First Iowa were in the rear, held in reserve.

We put up a temporary line of works under fire of the enemy, and at 2 o'clock I received orders to charge the enemy's skirmish line, 150 yards in my front, in good skirmish pits. We captured the pits with but slight loss, but the enemy evinced so much determination to regain them that the fighting became very sharp. The enemy's main line of battle, behind good works, was by actual measurement but 100 yards from these skirmish pits, and he fired from the works by volley. At three different times they followed up the fire by volley by an assault on my skirmishers. Their men swarmed over the works and charged gallantly, but I had reinforced the line until I had nearly a line of battle, and our incessant firing prevented him from charging as a perfect organization, and every charge was repulsed.

The order came to me so positively, from Generals Howard and Logan, to hold the ground I had already gained, that I should have done so, or ruined the brigade.

At night I relieved the skirmishers' line with the Thirty-first Iowa, Lieutenant Colonel Jenkins commanding. Colonel Jenkins managed the new line admirably. It rained a good deal during the night, but his men worked faithfully, and he put up quite a strong line of works so near the enemy that the conversation had to be carried on in whispers . . .

The loss in the skirmish line was quite severe. I sent you an official list of casualties the same night, and of the prisoners captured.

* * * * *

On the morning of the 22nd, [March 22, 1865] half an hour before day, I rode out to the advanced post, and ordered a patrol forward to feel of the enemy but it was discovered that he had left during the night. I at once sent word to the General commanding division, and, with a detachment of the Thirty-first Iowa, followed him. Everything indicated a precipitate retreat; a few stragglers were picked up; some of their dead and wounded were found near the roadside uncared for, and quite a number of small arms haversacks and clothing were found scattered in their deserted camp.

Just at sunrise I ran onto their rear guard, composed of cavalry, and my detachment being too small to fight it, I covered the road with a few men to make an effect, and ordered some ten or fifteen men as skirmishers to annoy the enemy until a regiment, the Thirty-first Iowa, which I had just ordered up, should arrive. Very soon after this our entire division moved to Bentonville, where we remained during the day and, at sundown we returned to the camp we had left in the morning. The graves of 17 rebel officers in my front indicate that the enemy suffered severely in killed and wounded. (Roster and Record of Iowa Soldiers in the War of the Rebellion; *Published under the authority of the Iowa General Assembly)*

- The Union losses at the Battle of Bentonville were 1,604. 1,196 of these were in Slocum's Left Wing. Reported Confederate losses vary, but were probably closer to 3,000. (Jacob Cox, *Sherman's March to the Sea*, page 196)

Occupation of Goldsboro

Historical Sketch—25th Iowa Infantry

[Report from Brevet Brigadier General Stone] On our march to Goldsboro, on the 23rd inst. [March 23, 1865], I had the good fortune to have the post of honor—rear guard for the "Army of the Tennessee." The rear of my command fell upon the Twenty-Fifth Iowa.

On the 24th inst., I was ordered to remain at the pontoon bridge over the Neuse River, near Goldsboro, to cover the crossing of our corps train, and, on the 26th inst. I rejoined the division in camp near Goldsboro.

Brevet Brigadier General Stone's Thanks

Historical Sketch—25th Iowa Infantry

[Report from Brevet Brigadier General Stone] During the campaign just closed, this brigade has been in four engagements with the following loss: Killed, 7; wounded, 64; missing, 12. We have captured, and turned over to the provost marshal, 145 prisoners of war. In taking Columbia, S. C., we captured 43 pieces of artillery, about 6,000 stand of arms, immense quantities of ammunition and ordnance stores, and released 40 officers confined there. We have marched 485 miles, built 16,037 yards of corduroy roads, and destroyed 3 miles of railroad. The brigade is in excellent health and spirits, but very ragged. My thanks are due to all my staff officers, Captain John N. Bell, Twenty-Fifth Iowa A. A. Q. General; Lieutenant Samuel W. Snow, Twenty-Fifth Iowa, A. A. A. General; Captain A. Bowman, Ninth Iowa; Lieutenant Baron H. Crane, Twenty-Fifth Iowa; Lieutenant D. Rorick, Thirty-first Iowa—now in the hands of the enemy—and J. W. Gilman, Thirty-first Iowa, A. A. Q. M., for the zeal and earnestness with which they have discharged their whole duty in the campaign just ended."

As will be seen from Colonel Stone's report, his regiment and brigade took a most conspicuous part in the battle of Bentonville, which was the last general engagement of the closing campaign of the war. The Iowa regiments composing his brigade had been assigned to the duty of holding a position of vital importance in that battle, and, under the immediate orders and direction of two of the most distinguished officers of the Union Army, they nobly performed their duty and upheld the honor and credit of their State, whose soldiers had won distinction in all the hardest fought battles of the war. (Roster and Record of Iowa Soldiers in the War of the Rebellion; *Published under the authority of the Iowa General Assembly)*

Editor's Notes:

On March 25, Sherman left Goldsboro for a meeting with Grant at City Point, where they spoke for an hour before going to see Lincoln, who was nearby on the steamer *River Queen*. During this meeting, Lincoln, Grant, and Sherman discussed the terms of surrender to be offered to the Confederates, and Lincoln presented a lenient view, consistent with Sherman's own preference. Lincoln repeatedly stated that he desired to see no more blood shed. They also discussed what should be done with Confederate President Jefferson Davis, with Lincoln stating that Davis ought to "escape the country," implying that little effort should be made to capture him.

Grant also spoke to Sherman about his change of plan regarding Richmond and the Army of Northern Virginia. The Confederate Army was now shrinking from desertions and Grant felt that the Army of the Potomac could defeat Lee without the direct help of Sherman and the Western armies. Grant also expressed political reasons to credit that upcoming victory to the Eastern armies.

Sherman left the *River Queen* at noon on March 28 and never saw Lincoln again. He arrived back at Goldsboro on March 31 with the plan that his armies would begin a march on Johnston starting April 10.

On March 29, Grant began an attack that cut the last of Lee's railroad communications, provoking a counterattack by Lee on March 31 that failed. Sheridan responded with a victorious counterattack against Lee. On April 2, Jefferson Davis, on Lee's advice, fled Richmond, and Grant's army promptly captured Richmond, and pursued the fleeing Lee and the Army of Northern Virginia, forcing Lee to surrender on April 9 at Appomattox Courthouse in Virginia near the North Carolina border.

Sherman joyfully yet cautiously announced Lee's surrender to his men on April 12, but this did not end the war for them, as Johnston and his active army had not surrendered. Several in the Confederacy had vowed to continue the fight, including Jefferson Davis, who was now in Greensboro, North Carolina, with his cabinet.

Others in the Confederacy felt that continuing the struggle was murderous, including the current Governor of North Carolina, Zebulon Vance, and three former governors of North Carolina: David Swain (the current president of the State University at Chapel Hill), William Graham, and Thomas Bragg. Joe Johnston also felt in concert with this group of North Carolina statesmen, particularly since Richmond had been captured. Vance and Johnston met in Raleigh, but then Davis ordered Johnston to meet with him in Greensboro. In Johnston's absence, Swain and Graham met with Hardee, Johnston's second in command, and Hardee gave them a safe conduct order and provided a locomotive for their use in taking them to meet Sherman.

On April 12, Swain and Graham started their journey out of Raleigh through the taunts of certain Confederate officers who called out that the two cowardly traitors should be hung. At the outskirts of the city, Wade Hampton stopped them, trying to argue them out of their plans, but they produced Hardee's safe conduct order. After the train traveled another two miles, it was halted again by Hampton's men, who claimed that Johnston had written an order rescinding his previous authorization to meet with Sherman, and ordering them back to Raleigh. The two men later learned that it was Jefferson Davis, not Johnston, who orchestrated this late maneuver.

But as Swain and Graham argued, first with those stopping the train and then with Hampton himself, Union cavalry appeared and started shooting at the Confederates. Hampton and his horsemen fled, and the Union soldiers then captured the locomotive, along with Swain and Graham. The two former governors explained their purpose to their captors and requested permission to return to Raliegh, but the Union cavalrymen refused them, saying that the two first must meet with Sherman, which allowed them to do what they really wanted to do anyway. Swain and Graham spent the rest of the day talking to Sherman, and then to General Francis P. Blair, Jr., commander of the 17th Army Corps, who had been a student of Swain's in 1837.

On the morning of April 13, Swain and Graham returned to Raleigh only to find Vance had left, apparently fearing that Swain and Graham had been captured and were being held as prisoners. Vance had gone to Charlotte, where he found Davis talking "wildly about rallying the scattered troops around Johnston." But Johnston confronted Davis, telling him that "it would be the greatest of human crimes for us to attempt to continue the war." Davis finally agreed and wrote a message to Sherman that was delivered by one of Johnston's couriers.

When Johnston left to meet his men on the 13th, he carried with him an order from Jefferson Davis to arrest Graham for treason, but Johnston ignored this order. On April 16, Johnston opened Sherman's reply, and then planned to bring Jefferson Davis into the negotiations of the surrender, but Davis had departed. Johnston arranged to meet with Sherman on the 17th.

On April 15th, Sherman wired to Stanton his intention of offering the same surrender terms that Grant had given to Lee, guided by his recent meeting with Lincoln on the *River Queen*. On the 17th, after Sherman and his staff had boarded the train to take them to his meeting with Johnston, a messenger came running with a telegraph from Stanton. The message informed Sherman that Lincoln had been assassinated on April 14 and warned Sherman that assassins were now on his track. Sherman asked the courier not to reveal the contents of the telegraph until Sherman returned from his meeting with Johnston.

Sherman and Johnston met in a small frame house, and when the two were alone, Sherman presented the telegram to Johnston, who stated that he thought the assassination was "the greatest possible calamity to the South." As the talks continued, the two generals agreed on most points, and finally Johnston put forth a bolder move and a break from Davis when he proposed to settle "the fate of all armies to the Rio Grande." Johnston said that the Confederate Secretary of War, John C. Breckenridge, was nearby and could confirm this offer. Sherman was eager to accept this offer, and to prevent a continuation of hostilities by Confederate bushwhackers as would occur if anarchy prevailed. Those around Sherman, including Logan and Blair, urged him to accept terms that would prevent another march against Johnston.

On April 18, Sherman had his second meeting with Johnston, with Breckenridge in attendance. Sherman presented a document to Johnston that included the disbanding of Confederate armies, the recognition of state governments, the reestablishment of the Federal courts in the South, the guarantee of political rights and rights of personal property, and a statement that the war was to cease.

The agreement did not address slavery, an issue that both Johnston and Sherman considered dead, as did all Southerners to whom Sherman had spoken to lately. But this oversight and mistake would soon haunt Sherman and his peace effort. Sherman did address slavery in a letter to Johnston on April 21, where he wrote "I believe, if the South would simply and publicly declare what we all feel and know, that slavery is dead, that you would inaugurate an era of peace and prosperity that would soon efface the ravages of the past four years of war."

On April 23, Sherman received a telegram that Major Henry Hitchcock would come to see him the next day, but the telegram did not state why he was coming. At 6 a.m. the next morning, Hitchcock arrived, along with an unannounced U. S. Grant. Grant bore with him a letter he had written to Sherman that included the reaction of President Andrew Johnson and his cabinet, which refused Sherman's settlement with Johnston. Grant's letter, following Stanton's dictate, also instructed, "Please notify General Johnston, immediately upon receipt of this, of the termination of the truce, and resume hostilities against his army at the earliest moment you can, acting in good faith."

The Johnson administration, influenced by Radical Republicans, in particular, Secretary of War Edwin Stanton, rejected Sherman's peace proposal as too lenient toward the South. The Radical Republicans viewed Sherman's plan as allowing the return of slavery, and they also wanted harsher treatment of the Confederate military leaders, including the imprisonment of Lee and others. (Some historians agree with the Johnson and Stanton view that Sherman far exceeded his authority during the surrender process and that Johnson and Stanton were correct in their actions to reign in Sherman.)

Much of the response of the Radical Republicans grew from Grant's surrender terms proffered Lee, that had been backed, and some felt authored, by Lincoln. Sherman's terms to Johnston were similar to Grant's, and consistent with his understanding of Lincoln's wishes going back to their meeting on the *River Queen*. This had placed the Radical Republicans in an agitated state, and without a lenient Lincoln to oppose them, the Radicals succeeded in obtaining more stringent terms of surrender.

Part of the mix-up may have been due to Sherman being unaware of correspondence between Grant and Lincoln, in which Lincoln instructed Grant to let the politicians negotiate the surrender, not the generals.

But the worst part of the whole situation was Stanton's dishonest vendetta against Sherman waged in the nation's newspapers, where Sherman was being called a traitor. The May 3, 1865, *Burlington Hawkeye* referred to the initial peace agreement as "Sherman's capitulation" and the stories that reached Mt. Pleasant, as shown in Emeline's next letter, were that Sherman had actually surrendered to Johnston. Finally, this subsided and those that had joined Stanton's crusade against Sherman changed their stance and embraced Sherman, but Sherman never forgave Stanton.

On April 26th, Sherman executed a revised surrender agreement with Johnston, upon which Grant wrote his signature of approval. Grant then took the original back with him to Washington. (Lloyd Lewis, *Sherman, Fighting Prophet*, pages 526-564)

After the surrender, the Union Army granted Jacob his furlough, and he briefly returned to Iowa. Unfortunately, we do not have any of Jacob's letters describing the assassination of Abraham Lincoln. Nor do we have Jacob's impression of the long, drawn out surrender, and the reactions of Stanton and the Johnson administration to Sherman's peace proposal. Emeline wrote the following letter after Jacob had left Mt. Pleasant to return to the 25th Iowa Infantry near Washington, D.C.

The Rumor of Sherman's Surrender to Johnston

[Mt. Pleasant, Iowa]
May 4th, 1865

Dear Husband,
. . . I heard yesterday that Sherman's army was going to be mustered out right away. I shall expect you in a few weeks at furthest. Won't that be nice? What did you think of <u>Sherman's surrender to Johnston</u>? The people here are pitching into him like fury . . .

Today we are making soap, washing, scrubbing, baking, &c, &c. Young'uns all gone to school but Kittie . . . Goodbye. One hurrah and come home.

Yours, Em

(The following is Jacob's first letter after his furlough, as he made his way back to his regiment to participate in the Grand Review in Washington, D.C. All the Union troops were to be honored by a march in Washington past the President, the Cabinet, and the various generals, including Grant and Sherman.)

Camp 25th Iowa
Petersburg, Virginia
May 7, 1865

My Dear Wife,
This is Sunday evening. We have just got into camp at this

place. And have been notified that mail will be received for an hour. So I will write you a few lines in haste. I am well—and got back to the regiment in good time without any accident. If I had time I would like to tell you all about my trip. I had a pleasant time. But I will soon be at home to stay and can tell you all about it. Don't you know the war is over and we are all going home? Ain't that good news? I can hardly realize it yet. I got to Raleigh Saturday night and found our army had moved the day before and was then 12 miles north on the Neuce River, lying over Sunday. I hired a man to take me out in a wagon. I got to the regiment at noon and they are all well and in good spirits.

We started the next morning for this place and have done the hardest marching that we have done since we have been in the service. We made from 25 to 30 miles a day. There was a race to see who could get here first. Nothing was molested in the least on the way, and everything was perfectly quiet. We have neither pickets nor skirmishers but go where we please, like we would at home. It seems very odd to travel that way. We think we will get home some time in June—perhaps sooner—have heard nothing definite about it yet. Don't know whether we will go on to Washington by land or water. But the war is over, and I am going home to stay!! Won't that be grand? I want to get a letter from you and find out if you are mad at me for going home this time. How is your health, dear, anyhow? I hope there is "nothing the matter" with you. Give my love to the children. I want to know if Kittie had got that other "Pa" yet? Give my respects to Ma's, Tom's, Alvah's, and all the rest—Direct as usual.

Your own Jake

I will write more in a day or two if I have a chance.

Alexandria, Virginia
May 22, 1865

My Dear Wife,

I take my pen this evening to write you a few lines again. I am all well and hearty and hope you are, &c, &c. We got here all right last Friday evening and I am really ashamed that I have not written to you before this. But if you knew how we are situated and how poor a chance we have to do anything, you would not blame me.

On Saturday after we got here I was so tired and worn out that

I lay and slept all day. It seemed so good to feel that we were done marching that I couldn't help lying down and taking it easy one day anyhow. I thought I would be sure to write to you on Sunday. We were then 3 miles from here and had orders to fix up camp as we would stay there some time.

But Sunday morning we were woken up at 2 o'clock and marched at 4 a.m. and moved three miles and are camped now just in the edge of Alexandria. It commenced raining early in the morning and rained hard all day. We all got wet to the skin. Did not get our tents till night. So you see I couldn't write that day.

Today I have drawn and issued clothing to my company, and have a few minutes left to write to you! We had orders when we came here to go into permanent camp, to remain till we start home. But today we have orders to move tomorrow to the Long Bridge, where we will remain till the morning of the 24th inst. That day we are to be reviewed in the City of Washington. The Army of the Potomac is to be reviewed tomorrow, the 23rd, and our army the next day. It will be the grandest review that has ever been seen in the world. I wish you could be there.

I have seen a great many sights that I would like to have you see. I did go to Richmond[1] without a pass. I was in Libby Prison, Castle Thunder[2], and the Confederate House of Congress. Saw Jeff Davis' house, General Lee's house, the Monument[3], and the forts around the city, &c. We crossed the "Chickahominy," the Pamunkey, the Rappahannock, the Occoquan, and &c. We came through Hanover Court-House, Stafford Court-House, & Fredericksburg. Then we marched 3 miles out of the way to see Mt. Vernon. Our whole division was marched in two ranks and at shoulder arms through the grounds and past Washington's tomb, giving us all a chance to see everything that is to be seen. We also saw the old church where Washington was baptized. It has almost been torn down and carried away by relic hunters.

We are camped now on a hill just back of Alexandria, and have a splendid view of the city, and the Potomac, both above and below, and of the camps and forts across the river. We are 7 miles from Washington City but can see the Dome on the Capitol, the Monument, and some of the public buildings.

But I am tired of it all, and would rather see you than all the "pomp and circumstance of war" between here and kingdom come! And I still expect to see you before long, and stay with you! Won't that be grand. We have received an order that all troops whose time will expire before the 1st of October shall be mustered out immediately—that means us; we have just 3 days to go on. But in military, immediately means any time, when you get ready. I still expect to get home some time in June. We will be sent to Iowa to be mustered out and paid off. As soon as I find out where and when we will be there I will write or telegraph to you, and you must be ready and go and stay with me till I go home. I shall look for you certain. Bring $100.00 along at least; I am pretty near strapped already.

I got your letter of the 4th inst. the day we crossed the Pamunkey River. I was glad to hear that you were all well, and that Lib had come back to stay with you. I haven't time to tell you now about my trip back to Raleigh. Ask me when I get home.

I and all the rest of Sherman's army think that he is all right, and have just as much confidence in him as ever. And we think that the folks at home had better be a little careful about who they pitch into. No real friend of his country will say a word to his discredit[4]. Will Black has got here all right; the men are all well and hearty.

I suppose you have heard all about the capture of Jeff Davis. We had a big time over the news. I will send you his picture to put in your album. They say the reason he put on hoops[5] was because he expected to be "confined" soon!! . . .

Give my love to all the folks.

Your own Jake

1. When Sherman's men first reached Richmond on their way from North Carolina to Washington, General Halleck, who was in the city, did not allow them to enter for fear of destruction to that city. Guards from the Army of the Potomac were posted to prevent them from entering. Reportedly, soldiers from the 15th Army Corps threw stones at those guards, while General Logan watched and laughed. On May 11, Sherman marched his men through Richmond.

    Based on Jacob's comment, in violation of Halleck's orders, he sneaked into Richmond without a pass to do some sightseeing.

2. Libby Prison was the Confederate prison for officers located in Richmond. Castle Thunder was a civilian prison located near Libby prison.

3. The Monument was a huge statue of George Washington on horseback, located in the Capital Square in Richmond.

4. Jacob is referring to Sherman's mistreatment by politicians, primarily Stanton, and the press.

5. When Union troops captured Jefferson Davis on May 12, the telegraph message proclaiming the event stated that Davis "hastily put on one of Mrs. Davis' dresses and started for the woods, closely pursued by our men, who at first thought him to be a woman, but seeing his boots while running suspected his sex at once." This story quickly spread through the country, prompting a plethora of cartoons characterizing the events. But it was not a true story. Several months after Davis's apprehension, two Union men who participated in the capture, James Parker and Andrew Bee, came forward and said that the story was a "wicked __ lie" and that "He had on a military suit, cavalry boots and all." But the original story of Davis' capture in the woman's clothing persisted for decades. (Webb Garrison, *A Treasury of Civil War Tales*, pages 171-173)

Historical Sketch—25th Iowa Infantry

From Goldsboro, the Twenty-Fifth Iowa moved, with its brigade and division, to Raleigh, and thence, after the surrender of the rebel General Johnston and his army, to Washington, D. C. On the 24th of May, 1865, the regiment, with its brigade, under command of its gallant leader, Brevet Brigadier General George A. Stone, participated in that greatest military pageant of modern times—the Grand Review at Washington. (Roster and Record of Iowa Soldiers in the War of the Rebellion; *Published under the authority of the Iowa General Assembly*)

Camp 25th Iowa Infantry
Crystal Springs, D.C.
May 28, 1865

My Dear Wife,

This is Sunday evening and after "retreat," but I will try to write you a few lines. I am still well and hearty, and in good spirits at the prospect of getting home soon.

We had our grand review last Wednesday. It passed off first-rate and everyone says we beat the Potomacs marching and in military appearance[1]. I sent you some papers with an account of the pageant. I wish you could have been here to see it. But there was such a crowd you could not have had any satisfaction or been able to get any accommodation; I never saw the like for people. We "bivouacked" in the city south of the Capitol the night before the review, and then marched to our present camp, which is about three miles north of the city in a very nice pine grove. I got a wall tent this morning.

You can't imagine what a relief it is to me to feel that the war is over. We don't talk about anything else. I feel proud of the part I have taken in putting down this rebellion. And thank God that I have lived to see the end of it. I have followed it and fought it through every rebel state but two. I have pursued the enemy of our country from the prairies of Missouri and the waters of the Mississippi to the Atlantic Ocean. Summer and winter, over hills, mountains, and rivers, through swamps and jungles, night and day, in wet and dry, I have been after them. And at last I slept in peace with the remnant of my gallant company in the City of Washington, under the shadow of the Capitol. On the day of the grand review when I marched down Pennsylvania Avenue at the head of Company B, I felt like I weighed about a ton? You don't blame me if I do feel a little proud, do you? I can't help it.

We have orders to make out our muster-out payrolls immediately, and as soon as they are ready we will be sent to Harpers Ferry[2] and mustered out, and sent from there to some point in Iowa to turn over our arms and be paid off. I don't know how long it will take, but you may be sure we will hurry them up as fast as possible. I put up my tent this morning and thought I would do lots of work today. But first H. McMillen of Mt. Pleasant came out to see me, and we had a long talk, then came Judge Kilpatrick, who ate dinner with me, then Mr. D.C. Burnett and F. Sypherd came. And then Mrs. Wittenmeyer and Miss Mary Shelton and other "Sanitary" ladies and I had to go to a meeting with them. So you see I had a very pleasant time and passed the day very agreeably, but did not get much muster-rollmuster roll made.

I shall let you know what point in Iowa we go to as soon as I find out, and shall look for you to meet me there sure. But I must quit and go to bed. I will tell you the rest when I get home. I got your letter of the 18th inst. yesterday and was glad to hear from you, and to find that you are not "guilty." I suppose I can come home any time I please now. You won't be "afraid of me."

Give my love to the children and Ma and Lib, and everybody else.

Yours ever, Your own Jake

1. Actual reports of the Grand Review said that the Army of the Potomac looked better, but that the Western armies marched better.

   It was during this parade that Sherman publicly insulted Stanton. Stanton extended his hand to shake Sherman's, only to have Sherman reject the gesture, igniting a buzz of whispers.

2. Harper's Ferry was where John Brown, the abolitionist, made his last violent attempt before the Civil War at storming an arsenal to arm slaves. He was captured by Lieutenant Colonel Robert E. Lee, tried and later hanged for his crimes.

Historical Sketch—25th Iowa Infantry

It then went into camp near Washington, and was there mustered out of the service of the United States on the 6th day of June 1865. Soon after being mustered out, the regiment was provided with transportation to Davenport, Iowa, where it was formally disbanded, and the officers and men departed for their homes, there to resume and discharge their duty as citizens, with the same fidelity they had shown while serving their country as soldiers. Among all the splendid regiments from Iowa, which had marched and fought – under the folds of the dear old flag, none reflected greater honor upon the State than its Twenty-Fifth Infantry. None rendered more important or effective service.

The compiler [of the Historical Sketch] extends an old soldier's cordial greeting to the surviving members of the Twenty-Fifth Iowa Infantry. He has endeavored to perpetuate the memory of the men who composed the regiment and who were its history makers.

SUMMARY OF CASUALTIES.

Total Enrollment: 1,136
Killed: 39
Wounded: 187
Died of Wounds: 24
Died of Disease: 201
Discharged for wounds, disease or other causes: 164
Buried in National Cemeteries: 104
Captured: 18
Transferred: 71

(*Roster and Record of Iowa Soldiers in the War of the Rebellion*; Published under the authority of the Iowa General Assembly)

Chapter Seven
After the War: Jacob and Emeline,
Family and Friends

*After the war, Jacob returned to Mount Pleasant, where he assist-
ed Emeline's brother Thomas, who had became owner and editor of
the Mount Pleasant* Home Journal. *He also had a stint as a traveling
washing machine salesman, but his main efforts were in helping the
local school district.*

*On January 12, 1873 Jacob died, almost eight years after the end
of the war, never having fully recovered from its harsh effects.*

Obituary
Capt. J.B. Ritner.

Our community has been called during the last year to
mourn the death of several of its most distinguished citizens. This week, we mourn another, Capt. J.B. Ritner, who
after a lingering illness of nine or ten months, died on the
morning of Sunday, January 12. Captain Jacob B. Ritner
was born in Washington, Pennsylvania September 6, 1828
and was a descendant of the eminent family of that name
to which Governor Ritner belonged. At the age of 15, he
came with his parents to Danville, Iowa. Afterwards, he
was a student at Mr. Howe's Academy and taught school
in this and adjoining counties. He was married April 3,
1851 to Emeline R. Bereman, who with five children, sur-
vive him. On the first breaking out of the war in April
1861, he enlisted with the three months men and served in
the campaign of the 1st Iowa. Returning, he served sometimes as a Justice of the Peace and was active as an
enrolling officer. When the 25th Infantry was raised, he
entered as 1st Lieutenant of Company B of which on
Captain Smith's return, he became Captain. He served
with the 25th through the war taking part in 15 battles and
escaping with only one slight wound.

After his return, he was, for a time, engaged with T. A. Bereman, Esq., in the publication of the *Home Journal.* And since its sale, has been living retired in care of his vineyard.

Captain Ritner, was, at the time of his death, a member of the School Board and has been intimately connected with the educational interests of our city. At the age of 18, he united with the Baptist church, of which he remained a useful and consistent member to the close of his life. He was a man of pure and honest motives, of strong convictions and of firm determined purposes. Highly esteemed by all who knew him and best by those who knew him best, his presence in society will be missed and his loss to our community deeply felt.

The funeral was held at 1:00 on Tuesday. Rev. K.W. Benton conducted the services with a goodly number of people in attendance.

The following article appeared in the Home Journal*:*

In Memoriam

The Board of Directors of Independent School District at their meeting last Friday evening, adopted the following resolutions:

WHEREAS, It has pleased our Heavenly Father to remove from our midst Capt. J.B. Ritner,

Resolved, By the Board of Directors of Mt. Pleasant Independent School District, that by his untimely death we have lost one or our most faithful, capable and efficient members.

Resolved, That in his death, the cause of common school education has been deprived of one of its most steadfast friends and supporters, and that the State has lost a citizen who proved himself worthy of all honor by his bravery and valor as a soldier.

Resolved, That while we gratefully remember his great worth as a soldier, a citizen, and a neighbor, we tender to his sadly bereaved family our undivided sympathies in this their greatest earthly loss.

MRS. EMELINE RITNER

Mrs. Emeline Ramsey Ritner (nee Bereman), one of the oldest and most respected residents of this city, passed away at her home on Webster St., Tuesday evening, Sept. 28, 1909. She had been sick for many months, and through all her suffering bore herself with fortitude and patience.

She was born in Mercer County, Ky., Jan. 18, 1831, and was one of a family of nine, only one of whom is now living, William Bereman, of Bloomington, Ill. She and Mr. J.B. Ritner were married in Henry County, Iowa, 1851. They were blessed with seven children. Evangeline and Willie, who died in infancy, and Mr. T. J. Ritner, Atchison, Kansas; Mrs. Kate Bemis, Bondurant, Iowa; Mrs. Eulalie Chase, Iowa City, and Misses Nellie and Emma, of this city.

The Ritner and Bereman families have had an enviable war record, all those who could do so, both men and women, serving in the armies or as nurses in hospitals. Mrs. Ritner gave her husband at his country's call, and when he returned at the close of the war he bore the well-deserved title of captain. But the war broke his constitution and he died in 1873, leaving to her the care of their little family. Bravely she set herself to the work of love and reared her children in the fear of God and to be useful members of society. They repaid her by loving and tender devotion during her declining years.

She was for a great many years a member of the Baptist church and was faithful in the service of her Lord. Until illness made it necessary for her to tarry at home she was ever to be found in her place in the house of God. Her circle of friends was large and all held her in highest esteem for her beautiful and helpful life.

Funeral services were held at the home Thursday, Sept. 30, at 2:30. Her pastor, Rev. Frank E. Weston, spoke from Job 5:26, and made reference to her many excellencies. Members of the Baptist choir sang appropriate hymns. The house was filled with mourning friends. The remains were borne to Forest Home Cemetery and laid to rest amid members of her family already deceased. Mr. T. J. Ritner,

Mr. Wm. Bereman, Mr. ____ Bereman, Evanston, Ill, and Dr. C. S. Chase, Iowa City, were the pallbearers. Amid others that "sleep with Christ" she awaits the trumpet of her resurrection.

Nellie and Kittie Ritner became teachers at Howe's Academy, with Nellie becoming the head schoolmistress.

Jacob's daughter Lulie (Mrs. Eulalie Ritner Chase) became active in the Waterloo, Iowa, chapter of the Women's Christian Temperance Union, serving as Secretary in 1901-1902. She received the following postal card from another Temperance activist:

Chippawa Falls Wis
Sep 14 1904

My true sister

I left my comb and brush and Liquizone in the church. I speak at Eau Claire tomorrow afternoon. I park here at night. Churches are fixing for more meetings. Please leave the things at the depot I left, for I will get them as I pass through Monday or Tuesday. Loving and grateful.

Carry A. Nation

Eulalie (Lulie)   Carry A. Nation
Ritner Chase, Early 1900s

Tilghman "Till" Bereman and the 1st Iowa Cavalry served under the "boy general" George Armstrong Custer for a year after the close of the war, maintaining the peace in Texas while observing the French in Mexico. Custer was despised by the Iowans and at one point a captain in the 1st Iowa Cavalry drew his sword and threatened Custer. Till later married Rebecca Hulme and moved to Aurora, Illinois, when the Western Wheel Scraper Company left Mt. Pleasant and relocated there. (Jeffry D. Wert, Custer–The Controversial Life of George Armstrong Custer, *page 238;* The History of Henry County, *page 245)*

Samuel Steele, Jacob's close friend and first lieutenant of Company B, married Sarah Margaret Everts on May 27, 1866. They had one child, but tragedy struck as Sarah died October 26, 1868. Steele married again in 1872, to Martha D. Oaks, and they had five children. In 1887, he was elected as Representative to the State Legislature. During that year, he also helped organize and incorporate the Mt. Pleasant Manufacturing Company, where he served as General Manager. That company manufactured steel sled-runners, as well as steel farm, field, and yard gates. (Portrait and Biographical Album of Henry County, Iowa 1888, *pages 221-222, 678)*

Charles Wils Payne, who was the first white child born in Henry County, married Miss Maggie Patton and they had four children. Wils worked as a farmer, and also served in the Iowa State Legislature as a member of the 18th and 19th General Assemblies. (Portrait and Biographical Album of Henry County, Iowa 1888, *pages 474-475)*

*Baron Crane's younger brother, Eber Lane Crane, married Annette Stone, the daughter of General George A. Stone. (*The History of Henry County, Iowa, *page 165)*

*Baron Crane, the second Lieutenant of Company B, married his childhood sweetheart, Abbie Mellen, in 1866. He became a clerk in Hugh Pickle's hardware store in Mt. Pleasant, and in 1869 he bought the business from Mr. Pickle. The store remained in the Crane family for three generations. Baron and Abbie had nine children. (*The History of Henry County, Iowa, *page 163)*

*In 1889, Harriet Ketcham of Mt. Pleasant submitted the winning design for a monument honoring the Iowa soldiers and sailors who had participated in the Civil War which was later constructed in Des Moines. According to one version of this story, Harriet Ketcham used tintype photographs of two of Baron and Abbie Crane's children when making the drawings of the monument. Anna Crane's face was used to represent the Pioneer Woman depicting History, and Ralph Crane's likeness represents Young Iowa. (Harriet Ketcham's grand nephew Hank Ketcham was instrumental in supporting the restoration efforts of the monument in the 1990s). (*The History of Henry County, Iowa, *page 163; Handbook for Iowa Soldiers' and Sailors' Monument, page vii)*

*Joshua G. Newbold, Captain of Company C of the 25th Iowa, became Governor of Iowa from 1877 to 1878. (*Portrait and Biographical Album of Henry County, Iowa, 1888, *pages 143-144)*

Mt. Pleasant Free Press:
Died May 6, 1908
Mt. Pleasant, Iowa, Thursday, May 14, 1908
A War Family

The death of Miss Sallie Bereman, last week, recalls the remarkable war record of her family. The parents were Mr. and Mrs. Samuel Bereman, earlier settlers of this county.

When the Civil War broke out, six sons went into the army. Jonathan S. enlisted in the 25th Iowa Infantry, contracted chronic dysentery and was brought home and died in 1863.

Alvah H. was editor of a newspaper here and was appointed a Captain in the 18th United States Infantry and afterwards became Colonel of the 45th Iowa Regiment.

T. A. [Thomas] was major in the 1st Iowa Cavalry. Wm. A. was a 2nd Lieutenant in the 4th Iowa Cavalry. T. H. [Tilghman] was a private in the 1st Iowa Cavalry. S. O. [Ol] was a Sergeant in the 4th Iowa Cavalry.

Of the six brothers, only Wm. A. is living. He is a resident of Bloomington, Illinois. Alvah died in California and was buried there. S. O. Bercman went to Atchison, Kansas and died there.

Thus, you see, six brothers enlisted before the war and after they were all gone, the father enlisted in the 37th Iowa Infantry, the Grey Beard Regiment. He took sick and died in Memphis, Tenn. He was in the son William's tent when death came to him.

Every man of the household had gone to the front and the mother enlisted as a nurse. She gave all she had to her country.

And besides the sons and the husband, Mrs. Bereman had her two sons in-law in the army. One of them was Capt. J.B. Ritner Co. B, 25th Iowa Infantry. The other was James Freeman, 25th Iowa, who was killed in the assault on Vicksburg in 1863.

Appendix

Samuel A. Howe was an important teacher of the Ritners and Beremans in both academic studies and moral/political issues such as slavery. The following section, from the History of Iowa by Benjamin F. Gue, helps explain his prominence and influence:

"Samuel A. Howe, pioneer educator, was born in Vermont in 1808. He early removed to Ohio and engaged in teaching where John Sherman and William Tecumseh Sherman were among his pupils. He resolved to secure a liberal education and defrayed the greater part of his expenses through Athens University by work about the institution. He established a reputation as an educator and inspirer of youth, as we find General Sherman saying on his march to the sea: 'Professor Howe I consider to be the best teacher in the United States. I am more indebted to him for my start in life than to any other man in America.' In 1843 he removed to Iowa and located near Mount Pleasant, teaching in a log schoolhouse the following winter.

In 1843 Howe removed his school to Mount Pleasant and there being no other accommodation it was located in the upper room of the old log jail. In 1844 the school was temporarily removed to the Cumberland Presbyterian Church and the following year was transferred to the Academy building erected for this purpose, where it still remains, having an unbroken record of over fifty years of continuous existence, making it probably the oldest continuously operated school in the state. After the dissolution of the Whig Party, Professor Howe became a Free Soiler. In 1848 he became a stockholder in the only antislavery paper in the Northwest, the Iowa Freeman. During the presidential campaign of 1856 it was one of the most influential advocates of the principles of the Republican Party. He was a firm believer in women's suffrage, temperance, the abolition of the death penalty and was strongly opposed to land monopoly. During his early advocacy of abolition of slavery he suffered much persecution, having property destroyed and was finally mobbed by pro-slavery ruffians on the streets of Mount Pleasant. Professor Howe defied persecution, hatred, loss of property and social ostracism and stood firmly by his principles through life. He died in Mount Pleasant, February, 15, 1877."

Bibliography

Blue and Gray Magazine

Official Record, as published by the Guild Press of Indiana on CD-ROM

Portrait and Biographical Album of Henry County, Iowa—1888, Acme Publishing Company, Chicago, Illinois, 1888. Reproduction by Unigraphic, Inc., Evansville, Indiana, 1976.

The Burlington Hawkeye Newspaper, Burlington, Iowa.

The Mt. Pleasant Home Journal, Mt. Pleasant, Iowa.

Vicksburg, Official National Park Handbook, National Park Service, Division of Publications, 1986.

World Book Encyclopedia, World Book, Inc. a Scott Fetzer Company, Chicago, London, Sydney, Toronto, 1998.

Arnold, James R.
Grant Wins the War, John Wiley & Sons, Inc., New York, 1997.

Barrett, John G.
Sherman's March Through The Carolinas, The University of North Carolina Press, Chapel Hill, 1956.

Bearss, Edwin
The Vicksburg Campaign, Volumes I, II, III, Morningside House, Inc., Dayton, Ohio, 1985.

Bradley, Mark
Last Stand in the Carolinas: The Battle of Bentonville, Savas Woodbury Publishers, Campell, California, 1996.

Brooksher, William Riley
Bloody Hill—The Civil War Battle of Wilson's Creek, Brassey's, Washington-London, 1995.

Castel, Albert
Decision in the West, University of Kansas Press, Lawrence, Kansas, 1992.

Coggins, Jack
Arms and Equipment of the Civil War, Broadfoot Publishing Company, Wilmington, North Carolina, 1990.

Cornish, Dudley Taylor and Hattaway, Herman
The Sable Arm: Black Troops in the Union Army 1861-1865, University of Kansas Press, Lawrence, Kansas, 1990.

Cottingham, Carl D.; Jone, Preston Michael; Kent, Gary W.
General John A. Logan, His Life and Times, American Resources Group, Ltd., Carbondale, Illinois.

Cox, General Jacob D.
Sherman's Battle for Atlanta, Da Capo Press, New York, New York, 1994 (First published in 1882 under the title Atlanta)

Cox, General Jacob D.
Sherman's March to the Sea, Da Capo Press, New York, New York, 1994 (First published in 1882 under the title The March to the Sea—Franklin and Nashville)

Cozzens, Peter
The Darkest Days of the War—The Battles of Iuka & Corinth, The University of North Carolina Press, Chapel Hill, 1997.

Crooker, Lucien; Nourse, Henry S.; Brown, John G.; Haney, Milton L.
The Story of the Fifty-Fifth Regiment Illinois Volunteer Infantry, Blue Corn Press, Huntington, West Virginia, reprinted 1993.

DeBolt, Margaret Wayt
Savannah Spectres And Other Strange Tales, The Donning Company/Publishers; Norfolk, Virginia Beach, 1984.

Elder, Dr. Don
A Damned Iowa Greyhound, University of Iowa Press, Iowa City, 1998

Farr, Dr. Henry
Diary of Dr. Henry Farr, Unpublished, Iowa State Historical Society, Iowa City, Iowa.

Faust, Patricia L.
Historical Times Illustrated Encyclopedia of the Civil War

Foote, Shelby
The Civil War, Volumes I, II, and III, Vintage Books, A Division of Random House, New York, 1958, 1986.

Garrison, Webb
A Treasury of Civil War Tales, Rutledge Hill Press, Nashville, Tennessee, 1988.

Garrison, Webb
Atlanta and the War, Rutledge Hill Press, Nashville, Tennessee, 1995.

Garrison, Webb
More Civil War Curiosities, Rutledge Hill Press, Nashville, Tennessee, 1995.

Gibson, Charles Dana and Gibson, E. Kay
Dictionary of Transports and Combatant Vessels, Steam and Sail, Employed by the Union Army, 1861-1868, Ensign Press, Camden, Maine, 1995.

Glatthaar, Joseph T.
The March to the Sea and Beyond, New York University, LSU Press Edition, 1985.

Grant, Ulysses S.
Memoirs and Selected Letters, Literary of the United States, New York, New York, reprinted 1990.

Henry County Bicentennial Commission; Ann Crane Farrier and others
The History of Henry County, Iowa, National ShareGraphics, Inc., Dallas, Texas, 1982.

Hertz, Dr. J. H., Late Chief Rabbi of the British Empire
The Pentateuch and Haftorahs, Hebrew Text, English Translation and Commentary; Soncino Press, London.

Kelbough, Ross J.
Introduction to Civil War Photography, Thomas Publications, Gettysburg, PA, 1991

Kennett, Lee
Marching through Georgia, Harper Perennial, A Division of HarperCollins Publishers, New York, New York, 1995.

Lewis, Lloyd
Sherman, Fighting Prophet, University of Nebraska Press, Lincoln & London, 1932, 1960, 1993.

Logan, Brigadier General Guy E.
Roster and Record of Iowa Soldiers in the War of the Rebellion; Published under the authority of the Iowa General Assembly, Volumes I-VI, Des Moines, Iowa, 1908, 1910.

Lowry, Dr. Thomas P., M.D.
The Story the Soldiers Wouldn't Tell–Sex in the Civil War, Stackpole Books, Mechanicsburg, PA, 1994.

Lyman, Darryl
Civil War Wordbook, Combined Books, Inc., Conshohocken, Pennsylvania, 1994.

Marshall-Cornwall, General Sir James
Grant as Military Commander, Barnes & Noble Books, New York, 1970.

Marszalek, John E.
Sherman, A Soldier's Passion For Order, Vintage Books, A Division of Random House, Inc., New York, New York, 1994.

Marvel, William
Andersonville, The Last Depot, The University of North Carolina Press, Chapel Hill & London, 1994.

McDonough, James Lee
Chattanooga, A Death Grip on the Confederacy, The University of Tennessee Press, Knoxville, 1984.

Meyer, Steve
Iowa Valor, Meyer Publishing Company, Garrison, Iowa, 1994.

Miles, Jim
A River Unvexed, Rutledge Hill Press, Nashville, Tennessee, 1994.

Randall, J. G. and Donald, David
The Civil War and Reconstruction, D. C. Heath and Company, Lexington, Massachusetts, 1969.

Schultz, Duane
Quantrill's War, St. Martin's Press, New York, 1996.

Sherman, W. T.
Memoirs of General W. T. Sherman, Literary Classics of the United States, New York, New York, reprinted 1990.

Sifakis, Stewart
   Who Was Who In The Confederacy, Facts On File, New York, Oxford, 1989.

Sifakis, Stewart
   Who Was Who In The Union, Facts On File, New York, Oxford, 1989.

Sword, Wiley
   Mountains Touched With Fire, St. Martin's Press, New York, 1995.

Ware, Eugene F.
   The Lyon Campaign and History of the 1st Iowa Infantry, Crane & Company, Topeka, Kansas, 1907. Reprinted 1991 by Press of The Camp Pope Bookshop.

Weed, Cora Chaplin
   Handbook for Iowa Soldiers' and Sailors' Monument, Press of the Camp Pope Bookshop, Iowa City, Iowa, 1897, 1994.

Wert, Jeffry D.
   Custer–The Controversial Life of George Armstrong Custer, Simon & Schuster, New York, 1996.

Wills, Charles W.
   Army Life of an Illinois Soldier, Southern Illinois University Press, Carbondale and Edwardsville, Illinois, 1996.

INDEX

About the Editor

Charles F. Larimer was born to an American father and Canadian mother in a U.S. Army Hospital in Trieste, Italy in 1953. He was raised in Sioux City, Iowa where he attended public schools, and graduated from the University of Iowa in 1975. Divorced, he now resides in Illinois with his son. Of Scotch heritage, Larimer is currently at work compiling a book of Scottish stories collected from a distant uncle who lives near Loch Ness.